Arsenal of Defense

ARSENAL OF DEFENSE

Fort Worth's Military Legacy

BY J'NELL L. PATE

Texas State Historical Association
Denton

© Copyright 2011 by the Texas State Historical Association.
First paperback printing, 2013.
All rights reserved. Printed in the U.S.A.

Library of Congress Cataloging-in-Publication Data
Pate, J'Nell L.
   Arsenal of Defense: Fort Worth's Military Legacy / by J'Nell L. Pate; Foreword by Kay Granger.
   Includes bibliographical references and index.
ISBN 978-0-87611-249-6
   1. Fort Worth (Tex.)—History, Military. 2. Defense industries—Texas—Fort Worth—History. 3. United States—Armed Forces—Texas—Fort Worth—History. 4. Fort Worth (Tex.)—Economic conditions. I. Title.
   F394.F7P37 2011
   976.4'5315—dc23

To the more than one million local military personnel and defense plant workers through the years, including my father, Vernon Rogers, who contributed to Fort Worth's military and defense legacy, and, as always, to my husband, Kenneth.

Contents

Illustrations

Foreword

E VERY CITY HAS A STORY ... FORT WORTH HAS A LEGEND.
For more than 150 years, this city has made a name for itself.
And it represents different things for different people. For most,
Fort Worth means the Old West, cattle drives and famous cowboys. For
some, Fort Worth is commerce, oil, and money. For others, Fort Worth is
art, culture, museums, and Van Cliburn.

In fact, Fort Worth is all of that ... and more.

Twenty years ago when I first entered public office, I began to realize
that perhaps nothing defines Fort Worth more than the one industry that
has done so much to create jobs and growth in the city for decades: the
military.

As a new Mayor in 1991, I found myself faced with a crisis: Congress was
threatening to close down the historic Carswell Air Force Base on the west
side of town. The community was outraged; the economy was threatened;
the future was endangered.

We launched a campaign to save our base. And in the process of telling
the story about Carswell, I learned how deep the military's roots run in Fort
Worth.

Most people credit Ripley Arnold for beginning the relationship. Major
Arnold was a rising star in the Army and hero of the Mexican War. Following the war he had been given command of Company F of the Second
Dragoons and had orders to create a military installation "at or near the
confluence of the West Fork and the Clear Fork of the Trinity River." On
June 6, 1849, he officially established Camp Worth, named in honor of his
former commander in the Mexican War. Eventually, the installation's name
was changed to Fort Worth.

It was the beginning of a long love affair between the military and this
city that continues to this day.

Throughout the last 150 years, the relationship has evolved and changed.
But one constant has always defined it: Fort Worth and the military are
good for each other.

Now, for the first time, all this rich history has been researched and presented in J'Nell Pate's beautiful new book, "Arsenal of Defense: Fort Worth's Military Legacy." The book chronicles the long, enduring relationship between the Armed Forces and Fort Worth.

Pate traces the history back to even before Major Arnold. General Edward Tarrant arrived in the area in 1841. But it was Major Arnold who returned years later and chose a site on the bluff overlooking the Clear and West forks as the site of the first military installation. Thus, it can be said that the military existed even before the city did.

In the following years the city and the military grew together. In the early twentieth century, America found itself involved in what was called the "Great War." And Fort Worth was right in the middle of it. First, pilots were trained at three airfields in the area. Then, the War Department opened a new base on the west side and named it after Texas Revolutionary War hero, Jim Bowie. On April 11, 1918, Camp Bowie sent the first 27,000 of its troops for France.

Years later, with World War II looming, Fort Worth leaders realized that military power was shifting from the ground to the air. They secured a B-24 production plant on the shores of Lake Worth. By 1943 with the war raging across the world, more than 200 planes were produced each month by the Fort Worth facility. The plant would change owners several times: from Consolidated Aircraft to Consolidated Vultee to Convair to General Dynamics to Lockeed Martin. No matter who has owned it, the plant has produced the best fighter planes in the world for sixty years.

Following the war, Fort Worth continued to be a home for other types of military aircraft production. In 1951, Larry Bell moved his helicopter operation to Fort Worth where it remains. And the local air field got a new name and a new mission. The re-christened Carswell Air Force Base became part of the new Strategic Air Command and was home to B-58s, F-111s and F-16s.

This was the same Carswell Air Force Base that I found myself fighting to save in the 1990s. And we did save it—by changing it. The Naval Air Station Joint Reserve Base is now a model for how to integrate all branches of the military and the reserves in a way that is practical and effective for a twenty-first century military.

As you read the pages in this book, you will learn how the presence of the military has shaped our economy, our city, and our culture. Now, this storied relationship is about to enter a new phase with the 2012 commissioning of the USS Fort Worth. It's only fitting that a city so closely aligned with the military would have a war vessel named after it.

I am grateful to J'Nell Pate for piecing together this important story. This book is well researched, well written, and well worth your time. I hope you enjoy reading it. And I hope you are as proud as I am of our great city's great military heritage.

Congresswoman Kay Granger

Preface

STANLEY COLE, FORMER EDITOR OF THE *Carswell Sentinel*, ONCE wrote, "since Major Ripley Arnold planted the U.S. flag at the fork[s] of the Trinity River, the fortunes of the military presence and the Fort Worth area have been interwoven and interdependent."[1] Although Major Arnold planted the flag in June 1849, one might actually push the military connection back at least eight years to the expedition of General Edward H. Tarrant in the spring of 1841, which included the Battle of Village Creek and the establishment of Bird's Fort that same year. These two events occurred in the eastern part of what in 1850 became Tarrant County, and they provide early evidence of the area's military associations.[2]

Local citizens left the area to fight for the South in the Civil War, then came home to develop Fort Worth as a supply town for thousands of cattle and their drivers moving north on the Chisholm Trail. Later, a railroad center emerged to support a booming stockyards and meatpacking industry. Although livestock, not the military, dominated the area's economy until the 1940s, an early twentieth-century local interest in aviation previewed the shift to military-defense institutions that arrived with World War I, greatly expanded in World War II, and remained an important mainstay thereafter.[3]

In a special June 1949 issue of the *Fort Worth Star-Telegram* commemorating the city's one-hundredth birthday, a writer suggested, "Fort Worth has seen miracles happen to itself in a hundred years, but few have come with the almost magical suddenness of its transformation from an oil, cattle, and agricultural center to one of the world's focal points of aircraft manufacture and aviation."[4] Surprisingly, when that statement appeared, Bell Helicopter's arrival had not yet even been imagined. Thus, when Bell came the next year, Fort Worth acquired even more aviation- and defense-related manufacturing.

Because military institutions provide numerous jobs, it is logical that most local citizens enthusiastically support government procurement contracts and cheer loudly upon their announcement. Much of Texas shares that sentiment, for in a Scripps-Howard Data Center poll done in Texas in April and May 2001, results revealed that 85 percent of respondents approved of the military, with 75 percent saying the military would be a good career.[5]

My purpose in writing this book is to chronicle what the military has meant to the greater Fort Worth area and to cite the many contributions the local community has made to the national defense. This is a layman's—albeit an academic layman's—military account. I formerly knew little about military affairs, but I love Fort Worth and its history. During my extensive research, I have become enthralled with the stories of people I "met" in the pages of books and fragile documents from numerous libraries and archives. I grew up on Camp Bowie Boulevard on property that had been a part of the camp, and I attended a primary school located two blocks from Camp Bowie's former headquarters. As a child our route to church each Sunday and Wednesday night followed Camp Bowie Boulevard to Arlington Heights Church of Christ and returned home traveling east on Pershing Street. I did not know then that the latter was named after General J. J. Pershing from World War I. At age ten when I was feverish with two-week measles, the loud engines of a B-36 from Carswell really bothered me. Later, I drove by Veterans' Memorial Park in the 4200 block of Camp Bowie Boulevard many times without noticing the memorials there to military men of World War I. While I lived in the midst of much local military history, I took it for granted; after many years, I am now paying homage.

Fort Worth's city planning director in 1988, Bruce McClendon, told an audience that Fort Worth "hasn't been an accidental city."[6] It took planning to develop the way it did. I think readers will enjoy learning the stories of the people who urged and cajoled innumerable officials to acquire various military installations for Fort Worth—and often used the same means to keep them here. Yes, Fort Worth is "Cowtown," and I appreciate the stockyards that made it so. However, military establishments and defense manufacturing plants have brought as much, if not more, attention, money, and population growth to the area than the previous emphasis on livestock. A Fort Worth Chamber of Commerce article once even called the city an "arsenal of defense."[7]

Acknowledgments

IRST, I MUST THANK THE LEAVE OF ABSENCE COMMITTEE OF Tarrant County College, Fort Worth, Texas, for granting my request for a sabbatical for the 1996–97 school year. As a result, I spent two full semesters of research time on the topic of "The Impact of the Military on Tarrant County." Other projects interfered, and years passed before I returned to the massive task that I had set aside.

I am most grateful to Norman Robbins, director of community relations at Lockheed Martin, for reading the two "bomber plant" chapters and for helping me with Lockheed photographs. I also want to thank the ladies at the Lockheed Martin Library who were there when I did my earliest research: Gale Harris, Linda Brown, Virginia Smith, Maxine Merriman, and Debra Johnson. At Bell Helicopter, my thanks go to Terry Arnold, who headed public relations at the time I did my sabbatical, and to Sheldon Cohen, Ron Whitley, Ben Gilliand, and Bridget Hall for photographs. I appreciate the kindness of Webb Joiner, former president and CEO of Bell, for taking time from his retirement to read the Bell chapter and for granting me an interview a decade earlier. Dominick J. Cirincione also made suggestions concerning the Bell chapter. Bobbie Skipper at the Naval Air Station Fort Worth Library (formerly the Carswell Library) was also a great help to me.

I want to thank several people at the Special Collections Library at the University of Texas at Arlington: Gerald Saxon, Kit Goodwin, Sally Groce, Jill Jackson, Brenda McClurkin, and Carolyn Kadri. My appreciation goes also to Jane Dees, former research librarian and archivist at the Fort Worth Museum of Science and History, and Christina Hardman, who took her place; Erik Carlson, former coordinator of the Special Collections Department at the McDermott Library at the University of Texas at Dallas, and Paul Oelkrug, senior curator there. My appreciation goes to Meg Hacker, director, and Barbara Rust and Rodney Krajca at the National Archives and Records Administration, Southwest Region, in Fort Worth for their help. At the Tarrant County Law Library in Fort Worth my thanks go to Peggy

Luttrell Martindale, assistant director; at the DeGolyer Library at Southern Methodist University in Dallas to Cammie Vitale; and at the Southwest Collection at Texas Tech University in Lubbock to Janet Neugebauer and Victoria Jones.

At the Fort Worth Chamber of Commerce I want to thank Andra Bennett, Marilyn Gilluri, and Lauren Turner. I also appreciate the help of Loyd L. Turner, former special assistant to the president of General Dynamics, who steered me to many interesting people to interview. He also helped me locate Beryl A. Erickson, chief test pilot for Convair, who sent me clippings from his own files. Gene Schulte of Bridgeport allowed me to go through his 1938–42 issues of *Southern Flight Magazine*. Thanks to Dalton Hoffman who shared his military photographs with me.

Stanley Cole of Target Marketing, former publisher of the *Carswell Sentinel*, graciously allowed me to sort through and copy many stories from his bound back issues. Also helpful with my Carswell research were Tate Reid of Congresswoman Kay Granger's office, Captain Paula Bissonette, and Master Sergeant Robert Romanelli, the latter two stationed at Dyess Air Force Base in Abilene where some Carswell records were moved. Dr. Griffin T. Murphey shared his information with me about the Canadian fliers in Fort Worth during World War I, and invited my husband and me to the biannual Memorial Day observance in their honor. Fellow Azleite Harry Evans, who worked at General Dynamics for many years, allowed me to interview him and put me in touch with a chain of people. Gretchen Barrett, daughter of Harry Brants, and Lucy Brants, his great-niece, helped me track down the story of their relative who was a World War I Fort Worth flier. Dee Barker of the Tarrant County Historical Commission shared information with me that she had researched on Bird's Fort, and Susie Pritchett of the Tarrant County archives helped considerably.

One of the most memorable events of my sabbatical was when Max Schelper took me on a tour of Lockheed and then introduced me to the Carswell and "bomber plant" retirees who were completing a total of 94,000 hours restoring five airplanes. They had spent 43,000 of those hours on the last B-36 to be built in Fort Worth. I was even invited to climb up into the cockpit of the restored B-36. As a result of that tour, I joined the B-36 Peacemaker Museum, Inc. group and briefly became involved in trying to save the restored B-36 for Fort Worth. Sadly, we lost it to the Pima Air and Space Museum that is adjacent to Davis-Monthan Air Force Base in the southern Arizona desert. I want to send my appreciation to all those who tried to save it for Fort Worth and who sought to build an aviation museum to house it. Their museum efforts with other airplanes continue. Don Pyeatt of the B-36 Group assisted me with photographs.

Most recently the editing work of Dr. Randolph B. Campbell, Chief Historian and Publications Director for the Texas State Historical Association, and Ryan Schumacher, Associate Editor, have made this a better book. They have my sincere appreciation and thanks.

CHAPTER 1

A Fort Begins the Military Tradition

S ETTLERS ARRIVING IN NORTH TEXAS IN THE FIRST HALF OF THE
nineteenth century never could have imagined that on the vacant
prairie lands they saw stretching westward from the ninety-eighth
meridian their descendants would one day manufacture and sell massive
numbers of military aircraft. Those early pioneers had left the United States
and its well-established cities behind to come to Texas, but within a century and a half the community they began—Fort Worth—grew into a large
city that ranked as one of the world's leading producers of defense materials. The story of Fort Worth is an example of a community's contribution
to, and the impact of the military on an American city that was repeated
numerous times across the country, but most frequently in the West. Fort
Worth, established where two forks of the Trinity River meet, began, of
course, as a military outpost.

In the 1840s four military men helped bring the first settlement activity
to the area that would become Fort Worth and Tarrant County. These men
were General Edward H. Tarrant, Brevet Major Jonathan Bird, Ranger
Captain Middleton Tate Johnson, and Major Ripley A. Arnold. The county
became Tarrant and the major city Fort Worth, honoring General William
Jenkins Worth, who never came to the area and died without knowing the
fort had been named for him.

Fort Worth's story actually started a little to the east. In the spring of
1841, a man named Ripley was killed by some unidentified natives on Ripley
Creek in Titus County (in East Texas). As a result, Mirabeau B. Lamar,
president of the Republic of Texas (1838–1841), ordered an expedition of ten
companies of troops north to the Trinity River to build a military road and
create a line of forts along the frontier. Following common practice at the
time, men on the expedition elected their officers. However, because of his
rank, Edward H. Tarrant, general of the Fourth Brigade of Texas Militia,
headed the expedition, despite not being elected. Sixty-nine men under
Tarrant left Fort Johnson (near Sherman in present Grayson County) on
May 14, 1841, and searched the land between the Brazos and Trinity Riv-

ers. On May 23 they captured one native and tied him to a tree. When they threatened to kill him unless he revealed the location of his village, he talked.

The next morning Tarrant led the attack on the native camp, which was on a tributary of the Trinity subsequently known as Village Creek (present Arlington). Rangers charged the native village as its residents fled, and when the soldiers pursued, they found two more villages along the creek and attacked these as well. Captain John B. Denton was the only Anglo killed, but nine other men in the expedition suffered injuries. General Tarrant later estimated that the three villages contained a total of 1,000 warriors, half of whom had been away hunting. He ordered his men to destroy the Indian camps and withdraw before the warriors returned. Two months later when General Tarrant returned to the area with a larger expedition, he encountered no Indians whatsoever, for they had not reestablished their homes on the creek.[1]

Because of this encounter with Native Americans, General Tarrant on August 7, 1841, commissioned Jonathan Bird as a brevet major and ordered him to raise 150 men for a three-month enlistment of Rangers to build a fort on the Trinity and establish a settlement. Bird, who only recently had moved to Texas from Alabama, spent a month trying to raise the 150 volunteers, but was able to persuade only forty-two men to join him. Mustered into service on September 19, the men proceeded to the site designated for their fort—near a crescent-shaped body of water surrounded by trees north of the West Fork of the Trinity. Bird ordered seventeen men to remain at the new fort—known to history as Bird's Fort—to protect the stockade. Its namesake then left to escort ten families from Bowie, Red River, Lamar, and Fannin Counties to the fort. He had promised 1,200 acres of land to each family under the 1840 Military Road Act. These ten families became the first Anglo settlement in North Central Texas.[2]

Any permanent plans the families entertained were short-lived because Bird soon learned that the 1841 Peters Colony contract included the land around Bird's Fort. Only Peters Colony officials could distribute the land and issue titles. The settlers involved were very upset about the misunderstanding over the land, and Major Bird began a letter-writing campaign on their behalf, which failed. Both he and the settlers abandoned Bird's Fort by March 1842. Some returned to the east, while others acquired Peters Colony land in Dallas and elsewhere.

From his home in Red River County, Bird wrote more letters, trying to obtain reimbursement for the $653.50 in expenses he had incurred while escorting the families to the fort. Even though the Congress of the Republic voted to authorize the reimbursement, the financially conservative Sam

Houston, who had succeeded Lamar as president, vetoed the bill, saying that others had spent money protecting their families and "asked no remuneration from the Government." Bird persisted. Finally, in January 1845, the Texas Congress passed a bill giving him drafts for $600 against his taxes in Bowie County to be used over a period of three years. Not waiting for the credit, he sold the drafts at a discount for cash. Brevet Major Jonathan Bird died in 1850, having never returned to the abandoned fort that bore his name. Because Bird's Fort was a civilian settlement with no permanent soldiers to protect it, it was not technically a military installation. Yet the actions of two military men—General Tarrant and Brevet Major Bird—had been instrumental in its establishment.[3]

In his second term, President Sam Houston followed a different political course than his predecessor Mirabeau B. Lamar. While Lamar fought Indians and even drove the Cherokees out of Texas, Houston sought to placate them so that Texas citizens and Indians could live side by side in peace. Houston's earlier friendship with the Cherokee in Tennessee shaped his later policies. On July 5, 1842, Houston appointed a commission to arrange meetings with the Texas tribes on the frontier. Nine tribes met with commissioners at a Caddo village in March 1843 and agreed to meet with Houston at a Grand Council at the abandoned Bird's Fort in August. Houston arrived at the appointed time and waited several days for the various tribes. The Indians finally began arriving in mid-September, by which time Houston had given up and returned to the capital. General Tarrant and General George W. Terrell, representing the Republic of Texas, signed a treaty with the tribes on September 29, 1843.[4]

The Bird's Fort treaty established a vague boundary between the white, or Anglo, settlements and Native American lands on the Texas frontier. Part of the Bird's Fort agreement stated that the tribes would move and remain west of a line of forts to be constructed along the northwest frontier. While it took a long time to implement (because of Texas annexation and the federal government's assumption of frontier protection), the selection of a site for the future Fort Worth can be seen as one consequence of the Treaty of Bird's Fort.[5]

A third military figure important to Tarrant County and Fort Worth arrived in the person of Ranger Captain Middleton Tate Johnson. A South Carolinian, Johnson came to Texas in 1839, served in the Texas Congress, and fought in the Mexican War. After reenlisting in April 1847, Johnson and his company received an assignment to the northwest Texas frontier at Kaufman Station, which would become Marrow Bone Spring.

Marrow Bone Spring, a trading post two or three miles southeast of the west fork of the Trinity River, had been established in 1845 when Texas

Middleton Tate Johnson arrived in Tarrant County with Texas Rangers earlier than the federal dragoons, who in 1849 established the army camp of Fort Worth. *Photo courtesy of the Genealogy, History, and Archives Unit, Fort Worth Public Library.*

president Anson Jones gave a license to Matthias Travis and assigned Isaac C. Spence as Indian Agent. The thirty-six–by-sixteen foot picket building officially became the Trading House at Marrow Bone Spring. In July 1846, fifty mounted Rangers under the command of Andrew Stapp arrived at the post for a six-month enlistment. Middleton Tate Johnson's company of Rangers replaced Stapp's.[6]

Once there, Johnson liked the area and began building a large two-story home to accommodate his family, which eventually included nine children. Shelby County, where Johnson had first settled when he came to Texas, did not appear to be growing and prospering, so he moved his family to the western Texas frontier. In order to establish a plantation, Johnson purchased and traded for land until he acquired several thousand acres. His plantation, in what later became the city of Arlington in Tarrant County, housed the Ranger headquarters. Johnson set up a gristmill, sorghum mill, blacksmith shop, general merchandise store, a large barn, and slave quarters. He was mustered out of the Rangers on February 3, 1849, and his wife and family arrived later that spring.[7]

Johnson greeted a small but welcome delegation of U.S. military troops at his plantation sometime in late May 1849. These were men of the Second Dragoons, led by Major Ripley A. Arnold who stopped at Johnson's Station to request assistance in situating a fort. Major Arnold carried a letter of introduction from General William Jenkins Worth, commander of the Eighth and Ninth Military Departments, covering the state of Texas and New Mexico Territory.[8]

General Worth, a New Yorker, began his military career at age seventeen at the outset of the War of 1812. The Seminole conflict in Florida, the Mexican War battle of Monterrey, and his capture of Mexico City in 1847 brought him promotions and fame. Worth was commander at Army headquarters in San Antonio when in February 1849 he issued orders that would create a line of federal forts along the Texas frontier to replace the former system of small Ranger stations. More permanent installations were necessary because settlers continually pushed west of the frontier line, where they encountered raiding Comanches, Kiowas, and other plains tribes, who challenged the newcomers on their hunting grounds. Because the government had placed 1,500 Army troops at General Worth's disposal, he possessed the means to defend the frontier. In effect the federal government finally planned to build the line of forts that the Republic of Texas had authorized at the Treaty of Bird's Fort six years earlier. Worth ordered Brevet Brigadier General William S. Harney, commander of the Second Dragoons, to inspect the North Texas frontier and recommend a general location for a fort in that area. Because General Harney believed that the West Fork of the

General William Jenkins Worth, after whom Fort Worth was named, died before even learning that Major Ripley Arnold had established the post and named it after him. Worth was Ripley's commanding officer in the Mexican-American War. *Photo courtesy Fort Worth Museum of Science and History.*

Trinity River would serve the military need, he ordered Major Arnold to select an exact site and establish the fort.[9]

On the day when Major Arnold arrived in late May 1849, M. T. Johnson greeted him and offered advice on where to establish a fort. Johnson suggested a location several miles to the northwest where the Clear and West Forks of the Trinity merged. He and some ex-Ranger settlers led Major Arnold and his Dragoons to a site on the bluff overlooking the confluence of the two streams. The men arrived in the early afternoon and someone shot a deer, which the group enjoyed for supper. One of the men, Simon B.

Farrar, wrote that they could have killed more deer, but they did not want to be "encumbered" with them.[10]

The next day the men stood on the bluff contemplating the site. Farrar wrote later, "while at that place and in view of all the advantages of a natural point of defense, and thinking of our late experience at Monterey [*sic*] where in the strategic action of General Worth had so terribly defeated the Mexicans, we there, in honor of that grand old hero, named the point Fort Worth." Whether Farrar meant that they named it on that first visit or when they returned a couple of weeks later is not clear. Some sources state that Colonel Johnson and Archibald Robinson owned the land on the bluff, but they donated the location for a fort with the provision that it would revert to them if, or when, the military abandoned it. No records have been found to substantiate this. At any rate, Major Arnold named the site Fort Worth after the superior officer who had sent him on the expedition and under whom he had served in the Mexican War.[11]

Major Ripley A. Arnold, thirty-two and a graduate of West Point, had been cited for "gallant conduct" in the Seminole wars and for "gallant and meritorious conduct" in the recently concluded Mexican War. Arnold's first assignment following the latter was to Fort Graham, west of present Hillsboro. Well-organized and efficient, Major Arnold, after taking M.T. Johnson's advice to locate the proposed fort on the bluff, returned to Fort Graham to move his troops north to the new site, which was ready for construction. With him rode troops of the Eighth Infantry and Company F of the Second Dragoons. Arnold and his men set up camp on June 6, 1849, at Terry's Spring (present Cold Spring), about a mile northeast of the bluff at a spot near the Trinity where the two forks united (near present Pavilion Street and Samuels Avenue). A grove of live oak trees provided shade for their tents, so the men called the site Live Oak Point. This became their camp while they constructed the fort, and by the first of August, Company F of the Dragoons moved up to the completed fort on the bluff.[12] A 250-by-300-foot parade ground stood about one block west of the present-day courthouse square in downtown Fort Worth. On the north side stretched a double row of soldiers' quarters; to the south officers' quarters; to the east stables; and to the west a hospital, quartermaster offices, the commissary supply, and warehouses. Unfortunately, the dragoons used green wood that shrank when it dried, leaving cracks and leaks in the buildings. In 1851 and 1852 many of the structures began collapsing and needed to be rebuilt. No wooden stockade surrounded the fort, only a rope fence. Major Arnold could congratulate himself, however, or thank Colonel Johnson for his advice, for the waters of the Trinity surrounded three sides of the fort on the bluff. Only to the south was the land flat and vulnerable to attack.[13]

Fort Worth architect Preston Geren drew this conception of the commanding officer's quarters at Fort Worth. The wooden building did not survive very long after the fort closed. *Photo courtesy of the Genealogy, History, and Archives Unit, Fort Worth Public Library.*

Fort Worth would be one in a line of forts established by the Army that included Fort Martin Scott (December 1848); Fort Croghan (March 1849); Fort Inge (March 1849); Fort Graham (April 1849); Fort Gates (October 1849); Fort Lincoln (July 1849); and Fort Merrill (March 1850). By 1851, Colonel Persifor F. Smith, commander of all forces in Texas, decided that he needed a second tier, a second line of federal forts, 100 to 150 miles west of the current line to intercept Indian raiders before they got to the area. Consequently, between June 1851 and March 1859, the federal government established an additional sixteen posts, some of which closed quickly. The forts had to be supplied from San Antonio, which received goods from quartermaster depots on the Texas coast. By 1856, one-fourth of the U.S. Army—4,047 soldiers—occupied eighteen Texas posts. The forts were not completely effective, and in 1861 the United States abandoned them, leaving to the Texans and the Confederates the job of protecting the frontier.[14] At full strength Fort Worth held eighty-six enlisted men and three officers.[15]

Major Arnold proved to be a strict disciplinarian. Private Joseph Murphy felt the brunt of Major Arnold's ire in May 1851 after being found drunk near the sutler's store. Arnold ordered a punishment known as bucking, which consisted of seating a man on the ground with his knees bent touching his chest. His hands were then tied together in front of his knees, forcing him to hunch over. Soldiers then inserted a pole like a broomstick between his knees and his elbows. The man being punished had to remain in that uncomfortable position until the commander decided to order his release. Major Arnold made the unfortunate Private Murphy endure this punishment for two days. One assumes that Murphy thought things over very carefully before allowing himself to become drunk on fort grounds again.[16]

Either the military overestimated the Indian threat, or the presence of the troops in Fort Worth kept the peace. Apparently only one raid occurred in the vicinity during the four years of the fort's existence, and even that was not reported. Former sergeant major Abe Harris related the event many years later. He did not remember the date, if indeed his memory of the

Fort Worth became the most northern post in a frontier line that stretched from Fort Duncan on the Rio Grande. Within a decade settlement moved 100 miles farther west. Adapted from a map drawn by Jack Jackson for Robert Wooster's *Soldiers, Sutlers, and Settlers: Garrison Life on the Texas Frontier* (College Station: Texas A&M University Press, 1987).

battle was correct. Mounted Caddos and Comanches attacked a band of Tonkawas several miles west of the fort in a live oak grove west of the present city of White Settlement. (The site of the battle was two or three miles due west of what during World War II would be the largest defense plant in the United States). Major Arnold sent a Lieutenant Bowles out with a squadron to investigate and they found human bones. The Tonkawas asked Major Arnold for protection, and he sheltered them in the camp commissary and refused to turn them over to Chief Towash of the Caddos. Arnold sent the Tonkawas three beeves for food. During the four years the fort was in operation, friendly Caddos, Wacos, and Ionis visited the fort to trade.[17]

Settlers felt safe in moving to the area because of the presence of the fort. The 1850 census showed 689 settlers in Tarrant County and 65 slaves. Not all of the newcomers settled adjacent to the fort; they spread out all over the county.[18] However, late in 1853, four years after the fort was built, orders arrived to close it. Troops had been constructing new buildings even as the Army made the decision to close it. The military abandoned seventeen buildings, all but two of which were made of logs covered with pecan clapboard. About one hundred civilians lived nearby when the fort was ordered closed. The settlers quickly took possession of the fort buildings, which formed the core of the new town. The community grew and developed on the site, still calling itself Fort Worth. As Leonard Sanders wrote in *How Fort Worth Became the Texasmost City*, the fort had created an "instant community." Apparently M. T. Johnson and Archibald Robinson, co-owners of the bluff site, did not press their claim to the land when the military abandoned the fort, if indeed they owned it.[19]

The troops of Company B, Second Dragoons, remained in Fort Worth even after Major Arnold departed for Fort Graham. Brevet Major H. W. Merrill assumed command with orders to move the troops to Fort Belknap. In September 1853 he was still waiting for transportation when Lieutenant Colonel W. G. Freeman came to inspect the troops. Freeman wrote, "I was gratified to find—it was the solitary exception throughout my tour—the guardhouse, that saddest of all places in a garrison, without a single *prisoner*. But Major Merrill informed me that most of his men belonged to the temperance society and that he has rarely occasion to confine any of them."[20] Perhaps Major Arnold's earlier strict punishment had worked. Private Murphy no doubt joined the Temperance Society rather than endure a bucking punishment again.

At Fort Graham Major Arnold was involved in a dispute with the post surgeon, Dr. Josephus Steiner, whom Arnold accused of being drunk. As a result, on September 6, 1853, Steiner shot and killed the thirty-six year old Arnold, who left a wife and two children. Dr. Steiner, who had many friends in the Hill County area of Central Texas, used the argument of self-defense and was not charged with a crime. In 1855 a group of men that included M. T. Johnson traveled to Fort Graham and brought Major Arnold's body back to Fort Worth for burial alongside two other of his children who had predeceased him. Thus, the military man who carried out the orders to establish Fort Worth lies buried within its boundaries.[21]

General Tarrant, associated with Fort Worth because of his participation in one of the first military forays into the area, was honored on December 20, 1849, when Governor George T. Wood signed a bill creating Tarrant County out of land taken from the northern part of a larger Navarro County. General Tarrant also is buried in Pioneer's Rest Cemetery, having been moved there in 1928 seventy years after he died. Of the four military men who led troops into the area between 1840 and 1850, General Edward H. Tarrant's name is immortalized in Tarrant County, and Bird's name lives on in the northeastern school district—Birdville, ISD. On the other hand, Johnson Station was absorbed into the city of Arlington, and the low income apartments named after Ripley A. Arnold in downtown Fort Worth gave way to big city development. Those four military men who led troops into the area between 1840 and 1850 could not know the military tradition that would follow, but they planted the seed that took seven decades to germinate.[22]

After the Fort Worth garrison closed, the federal government eventually shifted from massive involvement on the Texas frontier with eighteen military forts, to no presence at all shortly after Texas's secession from the Union in early 1861. During the Civil War neither side maintained a military post in Fort Worth or Tarrant County, nor did any battle occur nearby. Several months elapsed after southern secession before local men collectively began to support the war effort. Early in the conflict, individual volunteers traveled to East Texas to enlist with units heading east toward where the armies of North and South clashed. Colonel M. T. Johnson, who like many prominent local citizens was an early opponent of secession, organized a brigade and later supervised a fleet of blockade runners. Local men who did not volunteer for units leaving the state joined the Frontier Guard to protect settlers from any Indian attacks from the northwest. After federal troops abandoned the forts along the frontier line, Comanches and Kiowas became bolder and raided in Parker, Wise, and Jack Counties located just to the west and northwest of Tarrant.[23] During the war the population of Tarrant County declined from an estimated 6,000 to approximately 1,000. Only about 250 people resided in Fort Worth during the Civil War. The local economy was affected seriously as merchants struggled to obtain supplies. County officials issued certificates to substitute for money because of the scarcity of hard currency, and mail service also proved difficult.[24]

Despite its wartime decline, Tarrant County still remained an attractive place for migrants. Major Khleber M. Van Zandt, who lived in Marshall, Texas, when he enlisted in the Confederate Army, decided to strike out farther west after the war. He brought his talents to Fort Worth in the late summer of 1865 as a twenty-eight-year-old lawyer. Historian Sandra Myers writes that "Most modern authors agree that it was the influx of ex-Confederates like Van Zandt that saved Fort Worth."[25] As a result of this postwar migration, Fort Worth's population doubled by 1868 to approximately five hundred residents.[26]

By the time Reconstruction ended in Texas, the U.S. Army had returned in force to the western frontier they had abandoned so quickly nearly a decade earlier. This time Fort Worth did not need soldiers for protection, for the line of settlement truly had moved one hundred miles farther west. Forts established or reoccupied during this federal return included a new post, Fort Richardson, located sixty miles northwest of Fort Worth at Jacksboro in 1868; Fort Griffin, near present Albany, established in 1867; Fort Concho, near present San Angelo, established as a new post in December 1867; Fort McKavett, in southwest Menard County, reactivated in 1868; Fort Duncan on the east side of the Rio Grande above Eagle Pass, reoccupied in 1868; Fort Clark on the Rio Grande border, reoccupied, December 1866; in the Big Bend area, Fort Stockton, reoccupied, July 1867; and Fort Davis in Jeff Davis County, reoccupied 1867. Texas military historian Thomas Smith affirms that in the second half of the nineteenth century the U.S. Army became the largest "corporate organization," in the United States and that after the Civil War, its "largest geopolitical structure" was the state of Texas. Texas received up to 30 percent of the U.S. Army's operating budget. By establishing the forts, the U.S. government and its federal dollars helped settle the frontier as construction moved in to provide support to the scattered military posts. Smith calls it a "military commercial cooperative." One could not yet call the arrangement between Texas and the military a "military industrial complex," for Texas had little industry. Fort Worth took no part in the later nineteenth-century Texas military presence. The city's involvement with both the military and the defense industry would have to wait until the twentieth century.[27]

Livestock, cattle drives, meatpacking plants, and stockyards dominated Fort Worth's economy during the years from the Civil War until nearly the mid-twentieth century. Although little or no military activity occurred in the 1890s, two civilian groups—the Fort Worth Fencibles and the Lloyd Rifles—organized military drills. They provided exercise, entertainment, and social activities, with probably little thought of protection. One can imagine the pride and friendly ribbing that took place when the Fencibles won the post of honor in the inaugural ceremonies for President-elect Grover Cleveland in March 1893. To prepare for the event the forty-five members—ten commissioned and non-commissioned officers and a special surgeon—purchased new uniforms. Five years later when the Spanish-American War erupted, the two trained units volunteered for duty. They still awaited ships to carry them to Cuba, or elsewhere, when the brief four-month war ended.[28]

After the Fencibles and Lloyd Rifles activities and some local participation in the Spanish-American War, a bit of interest in things military continued. Names applied to the present University of Texas at Arlington during its early years represented military training, specifically from 1901 to 1917. In 1901 Dr. J. M. Carlisle launched Carlisle Military Academy, which evolved into the Arlington Training School by 1913. As a branch of Texas A&M University from 1917 it became Grubbs Vocational College, then North Texas Agricultural College and Arlington State College. In 1965 the institution became part of the University of Texas System. Academics won out over the military in its curriculum. Fort Worth University and Polytechnic College (later Texas Wesleyan) both formed college militia units. The militias served a social as well as military function, parading and practicing military arts.[29]

Veterans' reunions from the Mexican War, the Civil War, and the Spanish-American War also kept military affairs on the minds of various Fort Worth citizens through the years. In addition, in May 1902 three people who had lived at the original fort during its four-year existence returned to the city on the bluff for a reunion. These were Mrs. Kate Arnold Parker, a daughter of Major Ripley A. Arnold; Colonel Abe Harris, a former sergeant-major at the fort, and J. L. Leftwich of Weatherford, a former dragoon. They and others enjoyed reminiscing.[30]

The old nineteenth-century frontier army, which the three visitors fondly remembered, would in the twentieth century slowly, then wholeheartedly, adopt air power. Because aviation became so closely allied with the military in Fort Worth, early glimpses of the development of aircraft in and around the city are important for understanding of the community's later embrace of that industry. Aviation aroused an interest that endured. As the first decade of the twentieth century drew to a close, less than 2 percent of the U.S. population had ever seen an airplane. Among Fort Worthians the percentage stood at nearly zero. Events soon changed that statistic. In 1909 some prominent local citizens attended an International Air Meet at Belmont Park, New York. They returned home with exciting stories of seeing a man "in a flying machine" actually leave the ground and land without killing himself. Of course, Wilbur and Orville Wright had accomplished that feat six years earlier at Kitty Hawk, North Carolina, but no Fort Worthians witnessed that incredible flight.

As a result of their excitement, Fort Worth men with an early interest in aviation formed the Southwestern Aeronautical Association in 1909. Officers that first year were R. E. L. Costan, president; B. G. Leak, vice president; J. H. Price, secretary-treasurer, and H. H. Martin, corresponding secretary. Meetings included programs on aviation to acquaint members with the new phenomenon. In 1909, association member Amon G. Carter and other investors consolidated two local newspapers into the *Fort Worth Star-Telegram*. Carter's venture grew into the largest newspaper circulation in the South during his lifetime and helped publicize Fort Worth aviation activities. At Carter's suggestion, the local Southwestern Aeronautical Association decided to try to bring some international flyers to the area within the next eighteen months. Over the coming years Amon Carter was proactive in aviation, the military, and anything else that he believed would benefit the growth and popularity of his chosen town and the circulation of his newspaper.[31]

During the next two years as Carter promoted his new newspaper, he also helped bring an international flying demonstration to Fort Worth. Two visits to Fort Worth by national and international pilots in 1911 did not represent the military, but they did a great deal to stimulate the community's interest in aviation, which would serve it well later. The first visit occurred after a couple of Fort Worth men witnessed a flying exhibition by some French pilots in Dallas and returned home to urge local businessmen to invite the Frenchmen to repeat their efforts in Fort Worth. On very short notice the Fort Worth Board of Trade (forerunner of the Chamber of Commerce) and the Fort Worth Manufacturers and Jobbers put the project together in just three days. President Costan of the Southwestern Aeronautical Association traveled to Dallas and persuaded the fliers to come to Fort Worth, guaranteeing to pay them at least $5,000 for a flying exhibition, and if gate receipts warranted, up to $10,000. Costan, Carter, and others hustled contributions from local businessmen to reach the promised minimum.[32]

The fliers agreed to an exhibition in Fort Worth on January 12 and 13, 1911. City officials met the fliers' train as it arrived in Fort Worth on the morning of January 8, to prepare for the event scheduled later in the week. Newspaper publicity in Carter's paper and others attracted a crowd of thousands to the event itself, which was held at the racetrack (present West Seventh Street north of the Montgomery Plaza development). Schools agreed to give their students half-day holidays so the youngsters could see the pilots. Many stores closed early, and railroads offered discounted fares to people in outlying communities so they could attend. The traction company (streetcar line) worked overtime to move the huge crowds to the site of the demonstration The crowd of 15,000 waited for hours to witness what for most would be their first view of an airplane flight.[33]

Like a traveling circus, the fliers and their crew assembled their airplanes from crates that had come with them on the train. Four pilots made up the team: Roland Garros, Rene Simon, Edmond Audemars, and Rene Barrier. Later, in World War I, Garros became the first pilot to earn the title "ace" for shooting down three enemy airplanes and forcing two to land. ("Ace" was a French slang word that honored an outstanding performance in any endeavor.) Unfortunately, a strong wind threatened any attempt at flying on the first day the pilots were in Fort Worth, but Garros did not want to disappoint the crowd, which had paid admission fees of fifty cents for adults and twenty-five cents for children to see the show. Four mechanics held Garros's airplane while another turned the propeller to start the engine. Garros's "mosquito-like Demoiselle monoplane" bounced down the track. The crowd cheered as he gained speed, but groaned when it appeared he would hit a fence at the end of the field. The little aeroplane, as they called it, barely lifted before demolishing the fence and hitting some telephone wires.[34]

On the second day—Friday the thirteenth—only Rene Simon was able to complete a successful flight because wind conditions were even worse than they had been the day before. Audemars wrecked a plane in an attempt to get it off the ground. The crowd on the second day was down to 10,000 spectators, but they waited until 6 p.m. for Simon's flight. Men and women flew large kites to keep the crowd entertained while it waited. After Simon's brief flight, the fliers packed up and left on their special train. Gate receipts only brought in $6,300, and local organizers had to pay $400 to rent the grounds, erect seats, employ musicians, and hire ticket sellers.[35]

Those who missed the touring international fliers got a second chance to see an airplane flight later that same year. Wealthy newspaperman William Randolph Hearst announced on October 9, 1910, that he would give a $50,000 prize to the first aviator to fly coast-to-coast in thirty days or less. He gave participants a year to make the attempt. Few men, or women, were in a position to take up the challenge, but one who chose to try was Calbraith Perry (Cal) Rodgers, who came from a lineage of adventurers. His great-great grandfather, Commodore Matthew Calbraith Perry, opened Japan to the Western world for trade in the 1850s. Commodore Perry's brother, Oliver Hazard Perry, made the famous statement, "We have met the enemy and they are ours" on Lake Erie in the War of 1812.[36]

Cal Rodgers had aspired to a naval career like his ancestors, but scarlet fever at age six so affected his hearing that the United States Naval Academy turned him down. However, Rodgers did not let his partial hearing loss stand in the way of accepting William Randolph Hearst's contest challenge. Rodgers decided at age thirty-two that he would learn to fly so he could participate in the challenge. In June 1911 he attended the flying school Orville and Wilbur Wright operated in Dayton, Ohio.[37]

Once Rodgers decided to enter the contest, he needed a sponsor. Armour and Company, one of the largest and wealthiest meat packing firms in the nation, with plants in most of the major stockyards, including Fort Worth, offered their support. Armour produced more than slaughtered beef, specifically a new grape drink that they called "Vin Fiz." The name of the airplane they sponsored for Rodgers thus became the *Vin Fiz Flyer*. The airplane was a white EX-Flyer with thirty-two foot wings and a thirty-five horse-power four cylinder, water-cooled engine weighing 196 pounds. The airplane, capable of flying at fifty-five miles per hour, had no throttle so only two speeds were possible: wide open or stop. A mechanic could make some adjustments in speed by advancing the spark, but that was it. The plane had no windshield and no armrests.[38]

Because Rodgers was not even ready to take off until September 17, 1911, he probably realized that he could not win Hearst's $50,000 prize, as less than a month remained in the year given for the contest. By then, however, Rodgers simply wanted to see if he could be the first to fly from coast-to-coast. Mainly following railroad lines, Rodgers headed west, traveled to Chicago, and turned south across the plains to Kansas, Oklahoma, and down to North Texas. Having already missed Hearst's deadline there was no need to hurry.[39]

Amon Carter in his *Fort Worth Star-Telegram* gave Fort Worth citizens five days advance warning that the *Vin Fiz Flyer* was on its way south, calling Rodgers "Daredevil Cal." Carter placed a *Star-Telegram* reporter on board the train pulling Rodgers' special car, and the reporter wired from Denison, Texas, that Cal, following the Missouri, Kansas, and Texas tracks south from Gainesville, was sixty-five miles north of Fort Worth.[40]

On October 17, more than 8,000 Fort Worthians waited four hours in a pasture near the Ryan Place Addition south of downtown. The crowd had been larger, but many gave up and left before someone spotted the *Vin Fiz*. People yelled and whistles blew. Unfortunately, people in the crowd became so excited that they ran out into the pasture, and Rodgers had trouble landing. Mounted patrolmen could not effectively control the large crowd. Cleverly, Rodgers pretended to descend at one edge of the pasture, and the crowd moved there; then he flew to the other side of the field, and finally, at 4:16 p.m., set down his plane. Amon Carter and J. M. North Jr. (editor of Carter's paper), both members of Fort Worth's welcoming committee, met Rodgers at the airplane to shake his hand. Because the exhibition fliers the previous January had arrived in Fort Worth by rail and then assembled their airplane, Cal Rodgers became the first person ever to fly into Fort Worth. When he presented a letter to North from McAlester, Oklahoma, his flight also became the city's first airmail postal delivery. While Rodgers' crew tuned up his airplane's engine, the Fort Worth host committee took the celebrated pilot and his wife Mabel, who had arrived by train, to the Westbrook Hotel for a grand dinner sponsored by the Southwest Aeronautical Association. The Rodgerses were also guests at the Majestic Theatre that evening.[41]

Rodgers finally completed his cross-country flight on December 10, 1911, the first person ever to do so. It took him nearly three months to make the 4,231-mile trip from ocean to ocean. His actual flying time was eighty-two hours, four minutes, with an average speed of 51.56 miles per hour, and more than eighty landings en route. Rodgers' mechanic repaired the airplane so many times and replaced so many parts because of his nineteen crashes that at the conclusion of the trip only one strut and the rudder remained from the original airplane. Nevertheless, his airplane today is housed in the Smithsonian in Washington, D.C., for all to see.

Cal Rodgers inspired citizens of Fort Worth both to become aviators themselves and to help create an aviation city. One of the youngsters who saw Rodgers fly that day in Fort Worth was Ormer Leslie Locklear. Even the news on April 3, 1912, that Cal Rodgers had crashed into shallow water on Long Beach and died a few feet from where he had completed his famous trip four months earlier did not deter the young Locklear from his fascination with airplanes. Locklear's flying career would begin in Fort Worth with World War I.[42]

Locklear was not the only North Texan looking to the skies after Rodgers' flight. Two aviation enthusiasts in Decatur created a business. Jay Ingram, 26, was a Model T Ford dealer and mechanic in 1914 when he met an early stunt flier named Charles A. Foster in Dallas. Ingram offered to help Foster build an airplane at his shop. The two men bought a six-cylinder Port Roberts motor and used spruce wood for the fuselage. They called themselves the "Pioneer Aeroplane Exhibition Company." Foster flew their first plane on June 4, 1915, but Ingram and his two brothers learned to fly as well. Foster and Ingram took an airplane to county fairs all over Texas, Oklahoma, and Arkansas. After 1916 when airplanes became more common because of World War I, the two men could not get bookings and ceased operations. Jay Ingram became a flying instructor. But Ingram and Foster's activities put Decatur on the map as the first airplane factory in Texas, for they produced several flying machines.[43]

The next opportunity for citizens to view live airplane flights came

Captain Benjamin Foulois led the five fliers and airplanes that represented the entire air power of the United States in 1915. On a flight between Fort Sill in Oklahoma and Fort Sam Houston in San Antonio, Foulois and his men spent a night in Fort Worth to the delight of airplane enthusiasts in the city. *Photo courtesy Fort Sam Houston Museum, San Antonio.*

when Captain Benjamin D. Foulois and his six-man, six-airplane Army Air Squadron became the first military airplanes to arrive in Fort Worth. They landed on November 20, 1915, in the pasture where Cal Rodgers had set down his *Vin Fiz* four years earlier. Foulois taught himself to fly after receiving fifteen minutes of instruction from Orville Wright through the mail, and thus officially became the first, and at that time only, pilot in the U.S. military. The government allowed him $150 per year to maintain his airplane, but he spent $300 out of his own pocket the first year. In mid-November 1915, Captain Foulois and his men took five days to fly the 439 miles from Fort Sill in Oklahoma to Fort Sam Houston in San Antonio. They stopped to refuel and spend the night at Wichita Falls, Fort Worth, and Austin.[44]

Flying into Fort Worth with Captain Foulois were Lieutenants J. E. Carberry, T. S. Bowen, T. D. Milling, C. G. Chapman, and I. A. Rader. Captain Foulois's airplane bent an axle while landing, but he was not injured. The men flew their six ninety-horsepower Curtis JN 3 biplanes the 113 miles from Wichita Falls in two hours. Because of the damage to Foulois' airplane, the men stayed in Fort Worth longer than they had intended. The 3,000 people who turned out to see their machines were thrilled, as were Amon Carter and other prominent Fort Worth businessmen. Chamber of Commerce president Ben E. Keith organized an event to entertain the military men with a banquet at the Metropolitan Hotel, located at Eighth and Commerce Streets. The businessmen and the entire U.S. Air Corps gathered in a private dining room and enjoyed a long, relaxed dinner. Captain Foulois predicted that in case of war the U.S. government would spend $100 million to use air power in warfare, but the local citizens did not believe him. He urged them to write their congressmen to begin to build up the flying corps immediately. Prominent citizens of Dallas threatened to protest to Washington if Captain Foulois and his squadron did not also stop there, so after leaving Fort Worth they did exactly that.[45]

Early fliers called their machines aeroplanes. The Greek word *dromos* means a race or race course, so early airfields came to be called aerodromes.[46] Because of World War I and Captain Foulois, Fort Worth would soon acquire three of those new aerodromes. In fact, the city's success in obtaining three airfields in World War I most likely was the result of businessman Ben E. Keith having entertained Captain Foulois at that fancy dinner in 1915 at the Metropolitan Hotel. A second dinner the two men shared in Washington, D.C. two years later changed Fort Worth's future focus considerably.

CHAPTER 2

World War I: Three Air Fields

EN E. KEITH, WHO CONTINUED TO SERVE AS PRESIDENT OF THE Fort Worth Chamber of Commerce in 1917, wanted to bring military money into the city. With Louis J. Wortham, an editor of the *Fort Worth Star-Telegram* and a former state legislator, Keith traveled to Washington, D.C., early in the year to confer with the secretary of war. He wanted to convince military officials that Fort Worth possessed plenty of anything they might need: railroads, work force, mild climate, and food.[1]

Keith would have known about food supply, for not only did Fort Worth have the stockyards, in 1906 he began driving a truck for local produce company Harkrider-Morrison. By 1918 Keith would rise to controlling partner and continue to build the business under the name Ben E. Keith Company, using the latest technology in food wholesaling. By 2006, it would rank as the ninth largest broad line food distributor in the United States.[2]

In Washington, Keith saw Benjamin D. Foulois, the military man for whom he had organized the banquet in Fort Worth two years earlier, and Keith again gave a dinner for him. Foulois, now a major, had just returned from accompanying General John J. Pershing to Mexico with the First Aero Squadron. Keith told Foulois about his mission to bring military installations to Fort Worth. At dinner Foulois wrote on a piece of paper: "Do what you can for this Texan," and at some later point presented Keith and the note to Brigadier-General Cuthbert G. "Frog" Hoare, commander of the Royal Flying Corps Canada, which had been founded in April 1912. In early 1917, General Hoare was having problems recruiting enough Canadians for pilot training, and so welcomed Americans. Because the Canadian winter allowed fewer flying days than would a location in the southern United States, Hoare formulated a plan that he presented to Brigadier-General George O. Squier, Chief Signal Officer, U.S. Army, the commander of the American Air Service. Squier told Hoare that he needed instructors for the military flying schools the U.S. Army wanted to open. The two men reached an agreement for Canadians to train one hundred U.S. cadets to fly if a winter camp and airplanes were made available in the United States.

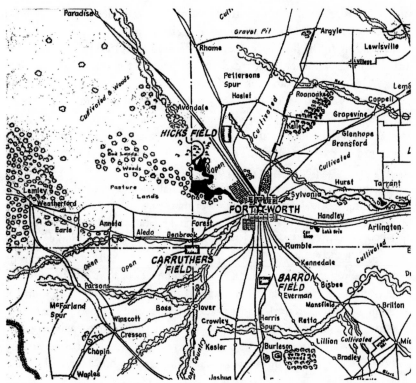

This Tarrant County map features the three Canadian-American pilot training fields that were located north, south, and southwest of Fort Worth called Taliaferro (Hicks), Barron, and Carruthers Fields, respectively. *Map courtesy Harold Langley.*

A Royal Flying Corps Canada wing would also move south for the winter. The two generals obtained all the necessary permissions, and General Hoare returned to Washington in June to finalize plans. Both generals signed the agreement, which was ratified by the U.S. War Department and the British War Office in June 1917. The final plan actually included a second Canadian wing.[3]

The reciprocal agreement stipulated that the RFC would train ten squadrons for the U.S. Signal Corps. This meant 300 pilots, 144 other flying officers, 20 administrative and equipment officers, and approximately 2,000 mechanics. The Americans would begin their training in Canada and complete it in the United States. The RFC would provide all equipment for the Canadian part of the training, and the U.S. Army would supply equipment for training that took place in the United States. Each service would provide pay, clothing, and transportation for its own soldiers, and draw rations to be repaid while in the other's country. As a result, 1,400 U.S. cadets traveled to Canada in July 1917 to begin flight training.[4]

According to the final agreement, the United States would provide three airfields in the southern United States instead of the one originally proposed. General Hoare and his staff began inspecting cities in Florida and Texas for possible sites. In Texas they considered Dallas, Midland, Wichita Falls, Austin, Waco, San Antonio, and Fort Worth. General Hoare liked San Antonio, but U.S. officials warned him that a labor shortage there might prove to be a problem. The Canadian general was said to have only "reluctantly" accepted Fort Worth over San Antonio.[5]

All three airfields were established in small sparsely populated suburbs surrounding Fort Worth: Hicks, Everman, and Benbrook. Hicks (near present Saginaw) took its name from Hicks Station on the Fort Worth and Denver City Railroad and the Charles E. Hicks family, which owned the land. The Fort Worth Chamber of Commerce rented the land from its owners, paying them only a small amount. The city of Fort Worth provided water, sewer, electricity, and telephone connections free of charge, and it constructed hard surfaced roads, graded streets, and railroad connections. The airfield at Hicks served sixteen squadrons of 250 men each, in addition to the cadet fliers. The field covered two and a half sections of land and consisted of twenty-four hangars, an ammunition building, and several other structures.[6]

Because the military chose Hicks on the rolling upland prairie north of downtown Fort Worth for bombardment training, it constructed concrete bombing sites shaped somewhat like the German Fokker airplane. German aircraft reigned supreme in the air during World War I, so early in the war people began to refer to Allied aircraft as "Fokker fodder." Buried a foot deep, level with the ground, the walls of the Fokker-shaped bomb sites were made of concrete, and the hollow insides could be pumped full of water by means of a nearby windmill. Slightly bigger than an actual Fokker, the targets had a forty-foot wingspan, and a body six and a half feet wide. Twenty of these concrete "Fokkers" were scattered over the gunnery range.[7]

Canadians, and later Americans, enjoyed training at the aerial gunnery field. During one stage of training a plane was equipped with Marlin machine guns mounted over the engine and synchronized to shoot between the propeller blades as they rotated. Also a Lewis machine gun was mounted on a turret in the rear cockpit of the airplane. Pilots flew over the Fokker-shaped targets, strafed with their machine guns, and cheered when they saw the water-filled targets splash. They also had the opportunity to drop "pretend" bombs. The targets reminded the young airmen why they were fighting.[8]

The gunnery range extended northwest over the waters of Lake Worth for live air-to-ground and air-to-air firing. An advanced landing ground was constructed on the shore of the lake so that the planes would not have to fly back to the field to exchange pilots and gunnery crews. This extension of the range meant that RFC Canada was able to participate for the first time in live air-to-air gunnery. The airplanes carried Lewis B machine guns loaded with cameras instead of cartridges and student pilots simulated air fighting with another airplane. An instructor flew the plane while the cadet acted as gunner. The cadet aimed the camera gun as though shooting down the opposing airplane. When developed, the photos revealed how accurate the cadet's aim had been.[9]

To provide land for the airfield in Everman, J. Martin Scott leased his 222-acre farm to the U.S. government for $3,220 for two years beginning in August 1917. He later extended the lease. Construction of the airfield began in the fall. The one-square-mile airfield and buildings were located ten miles south of Fort Worth and about one mile southwest of the town of Everman. The completed airfield resembled a town with its own railroad spur, fire department, police department, water supply, sewage system, and disposal plant. From the air, cadet pilots saw miles of asphalt roads, tennis courts, a baseball diamond, a football field, and a lake for swimming. For the important military training one also could find sixty-one permanent buildings, nineteen hangars, and the landing field—the aerodrome. The maximum number of service people housed at the Everman field at any one time was 103 officers and 2,157 enlisted men. When the first Royal Flying Corps cadets arrived, a detachment of American cadets that had received ground training at the University of Toronto arrived with them. After the Canadians left in April 1918, the Americans added a gunnery school, a radio detachment, and a photographic section.[10]

The third airfield was developed near the former home of James M. Benbrook. Called "Squire" by his neighbors because of his English heritage, he had been one of the earliest settlers southwest of Fort Worth. Arriving in Texas in 1874 from Illinois, Benbrook two years later petitioned the Texas and Pacific Railroad to place a station and watering stop along Mary's Creek near his land. He constructed a large Victorian house for his six children on Walnut Creek to the east in a little community then called Miranda (or Marinda). In 1880 the railroad complied, naming the station—and thus the community that grew up there—Benbrook. Before the Canadians arrived, the last excitement in Benbrook had been in 1896 when one of the West's last train robberies occurred there.[11]

Similar to the two other training airfields, workers at Benbrook built six cadet barracks, each with a mess hall, five commissioned and non-commissioned officers quarters, and one bachelor officers' quarters. In addition, there was an officers' club, an administration building, and a commanding officers' quarters. The base also had a hospital, a fire hall, a bakery, a post exchange, and to accommodate married officers with families, a school. Enlisted men worked in the aero repair shop, garage, machine shop, blacksmith shop, and motor test shed. Three "oil houses," perhaps what later were called filling stations, also provided service to the base. Major George Wellesby arrived in November 1917 to take command even though early-arriving officers had already begun flying instruction.[12]

Captain Murton A. Seymour of Vancouver, British Columbia, commanded the advanced RFC headquarters staff that left Canada in late September 1917 and began arriving in Fort Worth in October. The cadets were grouped into the 17th, 22nd, 27th, 28th, and 139th Aero Squadrons, composed of Canadians and Americans, the latter having volunteered to fight with the British before the United States officially joined the war. A new squadron arrived each week. Lieutenant Colonel Dermott Allen, chief of staff to General Hoare, remained in Texas to command the fifteen Canadian and ten American squadrons. Allen, the son of an Anglo-Irish barrister posted to Calcutta, had studied at the Royal Military College at Sandhurst in England, and joined the Royal Flying Corps in 1912. He flew patrols in France during World War I and received several promotions. Although he retired from the military in 1933 and later worked for British Airways, he often referred to his command in Texas at age twenty-seven as the high point of his career.[13]

The last Canadians to reach Texas were staff and cadets of the Forty-second and Forty-third Wings, which left Toronto on six special trains and arrived in Fort Worth on November 17. Their airplanes were crated in boxcars, ready for the mechanics to assemble as the men arrived and settled in. Many of the bi-wing airplanes (which they called airships) were Curtis JN 4s, which cadets nicknamed Jennys. B. Douglas Thomas of the British Sopwith Company designed the Jennys, which became the primary pilot-training airplane. Instructors, many of whom lacked experience themselves, yelled instructions over the sound of the engine because airplanes were not yet equipped with speaking tubes or ear attachments.[14]

Initially the British and Americans referred to their entire Fort Worth pilot training operation as Camp Taliaferro, calling the three aerodromes Hicks, Everman, and Benbrook Fields, after the suburbs where they were located. The camp was named in honor of Lieutenant Walter R. Taliaferro. One of only forty-nine U.S. officers assigned to aviation training between 1908 and March 1914, Taliaferro died in an air accident in 1915.[15]

The Forty-second and Forty-third Wings occupied Everman and Ben-

American pilots learned to fly using the Curtis JN 4 flying machines photographed here in July 1918. A British pilot standing by the first "Jenny" remained as an instructor after his own countrymen left. *Photo courtesy Dalton Hoffman, Local History Collection.*

brook respectively, while five squadrons and an Aerial Gunnery School were established at Hicks Field. Later the Canadians called the three fields Taliaferro #1 (Hicks), Taliaferro #2 (Everman), and Taliaferro #3 (Benbrook). Plans had moved so rapidly for this joint effort between the Canadians and Americans that the land and accommodations were not ready when the cadets began to arrive. Workers had completed only half of the construction on each of the three aerodromes. The water supply was insufficient; the sewage systems were not yet operating, and one field lacked electricity. Cadets lived in canvas tents until workers completed the barracks; in fact, cadets helped the civilian carpenters finish the sleeping quarters. Flight training began as soon as mechanics assembled the airplanes, even though the entire training organization still was not fully operational.[16]

Flying weather remained fine for a couple of months, but early in 1918 high winds brought "northers" with a rapid drop in temperature, heavy rain, and occasional snow. Student pilots deplored the heavy mud that filled the aerodromes' fields. On just one day forty propellers were smashed by mud thrown up from the wheels of the undercarriage. Over a period of a month an average of ten propellers broke each day. Fortunately, the weather soon improved, and a Texas winter remained much milder than a Canadian one.[17]

"For the most part, the facilities provided by the Americans were good, and in the case of the School of Aerial Gunnery, they were superior," General Hoare wrote the British war office. Facilities certainly represented a great improvement over what they had seen in Canada. "The U.S. have done everything we asked for in the way of ranges, etc., and in fact have spent a great deal of money for us," he added. The Canadians liked the "vast open prairies" that "offered an unobstructed view for miles." Fort Worth's location on the edge of the Grand Prairie was part of its advantage.[18]

The vast open spaces proved too tempting for one young Canadian cadet, Cecil J. H. Holms, who once took off heading west from Taliaferro #3 (Benbrook) without permission to deviate from his flight pattern. Having received only four and one-half hours of instruction before soloing, he became tired of flying around and around over the airfield and so headed west. He had flown about ten miles when the wind strengthened and dust began hampering his ability to see. He decided he had better land in a farmer's pasture. The farmer drove out in a Model T to check on him and invited him in for lunch. Luckily, the farmer owned a telephone, so Cadet Holms called his instructor and confessed what he had done and where he went down. Asking to speak to the farmer, the instructor advised that all airplanes were grounded because of the high winds. Consequently, the farmer and his wife invited Holms to stay overnight. The next morning the instructor and a mechanic flew in, inspected the plane, and changed a spark plug or two. The instructor did not yell at Holms in front of the farmer or the mechanic, but when they got back to the field, he lambasted him for flying farther afield than he was authorized. In relating the story later, what the young cadet remembered most about the incident was the home-cooked meals the farmer's wife prepared, a welcome change from military food.[19]

Where only three hours of training per day had been available at Camp Borden in Canada, students received an average of six and a half hours after their arrival in Texas. From November 17, 1917, until April 12, 1918, just before the Canadians left, they logged a total of 67,000 flying hours. One cadet, Floyd Lewis, remembered, "Texas was a short, pleasant interlude between learning and overseas action." However, there were many accidents and one Canadian later said that he believed that so many fatal accidents occurred because of "the daredevil spirit instilled by the R.F.C. pilots." Word spread to "hush up" news of accidents to keep from scaring the cadets still in training.[20]

The original agreement between the United States and Canada called for the Canadians to leave in mid-February 1918. General Hoare knew that the northern winter was not yet over, so he persuaded General Squier to let the Canadians remain until mid-April. In exchange, Hoare agreed to train eight additional American squadrons consisting of 144 pilots, 1,200 men, and a number of ground officers. When the Canadians left Fort Worth, training of the additional eight squadrons was incomplete, but all in all, the Canadians had instructed, or partially instructed, more than 4,800 men, both officers and other ranks of the American services. Over 400 pilots had graduated, and another fifty soon followed. More than 2,500 ground tradesmen trained in Fort Worth and another 1,600 gained some instruction before the Canadians left. In addition, the Canadians gave flight training to 1,500 of their own cadets. Both countries appeared satisfied with the outcome of the joint training arrangement; so also were the citizens of Fort Worth, who acquired three fully operational airfields once the Canadians left. Major General W. L. Kenly, Chief of the U.S. Air Service, wrote on May 17, 1918:

> By its faithful and efficient work in the training of our cadres and enlisted personnel, the Royal Air Force has conferred great and practical benefit on the United States Air Service. Equally important is the imponderable but undoubted benefit which has accrued to our men by instruction by, and association with, officers and men who have had practical experience at the front and with conditions we are preparing to meet.[21]

When the Americans took possession of the three airfields from the Canadians, they officially changed the names of the three Tarrant County airfields. Major Delos C. Emmons, Chief of the Air Division, Signal Corps, recommended that the field at Benbrook be named Carruthers Field in honor of Cadet W. K. Carruthers who had been killed in an airplane accident at Mineola, Texas, on June 18, 1917, even before the Fort Worth location was decided. The field at Everman became Barron Field in honor of Cadet R. J. Barron who drowned at Chandler Field, Essington, Pennsylvania, on August 22, 1917, after his airplane fell into the water. Taliaferro Field at Hicks kept the same name. The three fields received telegrams advising them of their new official names on May 1, 1918. Local citizens, however, found it difficult to remember to use the new names, so in newspaper articles, letters, and reminiscences people continued to call them Hicks, Everman, and Benbrook, or even Taliaferro 1, 2, and 3.[22]

When Major Theodore C. Macaulay arrived as the new U.S. commander of Taliaferro Field early in September 1918, he expressed concern that the name was not more widely used. Local residents still called it Hicks Field. Macaulay had known Lieutenant Walter R. Taliaferro and he wanted his friend's name honored. When someone told Macaulay that the name was hard to pronounce, he set them straight on that as well. It was pronounced as though it were spelled "Tolliver." He wrote a long article about the field's namesake in the *Taliaferro Target,* the field's weekly newspaper. Under Macaulay, Taliaferro Field aspired to be the best gunnery school in the country and it trained cadets from Barron and Carruthers Fields, as well as other nearby installations. In fact, officers from five other fields came to Taliaferro to complete the aerial gunnery course.[23]

Lieutenant Colonel Thomas C. Turner, took command of Barron Field in Everman in May after the Canadians left. He had enlisted in the Marine Corps at age eighteen and within a year and a half became a second lieutenant. He served in the Philippines, Puerto Rico, and Mexico, and in April 1917 began flight training in San Diego. He won his wings at Pensacola, Florida, in February 1918 and became a lieutenant colonel later that year.[24] At a later reunion of veterans of Barron Field someone reminisced about an incident when a rookie failed to salute Lieutenant Colonel Turner. As a Marine Turner wore a different shaped cap from most of the other officers, who were Army. Colonel Turner stopped the private and asked, "Don't you salute officers?" "Yes, sir," the recruit replied. "Then why didn't you salute me?" Turner asked. "Because I thought you were a Y.M.C.A. secretary," was the answer. The young man learned quickly that the commanding officer of Barron Field was a Marine and demanded respect.[25]

Wives of some of the American pilots came to the area near Taliaferro Field to find rooming houses so they could be near their husbands. Cecil Bush and Mina Vason boarded with Mr. and Mrs. Sam Gross of Saginaw while their husbands were in training. The Gross family became so well acquainted with the two young women that their daughter and son-in-law, Ione and Joe Rider, named their baby girl born in 1918 Cecil Mina. Later as an adult the girl added an "e," making a more feminine name in Cecile.[26]

Local residents kept fond memories of Carruthers Field. William Yeager, who as a boy lived on a ranch south of Benbrook, described the airplanes in his reminiscences: "It was breathtaking to watch those two-winged craft fly over the pastures shooting at rabbits and sometimes a wolf. They were supposed to aim at regular targets, but they must have had more fun shooting at rabbits." When the Americans took over the field, they proved a bit stricter about what the fliers could shoot at from their airplanes. A directive from the division of Military Aeronautics on December 31, 1918, ordered: "The shooting of wild fowl with machine guns from airplanes is absolutely forbidden." Offenders would be brought to trial.[27] Yeager remembered another time when a cadet provided some unintended excitement:

> One day, we were driving on a ranch road through the north pasture, which was about three miles south of Benbrook, when a

young cadet landed his plane in front of our Marmon Touring car. He borrowed some pliers, went over and fixed his plane, returned the pliers with thanks and took off back towards Benbrook, while we watched wide-eyed as if we had seen a visitor from Mars.[28]

Children who attended school in Benbrook at the time took delight in waving at the pilots as they flew over the schoolyard. Teachers probably had trouble getting students back inside the school building after recess. Mary Stallard McGaughy remembered the time she and her friends were walking to school and saw an airplane in the road ahead of them. They all helped push the plane until the pilot finally got his engine started and flew off into the sky.[29]

Several commanding officers served at Carruthers Field while under American jurisdiction, but Lieutenant Colonel Jacob E. Fickel would become the best known. Although he only commanded the field from October 22, 1918, to January 24, 1919, when he was transferred to Washington, D.C., he remained in the army and became a general by World War II.[30]

Pilot training was similar at all three fields, although only Taliaferro featured a bombardier school. Flying hours for the student pilots and their instructors, as of June 19, 1918, were 5:30 a.m. to 11:30 a.m. and 5 p.m. to dark. A training report for Barron Field listed the seven stages of flight training for a Reserve Military Aviator:

1. dual, an officer-instructor flew with trainees;
2. primary solo, flying only in a circle around the field;
3. advanced solo, flew a route farther away;
4. cross country, to a distant point and return;
5. formation, several airplanes;
6. accuracy, bombing and machine gun practice; and
7. acrobatic, leave the cockpit in flight.

Some accounts report that the seventh stage occurred only at Barron Field.[31]

A War Department memo urged cadets when not in flight to utilize proper flying terms and not colloquialisms, because civilians might get the wrong impression. For example, instead of "joyride" they were told to say practice flight; instead of "stunt" flying or "trick" flying, acrobacy, and "exhibition" flights were really demonstration flights. In the *Cadet Note Book*, Instruction No. 5 stated that no flyer could do acrobatics unless he was in the acrobatics unit and had been approved for such flying. Instruction No. 51 in the same book stated that "No machine will fly over Fort Worth or Camp Bowie." Apparently cadets did not scrupulously obey this instruction, as a story about Eastman Kodak reveals.[32]

The Eastman Kodak Company of Rochester, New York, wanted to help the war effort and in cooperation with the army set up a training school of photography, inviting the fields to send cadets to the school. The company gave each cadet five folding cameras—one for himself and four to take back to friends. Of course, to use the cameras, the men would have to purchase Eastman film and let Eastman process it. As a result of the photo department at Barron Field, "unauthorized" aerial photos were taken of much of Fort Worth that later proved valuable in many ways, especially in real estate development.[33]

Unfortunately, numerous air accidents caused deaths at all three fields. The first fatal collision at any of the three installations by cadet pilots in the air occurred at Carruthers early in the morning on December 21, 1917, when three members of the Royal Flying Corps were killed. The most famous pilot killed at any of the three local flying fields was Vernon Castle, a well-known dancer who had appeared on Broadway with his wife Irene. Born in Norwich, England, in 1887, Castle came to the United States in 1906 and learned to fly at the Curtiss school in Virginia at his own expense. He and his wife were starring in a stage show for Irving Berlin when Castle dramatically announced he was leaving the show to go to war. Having kept his British citizenship, he joined the RFC in 1916, flew 300 missions over German lines, and won the Croix de Guerre. In 1917 he was transferred to Canada as an instructor and thus became a part of the reciprocal agreement with the United States that brought Canadian instructors to Fort Worth.[34]

Castle died when the plane he was in crashed at 10:30 in the morning February 15, 1918, while he instructed an American cadet. As Castle headed in for a landing he was forced to pull his plane up sharply to avoid another airplane flown by an American student that was about to collide with him. This caused Castle's Jenny to stall for a second and then "slam into the ground" forty feet below. While the Canadian trainers had placed student pilots in the front seat and the instructor behind, at Benbrook, Castle insisted that students sit in the safer rear seat. Consequently, the thirty-one-year-old Castle died instantly when the plane crashed, but the cadet in the second seat behind him suffered only slight injuries. The two passengers in the other plane also survived. Because the Castles had been so well known before the war, the story quickly spread across the nation via telegraph. An elaborate funeral procession took place the next day as Castle's coffin, draped with the British flag, rode in a horse-drawn artillery caisson to the Texas and Pacific Railroad Station. A Royal Flying Corps honor guard followed the caisson with their rifles pointing to the ground in the British tradition.[35]

Across all three aerodromes in nearly 100,000 hours of flying time, a total of 106 fliers died in air-related accidents between January 1 and December

17, 1918. Of this total, at least thirty-eight were Canadian or British pilots. A British War Graves Commission purchased burial spots in Fort Worth's Greenwood Cemetery in 1924 for eleven Canadians who had died and were buried in Fort Worth. In the 1930s a World War I Fliers Club began holding an annual memorial service at a monument the Canadian government erected in honor of the dead fliers. A ceremony at the monument continues to this day, held in alternate years on Memorial Day, the most recent in 2011. Flying fatalities gave Taliaferro the highest number of accidental deaths of any field nationwide. Incidents also occurred that damaged the "airships" but did not seriously injure the pilots. Pilots filed accident reports almost daily. Two from Barron Field offer some insight: "Taxyed [*sic*] into ditch, ship nosed over but balanced with one end of propellor [sic] stuck in ground;" and "Hit tree while taking off." Local residents remembered "lots of crashes."[36]

Although flying was dangerous, influenza represented the major medical threat facing all local soldiers as the deadly Spanish influenza swept the country in 1917–19, killing civilians and military personnel. As the epidemic spread nationwide, commanders at military bases took precautions. At the behest of Major A. F. Stotts, medical officer at Barron Field, the field's commander issued orders telling the men to avoid public places like movie theaters and keep the barracks well aired. In addition incoming troops were to be quarantined for two weeks, and spitting on floors was "strictly forbidden." Orders also suspended all dances, hops, and other gatherings on military reservations. Despite precautions, fully one-third of the people at Barron field caught the flu in the winter of 1918–19. A quarantine kept cadets at Taliaferro Field from leaving the base for several weeks, but officials lifted it in October 1918 when the health on the post was cited as "still excellent."[37]

Young women who chose to help the war effort by serving as nurses resided at all air fields and military bases and provided skilled care during the influenza epidemic. One of those at Barron Field was Alice Collins. She took her four-year nurses' training at a Sisters of Charity Hospital in St. Louis, Missouri, and began working at Jefferson Barracks in the outskirts of St. Louis after the war started. When she received a telegram telling her she was being transferred to Barron Field in Everman, Texas, she had never heard of either place, but someone finally told her the field was close to Fort Worth. Alice was picked up at the railroad station in Fort Worth and brought to Everman. She became one of five nurses and three doctors assigned to care for 1,000 men. The hospital had a capacity of seventy beds and served a total of 1,325 patients during the years Barron Field was active. Alice later recalled, "We worked sometimes twenty-two hours a day." She and other nurses also wrote letters home for sick soldiers and sometimes would have to "write to the parents and say that your son John died [of influenza] and so and so."[38]

When the influenza epidemic did not require quarantines, numerous activities existed for off-duty cadets. Perhaps these activities helped to keep their minds off the dangerous aspects of their training and the European war they soon would enter. On April 18, 1918, a memo went out at Barron Field announcing a minstrel show and asking for volunteers to sign up to perform. The soldiers also engaged in sports and challenged teams from the other airfields and Camp Bowie. One unusual activity, certainly not one planned for the pleasure of the soldiers, took place when someone in authority at Barron Field assigned everyone to weed-pulling duty. The weeds had grown so high that airplanes often broke their propellers when landing. At least one time the entire personnel of the field lined up, shoulder to shoulder in a formation more than a mile wide, and swept across the field pulling weeds.[39]

Cadet-inspired publications provided an outlet for the creative energy of the men and kept them informed about current activities. The first issue of a magazine called *The Strut* appeared in September 1918 at Carruthers Field. It contained poems, jokes, gossip, and more serious articles about airplanes and flying written by officers stationed at the field. Dances and other musical events provided yet another form of entertainment. The men compiled lists of those who could play the piano, violin, or other instruments and could be asked to contribute when the need arose. For example, the enlisted men at Taliaferro invited the enlisted men at Carruthers to a dance on Friday, September 17, 1918. "Pretty girls will be here and delicious refreshments will be served," said the invitation. The men also enjoyed venturing to dance halls away from the airfields for entertainment. When someone reported that Barron Field officers frequented dance halls where enlisted men were present in large numbers, the department commander "instructed [the officers] as to the impropriety of such practices and trusts that further action will be unnecessary." He felt such activity was "subversive to discipline."[40]

Officers sometimes received a different duty when they were invited to fly an airplane to a state fair nearby. Fair promoters requested fliers because spectators loved them. Colonel Turner at Barron Field turned down most such requests; however, Colonel Fickel at Carruthers was more accommodating. When the commanding officer of Rich Field in Waco asked Fickel to send airplanes for an exhibition, he sent seven "ships."[41]

The person who best combined flier and entertainer was Second Lieutenant Ormer Leslie Locklear, who was stationed at Barron Field. A local Fort Worth resident and daring pilot who survived his flight training and went on to be a successful instructor, Locklear managed to turn the flying

Barron Field utilized a truck made out of a Model T automobile and pulled a wagon across their parade ground during training maneuvers. *Photo courtesy National Archives and Records Administration, Southwest Region, Fort Worth.*

skills he developed at Barron into a successful, though short-lived movie career. Born in Gainesville, Texas, in 1891, Locklear moved with his parents to Fort Worth while still a youngster. Seeing early flying demonstrations in Fort Worth sparked an interest in learning to fly. He and his brothers constructed a crude glider, which they pulled behind an automobile until it rose in the air. His daredevil spirit was in early evidence when he raced for a local motorcycle club and when he fearlessly climbed to the tops of buildings while working in construction with his father.[42]

Locklear enlisted in the Air Service on October 25, 1917, taking his flight training at Fort Sam Houston in San Antonio. He finished ground school at the Texas School of Military Aeronautics in Austin and was commissioned a second lieutenant. His orders sent him back to Fort Worth to complete his flight training. The first indication that Lieutenant Locklear might reveal his daredevil nature while flying at Barron Field came during a test when student pilots were asked to read ten words flashed from the ground while flying at 5,000 feet. The wing obscured part of the view, so Locklear climbed out on it while his instructor flew the airplane. He was the only student pilot to read all the words and receive a perfect score. Another time he climbed forward on the fuselage to replace a radiator cap that had come loose and caused hot water to spray in his face.[43]

From that beginning Locklear and his friends began stunt flying. A fellow pilot would control the airplane, and Locklear would walk on a wing or balance himself while standing. Eventually someone told Colonel Turner, and he made a point of viewing their antics. Instead of ordering punishment, he asked them to do their wing-walking demonstrations to show the stability of the Curtiss (Jenny) airplanes. Lieutenant Locklear and two of his daredevil friends were kept at Barron Field as instructors and not sent overseas to France. They complained, but to no avail. One of the stunts they perfected was done with Lieutenant James Frew flying his airplane directly above the one flown by Lieutenant Milton "Skeets" Elliott. Locklear would then jump from Frew's plane to Elliott's. When then General Benjamin Foulois, who had been named head of the U.S. Flying Service forces in France, visited Barron Field in September 1918, he was *not* pleased at Locklear's stunt flying demonstration.[44]

When the war ended, Frew accepted a discharge and went home, but Locklear and Elliott remained in the service. They persuaded Lieutenant Shirley J. Short to join their acrobatic flying team and they attracted local newspaper attention. Colonel Turner sent Locklear to Chicago on April 22, 1919, to perform maneuvers in the fifth Victory Loan Drive. Locklear loved it, and realized that he might make money from stunt flying after leaving the service. Back in Fort Worth, Locklear made a deal with a promoter named William Hickman Pickens to handle him and his friends Elliott and Short when they got out of the service. On May 5, 1919, after Locklear received his honorable discharge, Pickens began advertising "Locklear's Flying Circus," which traveled to cities and towns where Locklear would jump from one airplane to another at 5,000 feet. Pickens invested in two new airplanes for Elliott and Short to fly. Newspapers quoted Locklear belittling the danger, saying that he was as likely to be killed "falling off a curb."[45]

In July 1919 Locklear made his first foray into acting when he signed a Hollywood contract for a movie called *The Great Train Robbery*. After the film concluded shooting, he returned to stunt flying, sometimes making $3,000 for a half-hour appearance. As many as 75,000 spectators watched Locklear perform at the State Fair in Dallas on Friday, October 17, 1919. His appearance even outshone the annual Texas-Oklahoma football game the same day. Locklear earned $1,650 per week working for the William Fox Studio to make his second film, *The Skywayman*. The studio told him that he did not have to do the stunts for the movie live; they could be staged. But Locklear insisted on the real thing. The last scene of *The Skywayman* was to be a night flight nosedive and crash filmed on August 2, 1920. Ground lights were to go out to signal Locklear when to pull up so he would not hit the ground; however, something went wrong and the light did not go out. Locklear crashed into the ground at 150 miles per hour. Huge crowds followed his funeral procession to the train station in California, and another large crowd gathered the day of his funeral in Fort Worth—the young daredevil had returned home.[46]

Shortly after the armistice was signed on November 11, 1918, pilot training gradually wound down and men slowly began heading home. Some men, however, chose to remain long enough to finish their training and earn their wings. Both British and French officers, who had trained American pilots after the United States entered World War I, began leaving the Texas airfields even before the war ended. After the armistice, the Americans eagerly awaited discharge, but none of the fields closed immediately. The last issue of the *Taliaferro Target*, dated January 10–17, 1919, explained that officers were being discharged and the number of enlisted men soon would be reduced to the base minimum of 200.[47]

After the war ended and his responsibilities lightened, Taliaferro commander Major Macaulay traveled west with his mechanic, Private Staley, late in December 1918 to take part in a transcontinental flight that commenced at Rockwell Field in San Diego in January 1919. Macaulay flew a De Havilland DH-4 carrying tanks for fifty-seven gallons of extra gasoline and ten gallons of oil. Unfortunately, as they flew eastward the failure of the generator and later the battery forced them down in far West Texas near Hot Wells (in Hudspeth County east of El Paso). Changing the connections to the lighting battery allowed them to reach Pecos, Texas, where they got a new battery. From there they continued and reached Baton Rouge, Louisiana, on January 23. Their route then carried them to Americus, Georgia, and then Arcadia, Florida, which they reached on January 24. Motor trouble developed the next day while en route to Jacksonville, forcing Macaulay to land in tall weeds at the north end of Lake Okeechobee. He and his mechanic enlisted a barge to bring the airplane to Fort Lauderdale and then to Miami where workers at the Marine base there restored it to flying condition.[48]

On the way back, Macaulay hit a wire fence in Georgia, turning the airplane over and damaging the propeller, radiator, and three wing sections. At Souther Field, Georgia, Macaulay picked up another De Havilland and continued west. Rain damaged the propeller, so he replaced it with a new one at Payne Field outside West Point, Mississippi. The field was too soft for take off, so Macaulay and Staley boarded a train to Fort Worth to wait for better conditions. A JN-4H from Taliaferro took Macaulay back to Mississippi on February 16 where he boarded the DH-4 and flew it back to Taliaferro Field the next day. Despite the problems Macaulay and Staley faced, they completed what the Air Service called the "first round trip across the United States."[49]

Seen from the air are fifteen hangars with long barracks buildings on the side as they stood on January 31, 1918. While officially Taliaferro Field #1 under the Canadians, locals called it Camp Hicks Aviation Field. *Photo courtesy Dalton Hoffman Local History Collection.*

With the mishaps and delays, it had taken not quite two months for the round trip. No doubt many people in Fort Worth remembered the transcontinental trip of Cal Rodgers eight years earlier, which had taken him three and a half months, traveling only one way. Major Macaulay, however, was not satisfied and knew he could do better. He left Fort Worth on Saturday, April 12, 1919, and flew to Tucson, Arizona. On Sunday he flew to San Diego and back to Tucson, and then to Fort Worth on Monday. Bad weather delayed him, and he did not reach Jacksonville, Florida, until Thursday. He headed back at once, had motor trouble in Mississippi and reached Fort Worth on Friday, April 18, a round trip of seven days. He was actually in the air forty-four hours and fifteen minutes, and his average speed was 138 miles per hour.[50]

Soon after the completion of Major Macauley's second trip, the three airfields began closing. When Taliaferro Field shut down in mid-1919, the government sold surplus buildings at auction to local residents. Of the three training fields in Tarrant County, Taliaferro retained its field and a few buildings longer than the other two and was the only one to reopen twenty years later when World War II erupted. At that time the name Hicks Field stuck. The hospital at Carruthers Field remained open until May 3, 1919, and the post officially closed on November 8, 1919. The last of the three fields to close was Barron Field. Many cadets found themselves in the middle of their flight training when the armistice came. Post commanders received a telegram on November 18, 1918, advising them to instruct their men that they could apply for a discharge and discontinue flying, or they could stay, complete their flying course, and obtain their commissions. In one cadet detachment of 214 men, 185 asked for immediate discharge. Government red tape meant that the discharges came more slowly than the men and their families wanted. Finally the word got out that men needed at home could be discharged first.[51]

The Air Service Flying School was still in operation in October 1920, but the total flying time for the week ending October 2 was only nine hours. A flood of requests from chambers of commerce and other civilian groups asked for pilots and airplanes to participate in aerial exhibitions, but a War Department memo prohibited such flying "unless the same be involved in a governmental or national project." An airplane company named National Airplane had considered buying Barron Field as a factory location in the summer of 1919, and its president R. H. Pearson made a speech to the Fort Worth Chamber of Commerce to that effect. The purchase, however, never materialized. Memos sent in October 1920 urged the commanding officer of Barron Field to "expedite" the abandonment of the field. Equipment went to Montgomery, Alabama, and Americus, Georgia. Most of the activity that year consisted of counting inventory and making reports. By January 1921 all but a few wooden structures had been dismantled. The military ordered its complete abandonment by June 30, 1921. Tarrant County residents who had worked at the field as civilians or who had been stationed there with the military formed a Barron Field Club and met periodically to picnic and reminisce. They met until at least 1931.[52]

The concrete munitions building with walls one foot thick was the last to remain standing, and residents used it as a school for African American children from 1925 to 1936 as a part of Everman Independent School District. Later, businessmen constructed an industrial park nearby. As a 1976 U.S. Bicentennial project the Everman Garden Club saved the small former munitions building-school and acquired a historical marker.[53]

Many men who had come to Fort Worth as a result of being stationed at one of the three airfields remained or returned to the city to make their homes here after the war. The story of Harry E. Brants and his subsequent life in Fort Worth is just one example. Although an American, born in 1895 in Yorktown, Illinois, Brants was living in Canada when the British entered World War I. His grandfather originally had emigrated from Germany to Canada, and then the family moved to the United States before Harry was born. After hitting hard times as grain farmers, they returned to Canada and settled near Winnipeg. Harry enlisted in the Royal Canadian Air Force in 1915. When the United States entered the war in April 1917, Harry Brants was commissioned into the U.S. army within a month and became a pilot instructor at Taliaferro I. The Americans called him "Canuck" because of his earlier connection with the Canadians, and many mistakenly thought he actually was Canadian. When the war ended, Brants remained in Fort Worth, working as a clerk in a local bank. Not long after, he married Elizabeth Humble, the daughter of a local farmer.[54]

Brants eventually brought every member of his immediate family to Fort Worth. He built houses for them near where he and Elizabeth and their daughters lived on the Humble farm. In 1920 Brants and his father helped organize the Ryan, Brants and Company General Insurance, and six years later formed the Brants Company, also insurance, with his two brothers, Howard and Burdette, and his brother-in-law D. T. Costello. By 1940 Brants was raising registered Hereford cattle and fine riding horses on the farm and had become senior partner in the Brants Company, which still operates in Fort Worth.[55]

A wide variety of benefits came to Fort Worth and Tarrant County as a result of the three air training fields that came to the empty fields and sparsely settled suburbs surrounding Fort Worth during World War I. Local businesses of all kinds welcomed the cadets as customers. For example, Haltom's Jewelers in downtown Fort Worth sold gold aviation wing pins to the men once they completed their training. Local residents interacted with personnel at the three fields, selling produce from their farms, delivering groceries, and providing the men ten-cent packages of cigarettes. But larger businesses benefited as well. The Fort Worth Stockyards and the huge grain elevators north of the city near Taliaferro Field gave easy access to meat and grain for feeding the hundreds of cadets that trained locally. Numerous oil refining plants provided the fuel the airplanes needed for the thousands of hours of flying time. Other benefits were more intangible personal or social ones. Children walking to and from school excitedly scanned the skies for airplanes from the field, and families welcomed the newcomers to Fort Worth and to Texas.[56]

Clell Wakefield is a good example of how a local Saginaw family benefited from Taliaferro Field. Wakefield was a farmer who had been a blacksmith, operated a thresher, owned a dairy, and sold butter and ice cream. In 1916 he opened a general merchandise store and ice house on the west side of what is now Saginaw Boulevard. His business grew as he filled grocery orders for families working and living near the field. After Taliaferro Field closed, Wakefield purchased a surplus building, moved it across the highway, and opened Wakefield's Cash Grocery. He became postmaster for

Saginaw and had a postal window in a corner of his store. Even after Wake-field died in 1924, his wife continued as postmaster and ran the business.[57]

The Great War, as World War I was called at the time, placed Texas on the map as a good place to train pilots. The relatively flat terrain and warm climate—combined with the favorable work force and good economic con-ditions—proved hospitable to aviation; Fort Worth benefited as did the other Texas cities with World War I military installations: San Antonio, Houston, Dallas, El Paso, Waco, Wichita Falls, Port Arthur, and Austin.[58]

In the nineteen months after the United States declared war, American military aviation made great progress. It went from being a flying branch of the Signal Corps having sixty-five officers and 1,000 enlisted men to an Air Service of 20,000 officers and 170,000 enlisted men. In 35,000 combat flying hours, American pilots overseas shot down 781 enemy airplanes. Fort Worth's three training fields contributed greatly to this successful effort.[59] Fort Worth business leaders proved that they could attract and support suc-cessful military installations. The community arranged land, utilities, roads, and whatever else the military needed. They learned an early lesson that federal money brought prosperity and jobs. Not only did the city fathers support the three airfields, but they also sought and won the establishment of an army infantry training camp—Camp Bowie—located due west of downtown Fort Worth.

CHAPTER 3

World War I: Camp Bowie

UST DAYS AFTER PRESIDENT WOODROW WILSON SIGNED THE declaration of war against Germany on April 6, 1917, Fort Worth businessmen expressed the hope that an army training camp might be located in their city. Chamber of Commerce president Ben E. Keith and Mayor W. D. Davis met with Brigadier General James Parker, commander of the Southern Department at Fort Sam Houston in San Antonio, to present the case for Fort Worth.[1]

The two men displayed maps of the city, which possessed excellent rail facilities, was the leading grain center in the Southwest, and boasted two large meat packing plants with the largest stockyards facility in the Southwest. General Parker was impressed enough to send a three-man inspection team headed by Brigadier General Charles G. Morton to Fort Worth to look at prospective sites. Keith and Davis took the team to two locations: one south of the Southwestern Baptist Theological Seminary and the other near Lake Worth.

Dr. Holman Taylor, a veteran of National Guard service on the border, previously had surveyed a site two and a half miles west of Fort Worth for the National Guard. "Man, I know the best site in Texas for an army camp," Taylor told the local committee. "It's there in Arlington Heights between the street car line and the Stove Foundry Road." Taylor convinced the chamber of commerce committee to take General Morton there. Unfortunately, while General Morton was in Fort Worth, rain began pouring down, and the local businessmen feared that their chances to obtain the army camp would be slim. The downpour that dampened the visit of the city delegation and the military to Arlington Heights surprisingly revealed good drainage in the area, which was on high ground and possessed gravel just under the topsoil. The city committee offered the land, a railroad spur, a hard surface road built from downtown, and telephone and utility connections—all free to the government if they would build in Arlington Heights.[2]

The site, which Taylor showed the delegation, belonged to the estate of wealthy Denver financier H. B. Chamberlin who had owned American

Land and Investment Company. In 1889 he bought 2,000 acres in what became Arlington Heights, built a large hotel called the Arlington Inn, a lake resort called Lake Como, a streetcar line, and two power plants. River Crest Country Club, constructed in 1911, became the centerpiece of Chamberlin's planned upscale community, with Arlington Heights Boulevard running through it slightly southwest to northeast. Chamberlin only just began developing the area into residential lots when he was killed in London in an accident, so his dream project came to a halt after only a few homes were built.[3]

On June 11, 1917, the city learned that the military had accepted their offer. The War Department named the new base Camp Bowie after Texas revolutionary war hero Jim Bowie of Alamo fame. The new camp would cover 2,000 acres from University Drive on the east to Merrick Street on the west and from White Settlement Road on the north to Old Stove Foundry Road (later Vickery) on the south. The War Department signed a construction contract with Thompson Construction Company of Dallas on July 18, 1917. The Army moved quickly, establishing a quartermaster headquarters on July 23, and a timekeeper office two days later. However, in August the city still was in the process of acquiring land.[4]

Soon almost 3,500 workers began construction, laying out forty miles of streets and locating sites for buildings. By August 21, 900 structures, including mess halls, warehouses, bathhouses, and latrines covered the land. The city continued laying water pipes, and the Texas and Pacific and Frisco Railroads built a spur. The city spent $50,000 for water mains, Tarrant County provided $65,000 to improve a road, and Northern Texas Traction Company spent $125,000 to extend the streetcar line.[5]

Officials announced August 24 as Camp Bowie's opening date, although construction on the base hospital had not even begun. Tent floors and walls, the guardhouse, a gas instruction chamber, and a remount station were not completed until November 1917. The final site covered 1,410.5 acres and cost the government $2,235,504 to construct, which did not include the costs to the city and county for infrastructure. Camp Bowie had a capacity of 27,000 officers and men.[6]

Four hundred fifty men representing four troops of the First Texas Cavalry arrived by train on July 26, 1917, and became the first soldiers at Camp Bowie. Coming from Amarillo, Corsicana, Houston, and San Antonio, they and their commander, Major (soon to be Lieutenant Colonel) John B. Golding, arrived with horses and equipment from recent service in the Big Bend. Their job was to guard the camp during its construction. Major Golding thus became the first commander of Camp Bowie.[7]

Early arrivals among the enlisted ranks posted to Camp Bowie stayed in

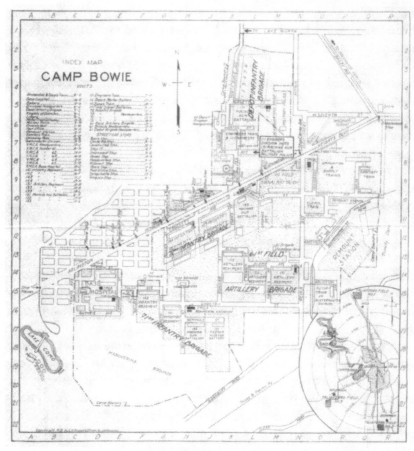

Map of Camp Bowie. *Map courtesy North Fort Worth Historical Society and Pete Charlton.*

wooden-sided Sibley tents meant for eight men, but ten soldiers soon were crowded into each one. One of the first enlisted men at the camp was Hubert W. Hodges, who had volunteered June 16, 1917, in Sweetwater, Texas, and became a corporal in Company C, 111th Engineers. He remembered carpenters scurrying all over the base still working. He and his fellow soldiers drilled in their civilian clothes for several weeks before they received military uniforms, and they trained with wooden guns. Although there was a food line, soldiers had to eat out of their own mess kits and wash them up afterwards. Wooden guns eventually were replaced with real ones, including Springfield rifles, Enfields, Colt and Smith & Wesson revolvers, and twelve-gauge shotguns. Wool uniforms began arriving September 15 while temperatures soared, because some officials in Washington, who had never been to Texas, reasoned, "It's fall isn't it?" A cold front hit before all the uniforms arrived, however, so the Red Cross put out a call for blankets and other clothing. Local civilians responded generously.[8]

One soldier, Reed Craig Collier, a local boy whose parents lived in Forest Hill, vividly recalled the privation of those early days. He remembered that the only equipment the Camp Bowie soldiers had available for their horses consisted of bridles and saddle blankets. They took the horses out each morning for exercises, and in the afternoon they undertook dismounted drill and guard duty. He also remembered that the camp possessed only four field pieces for two regiments to use.[9]

Major General Edwin St. John Greble, a career army man, assumed command of Camp Bowie on August 23, 1917. Born at West Point, New York, in 1859, he returned to the United States Military Academy there as an appointee from Pennsylvania, following a family tradition. Graduating in 1881 as a second lieutenant of artillery, Greble later taught at West Point, toured Europe as an observer, and served two duty assignments in Cuba. He also served on the Mexican border during the Mexican Revolution. Greble became a brigadier general in 1916 and a major general in 1917. When he arrived in Fort Worth, a Chamber of Commerce delegation met him and offered their assistance in his command. "It is a unique experience to find awaiting me a committee that desires to cooperate with me and do what I feel is best. Usually I am told what the local committee wishes me to do. I feel delighted that Fort Worth wants to comply with the best interests of the camp," General Greble said. He established his divisional headquarters in a tent north of Arlington Heights Boulevard, which the city fathers renamed Camp Bowie Boulevard after the war.[10]

Brigadier General E. St. John Greble commanded the newly organized Thirty-sixth Division at Camp Bowie before leading them to France in World War I. *Photo courtesy Dalton Hoffman, Local History Collection.*

Initially, plans called for Camp Bowie to utilize National Guardsmen with volunteers and draftees to be added later. Because the camp was not ready for full operation in September 1917, General Greble rearranged schedules to stagger the arrival of the various guard units. He ordered forty-five special trains to bring the entire Oklahoma Guard and 10,399 troops of the Texas Guard. Some guardsmen provided their own transportation to Fort Worth, but by the end of October most of the men had arrived.[11]

Although Oklahoma guardsmen complained because they were not allowed to train in their home state, the decision to combine the Texas and Oklahoma Guards created a new military unit that became the Thirty-sixth Division—a proud group that fought bravely in World War I, World War II, and later conflicts. Because the Thirty-sixth so closely identified itself with Texas, some members considered it the first Texas state volunteer unit and traced its origin to the Texans who rose to fight Mexico in the Texas Revolution. They looked at Texas troops who fought in the Civil War as precursors of the fighting Thirty-sixth as well. Technically, however, the division began August 5, 1917, with the federalization of the Texas and Oklahoma National Guards.[12]

An important detail for the men of the Thirty-sixth Division at the time was the design of a patch for their uniforms to identify their combined Texas and Oklahoma unit. Although someone suggested the Lone Star of Texas with an Indian head in the center, the final patch depicted a large blue arrowhead inside a circle, with a large gold T for Texas in the arrowhead's center. As a result, the men began calling themselves "T-Patchers." Graduates and students of Fort Worth's Arlington Heights High School, whose campus is located on part of the original Camp Bowie, may note that their colors are the same gold and blue of the T-Patchers.[13]

Nationalities of the men in the Thirty-sixth varied greatly, with the 600 Native Americans from Oklahoma heavily influencing the choice of the arrowhead patch. Certainly, the Thirty-sixth had more Native Americans in it than any other division. The Oklahoma Indian tribes represented were Arapahoe, Caddo, Cherokee, Cheyenne, Chickasaw, Choctaw, Comanche, Creek, Delaware, Kaw, Osage, Pawnee, Peoria, Ponca, Quapaw, Seminole, and Shawnee. Besides Anglo American, the rest of the division's men came from many backgrounds: Assyrian, Bohemian, Danish, German, Filipino, French, Indian, Italian, Mexican, Polish, and Turkish. Actually, National Guardsmen from Texas and Oklahoma comprised only about two-thirds of the Thirty-sixth, but the government added recruits and draftees from those two states to the division, so it retained its bi-state composition.[14]

Commissioner of Indian Affairs Cato Sells visited Camp Bowie late in 1917 and again in March 1918 to see how his charges were adapting. He found their morale high, their treatment satisfactory, and their reputation as soldiers excellent. Some Native leaders had wanted all-Indian subunits, but the War Department scattered them throughout the division. The assimilation policy of the federal government that had gained strength in the late nineteenth century remained the guiding force. In fact, Commissioner Sells expressed disappointment when he learned that Company E was almost entirely Native Americans. He preferred integrated units so that the Indians could absorb white language and habits. Some Native Americans in the Thirty-sixth received royalty checks because of the oil boom that had swept through northeastern Oklahoma a few years earlier. Roy Mitchell, a Pawnee, got a $66,000 check while at Camp Bowie. Others received government allotment money for their tribe. Soldiers called Company E the "Millionaire Company" even though some did not get any extra checks at all.[15]

People began calling the Thirty-sixth the Panther Division because Camp Bowie was in Fort Worth, nicknamed "Panther City." (It gained the nickname in the nineteenth century when a Dallas newspaper reporter said that Fort Worth was so dead a sleeping panther had been seen on Main Street.) The division's marching song became *The Campbells Are Coming*, a Scottish air the men changed the words to "The Panthers Are Coming." Unlike most other divisions of World War I, the Thirty-sixth retained its regional identity for several decades.[16]

National Guard divisions were triangular with three brigadier generals under the major general. This arrangement created a division of 991 officers and 27,114 men. The brigade commanders under Major General Greble at Camp Bowie were Brigadier Generals Henry Hutchings (Seventy-first Infantry), John A. Hulen (Seventy-second Infantry), and George Blakely (Sixty-first Field Artillery), who was the only regular army brigade commander. Of these three brigadier generals, Hulen's name will be the most recognizable to Fort Worthians because of the twelve-mile-long street and large shopping mall that bear his name. Hulen served in the Spanish-American War but retired from the military early in the twentieth century; however, unrest in Mexico and Pancho Villa's raid into the United States at Columbus, New Mexico, on May 9, 1916, brought Hulen back into the military. He assumed command of the Sixth Separate Brigade, which patrolled the U.S.-Mexican border.[17]

Among General Hulen's junior officers was a young second lieutenant of the 131st Field Artillery named James Frank Dobie, who later rose to fame teaching southwestern literature at the University of Texas and writing numerous books as J. Frank Dobie. Born in 1886, he already was teaching at the University of Texas when the war began. Although he had only been married for a year, he took a leave of absence from the university in

General John H. Hulen (left) and a fellow officer named Matthews pose in front of one of the hundreds of Camp Bowie tents. *Photo courtesy Texas State Library and Archives Commission.*

1917 and joined the Army. Another of Hulen's junior officers was Captain James Claude Wright. Born in 1890, Wright was captain of a company from Weatherford and served on the Mexican border before his duty at Camp Bowie. His son Jim later would be a U.S. Congressman from Fort Worth, eventually serving as majority leader and then speaker of the U.S. House of Representatives.[18]

The Thirty-sixth Division trained for seven months at Camp Bowie before departing for the warfront in France. During their time at the camp various entertainments kept the men occupied while off duty. Because stamps for first class mail cost only two cents, many servicemen often wrote home to wives and girlfriends. Those letters persuaded many young women to move to Fort Worth to be near their sweethearts or husbands. Many weddings took place at the Tarrant County Courthouse in downtown Fort Worth, and young couples then rented houses or rooms to set up housekeeping. In fact, the demand became so great that some landlords charged as much as $75 per month, an expensive rent at that time.[19]

In 1917 the secretary of war created the Fosdick Commission on Training Camp Activities and invited seven organizations to provide activities for the "comfort and welfare" of the men at Camp Bowie. These organizations were the Young Men's Christian Association (YMCA), Young Women's Christian Association (YWCA), National Catholic War Council, American Library Association, Salvation Army, Jewish Welfare Board, and War and Camp Community Service. Congressional appropriations, donations, and sale of the *Smilage Book* financed the activities of the Fosdick Commission. The *Smilage Book* contained coupons the purchasers could give to soldiers for admission to Liberty Theaters, which were located in military camps. Sales of these books nationwide raised approximately $3 million. In addition, the Fosdick Commission helped servicemen while they were abroad, and assisted them in finding jobs after the war ended.[20]

The YMCA provided activities, and the local YWCA sponsored strictly chaperoned weekly excursions of young ladies to the recreation hall at Camp Bowie to help entertain the soldiers. Couples were not allowed to go outside the hall together. Chaperones had a more difficult job during warmer months because soldiers propped the sides of the building open to provide better ventilation. The YWCA provided similar excursions to entertain the enlisted men at Taliaferro, Barron, and Carruthers Fields.[21]

The local Salvation Army called their two-story building a "hut," and the one they opened at Camp Bowie was the second they opened in Texas. Eventually others were opened at most bases. The welcoming sign over the hut's entrance read: "The Salvation Army Canteen" and below that "Soldiers Rest and Reading Room." Adjutant and Mrs. H. G. James of Fort

Worth supervised the Camp Bowie facility. Salvation Army huts all followed a similar layout—60 or 70 feet wide by 110 or 126 feet deep. Large social halls covered the ground floor and provided writing desks, tables, a library, magazines, games, a Victrola, and a piano. A canteen served meals at cost. Religious services and entertainments were held in the auditorium. A porch with rockers and swings surrounded the ground floor. Upstairs, Adjutant James and his assistants kept their offices. In addition, several well-furnished bedrooms provided accommodations for mothers, wives, sweethearts, or other relatives visiting soldiers at the camp.[22]

Additional responsibilities of the Fosdick Commission included temporary care and protection of young girls in cities where Army camps were located. Sometimes young ladies followed a soldier to camp with false hopes of marriage, and became stranded, unable to find jobs or decent places to stay. Because of the military camps in Tarrant County, Fort Worth qualified to receive money from the government program. Consequently, Mrs. John Waples chaired a committee of five local women who established the Girls' Protective Bureau in April 1917, using the federal money to deal with the local situation. Federal support ended in 1919, but the group continued to assist young women under the name Girls' Protective Association. The Fort Worth Welfare Association eventually added the group as a new department. In 1922 the society ladies purchased a nine-room frame house at 917 North Henderson, which they called Worth Cottage, as a temporary home for young women who needed help. The philanthropic group was still in operation and assisting young ladies during World War II.[23]

The Liberty Theater provided some on-base entertainment. Located in front of the Thirty-sixth Division Headquarters, it could seat 2,000 soldiers. The soldiers attended concerts there, watched vaudeville acts, heard lectures, and saw silent movies. Margaret Wilson, daughter of President Woodrow Wilson, sang at the Liberty Theater at Camp Bowie on April 3 and 4, 1918.[24]

Each regiment organized its own band. As more recruits arrived at Camp Bowie, the membership in each band increased from twenty-eight to forty-eight members. Bandmasters held commissioned rank. In addition to official performances, bands provided listening entertainment for the troops. A soldier named Brooks Morris did not join a band, but he played the violin on the Monday nights when he was in charge of recreation. He could also play any tune on the piano that was requested for a sing-a-long, including the two most popular at the time: "Over There" and "Grand Old Flag" by George M. Cohan. Morris later organized the Fort Worth Symphony Orchestra and directed it for twenty years.[25]

Because of the Texas-Oklahoma makeup of the Thirty-sixth Division,

TENT SCENE, CAMP BOWIE, FORT WORTH, TEXAS.

This World War I postcard allowed soldiers to write home to family and show the tents in which they were living at Camp Bowie. *Photo courtesy Dalton Hoffman, Local History Collection.*

their newspaper at Camp Bowie was called *The Texahoma Bugler,* and it provided news from the various units. Most editions included a long list of marriage licenses issued. Local merchants supported the *Bugler* with advertisements urging soldiers to patronize their movies, buy Army lockers, and eat at their cafés. Nearby churches used the *Bugler* to invite soldiers to attend their services. Another publication called *Pass in Review* appeared twice a month and provided more literary fare than the more newsworthy *Bugler.* Sports competitions between units also provided activities for many servicemen and the results were reported in the camp newspapers.[26]

Passes at Camp Bowie were not difficult to obtain until the Spanish influenza epidemic of 1918 placed the local military bases under quarantine. Before that, the soldiers traveled into Fort Worth as often as three times a week, paying five cents to ride the streetcar to downtown Fort Worth. Enlisted man Hubert W. Hodges remembered social activities at nearby Lake Como. After obtaining a pass to leave camp, he and his friends could catch a city streetcar on Arlington Heights Boulevard and ride to the lake where there were several concessions and a place to swim. Sometimes they traveled to downtown Fort Worth for movies or other types of shows. He noted that the area around Camp Bowie remained "sort of a bare prairie"; not much residential development surrounded it, and soldiers on guard duty occasionally encountered prowlers.[27]

Local country clubs such as Glen Garden and River Crest invited officers to dances and welcomed soldiers accompanied by family members and friends on Sundays for dining. Officers also enjoyed golf on the clubs' courses. Because River Crest was only a few blocks from the Camp Bowie headquarters, local residents began to remark that Camp Bowie probably was the only Army base in the country located next door to a country club. People often enjoyed a laugh when they noticed the destination sign on the Fort Worth streetcar: Army Camp/Country Club. Although they were, of course, two different destinations, people enjoyed telling the story anyway. Fort Worthians often rode the newly extended streetcar line to Lake Como on Saturday nights to meet and entertain soldiers. Local merchants supported the war effort by giving needed items to the soldiers, and even national corporations joined the effort. Because they knew that regulations required soldiers to be clean-shaven, the Gillette Safety Razor Company gave razor kits worth fifteen dollars—almost a month's pay for enlisted men—to servicemen at no cost.[28]

Perhaps the most notable off-base excursion for Camp Bowie soldiers occurred at the 1918 Fat Stock Show (later the Southwestern Exposition and Livestock Show and Rodeo). General Greble asked Sergeant Joe S. McGuire, a soldier from Oklahoma, to prepare a mounted demonstration of cavalry skills. McGuire's exhibition included Roman riding, bareback riding, and trick riding. Other military equestrians entered their horses in a competition called Soldier Stunts in which officials judged their horses for their manners, handiness, and conformation. The riders won prizes ranging from fifteen dollars to thirty-five dollars. Servicemen were admitted to the stock show at a discounted rate of thirty cents, and the commanders of Camp Bowie and the three airfields cooperated by providing off-base passes good until midnight on the night a soldier attended.[29]

One entertainment that proved troublesome for some soldiers was drinking alcohol. Numerous saloons existed in Fort Worth in 1917 as well as an energetic bootlegging trade. Company commanders quickly curtailed an early freedom to overindulge, however, by punishing men who imbibed too much. The Anti-Saloon League, pressing for the prohibition amendment, convinced the War Department to ban the sale of alcohol in the vicinity of training camps and to forbid any man in uniform from buying a drink. In fact, on April 15, 1918, the Texas Legislature passed a law that forbade the sale of liquor within ten miles of any place where troops were quartered. Shortly thereafter, a Texas law closed all saloons. The war ended and most soldiers returned home before the Eighteenth Amendment to the U.S. Constitution passed on January 16, 1920, making prohibition a national policy. Perhaps the threat of the soldiers' overindulgence in spirits inspired the minister of the First Baptist Church in Fort Worth, J. Frank Norris, to hold a revival at Camp Bowie in mid-1917. Or, perhaps Norris assumed that soldiers soon to face a battlefield needed spiritual assurance of the heavenly sort.[30]

Soldiers who chose to avoid organized activities, religious or otherwise, could sneak off on a Sunday, or any other day, to a swimming hole they had discovered near the camp. A dam on the Trinity River near a railroad trestle created a pond that backed up almost to present University Drive. Locals later called it Soldiers' Dam because so many of the men from Camp Bowie swam there. A young student of West Van Zandt Elementary later remembered that a lot of youngsters his age swam there too.[31]

Officials in Washington named the American Red Cross Nursing Service as the recruiting agency for both army and navy nurses as soon as the war began. Major A. W. Connery, a twenty-five-year resident of Fort Worth and an insurance executive, gave up his job to become the local field director for the American Red Cross during the war. He served Camp Bowie and the local airfields from November 30, 1917, to December 15, 1918. Initially, he supervised the construction of the Red Cross Convalescent and Nurse's Recreation Hall at Camp Bowie during the fall and winter of 1917–18. Eighty-eight women served as nurses at the Camp Bowie hospital. The nurses at Camp Bowie came to Fort Worth from all over the country, even from Canada. Only a few were local women. All, however, had graduated from hospitals of good standing. Although most received accolades for their support of the war effort, a handful faced discrimination because of increased hostility toward Germans.[32]

Gertrude Lustig, a veteran of eleven years of army service, became chief nurse. She had been on a pleasure trip in Egypt when the European war broke out in 1914. She returned to serve at Walter Reed Army Hospital in Washington until she came to Fort Worth in 1917. Unfortunately, Lustig, a native of Breslau, Germany, permitted fellow German nurses to sing their favorite native songs in the ward. As a result she was charged with being pro-German and failing to register as an enemy alien. Local newspapers played this up and eventually she was deported.[33]

Another German nurse who faced discrimination was Ella Behrens, whose family had lived in northeast Tarrant County for several years before World War I began. A Red Cross representative asked Behrens, a registered nurse, to help out at Camp Bowie's hospital, and she did. Eventually she was mustered into the Army Nurse Corps. Partially disabled, Behrens worked the supervising desk in the hospital kitchen and never missed a day on the job. Her problems began when someone overheard her softly singing a German folk song. Also, she was heard speaking German to another nurse, perhaps Gertrude Lustig. During the influenza epidemic, someone accused Behrens of slipping flu germs into the food that she served and made a statement to Secret Service agents. The agents arrested Ella and placed her in the Fort Worth city jail, not allowing her to inform her family of her whereabouts. Eight days later she was released and allowed to go home but was told not to tell anyone what had happened to her. Behrens was so frightened she did as she was told.[34]

Officials at Camp Bowie gave Behrens a dishonorable discharge causing her to forfeit her pay. Although she appealed and even asked for a court martial to clear her name, government officials ignored her. The dishonorable discharge made it difficult for Behrens to obtain jobs in later years. Finally, in 1946, the newly elected congressman from Grapevine, Wingate Lucas, persuaded an army board to review Behrens's case. On January 29, 1949, the board cleared her of all charges, changed her discharge to honorable, and restored all her back pay. At age sixty-seven, Behrens received a formal apology from the U.S. government for the unfair treatment she had faced more than thirty years earlier.[35]

The Spanish influenza (flu) swept through the Fort Worth military installations in the fall of 1918. Nationwide during World War I, disease (pneumonia or influenza) killed more soldiers than did war injuries. Of all U.S casualties, 66,751 were from disease, while 48,909 soldiers were killed in action. When a number of soldiers found themselves in the base hospital with measles, the officer in charge reported: "the stricken ones are patriotic, claiming they have just plain old American measles and not German measles." During the influenza epidemic in the fall of 1918, it became news *not* to have daily deaths. The *Fort Worth Star-Telegram* reported on October 23, 1918: "Not a death occurred at Camp Bowie Base Hospital during the 24-hour period from noon Tuesday until noon Wednesday. It has been over a month since a similar report came from the hospital." Lieutenant Colonel Louis Hanson, commanding officer of the hospital at Camp Bowie, along with his army doctors and Red Cross nurses, placed sick soldiers in the four contagious wards. In addition, a special physician supervised an insanity ward. The hospital sometimes became so crowded that men slept on the reception room floor until beds could be made available. Lieutenant Joe Driskell of Company E, 143rd Infantry, became so concerned for the men under his command that during the epidemic, he wrote home for blankets and quilts as well as aspirin. He lost three men out of his company. Even at Camp Bowie, not all deaths were influenza related. On May 18, 1918, Company I, Headquarters Company of the 142nd, was firing a trench mortar when a shell jammed and a soldier dropped another on top of it. Both shells exploded, killing fifteen soldiers and wounding twenty.[36]

Reed Collier is the dark-headed soldier sitting on the far right on the steps of the base hospital at Camp Bowie. *Photo courtesy of the family of Reed Craig Collier.*

This Red Cross parade took place in downtown Fort Worth on May 20, 1918, in honor of the troops. *Photo courtesy of Dalton Hoffman Local History Collection.*

Soldiers trained at Camp Bowie would join an American army eventually four million strong. A year earlier, when the United States declared war, the total strength was less than 200,000 with 127,588 in the regular army and 66,554 National Guardsmen on the Mexican border. The National Defense Act of May 1916 provided the initial impetus for increasing the nation's military strength, and the Selective Service Act of 1917 mandated that young men ages twenty-one through thirty register for the draft. In August 1918 the government enlarged the range to eighteen to forty-five, eventually drafting nearly three million of the twenty-four million who registered.[37]

The first trained group of 27,000 Camp Bowie soldiers left for France on April 11, 1918. The city of Fort Worth and the military planned a downtown parade to send them off with great fanfare as families of the soldiers arrived from Oklahoma and North Texas to say goodbye to their loved ones. Estimates varied as to whether the parade lasted two or four hours, but most writers agree that over 100,000 spectators came to see the "doughboys" march down Main Street, and that the cheering never stopped. Schools, banks, factories, and most Fort Worth businesses closed for the event. Governors R. L. Williams of Oklahoma and William P. Hobby of Texas sat on the reviewing stand with Major General Greble, recently back from Europe, and his Thirty-sixth Division staff. The men boarded trains for the four-day trip to New York. "Sixteen men did not share the patriotic enthusiasm of their comrades and went over the hill." The military tracked down the deserters, court-martialed them, and sentenced them to long prison terms at Fort Leavenworth, Kansas. Meanwhile, back in Fort Worth, the Red Cross discovered that some families spent all of their money traveling to Fort Worth to see their men off and needed financial help to return home.[38]

Greble led the first group of soldiers who left Camp Bowie on their way to Europe. Replacing him in Fort Worth was General Hulen, who supervised the remainder of the training program. Major General William R. Smith, age fifty, an 1892 West Point graduate, was transferred from the Thirty-seventh Division to the Thirty-sixth and ordered to join the division in New York as they embarked for France. On August 1, 1918, General Hulen and his men arrived in France. The Thirty-sixth Division fought with the Fourth French Army in the Meuse-Argonne offensive—the last major campaign of the war. The Thirty-sixth advanced twenty-one kilometers, captured 813 prisoners, and lost 2,601 men killed or wounded. Private Hugh J. Kent, a former *Dallas Evening Journal* employee, published their division newspaper, *The Arrow Head,* weekly while they were overseas. Back in North Texas local newspapers reported that the Thirty-sixth Division experienced "much severe fighting and its losses have been quite heavy. The men fought continuously for sixteen days." Their commander praised them as they "withstood the most bitter German counterattacks without flinching."[39]

After the Thirty-sixth Division left for France, several hundred officers and men remained at Camp Bowie. General Greble had kept back seventy clerks and stenographers at his headquarters because he expected to train another division, the 100th. General Greble, however, took disability retirement in September 1918, and two months later the War Department canceled further training because of the armistice on November 11. A story circulated among the men in Europe that the Thirty-sixth would remain in Germany for some time with the army of occupation, but this angered General Hulen and he pulled strings. He argued that as National Guardsmen his men had served in Mexico for two years before the Great War began and they deserved to go home.[40]

In May 1919 the Thirty-sixth Division sailed from Brest, France, on the *S.S. Finland*, arriving in Newport News, Virginia, early in June. Trains brought them directly to Fort Worth. As the men marched from the train station to return to Camp Bowie, huge crowds cheered, tossed roses, and rang bells. Celebrations continued for days with dances, parties, band concerts, and buildings decorated with patriotic banners. The war was over, and their "boys" were home. Each doughboy received a bonus of $60 and a discharge, being deactivated June 18. The T-Patchers had earned thirty Distinguished Service Crosses and 128 Croix de Guerre medals. Proud Texans reorganized the unit in San Antonio in 1923 as the Thirty-sixth National Guard Division.[41]

By the end of the war more than 100,000 men had trained at Camp Bowie. General Smith, still in command on June 22, 1919, wrote the *Fort Worth Star-Telegram* to thank the men of the Thirty-sixth Division for their patriotism: "On the training ground and on the battlefield you have a acquitted yourselves as soldiers worthy of America's best traditions and have left a record behind you second to none, one upon which your country will look with the greatest pride." A granite marker honoring the Thirty-sixth Division stands in Veteran's Park, a triangular-shaped block on the former headquarters site, surrounded by Thomas Place, Crestline Road, and Camp Bowie Boulevard at the latter's 4200 block. The marker reads: "To those gallant men who composed the original Thirty-sixth Division of World War I, and who trained here before departing for service overseas, where many of whom made the supreme sacrifice, this marker is reverently dedicated." Local Fort Worth artist Barvo Walker sculpted a fifteen-foot high bronze statue of a soldier holding his wounded comrade. The statue was dedicated on November 11, 1987.[42]

Not until the summer of 1919 did the work of dismantling Camp Bowie begin. The growth of residential homes, interrupted two years earlier, returned. Many houses built in Arlington Heights shortly thereafter contained materials from former army structures. Local resident Porfirio Lopez bought one of the officers' clubs and hauled it in pieces to the North Side where he turned it into a home for his family. Because the streets and utilities remained, once workers had dismantled the buildings of Camp Bowie, the neighborhoods of the addition known as Arlington Heights quickly began filling. Former soldier Joe Driskell helped develop the area. Street names such as Hulen and Pershing honored well-known generals from the war. El Campo Street, Sanguinet Street, and Camp Bowie Boulevard all remind residents of people and places from the base's history.[43]

Two very different occurrences indicate ways in which Camp Bowie boosted the economy in Fort Worth. George Mallick, a local youngster not old enough to join the army in 1917, sold ice cream cones and fried pies for five cents apiece across the fence to soldiers at the base. Far away in Washington, D.C., Congress passed a law on October 6, 1917, providing monthly payments to military dependents. A soldier would receive additional pay of $15 if he was married; $25 if he was married and had one child; and $32.50 if he was married and had two children. The government later provided for an additional $5 for each child, up to a maximum total of $50. These are but two examples of ways base activities during the war helped to put money into the local economy.[44]

World War I marked the first time military and defense matters assumed major significance in the Fort Worth area since the founding of the fort in 1849. Three economic strengths that would figure prominently in the city's growth then and in succeeding decades came together during the war years: livestock, oil, and the military.

The livestock industry remained the city's largest economic support, and World War I purchases enhanced receipts. The Fort Worth Stockyards broke records during World War I, receiving three and a half million animals in 1917. Fort Worth became the largest horse and mule market in the world in 1915, even before the United States entered the war, because European governments began buying the animals for food and for military mounts. By June 1916 Fort Worth dealers had shipped over 100,000 horses and mules to Europe for which they received $11 million. Oil emerged as a new source of revenue for Fort Worth in October 1917 when a wildcat well on the John McCleskey farm in Eastland County ushered in an oil boom in West Texas. Pipelines from the boomtowns of Burkburnett, Desdemona, Eastland, Ranger, Cisco, and Breckenridge directed the oil to new refineries in Fort Worth, and the fuel assisted the war effort. The influence of Camp

Bowie and the three airfields, however, challenged the livestock base of Fort Worth's economy and its new oil wealth. Nearly $2.5 million in new money entered the Fort Worth economy for construction costs for the army camp and street and utility infrastructure. Annual salaries of military personnel at Camp Bowie during World War I totaled $6 million, twice the annual wages paid at the stockyards; however, because of animal sales, the stockyards produced more income for the city.[45]

Military and defense activities and income were becoming important to Fort Worth and Tarrant County during World War I, but they would not become *the* primary force in the local economy until World War II. Cattle and other livestock would reign supreme a little longer. Aviation, however, remained an abiding interest of Fort Worth's city fathers in the years between World War I and World War II.

CHAPTER 4

Local Aviation between the Wars

A FAMILIAR TRUISM AFTER WORLD WAR I WAS THAT AFTER American farm boys became doughboys and viewed a larger world—Gay Paree or elsewhere—they really did not want to go back to the farm. For this and other reasons many men who returned from the war to be discharged in Fort Worth never left there. Others who enjoyed flying remained in the military until 1920 when all three local airfields shut down completely. These young fliers often accepted invitations to do exhibitions for country fairs and other events simply to maintain public interest in the Army Air Service. The popularity of airplanes after the war was a direct result of their increased use by the military during the war. Their continued popularity and progress in the Fort Worth area during the two decades between the world wars inspired a much greater emphasis on military defense activity later. Immediately following World War I and as late as 1923, most aviation fields in the United States remained military bases. The U.S. government created what they called the Model Airways System as an experimental project to link military bases. The first connection came in 1920 linking Washington, D.C. to Dayton, Ohio, St. Louis, Kansas City, Salt Lake City, and finally San Francisco. Later, officials proposed a north-south route from St. Louis to San Antonio. The ongoing rivalry between Fort Worth and Dallas became an issue, and Fort Worth's Aviation Club persuaded the Army to include Fort Worth on the route. Organizers solved the problem of pleasing both cities by making Dallas the stop on the flight north, and Fort Worth the stop on the flight south.[1]

Some returning World War I fliers created a short flight airline service in Fort Worth in 1919. Russell Pearson, K. C. Braymen, and D. H. McClure formed the Fort Worth Aerial Transportation Company and purchased thirteen surplus JN-4s. They made their first flight from River Crest Country Club with a plan to specialize in transporting gift packages from manufacturers like Fort Worth's Pangburn Candy Company to mayors of neighboring cities. They apparently tried to be too specialized, for their company closed after only a few months. Despite their failure, this pioneering effort in commercial aviation would not be Fort Worth's last.[2]

In order to encourage commercial aviation, Congress passed the Air Mail Act of 1925 (also known as the Kelly Bill), which authorized the postmaster general to contract for airmail service. This began the process of turning over government airmail routes to private contractors and marked the beginning of commercial aviation. In 1926 the Air Commerce Act gave the secretary of commerce responsibility for fostering air commerce through the establishment of airports and navigational assistance, and authorized the registration of aircraft and the certification of pilots. The Air Corps Act authorized the continued existence and expansion of the Army's Air Service over a five-year period, changing the name from Air Service to Air Corps. The act authorized 1,518 officers, 2,501 cadets, 16,000 enlisted men, and 1,800 aircraft.[3]

These were part of the reason the Army sent Air Service Staff Sergeant William G. Fuller from Love Field in Dallas to Fort Worth to find a suitable site for military landings. The former Barron Field location southeast of Fort Worth seemed appropriate. However, military and city officials ultimately chose an area closer to Fort Worth near the abandoned Taliaferro Field. Located four and a half miles due north of Fort Worth (on North Main Street) the new field originally was called Fort Worth Airport when it opened in 1925, and the United States Army became its main user. The city of Fort Worth assumed control from the Army on April 1, 1926, and in 1927 city officials changed the name to Meacham Field in honor of Mayor H. C. Meacham who had urged its creation. Fuller, after his Army enlistment ended in 1927, became airport manager, a job he held with the city of Fort Worth (except while he was on active duty during World War II) until his retirement in 1961.[4]

Fort Worth leaders continued their love affair with air flight, holding regular meetings of the Fort Worth Aviation Club that had begun in the mid-1920s. The club was a legacy of the Southwestern Aeronautical Association, which city leaders formed in 1909. The Model Airways program was not the only post-war military activity in Fort Worth. During the war Congressman Fritz Lanham, in response to local efforts, had helped bring helium extraction to Fort Worth. The Navy authorized construction of a gas plant to manufacture helium on the city's north side. Contracts for the project totaled $4 million and created the world's first helium production plant. The plant extracted helium from natural gas, returned the gas to the pipelines for commercial use, and bottled the helium for use by the Air Service.[5]

North Side helium plant for U.S. dirigible fleet.

Helium Gas Plant being built by the U.S. Government at a cost of $5,000,000.

For complete 64-page booklet, go to Portal to Texas History website.

The Fort Worth Chamber of Commerce, proud of its new five million dollar helium facility on the north side of Fort Worth, touted its praises in a brochure in 1919. Finished toward the end of the war, the plants captured the helium used in dirigibles from West Texas gas wells. *Photo courtesy United States Navy.*

Experimentation in helium production continued after the war with the Linde Company and the Air Reduction Company pumping from $250 to $400 million into the local economy. Early in 1929 the Bureau of Mines in the Department of Commerce moved the helium plant from Fort Worth to Amarillo, Texas. The Fort Worth plant buildings and considerable shop equipment became the property of the Bureau of Air Commerce (later the Federal Aviation Administration) and became their district headquarters.[6]

The city of Fort Worth received a great deal of media attention when the Navy dirigible *Shenandoah*, filled with helium, completed a 9,000-mile mission, logging 258 hours of flying time. Fort Worth represented the midway docking point on each phase of its flight across the continental United States. Unfortunately, the *Shenandoah* crashed in a heavy thunderstorm over Ava, Ohio, on September 3, 1925, killing eighteen of the thirty-five crew members. Two who survived were Fred J. Tobin and the ship's commander, R. G. Mayer. After serving together in the Navy for many years, the two men later settled in Fort Worth and worked for the defense plant in west Fort Worth that ultimately became Lockheed Martin. Mayer became

Fort Worth Division Manager, and Tobin an assistant foreman in the 1950s when the plant was called Convair.[7]

Whether officials of the Chamber of Commerce were farsighted enough to envision Fort Worth as a future aviation hub and stronghold of military defense assembly plants, their actions in the 1920s and 1930s contributed to that outcome. The chamber welcomed anything that publicized that new machine—the airplane. In May 1927 Charles Lindbergh completed the first non-stop flight over the Atlantic, so naturally his landing at Meacham Field on September 27 in his plane the *Spirit of St. Louis* created much excitement.[8]

In 1928 Amon G. Carter, publisher of the *Fort Worth Star-Telegram*, served as president of the Fort Worth Aviation Club. The Chamber of Commerce added an aviation department to its organization to promote air flight. Headed by D. W. Carlton, the new department planned an "Aerocade" trip to West Texas in 1928. Carlton and his committee enlisted fourteen airplanes and pilots for a nine-hundred-mile swing around the Fort Worth trade territory. The Aerocade was so successful that the chamber planned a second one in 1929. For that one, twenty airplanes and seventy-three passengers flew over South Texas, the Rio Grande Valley, and even as far as Monterrey, Mexico. Unfortunately, the plane carrying Jack H. Hott, manager of the Chamber of Commerce, and his pilot, Bert Pidcoke of the Texas Company, went missing. The chamber organized a search of the area around Monterrey. The two men eventually rode into civilization on mules, having made an emergency landing in an isolated spot in the interior of Mexico after their airplane ran out of gas.[9]

Private enterprise also aided the aviation industry in Fort Worth. Seth Barwise and other Fort Worth businessmen pledged $57,000 to form Texas Airways Corporation in August 1927. Underfunded, the company struggled, so Temple Bowen, a Fort Worth aviation pioneer, took over the company permit in 1928 and established Texas Air Transport. He began limited mail, cargo, and passenger service to Fort Worth. Then in October of that same year A. P. Barrett acquired the company from Bowen. Barrett expanded, creating Southern Air Transport. As of 1930 the company, which was headquartered in Fort Worth, provided day and night airmail service to the north from Fort Worth and operated two airlines to the south.[10]

In 1930 Southern Air Transport joined three other fledgling airlines to create American Airways, Inc. A spokesman claimed in April 1930 that it "operates more daily scheduled mileage than any other system in the country. Fort Worth is now but twenty-six hours from New York." American Airways would become American Airlines in 1934, but while it was still Southern Air Transport, Fort Worth newspaperman Amon G. Carter owned stock, which he retained. His part ownership of the new American Airlines fulfilled his need to be a part of the growing aviation industry and brought him wealth as well.[11]

By the 1930s, isolationism and various peace movements kept the U.S. government from spending very much money on military airplanes. Even so, an interest in aviation remained strong in Fort Worth, especially for airmail contracts. A great deal of airmail came through Fort Worth because it was a crossroads on both the east-west and north-south routes of the federal Fourth Airways District. The district extended from California to the Mississippi River and from the Mexican border to Kansas City. The district was responsible for airways maintenance, as well as teletype service, radio, and airline inspections. Meacham Field airline schedules for 1933 reflect thirty-two flights in a twenty-four hour period. Meacham covered 325 acres with an estimated value of $1 million, three hard surfaced runways, two hangars, and a $150,000 American Airlines building. The government also maintained a small radio facility at the field. Many people, including newspaper reporters, referred to the airfield as Fort Worth Municipal Airport because of the city's ownership rather than Meacham Field. The volume of airmail handled at Meacham Field in 1935 ranked it third in the nation, behind only New York City and Chicago. By 1939 the three major airlines in Fort Worth were American, Braniff, and Delta.[12]

For some enthusiasts, building airplanes soon became as compelling as flying them. However, few airplane manufacturing companies existed in the United States in the 1920s and 30s. Texan George Williams and his Texas Aero Corporation, located in Temple, was one of the first. Williams acquired a government license for the manufacture and sale of new aircraft as early as 1928. Unfortunately, when he died in an airplane crash in 1930 his company closed. The tumultuous events of the 1930s would bring more opportunities to aircraft manufacturers.[13]

After the infamous appeasement of Adolf Hitler by Britain and France, granting him the Sudeten area in the Munich Agreement of September 30, 1938, and Hitler's seizure of Austria earlier that year, President Roosevelt met in the White House with his military advisers where he appointed General Henry "Hap" Arnold as Chief of the Air Corps. Arnold had graduated from West Point in 1907, and four years later became a flier when the Army sent him and another second lieutenant to Dayton, Ohio, to train under Orville Wright. Coincidentally, Arnold trained in the same 1911 flying class with Cal Rodgers, the ill-fated flyer who made history in Fort Worth. When the Chief of the Army Air Corps Major General Oscar Westover died in an air accident on September 29, 1938, President Roosevelt promoted Arnold to major general and named him as Westover's replacement. Roosevelt either knew exactly what he was doing or made a lucky choice, for placing General Arnold in command of the Air Corps ultimately meant the successful adoption of the new philosophy of air power that the nation and the world needed at that time. Because of his position, General Arnold traveled with President Roosevelt to important conferences, such as the signing of the Atlantic Charter in August 1941 between Roosevelt and Winston Churchill, prime minister of Great Britain. Despite his travels with FDR, Arnold made several trips to Fort Worth during the war.[14]

Roosevelt wanted an annual production of 10,000 airplanes and the capacity to produce twice that many. He called a secret meeting at the White House on November 14, 1938, that would ultimately be important to the Air Corps and to the citizens of Fort Worth. FDR's top advisers attended along with General Arnold. The president informed them that Hitler would not be impressed by anything short of overwhelming air power. He planned to ask Congress for 20,000 planes, to be delivered in two years through private industry and also to request "seven new plants the government would construct." Roosevelt wanted to supply France and Great Britain with airplanes in order to protect the Western Hemisphere. General Arnold immediately drew up an expansion plan for more airplanes to present to Congress.[15]

Roosevelt, in his State of the Union address on January 4, 1939, announced his intention to strengthen air power, but he reduced his request from 20,000 airplanes to 10,000 in two years and even later to 5,000, perhaps with the hopes of more readily persuading Congress to comply. At that time the major U.S. aircraft firms—Consolidated, Martin, Douglas, North American, Curtiss, and Boeing each produced about forty airplanes per year.[16]

General Arnold, in January 1939, called officials of Consolidated to a meeting at Wright Field in Dayton, Ohio, where he told them that he needed a long range airplane similar to the B-17 Flying Fortress, which first flew in July 1935. He asked Reuben Fleet of Consolidated if his company could produce a heavy bomber with a speed of more than three hundred miles per hour, a flight ceiling of 35,000 feet, and a range of 3,000 miles. In other words, could it out perform all rivals? Fleet assigned I. M. Laddon, his chief engineer, to direct design work. Preliminary specifications, mock up, and wind tunnel testing of a model proceeded rapidly. The government signed a contract on March 30 for an XB-24 bomber. When the experimental model made its maiden flight over San Diego on December 29, orders already had started coming in. Consolidated thus acquired its wartime bomber to build. By the end of World War II the B-24 bomber became the most-produced four-engine aircraft in history because of wartime necessity and the fact that it was built by several different companies. Fort Worth factory workers would become a major part of that production.[17]

In Fort Worth, the continuing emphasis on aviation began to reap benefits as the U.S. government became increasingly interested in military aviation. The Civil Aeronautics Authority named North Texas Agricultural College (now the University of Texas at Arlington) as one of thirteen schools nationwide to train pilots under a National Youth Administration project. As early as December 1938, President Roosevelt proposed a plan to train 20,000 college students annually and then keep some of them in the Army and Navy Reserves. The courses began in January 1939 with plans to expand to more colleges later. Those at the Arlington campus took their flight training at the Grand Prairie Airport, six miles to the east.[18]

Both Democrats and Republicans criticized FDR's plan for pilot training, arguing that the danger of a foreign invasion "is much less than the danger of economic collapse from an unbalanced budget," "war mongers of the New Deal have unnecessarily alarmed the people," and America should forget "this silly war hysteria." Roosevelt accepted the criticism and continued planning. In January 1939 he asked Congress for $300 million in appropriations for the Air Corps. President Roosevelt's actions eventually brought massive defense measures to Fort Worth and to the nation. On April 3, 1939, he signed the National Defense Act of 1940, authorizing 6,000 airplanes for the Army Air Corps and increasing the personnel to 3,203 officers and 45,000 enlisted men. Congress had honored his request for the $300 million.[19]

Early in 1939 the Fort Worth Municipal Airport (Meacham Field) became the designated training field for a government sponsored Civilian Pilot Training Program (CPTP) with the aviation school located at North Texas Agricultural College. Students at NTAC still trained at Grand Prairie and other small county, city, and municipal airports. Soon Fort Worth Municipal Airport began turning out fliers with primary and advanced training with as many as thirty pilots in the advanced class. The school employed approximately thirty people.[20]

The government established the first airway traffic control center in the South at Meacham, operated as a division of the Civil Aeronautics Authority. The center, with its nine employees, directed traffic on all airways within a 200-mile radius of Fort Worth. The city's airport became one of only two fields in the United States equipped in 1939 with blind landing equipment. This distinction did not last long, however, once military preparedness accelerated. Some of the college students enrolled in the pilot training program on college and university campuses did become military aviators.[21]

When Germany attacked Poland on September 1, 1939, and the war officially began in Europe, the United States ranked seventh worldwide in military aviation. With the help of a quick military buildup that fortuitously placed Fort Worth solidly among the nation's plans, that ranking soon changed. Because Britain declared war on Germany in September 1939, Fort Worth officials conceived the idea of persuading Canada once again to establish a winter training program in the area, making use of the three training fields left from World War I.[22]

Fort Worth officials proposed training the Canadians as civilians, who could then go home to Canada to enlist in their own air service. Fort Worth Mayor I. N. McCrary attended a conference of mayors in Washington early in 1940 and learned that land had been leased near Roanoke, Texas, for a flying field. He suggested using the three Texas fields previously in service. To support this suggestion the Fort Worth Chamber of Commerce submitted data to the War Department about the three World War I fields in Saginaw, Everman, and Benbrook. A few hangars still remained in 1940, even though two decades had elapsed since the three fields had been in use.[23]

In the first indication that the Fort Worth Chamber of Commerce intended to seek defense military or industrial activity, William Holden, executive vice president of the Chamber, wrote members:

> Complete data on the three tracts near Fort Worth used by the government as aviation training fields during the world war has been assembled, including transportation facilities, water, fuel and power supplies, drainage, available housing, etc. Accurate maps of these areas have been prepared and all this data submitted to the Army Air Corps. Similar data and maps in regard to other areas available for use as aviation training camps have also been prepared and submitted. The same favorable conditions which brought to Tarrant County three aviation training fields during the world war exist today.[24]

The assessment of the fields concluded that the former Carruthers landing field, which by 1939 was located only three-fourths of a mile from the town of Benbrook, was too close to town. In addition, Fort Worth's Granbury Road crossed the site and there was other property development in the area. Barron Field, located west of Everman, was still available because the terrain there remained the same. Also, the former Taliaferro Field, then one and one-half miles north of Saginaw, remained practically unchanged from 1917 except for needing re-grading due to erosion. Two hangars, a headquarters building, and many concrete blocks remained. This site, which Fort Worth citizens continued to call Hicks Field, became the only one of the three former World War I fields that reopened and saw service in World War II.[25]

The Army Air Corps announced June 8, 1940, that a primary training school for pilots would begin at Hicks Field. It opened July 22, and cadets began arriving in large numbers in the fall. Called the Texas Aviation School and covering 500 acres, it became the first defense installation in Tarrant County in the months prior to World War II. Between 1940 and 1941 three large steel-framed hangars were constructed and old ones rehabilitated at a cost of $250,000. A new YMCA building housed a club room and a movie theater. Major W. F. Long, formerly in charge of the Dallas Aviation School at Love Field, operated Hicks when it first opened. Major B. S. Graham, a World War I pilot who had served nineteen months in France, later commanded. Plans called for the first class of 120 students to be in training by August 3, 1940, and a second class of 95 cadets to arrive on September 11, with about that same number every five weeks thereafter. Fifty student fliers remained from the first class to serve as instructors, working alongside 127 civilian employees.[26]

The Fort Worth Chamber of Commerce maintained its efforts to acquire as many military operations and installations as possible for the city. William Holden, executive director, made numerous trips in July and August 1940 to the West Coast, to Washington, D.C., and anywhere else he thought he could work to persuade the Army and Navy to select Fort Worth for their training fields, airplane factories, seaplane bases, or other related enterprises. He told city officials that Congressman Fritz Lanham and Texas Senator Morris Sheppard had been cooperating with him.[27]

The Civil Aeronautics Authority selected Lake Worth, on Fort Worth's northwest side, as a site to construct one of fifteen inland seaplane bases to be established in Texas. The National Youth Administration built it in early summer 1940 near Holden Boat Works on Lake Worth. Initially, the dock handled two seaplanes and provided gas, oil, and service as a mid-continent stop for Navy airplanes flying cross-country. A cyclone fence protected the visiting seaplanes from vandals or curious neighbors. The base utilized modern equipment and was one of the largest of its kind in the country. When complete, it could buoy twenty-eight airships at one time. In an eighteen-month period it serviced more than 1,200 seaplanes. Its gasoline pumps dispensed one hundred gallons of fuel a minute and could service three airplanes simultaneously. The Aviation Committee of the Chamber of Commerce also hoped to acquire another naval base at Eagle Mountain Lake, and they did.[28]

Even while officials made plans to reopen Hicks and the seaplane dock took shape, President Roosevelt increased the demands he had made on the American aircraft industry only months earlier. In a radio address on May 16, 1940, FDR issued what appeared to be an unrealistic request: "I should like to see this nation geared up to the ability to turn out at least 50,000 planes a year." This was five times what he had asked for after the Munich Agreement. He asked Congress for $896 million to fund this request. People called it "fantastic" and "too optimistic."[29]

Two weeks later, on May 29, 1940, Roosevelt appointed Ford Motor Company industrialist William S. Knudsen to head the U.S. military production of airplanes and arms and armaments. One of Knudsen's first tasks was to contract for the building of new factories that could quadruple existing aircraft production, and then to see that 500,000 new workers were hired. Congress passed a bill on August 22, 1940, creating the Defense Plant Corporation (DPC) to build new or enlarge existing factories. In the next five years the DPC constructed 344 new plants of all types—mostly in the Western part of the country—at a cost of $1.854 billion. Throughout the nation the government investment in a total of 446 plants was $3.265 billion. The government wanted inland plants located away from possible coastal attacks. North Texas, centrally located and at a distance from any coast, fit the government's requirements. The DPC also constructed a $65 million building at Willow Run, Michigan, in which the Ford Motor Company was to build B-24 bombers originally designed by Consolidated in San Diego. In September 1940 the War Department told the airplane industry to tool up for mass production orders and not to accept commercial orders without government approval. Texas acquired a Consolidated factory at White Settlement, near Fort Worth, and a North American Aviation plant at Grand Prairie near Dallas.[30]

Prior to the U.S. entrance into World War II, General Arnold's task became acquiring enough airplanes and men trained to fly them to create a large air force. He expressed a concern that the U.S. had given so many airplanes away to Britain under the Lend-Lease Act that it could not create an adequate air force for itself.[31]

Fort Worth's mainstay livestock industry and the city's burgeoning stake in aviation, met in the person of Scotsman John Kennedy, a livestock commission agent, who with partners would form Bennett Aircraft and later Globe Aircraft, a company that during World War II would produce military airplanes. (Aircraft manufacturers learned in the 1930s that when introducing new models it took a production of ten to twelve planes to bring the cost to a sustainable price range. With a larger airplane, often twenty planes had to be produced to reach a level cost. Manufacturers quickly realized that military orders, however scarce, would call for production of a larger quantity, so they hesitated to introduce new designs unless they had a guarantee of the larger military sales.)[32]

Kennedy had arrived in the United States in 1908 at age sixteen, sent by his recently impoverished father to a friend, John Clay, who owned a commission company at the Chicago stockyards. After several years, the hardworking young Kennedy found himself in Fort Worth as regional manager for Clay. Kennedy learned of a serum to prevent blackleg, an infectious bacterial disease, in cattle. He bought the rights to the serum, and created Globe Laboratories to produce it, in the process becoming quite wealthy. In about 1938 Kennedy became interested in aviation; working with an engineer he made an all-wood prototype of an airplane he wanted to build. Always optimistic and willing to venture down a new path, Kennedy sought investors to create an airplane manufacturing company, which would become the first such plant in the Fort Worth area. (The only other Texas airplane factory at the time was located in Houston.)[33]

The Fort Worth Chamber of Commerce had been for nearly three decades an enthusiastic supporter of aviation, and it wanted an airplane factory in Fort Worth. At a chamber dinner at the Hotel Texas on October 25, 1939, officials cooperated with Kennedy to announce plans for the Bennett Aircraft Corporation, named after Frank W. Bennett, a Dallas and Houston oilman who became a large investor. Livestock and aviation retained their connection, because W. L. Pier, president of the Fort Worth Stockyards, was also president of the Chamber of Commerce at the time. The airplane that Bennett Aircraft planned to produce would be called the Bennett Bimotor Executive Transport, a lightweight, two-seater made out of plywood. Construction of the factory began on the Kennedy farm, and Kennedy volunteered his large wooden horse barn as an additional facility. The new building covered 40,000 square feet and possessed its own adjacent airfield. Capitalization of Bennett Aircraft was $350,000 when it received its charter April 5, 1940, with directors listed as John Kennedy, C. A. Lupton, Harry E. Brants, W. P. Bomar, Dion L. Johnson, R. E. Harding, Jr., and R. L. Bowen, all of Fort Worth, plus Bennett.[34]

The directors hired aircraft engineers from all over the country. They even persuaded design engineer Max Spenger of Basel, Switzerland, who formerly worked in the German Messerschmidt factory, to sign on. Folks told stories that when the company first opened in Kennedy's horse barn, employees shoveled hay out of the loft to make room for offices. The officers of Bennett Aircraft were John Kennedy, president; vice presidents D. L. Johnson, F. W. Bennett, James Goodwin Hall; and Norman Nicholson, secretary-treasurer. The first factory manager was Lloyd Royer of Manhattan Beach, California, formerly with North American Aviation Corporation. Captain Frank C. Merrill, who had worked for American Airlines, headed sales. Hall, a World War I veteran and holder of a dozen flight records, served as chairman of the corporation's executive committee.[35]

Local efforts to attract a builder of civilian airplanes came toward the end of the 1930s with Bennett Aircraft. Later as Globe Aircraft the factory built AT-10 trainers during World War II. *Photo courtesy the University of Texas at Dallas.*

The engineers developed the company's signature model, the Bennett BTC-1, a bi-motor, mid-wing, plywood and plastic executive transport craft with a cruising speed of 196 miles per hour and a wingspan of forty-eight feet. With war once again underway in Europe, Bennett changed the BTC-1 to include a metal fuselage. The Bennett BTC-1 was the first airplane manufactured in Fort Worth. On April 11, 1940, the first Bennett BTC-1 left Fort Worth Municipal Airport (Meacham Field) with four passengers en route to Miami, Florida. Each Bennett BTC-1 would sell for $30,000. The directors of the new company hoped to sell three hundred airplanes to the United Kingdom as its first large order (a military one) but the sale would depend on the U.S. government dropping its arms embargo. With the Neutrality Act signed by President Franklin D. Roosevelt on November 17, 1941, this was accomplished. D. L. Johnson, chairman of the Fort Worth Chamber of Commerce's aviation committee, said at the announcement dinner that other nations besides the United Kingdom were interested in the Bennett plane, including China, Brazil, Mexico, and some Scandinavian countries. The U.S. Army planned to take a look at it as well.[36]

On August 1, 1940, Norman Nicholson of Bennett Aircraft conferred in Washington, D.C. with General H. H. Arnold, chief of the Army Air Corps, and General Jacob E. Fickel, assistant chief for training and operations, hoping to interest them in the BTC-1 as a trainer. As a lieutenant colonel more than twenty years earlier, General Fickel had been the commander of Carruthers Field in Benbrook, west of Fort Worth. Nicholson and Fort Worth's Congressman, Fritz Lanham, visited President Franklin D. Roosevelt's Advisory Defense Commission. Texas Senators Tom Connally and Morris Sheppard helped pave the way for Nicholson's Washington visit. He then went on to New York to meet with the British Purchasing Commission. This early in, Texas political leaders lent their influence to Fort Worth's aspirations to be an aviation center. They and their successors through the years became masters at such negotiations.[37]

Late in 1940 the officers reorganized Bennett Aircraft as Globe Aircraft Corporation because Kennedy had sold his Globe Laboratories and bought out enough of his investors to control the aircraft company. Early in 1941 he began building a lightweight commercial airplane that he called the Globe Swift. This first plane, called the CG-1 was completed May 21, 1941, and successfully passed its test flights. Production slowed because of World War II and the drop in civilian purchases of airplanes, and by the fall of 1941 the firm began accepting army contracts.[38]

Globe Aircraft would not be the only Fort Worth airplane factory supplying the war effort. Massive defense contracts came to the city during World War II, but not without a great deal of effort by local officials to court their government counterparts. John Kennedy's Globe Aircraft, however, remained the one important airplane manufacturer during the war that was locally owned. National preparations for the war presented local leaders with great opportunities.

North Texas during World War II would go from having no aircraft industry with the exception of Globe to becoming one of the three largest aircraft production centers in the nation. As FDR had requested, the output of airplanes from American factories—including some American-financed Canadian production—reached an astonishing 229,230. This represented over 50,000 airplanes for each of the four years that the United States geared up its massive war production efforts. What had seemed impossible in 1940 would be achieved by 1944.[39] The participation of Fort Worth and Tarrant County in this patriotic wartime effort makes for a fascinating and inspiring story. John Kennedy's Globe facility in Saginaw and the Consolidated bomber plant located west of Fort Worth in White Settlement became major Tarrant County players.

CHAPTER 5

World War II: The Bomber Plant

NY STORY OF CONSOLIDATED AIRCRAFT CORPORATION MUST begin with Major Reuben Fleet, the blue-eyed, six-foot war veteran with a commanding military posture who bought two struggling airplane companies half a decade after World War I and "consolidated" them to create his new company. The self-confident, stubborn Fleet built his factory into a major supplier of airplanes for the war effort with a division located in San Diego and a new one in Fort Worth in World War II.[1]

Fleet, who grew up in Washington State, became interested in flying and trained as a pilot during World War I. He remained in the Air Service at McCook Field in Dayton, Ohio, until 1922. In November of that year he accepted a position as general manager of the Gallaudet Aircraft Corporation in Greenwich, Rhode Island. Engineer Edson Fessenden Gallaudet created the company, but lost a Navy contract. The company foundered, and Gallaudet resigned in 1922, giving Fleet the chance to purchase it the following year.[2]

In May 1923, Fleet combined Gallaudet, the smallest World War I airplane manufacturer, with what remained of Dayton-Wright, the largest, using $25,000 of his own and his sister's money, to incorporate Consolidated Aircraft Corporation in Delaware. Fleet's purchase of Dayton-Wright included all of the company's designs. In addition, he hired their chief designer, Colonel Virginius E. Clark. Fleet also inherited an order for twenty models of a TW-3 basic trainer. In June, Fleet brought out the all-metal Gallaudet CO-1-Liberty 400 designed by Air Corps Engineering.[3]

In 1924 the Air Service contracted with Fleet to produce Consolidated's first original design, an improved version of the TW-3, which the company called the PT-1. The Army ordered fifty, giving Fleet justification to seek a better production facility, which he found in Buffalo, New York. He leased a large factory where Curtiss had manufactured airplanes in World War I. The Army eventually bought 170 of the new airplanes, the Navy purchased 300 of a different version, and Fleet sold various versions to twenty-two foreign countries. Because Fleet realized that the cold Buffalo winters made flying difficult for test pilots, he decided to move his factory to a warmer climate. He chose San Diego, hired an architect to design a plant, and between August and September 1935 he moved his entire operation on 157 railroad cars. This move seemed in keeping with the motto Fleet coined for his company, "Nothing short of right is right."[4]

Acquiring a defense plant for Fort Worth eventually would involve Fleet. Interest in bidding for a government-constructed defense plant in North Texas developed quickly after President Franklin D. Roosevelt announced his plans and defense goals for military aviation. Roosevelt made it clear that for security reasons the military construction industry needed to decentralize and build plants inland away from any coast. The local labor pool in North Texas, although untrained in aircraft manufacturing, nevertheless was plentiful, and housing problems could be solved more easily in North Texas than in the already crowded industrial areas on both coasts. In addition, the flat terrain, temperate climate, and ideal flying weather proved to be significant advantages.[5]

Again the rivalry between Fort Worth and Dallas came into play as officials of both cities tried to attract a defense plant to their city. Fleet's friend Tom Bomar, who had helped him move his plant from Buffalo to San Diego in 1935, accompanied him to North Texas to look at potential sites. In Dallas, officials from the Chamber of Commerce showed the two men around. In Fort Worth, Amon G. Carter, publisher of the *Fort Worth Star-Telegram*, headed a business group that showed Fleet and Bomar a site on Lake Worth. In Houston, Jesse Jones, U.S. Secretary of Commerce, showed Fleet where an artificial lake and plant site could be built and then entertained both men at a local country club. Fleet thanked him, saying he still had not seen anything that looked as good to him as Chula Vista on San Diego Bay. Later, the two Consolidated men flew to New Orleans and looked over Lake Pontchartrain; Fleet also sent the Consolidated vice president to examine sites in Oklahoma.[6]

J. H. Kindelberger of North American Aviation made a firm offer to the Dallas Chamber of Commerce group led by R. L. Thornton Sr. for a site west of Hensley Reserve Airfield, already owned by the city of Dallas. The city secured options for land adjacent to it for a factory. With Dallas in negotiation for the North American plant, Fleet then turned his attention to Fort Worth. Amon Carter claimed that from August 1939 forward he remained in almost daily communication with Fleet, the Army and Navy, and U.S. government leaders. When Carter learned that Tulsa and Atlanta would have airplane factories, he stepped up correspondence with FDR, as the men were friends of sorts. (Carter had entertained President Roosevelt at his home in Fort Worth). In trying to attract the defense plant, Carter relied for help on Harold Foster, manager of the industrial division of the Fort Worth Chamber of Commerce, who prepared an elaborate brochure touting the advantages of Fort Worth. The Chamber offered to deed 1,450 acres of land near Lake Worth, and the city of Fort Worth promised to clear the land and build all necessary roads. An ideal situation would be to have the new B-24 manufacturing plant constructed adjacent to an airfield that could train pilots to fly the airplanes. As a first step, the government agreed to the Lake Worth site on January 3, 1941, after receiving the offers from the Chamber of Commerce and city officials. Apparently, promises President Roosevelt made to Texas senators and local officials also helped Fort Worth win the favorable nod.[7]

"The fight to secure this great plant was long and strenuous," said William Holden, executive vice president of the Fort Worth Chamber of Commerce, in a January 1941 annual report. A couple of months later he wrote, "The bomber plant, together with the adjoining industrial airport, will mean more to the growth and progress of Fort Worth than any other project ever secured." Although the industrial airport had not yet become reality, his words would turn out to be prophetic. Events moved rapidly, and building the aircraft factory proceeded. The Austin Company of Cleveland signed a contract in March to construct the proposed $30 million Fort Worth plant. The U.S. Corps of Engineers arranged for field offices, and the L. J. Miles Construction Company of Fort Worth signed a contract to build the landing area for the adjacent airfield.[8]

For the city to fulfill its agreement to build new streets and improve existing ones, it asked citizens to approve a $3 million bond issue. Storm sewers, drainage, streetlights, and traffic signals added to costs. Voters on March 4, 1941, approved the bond issue needed to purchase the necessary land for Consolidated and the industrial airport by a thirteen to one majority. Included in the site was a 400-plus acre farm that the George and Sarah Grant family had owned since 1881. Earlier the Grants had sold some of their land to the city of Fort Worth for $38 per acre to become a part of Lake Worth. They did not want to sell additional land for the "bomber plant," but the government acquired the land through eminent domain, giving them a check that represented $187 per acre.[9]

During groundbreaking ceremonies for the new bomber plant on April 18, 1941, a downpour drenched the assembled dignitaries. Nevertheless, each designated person lifted the silver shovel and carried out his part of the official day. Major General Gerald C. Brant said as he put a silver shovel in the ground, "We're starting to dig Hitler's grave this afternoon." Colonel F. M. Hopkins, one of two Air Corps representatives who came to Fort Worth, agreed that the project was "one of the most important in the country to the nation's defense program."[10]

Although officials believed construction might take two years, after the December 7 attack on Pearl Harbor, the Austin Company worked around the clock in cooperation with Colonel John H. Anderson of the Army Corps of Engineers to finish the job. In less than nine months they completed construction of the huge factory. Stories persist that when Amon Carter learned that the Tulsa assembly plant would be identical to Fort Worth's, he persuaded the Army architects to add twenty-nine feet to the Fort Worth plant's dimensions to make it the world's largest airplane factory and longest straight assembly line. The building had no windows and workers installed the world's largest industrial air conditioning system.[11]

Because of all the "preparedness spending," Fort Worth's economy grew rapidly during the first half of 1941. Bank clearings were up $29 million from the same period in 1940 to a total slightly over $199 million. The county, state, and federal governments spent nearly $3 million building and improving roads to assist traffic flow to the factory. For Fleet's Consolidated Company itself, headquartered in San Diego, plant facilities doubled and then redoubled. While the company enjoyed sales of $3.6 million in 1939, sales for the first eleven months of the following year reached $95.5 million. It was the greatest one-year growth in the history of American business.[12]

Officials encountered numerous problems in setting up the aircraft factory and getting it operational. Because the North Texas economy previously provided more agricultural than industrial jobs, few skilled assembly-line workers existed. Consolidated hired a nucleus of one thousand workers in Fort Worth in July 1941 and sent them to San Diego for training. Fleet and his administrators also selected an executive group from the San Diego plant to organize the Fort Worth operation. When the United States declared war on Japan and its allies in the days after the attack on Pearl Harbor, the group was ready to move to Fort Worth and begin hiring workers. Fleet cut the original San Diego engineering staff in half to supply the second factory. He bought out a small company called Hall-Aluminus Aircraft Corporation of Bristol, Pennsylvania, in August 1940 and transferred key workers to wherever they were needed. Archibald M. Hall, former president of Hall-Aluminus, went to Fort Worth early in 1942 to oversee completion of the plant and assembly of the first B-24s.[13]

Throughout this process of organizing operations in Fort Worth, Fleet expressed his unfavorable opinion of bureaucratic red tape loudly and often, complaints that soon resulted in his leaving the company. He had not even wanted to set up the plant in Fort Worth. President Roosevelt promised the governors of both Texas and Oklahoma that each state would have a defense plant, but Fleet wanted to expand in San Diego with government money and did not want to construct and run two additional factories. For nearly two decades he operated his company his own way; consequently, government officials did not envision him as the kind of team player they wanted. One of his biographers called him an "iron-willed curmudgeon." Therefore, before Fort Worth began operations at its own Consolidated plant, officials persuaded Fleet to sell his company. Some accounts imply that someone in Washington pressured him because his "one-man style of management" would not work during wartime. He had operated as chairman, president, and general manager. Others claimed that labor disputes and Fleet's frustration over high taxes (The income taxes on businessmen of his bracket reached 93 percent!) slow reimbursement from the government, and bureaucratic meddling convinced him to sell. Once when Washington officials wired Fleet that they needed an immediate response to the latest questionnaire, one of many they had sent him, he is reputed to have replied, "Do you want airplanes, or questionnaires answered: you can't have both."[14]

Whether the government influenced the people involved or not, whatever the means were that convinced Major Fleet to sell Consolidated, Victor Emanuel, head of the Aviation Corporation (AVCO), acquired the company through a small subsidiary, Vultee Aircraft, Inc. of Downey, California. The fact that Consolidated recently had received a contract to build an experimental XB-36, convinced Emanuel to conclude the transaction. Vultee Aircraft purchased 440,000 shares, representing 34 percent of Consolidated common stock for $10.945 million in November 1941. Fleet remained in San Diego and served as a consultant both to Consolidated and to the Defense Department throughout the war.[15]

After Fleet left Consolidated, Emanuel persuaded Tom Girdler of Republic Steel to take over "and fast." Emanuel believed that Girdler was the man who could keep production moving to meet government requirements. Emanuel appointed him chairman of the board of both Consolidated and Vultee Aircraft. Harry Woodhead, president of AVCO and board chairman of Vultee, became president of both companies. When the transfer of Consolidated stock from Fleet to Emanuel took place on December 19, 1941, not even two weeks had elapsed since the attack on Pearl Harbor.[16]

Although the sale that forced Fleet out of Consolidated occurred in 1941, the name change and the merger were not fully complete until 1943. Officials of Consolidated and Vultee Aircraft, Inc. worked out the details during 1942, and directors of both companies approved an agreement in January 1943. The new company would be called Consolidated Vultee Aircraft Corporation. Shareholders approved the agreement on March 17, 1943, and it became effective the next day when officials filed articles of incorporation papers in Delaware. The merged company created thirteen divisions in ten states with a combined payroll of 100,000 workers. Fort Worth represented one of the largest divisions. Although someone coined the phrase "Consair" in the spring of 1943 as a shortened name for the company, it did not catch on. However "Convair" did. Over a decade later in 1954 the company made Convair its official corporate name.[17]

Production plans for Consolidated's B-24 orders called for a former Ford Motor Company plant in Willow Run, Michigan, to ship parts to Fort Worth for assembly. The Willow Run factory was behind schedule, so the San Diego Consolidated plant sent components to Fort Worth for the first 150 airplanes; production began in March 1942 with two parallel, fully powered assembly lines. Officials of the Army Air Corps accepted Fort Worth Consolidated's first assembled B-24 on May 1, 1942, one hundred days ahead of schedule.[18]

George J. Newman, who on March 3, 1942, became vice president in charge of operations for Fort Worth Consolidated, flew a locally built B-24 airplane for the first time on April 19 as many workers and dignitaries watched. Newman, a former test pilot for Consolidated, had flown every type of airplane the company built, having worked for Consolidated since he was fifteen shortly after Fleet created it. In February 1941 he set a non-stop flight record of nine hours, fifty-seven minutes flying from San Diego to New York with the first B-24 to be delivered to Britain. The Royal Air Force named the B-24s "Liberators" when they arrived.[19]

Once Newman flew that first Fort Worth-built B-24, production began in earnest. The assembly process for the airplanes started at the south end of the plant with the subassembly of smaller parts. Henry Ford's original assembly-line technology—as well as the auto industry's use of interchangeable parts—influenced airplane production. An east-west aisle, fifty feet wide, separated the production line into two parts. By the time the process reached the aisle, assembly of the airplane into one piece had begun. The structure moved on a monorail attached to the ceiling, and the station holding the plane moved every other day, or sometimes every third day. Once the airplane had wheels, it moved on its own. In the early days a tram ran down the middle south-north aisle pulled by a tractor-type vehicle, and workers could step on it, hold on to a bar, and ride. Officials used a broadcast system to call workers to a telephone to get instructions from a supervisor. Consolidated added a third shift in July 1942 and thus began a twenty-four-hour, seven-day work week that rapidly began sending B-24s and B-87s (a transport modification of the B-24) off the assembly line. The first B-87, ready more than thirty days ahead of schedule, rolled out on August 24, 1942.[20]

The B-24 Liberator was built at Consolidated Aircraft in Fort Worth. *Photo courtesy United States Air Force via Don Pyeatt.*

By the summer of 1943 the Fort Worth Division ranked second among all U.S. producers of heavy bombers in efficiency of production. By late 1943, more than 200 airplanes a month rolled off the assembly line as employment reached 30,574 by November. With improved machinery, the plant could produce more efficiently at a cheaper cost by the end of the war than it had at the beginning. The man-hours needed to produce one Liberator in 1940 in the San Diego plant could produce fourteen in 1943. In 1942 a B-24 cost $238,000, but by 1944 the cost had dropped to $137,000.[21]

The War Manpower Commission worked continually with Consolidated Vultee officials to train foremen and lead men to meet the ongoing employment needs. The plant wasted no production time in 1943 for holidays; Christmas Day was the only day of rest for workers that year. Board Chairman Tom M. Girdler announced that in 1943 Consolidated Vultee, all divisions combined, delivered more aircraft by number and weight than any other manufacturer and was the world's largest producer of airplanes. The company had produced 126 million pounds of finished product, with the second largest producer coming in at 115 million, and the third at 73 million. The peak production year for Consolidated Vultee was 1944. Combined, the Fort Worth and San Diego plants that year outproduced every other aircraft manufacturer in the world. However, when officials tabulated totals for the entire four years of war production, North American Aviation outproduced Consolidated Vultee. The War Department announced on August 9, 1944, that the Fort Worth Division had begun producing a B-32 bomber, although it revealed no specific information about it other than its nickname, the "Dominator." When production of the B-24 Liberators came to an end in December 1944, Consolidated Vultee then concentrated on the B-32 Dominators. In an effort to keep production high, the U.S. Army Corps of Engineers approved a $2 million expansion program for Consolidated Vultee's Fort Worth Division in 1944. By completion in the spring of 1945, the cost reached to $3 million. The largest additions were two new 100,000 square foot buildings that became raw materials and process materials warehouses. Construction expanded the existing warehouse for the salvage department and the cafeteria. Also added were a road from the plant to Clifford Street, a new employee parking lot, new road paving, relocation of floodlights along the west fence, and excavation, grading, and installation of underground fire mains for the new buildings.[22]

During peak employment at the plant, the city of Fort Worth ran short of buses to carry workers out to Consolidated. People began pulling trailers with sideboards behind their pickup trucks for workers to ride in, but they had to stand up for the entire twenty to thirty minute ride from downtown. Even with the great mass of people heading to the plants, none were expendable. In fact, company officials learned in May 1944 that the Texas headquarters for selective service had granted a moratorium on the drafting of all male Consolidated employees between the ages of twenty-six and thirty-seven if they were "regularly engaged in" an activity in war production or the national interest. One remarkable aspect of the stream of workers was the large number of women traveling to the plants.[23]

The aircraft plants also provided an opportunity for women to don pants and join the workforce in heavy industry for the first time. Before 1941 almost no women worked in aircraft, but by 1942 women already comprised nearly 40 percent of Consolidated's total workforce, and not just in Fort Worth. While women workers at a Boeing plant in Seattle claimed the distinction of inspiring the first "Rosie the Riveter" nickname, Fort Worth's women certainly occupied the forefront as well. The overall proportion of women in the workforce in the United States in 1940 consisted of about 25

These three "Rosie the Riveters" worked at Consolidated in Fort Worth building B-24 Liberators for the war effort. Some folks laughingly called the bomber plant the "bloomer" plant because of the female workers. *Photo courtesy Lockheed Martin.*

percent, but by 1945, at the peak of wartime production, women represented 36 percent of the total workforce. People all over Fort Worth began calling the Consolidated plant the "bomber plant," but Gloria Doyle, one of the women who worked there, recalls that people also called it the "bloomer plant" because of the women workers. Later in the war when even men with wives and children were drafted and left their jobs at Consolidated, women usually replaced them because few men remained who were available to work. One young Brownwood, Texas, woman convinced her brother to drive her to Fort Worth so she could get a job. "I remember watching my brother drive away. After he dropped me off at the boarding house, I almost ran after his truck to stop him. I was a little scared of being on my own."[24]

The Girls' Service League, a charitable organization supported by wealthy Fort Worth matrons, provided two boarding houses for young ladies, perhaps some of them "Rosie the Riveters," during World War II. The organization, created during World War I, became a part of the Fort Worth Community Chest in 1930 and changed its name to Girls' Service League, Inc. In 1940 they purchased the vacant Winfield Scott home at 1509 Pennsylvania (Thistle Hill) and created a boarding house. They bought a second house, Lassiter Lodge, on Penn Street nearby. During the war, extra rooms at Thistle Hill served as classrooms and workshops for defense nutrition classes or as Red Cross Sewing Rooms during the day. Both houses together provided homes for seventy young working women by December 1943. Because the residents often married and left, there was quite a turnover. Almost 500 young women enjoyed the safety and comfort of the two Girls' Service League boarding houses in World War II. Lois Barnett, a resident of Lassiter Lodge acquired not a riveting job, but nevertheless war work. She toiled at the Quartermaster Depot in a rubber storage room full of jeep and airplane tires and tubes of all sizes.[25]

Consolidated officials sought to keep workers' morale high. In the company newspaper, *The Eagle*, a letter appeared on May 20, 1943:

> TO MEN AND WOMEN OF CONSOLIDATED VULTEE AIRCRAFT
> FORT WORTH, TEXAS DIVISION
> Our fighting men, standing shoulder to shoulder with our gallant allies, the British and the French, have driven the enemy out of North Africa. In this victory the munitions made by American industry, labor and management, played a very important role. There is glory for us all in this achievement.
>
> Eisenhower, General, Commander-in-Chief
of the Allied Forces in Africa."[26]

For the first time since its opening a year and a half earlier, the plant scheduled an open house for its employees and guests. Each employee could invite one member of his or her immediate family, who was over eighteen, on an inspection tour between 9 a.m. and 6 p.m. on Sunday, June 27, 1943. Employees and visitors could "walk down the world's longest airplane double assembly line and view the 'air might' for which their kin are responsible," according to the invitation in the company newspaper. Plant officials wanted family members to be able to share the "pride in the planes" that their loved ones helped build to further the war effort. Family members and employees could tour a fully assembled B-24 and a C-87 as well. The next

Crowds flocked to Consolidated on Sunday, June 27, 1943, for an open house where workers could invite one family member over the age of eighteen to view construction of the B-24s. *Photo courtesy Lockheed Martin.*

issue of *The Eagle* reported that 32,400 visitors inspected the plant during the open house.[27]

During the course of the war, numerous visitors stopped by the plant, from soldiers touring the country to urge the purchase of savings bonds to government officials. The most important visitor, however, was President

President Franklin D. Roosevelt, his wife Eleanor, and his son and daughter-in-law made a surprise visit to Consolidated on September 28, 1942, to encourage the local workers. Also in the convertible were plant manager George Newman and Major General Donovan. *Photo courtesy Lockheed Martin.*

Franklin D. Roosevelt who made a surprise visit to Fort Worth's Consolidated plant on September 28, 1942. At the time, it was his only visit to a war factory in the Southwest. Roosevelt and his Secret Service detail arrived on a special train that pulled entirely into the building. Then he transferred to an open limousine that traveled through the plant at a very slow speed, surrounded by Secret Service agents. In the car with him were his wife, their son and daughter-in-law, Mr. and Mrs. Elliott Roosevelt, and the latter couple's children. The younger Roosevelts lived in Fort Worth. Also with them in the limousine were Newman, head of Fort Worth Consolidated, and Major General Richard Donovan, commander of the Eighth Army Corps.[28]

Before learning who might be visiting, workers realized that something special was happening when they saw maintenance workers draping extra American flags around the building, and the factory manager S. J. Powell scurrying about. "Must be a really big shot visitor," someone said, and indeed it was. Work stopped, and everybody lined up. Security was tight. No one was allowed on the balconies. Roosevelt's car did not stop; he was not inspecting airplanes. He just waved and made an appearance to encourage workers in the nation's largest aircraft factory. Besides that, he got to see his Fort Worth grandkids. News agencies did not report his visit until he was back in Washington.[29]

Another important visitor to the B-24 airplane factory, General Henry H. Arnold, chief of the Army Air Corps, made his first wartime trip to Consolidated in July 1942 while on a five-state inspection tour. "I look forward to the time when we can get the planes we need to win the war," he said while in Fort Worth. He also commented that he was "very favorably impressed with the plant, its type of construction, its layout, plans and production."[30]

Former U.S. Navy Commander Roland G. Mayer became manager of the Fort Worth Division in 1944 after serving as assistant division manager for fifteen months, succeeding George J. Newman, who resigned near the war's end for a peacetime job. Mayer had worked for Consolidated Vultee since retiring from the Navy in 1940 after twenty-two years of service. Mayer, an expert on lighter-than-air craft—dirigibles—held a license to fly them as well, and he was a survivor of the historic *Shenandoah* dirigible disaster in September 1925. Chairman of the Board Tom M. Girdler, who took over from Fleet in December 1941, resigned April 27, 1945, when he saw that the war was about to conclude. He explained that he assumed the chairmanship three and a half years earlier, "only in service of the nation and in support of the government war effort."[31]

As World War II indeed came to an end General Arnold sent a letter early in September 1945 thanking the workers for a job well done at what was now officially called Convair in Fort Worth: "Your plant in Fort Worth cooperated magnificently in meeting every changed or urgent production schedule. Without your outstanding services, our air plans against these two enemies could never have been accomplished." Mayer reminded employees that the work expected from Convair changed when the war ended. "During the war," he said, "the United States government wanted the best airplanes it could get the fastest—at any price. But our customers now—including the government—want the best airplanes they can get the cheapest." Mayer announced that production on the B-32 would stop, but the plant would continue to work on three important experimental projects— the XB-36, the C-99 six-engine transport, and a third type of airplane still classified by the war department. Mayer cut the workweek to forty hours, five days a week, down from forty-eight hours, six days a week. Only the Experimental Department continued to work two shifts per day. In a letter in the company newspaper, Mayer thanked the employees, who he had begun laying off, for a "military mission completed" and a "job well done." He said,

Those of our employees who have stayed with their war job until the end of hostilities should have a deep feeling of satisfaction
and pride in their loyalty to our nation and our fighting men. You
have done your part in the building of B-24 Liberator bombers and
C-87 Liberty expresses, as well as the B-32 superbomber war planes
which have played a vital part in our nation's victory. Possibly you
could have left earlier and 'jumped the gun' in getting a peace-time
job. You elected to stay until your job was done. Congratulations on
your patriotism! Now we have to readjust our lives to winning the
peace. —Our war mission has been completed.[32]

Indeed, during World War II Consolidated Vultee (all thirteen divisions) ranked second in production among all American aircraft manufacturers. From the day the first B-24 rolled off the assembly line in San
Diego until the war ended, the company produced 30,903 airplanes. The
Fort Worth division produced more than 3,000 warplanes—2,750 of them
B-24 bombers. Nearly 300 were C-87 transport versions of the B-24, and
then the rest B-32 heavy bombers. In addition, the entire company created
enough spare parts to equal 5,000 more airplanes delivered as spares. This
represented nearly 13 percent of the total output of the nation's industry.
North American Aviation ranked first in producing 41,188 airplanes, and
Douglas, Curtis, and Lockheed ranked, third, fourth, and fifth with 30,696,
26,154, and 18,926 respectively.[33]

Even though these figures represented the Consolidated Vultee output
nationwide, the impact of the Fort Worth plant's production on the city was
tremendous. In the decade from 1940 to 1950, the population of Fort Worth
increased 58.9 percent from 177,662 to 278,778, with wartime jobs bringing
thousands of workers from surrounding small towns and rural areas into the
city. Peak employment at the local plant, the city's largest employer, reached
nearly 31,000 during the war and brought many changes. Numerous airplane
parts suppliers began business in the city, also boosting Fort Worth employment. Convair helped train some workers who later accepted jobs at other
factories. Because many newcomers to the city from outlying towns and
farms chose to live near the plant, the west side of Fort Worth experienced
the largest population increase. As a result, several independent suburban
towns incorporated in order to protect the right to control their growth.[34]

After the cancelation of wartime contracts and the resulting layoffs and
plant closings, only five Convair divisions remained open. Three of those
closed in the next two years, leaving only San Diego and Fort Worth. According to historian John Rae, "The retention of the Fort Worth plant
deserves attention; Convair was almost alone in retaining a wartime gov-

The B-32 Dominator replaced the B-24 as Consolidated's major production airplane toward the end of World War II. *Photo courtesy United States Air Force via Don Pyeatt.*

ernment-built facility at a distance from its main plant." Fort Worth was fortunate that Convair had unfinished government projects, and workers were grateful it would remain open, at least for a time. By December 1945 only sixteen airframe plants still operated out of the sixty-six that had been busy a year earlier. Most of the branch factories that the major airline companies opened for war production shut down either before V-J Day or a few months after. However, three plants did not: the Columbus plant of Curtiss Aircraft, the Wichita plant of Boeing, and the Fort Worth plant of Convair. Citizens of Fort Worth, Chamber of Commerce members, and especially employees and officials of Convair who had not been laid off gave a huge collective sigh of relief. Even so, Convair employment at the Fort Worth plant dropped to 6,200 in 1946.[35]

Local citizens and company employees need not have worried too much, for Fort Worth had the B-36. General "Hap" Arnold as early as April 11, 1941 had asked the aircraft industry to develop a bomber capable of carrying a 10,000 pound bomb load to a target 5,000 miles away and returning to its base without refueling. The San Diego Consolidated plant accepted the task, but later gave the project to Fort Worth. Because Germany did not overrun Great Britain, such an airplane had not been needed during the war, but Congress authorized production following the war's conclusion.[36]

In anticipation of a longer runway being needed for the huge B-36, Army engineers as early as 1945 authorized the runway that was shared with Fort Worth Army Air Field to be extended by 1,000 feet, making it 8,200 feet long and one of the longest concrete runways in the country. At 300 feet wide, it also was wider than any other. The very first flight of the experimental giant—the XB-36—began on a swelteringly hot August morning in 1946. The cabin air conditioning was not working, and the temperature reached 140 degrees inside. A crowd of approximately 7,000 Convair employees gathered along Grant's Lane, lining the fences around the plant, to watch the takeoff. Test pilot Beryl A. Erickson released the brakes and slowly pushed the throttle forward. The big plane shuddered and shook as it accelerated. It lifted off at 10:10 a.m., and a cheer went up from the crowd. Erickson circled within sight for thirty minutes and landed at 10:47 a.m. He called it a "good flight."[37]

Erickson had hired on with Consolidated in San Diego in 1940 and spent his time transporting airplanes from the West Coast factory to the Pacific Theater to fulfill a contract between Consolidated and the Air Transport Command. Erickson eventually became the main test pilot for Consolidated's B-24, XB-32, and the new XB-36 programs. In 1942 he and his wife followed the B-32 program to Fort Worth where assembly of the B-36 had been shifted. Of all his piloting experiences, the scariest came in Fort Worth during the B-36's still experimental phase on its sixteenth flight on March 26, 1947. After takeoff the retract strut of the right landing gear exploded and the landing gear fell free, pulling the side brace out of the rear spar. The huge right landing gear hit the lower longeron of the No. 4 engine, rupturing the fuel and oil lines. Flames broke out but Erickson's crew put out the fire. "I recommended to the engineering department that we put the left gear and nose wheel down manually and put everybody out by parachute except for Gus Green, the co-pilot, and myself," Erickson explained later. Planning occupied four and a half hours, and because fuel could not be dumped, a total of six hours elapsed in the air to burn off fuel before the XB-36 attempted a landing.[38]

As it happened, the Convair board of directors was meeting in New York at the same time. When the directors got word that their airplane was in trouble, they broke up their meeting and anxiously listened to news reports. Later, Harry Woodhead, Convair president, explained, "Many people realized this was more than just another airplane in trouble. Production of B-36s is essential to America's safety, and the damage to the experimental model would have adversely affected both flight testing and production." What Woodhead did not say, but many others later did, was that if the XB-36 had crashed, the program would have ended, and Northrop's Flying Wing (XB-35) would most likely have received the contract. "If it

The XB-36 flight test pilot Beryl A. Erickson (left) and his co-pilot Gus Green remained on board the big airplane the day its right landing gear failed. The rest of the crew bailed out before Erickson landed the B-36 safely. *Photo courtesy Lockheed Martin.*

had crashed there probably would not have been a B-36 program in Fort Worth," Loyd Turner, special assistant to the Convair General Manager, stated many years later.[39]

Meanwhile, news of the B-36's in-air problems reached Fort Worth citizens via radio, and people began assembling as near as they could to the runway to witness the giant airplane's attempt to land. What they saw first were the twelve crew members parachuting out, two at a time, every fifteen minutes. J. D. McEachern, flight engineer, the last one to leave, first crawled out on the wheel well to look at the damage to the landing gear so he could radio back the information to Erickson. High winds gave the parachutists problems, but all survived, although four sustained broken legs and McEachern broke a vertebra in his back.[40]

One of the crew, Major Stephen Dillon, once on the ground, took a C-47 back up to fly behind the B-36 so that as it touched down on the runway he could radio Erickson and Green how to steer. Right before sunset at 6:15 p.m. as the XB-36 came from the northwest over Lake Worth and touched down, Erickson turned off the ignition switch "which de-electrified everything except the batteries. We were concerned that the plane would burn if we ruptured the wing." He had no brakes, so he also reversed the propellers and leaned the B-36 to the left to touch down on the good landing gear as much as possible. The big plane came to a stop with no further damage. It settled slowly to the right in some grass by the runway. The crowd on the ground, estimated at 100,000, cheered. During the scary flight Erickson's wife and children were in Los Angeles visiting her parents and did not know he was in danger until they turned on the radio for news that night. Billye Erickson remembers that "Gabriel Heatter [announcer for a national radio news show] came on and said, 'There's good news tonight!' and told about the incident, but the plane had already landed," The airplane did not fly for another three months while engineers at Convair redesigned the retract strut.[41]

Several takeover attempts, mergers, and name changes would occur at Consolidated in the years after World War II, including one just a year after the war ended. Events in the late summer of 1946 nearly brought the end of the Convair name when negotiations began to merge Convair into Lockheed Aircraft. Under consideration was a proposal for Lockheed to absorb the aviation divisions of Convair and for AVCO, Convair's parent corporation, to withdraw, taking a Nashville property that made kitchen ranges and freezer cabinets for Crosby Corporation as well as acquiring ACF-Brill Motors of Philadelphia. Convair stockholders were to receive one share of Lockheed for each one and one-sixteenth shares of Consolidated Vultee Aircraft Corporation (Convair). Victor Emanuel, AVCO chairman; Robert E. Gross, Lockheed president; and Irving Babcock, chairman of Consolidated since Girdler's resignation, all agreed to the merger. The plan, however, lost momentum before it could be put to the stockholders for a vote because of problems with Lockheed's major commercial property, Constellation airlines. The Civil Aeronautics Administration (CAA) had grounded Constellation in July 1945. There also were indications that the Department of Justice did not approve of the merger on antitrust grounds.[42]

Consolidated won the contract to build the B-36 Peacemaker in Fort Worth after the war ended. *Photo courtesy United States Air Force via Don Pyeatt.*

A slow-talking dude rancher named Floyd Bostwick Odlum took over a financially strapped Convair late in 1947. Owner of an investment company, Odlum wore Western work shirts, loud ties, suspenders, and wide-brimmed hats. Despite what people might have thought based on his appearance, Odlum was a shrewd investor who at the beginning of the Depression in 1929 renamed his business Atlas Investments and did not lose the company's $14 million value because he was able to get out of the stock market in time. The son of a poor Midwestern Methodist preacher, Odlum became adept at buying up businesses and selling their assets and by 1935 was worth $100 million.[43]

In January 1947 Odlum began buying Convair stock in the open market as he saw a "special situation" developing that looked like a challenge. Odlum defined such a situation as one in which the potential assets of a company seemed to be worth more than—and to outweigh—its immediate liabilities. He liked to try to turn things around. Therefore, Odlum and his Atlas Investments Corporation acquired 117,200 shares of Consolidated Vultee Aircraft Company stock, about 7 percent of the total, during the summer of 1947. Negotiations then began between the executives of Atlas and AVCO. (Victor Emanuel was the largest stockholder of AVCO.) As per the agreement, Atlas men would replace AVCO men on the board, and Atlas would acquire 10 percent of the stock after the retirement of the AVCO shares. AVCO had held controlling interest in Consolidated Vultee since its stock purchase of December 1941, but AVCO relinquished control to Atlas in November 1947. Stockholders ratified the deal at a meeting on November 6, 1947, and two weeks later Odlum became chairman of the board of Convair. At the time, Convair's Fort Worth plant exceeded the size of its nearest competitor by one million square feet.[44]

Odlum's intention, once he gained control, apparently was to improve the financial situation of Convair and then sell out. Naysayers predicted that he could not do it. Under Odlum's leadership by mid-1948, the plant cut the time needed to build a Convair 240 from 86,000 man-hours to 45,000. Odlum's managers improved ordering efficiency and planning, increasing morale and shortening the man hours on each airplane.

Another boon for the company occurred when orders started flowing in for the B-36. The U.S. government appropriated money for Convair's B-36 project after canceling orders with Boeing, Northrop, North American, Republic, and Kellett. Soon Convair held orders totaling $165 million. The B-36 became "the Air Force's favorite child." Convair's competitors made "broad hints of undue political influence and even of corruption." After an employee contest, the B-36 acquired the sobriquet "Peacemaker."[45]

Following his practice of selling off assets, Odlum shut down the Stinson Division of Convair on June 30, 1948, because sales had dropped the previous year. Five months later he sold the Stinson tools, design, name, and goodwill to Piper Aircraft Corporation. With only two divisions of Convair left by the end of 1948, Fort Worth's nearly mile-long plant under one roof was the largest. Although Convair reported a loss of $11.9 million in 1948, the next year Odlum saw his turnaround beginning, with profits of $3.7 million. Military sales of $173 million and commercial sales of $24 million fueled the slight rise in profits. Odlum and his stockholders credited the B-36 program in Fort Worth for the company's success.[46]

In June 1948 Odlum appointed Lamotte T. Cohu president and general manager of Convair. Cohu formerly served as president of Trans World Airlines, and before that general manager of Northrop Aircraft Corporation. He retained his office in San Diego, but he made frequent visits to Fort Worth. In April 1950 he came to town with new business cards saying Convair. He explained that the company was "making progress popularizing the 'Convair' name to shorten our lengthy corporate style of 'Consolidated

Vultee Aircraft Corporation.'" Apparently more than just the assembly line was being streamlined.[47]

Because of the B-36 program, the Fort Worth Convair plant increased its payroll from 14,000 in April 1949 to 16,000 in April 1950 to 28,000 in April 1951. This made the Fort Worth plant "the largest single aircraft family in the United States," and the "largest integrated aircraft manufacturing unit in the world," according to August C. Esenwein, division manager. The San Diego Convair plant employed 19,000 workers and was the fourth largest U.S. airplane plant. Only Fort Worth produced the B-36, and the large bomber brought employment levels at Convair to an all-time high of 31,000 in October 1951, surpassing even the wartime record of 30,609 set in November 1943. The production line averaged one B-36 each week.[48]

Convair did not depend solely on its B-36 contracts, however; by 1952 the Fort Worth plant began building two experimental models of the YB-60 swept back wing all-jet bomber, a modified version of the B-36. Eight J-57 jet engines powered it, and it made a first test flight in mid-1952. Earlier in 1952 a $650,000 engineering test laboratory had opened that allowed workers to simulate almost any environmental condition found anywhere— from the hottest Sahara winds and sandstorms to frigid Arctic blizzards. The lab could also simulate flying altitudes up to 80,000 feet. Unfortunately for Fort Worth, Boeing won out with its B-47s and B-52s, and Convair did not build its B-60.[49]

The era of Convair's B-36 was coming to an end when the Air Force announced on October 14, 1954, that it had ordered Convair's B-58 Supersonic bomber into initial production at the Fort Worth plant. The first flight of the delta-winged B-58 came on November 11, 1956, with test pilot Erickson at the controls. More changes came for Convair personnel when the company began an expanded recreation program for its employees and their families that featured as many as three dozen different activities—flying, horseback riding, square dances, hunting, archery, bridge, and pistol and rifle shooting, as well as the expected softball, basketball, and other team sports. In September 1955 the Convair Recreation Association began construction of an eighty-acre private recreation park for employees and their families. Included were a swimming pool, riding stables, picnic areas, athletic fields, and a recreation building. Recreation had been offered on a lesser scale during World War II, when a girls' basketball league called the Convair Bomberettes won first place in the Fort Worth Municipal girls' basketball league in March 1945, losing only one game in the entire season.[50]

In salaries as well as recreational facilities Convair employees indeed fared well. Payrolls in 1955 totaled $97 million for the 19,000 employees.

Once the Korean War ended, employment dropped temporarily. However, the next year the payroll jumped to $125 million with an increase in B-58 orders. Company officials bragged that their factory was the only one of the government-owned aircraft plants created for World War II that had remained in continuous operation. The U.S. government technically called the "bomber" plant Air Force Plant Four. Convair leased it from them in the 1950s, but the manufacturing facility's tenants would go through three more name changes during the next decades of the twentieth century: General Dynamics, Lockheed, and—after a merger with Glenn L. Martin's former company—Lockheed Martin.[51]

In Fort Worth and the nation World War II still needed to be won. The bomber plant was not the only addition to Fort Worth's infrastructure dedicated to defending the nation during the war and the years after. The construction of an Army Air Field adjacent to the "bomber plant" consumed much local effort—to acquire, construct, and operate.

CHAPTER 6

World War II: Air Power at Fort Worth Army Air Field

LOCATED ON THE EASTERN EDGE OF THE FLAT, LEVEL PLAINS OF West Texas, Fort Worth's destiny lay with air power. A pilot training center at an airfield adjacent to the "bomber plant" of World War II would contribute to that prominence. Pioneers in aviation also paved the way.

An army officer who had served his country since the Spanish-American War in 1898, William "Billy" Mitchell, became the first American to emphasize the importance aviation would have in future military conflicts. He became a major in the Aviation Section of the U.S. Signal Corps and learned to appreciate the value of air power during World War I.

Mitchell began an outspoken campaign that resulted in a court-martial in 1925 after he accused the military of "incompetency, criminal negligence, and almost treasonable administration of the national defense" after the crash of the Navy dirigible *Shenandoah*. The charges against him alleged that he had made statements "to the prejudice of good order and military discipline." A military tribunal found Mitchell guilty on December 17, 1925, and suspended him from his pay and rank for five years. The embittered Mitchell resigned, and as a civilian continued his fight for an increased emphasis on air power in the nation's military. He continuously argued the air power case for a Department of Defense with equal co-branches: army, navy, and air force. He wanted a separate air force to operate independently of the army.[1]

A separate air force was still more than seven years away, however, when Brigadier General Jacob E. Fickel visited Fort Worth in May 1940 with plans to inspect sites appropriate for locating a training base for army pilots. General Fickel was familiar with Fort Worth because twenty-two years earlier as a lieutenant colonel he had commanded Carruthers Field in Benbrook during World War I. What had been the Army Air Service in World War I had changed to the U.S. Army Air Corps on July 2, 1926. City fathers were excited at the prospect of an air base as well as a manufacturing plant.[2]

A member of the Civil Aeronautics Administration (CAA) in Fort Worth filed an application with the War Department in 1940, asking for a primary training base for the Army Air Corps. Others in Fort Worth agreed. San Antonio already had become an important center for aviation training at its Randolph and Kelly Fields, but a base in Fort Worth would give early training for "fledgling pilots" and prepare them for entrance into Randolph or Kelly.[3]

The Fort Worth Chamber of Commerce worked to persuade the U.S. military to select a Fort Worth site for a military base at the same time they courted the airplane factory. Once Fleet and Consolidated agreed to come, organizers went ahead and planned an industrial airport next to the plant. Newspaper reports at first referred to the airfield as "the proposed Lake Worth bomber plant airport." While still in its planning stages some accounts called it Lake Worth Industrial Airport. Then local promoters learned on March 21, 1941, that Consolidated officials had suggested to the Army Air Corps that they locate a heavy bombardment group on the airport adjacent to the plant. The vice president of Consolidated, C. A. Van Dusen, said "a heavy bombardment group operated adjacent to a factory that built heavy bombers would enable the manufacturer to learn things to contribute to improvement of the type [of aircraft]." In addition, he explained that personnel at the Air Corps base could benefit by being located where their planes were assembled. William Holden, executive vice president of the Fort Worth Chamber of Commerce, stayed in contact with Van Dusen after January when Consolidated made its request.[4]

City officials in the public works department faced bureaucratic red tape as they forwarded their plans to the state office of the Work Projects Administration (WPA) in San Antonio. They learned that the CAA must issue a "certificate of necessity and convenience" before the WPA could approve the airport project. They filed plans for concrete runways 7,000 feet long and 150 feet wide. The WPA officials told them to make them 5,000 feet long and 75 wide with asphalt. Fort Worth officials wanted to use the larger dimensions to please the Army Air Corps and help attract the military base. Local officials originally promised to spend $267,000 to build an airport adjoining the bomber plant and to give the government a 99-year lease on the land. When they could not reach an agreement with the WPA for funding, the city of Fort Worth—to speed production—deeded the land to the U.S. government for them to build the airport. City officials were relieved that the army took over the building because they then did not have to do it themselves. Captain John H. Anderson became resident army engineer.[5]

On June 16, 1941, President Roosevelt approved $1.75 million to construct an airfield adjoining what people were calling the Lake Worth Bomber Plant. The federal money provided for drainage, grading, runway construction, taxi strips, aprons, night lighting, boundary markers, fencing, and other features. Roosevelt and the military wanted to have the air base completed by the time the aircraft factory began production. Things moved rapidly, and a week later a group of 176 National Youth Administration workers with axes and shovels arrived to clear the airport site of trees, houses, and fences. Their numbers increased to 250 the next day. L. J. Miles Construction Company of Fort Worth began landscaping the landing area in preparation for the runways, moving approximately 250,000 yards of dirt at a cost of $475,000.[6]

Meanwhile, the War Department, on June 20, 1941, created the Army Air Forces from the old Army Air Corps with a General Headquarters Air Force to be a major component. They shortly renamed it the Air Force Combat Command and put Major General Henry H. "Hap" Arnold (who had headed the Air Service in World War I) in charge. General Arnold obtained permission to boost the overall pilot quota to 33,000.[7]

Although an airport next to the bomber plant seemed assured, the Army Air Forces still had not approved it for a pilot training base in the summer of 1941. They announced plans to build thirty bombardment wing bases across the nation, however. On September 3, 1941, the site board of the Fourth Air Force came to Fort Worth to examine locations, including the "the proposed Lake Worth bomber plant airport." For Fort Worth all of the red tape was not over. The city had not yet acquired all of the land needed by the military nor deeded it over to the government. At a special city council meeting on September 8, 1941, members formally passed the required motion to do so. That same day the Tarrant County Commissioners' Court verbally agreed to repave and widen two highways leading to the proposed airfield.[8]

The Texas Bitulithic Company of Dallas, the lowest of eight bidders, received a contract on November 3. Valued at $473,188, it called for the paving of two runways and a taxi strip. The company had to agree to complete the work within seventy-five days of receiving a notice to proceed. They began pouring concrete on December 1 and planned to work two shifts. In the end, the Army acquired the runways they wanted: one was 7,000 feet long and the other 7,300 feet, and both were 150 feet wide. Then on January 7, 1942, the Army Air Force chose the new base for its heavy bomber school, called at the time Tarrant Aerodrome or Tarrant Field. Within a month the 1,100-acre site became a hub of activity as hundreds of workers arrived.[9]

In May 1942 Colonel Bernard S. Thompson took command of the partially completed base next to the Consolidated plant. Colonel Thompson, formerly in command of a tactical group at the Will Rogers Air Base in Oklahoma City, located his temporary offices in the Air Force section of Consolidated's Administration Building. His intention was that the base would be operational by September 1. However, the base officially opened August 21, 1942, when Colonel David W. Goodrich took over as the first official commanding officer, and the first B-24s arrived.[10]

During September, calls went out for recruits for the new Army Air Field. Jobs would be available for mechanics, radio operators, airplane motor repairmen, maintenance workers, welders, and armorers, as well as for adding machine, typewriter, and comptometer operators. New recruits would be privates receiving $50 per month, plus additional pay for dependents. Early arrivals at what was still being called Tarrant Field saw a muddy prairie with a few scattered barracks, a sixty-foot control tower, and giant hangars. According to the recruiting notice, "All enlisted men are furnished food, clothing, lodging, and medical and dental care." However, they learned that the piped-in water supply was acceptable only for showers, not for drinking. Kegs located in the barracks furnished their drinking water.[11]

The Army Air Forces Combat Crew School officially opened on October 12, 1942—Columbus Day—at Tarrant Field. No formal ceremony acknowledged the grand opening of the base. Officials planned a brief ceremony two days later, however, when the first crew went aloft in the first B-24 flown from the base with Major John M. Schweiger, director of training, piloting it. His navigator, a Fort Worth man, was Lieutenant Alex Pentikis. Colonel James S. Stovall, a West Point graduate with more than twenty years of experience in the Air Corps, replaced Colonel Goodrich as commanding officer on September 14, 1942. Workers completed final construction of the field by December 31, 1942, at a total cost of about $6.5 million. The light gray buildings with green shingled roofs at Tarrant Field were covered with cement asbestos sheathing that looked like wood but was fireproof. The same style buildings, used as barracks, offices, and recreation rooms, were propped up off the muddy ground by short concrete piers.[12]

Nine-member crews were required to man each of the four-motored Consolidated B-24 Liberator bombers. A crew consisted of a pilot, copilot, bombardier, navigator, aerial engineer, and gunners. The crews ate, slept, and trained in each other's company twenty-four hours a day. This concentrated nine-week all-day—no matter the weather—training allowed the men to learn their airplane and each other's minds and reactions. Each day they flew five hours and had five hours of ground instruction. Student officers completed one class every four and a half weeks; mechanics ground school lasted four weeks. Crews completing training rotated either to the

Student pilots flock to meals at the General Mess Hall at Fort Worth Army Air Field during World War II. *Photo Dalton Hoffman Local History Collection.*

European, Middle Eastern, African, or Pacific Theaters. The Tarrant Field routine became familiar even to people living in the newly incorporated communities of Westworth Village, White Settlement, and River Oaks. A huge cannon in front of the post headquarters blasted everyone awake at 6 a.m. and boomed retreat at 4:45 p.m. Military ceremonies accompanied each firing, a small detail raising the flag each morning, and a thirty-five piece field band playing the "Star Spangled Banner" for retreat.[13]

The round-the-clock flying schedule created airplane maintenance problems because workers were not yet fully familiar with the B-24. In addition, the weather in fall 1942 was unusually cold and wet. Making the situation worse, a Del Rio training school for B-26 pilots had not yet opened, so its students also trained at Tarrant Field. Both training aircraft and flying instructors remained in short supply because Tarrant Field became one of the first B-24 schools to begin instructing pilots and time was needed to get organized. The field eventually acquired its own hospital, modern theater, chapel, and athletic facilities, and each squadron operated its own day-room for recreation.[14]

The army base next to the bomber plant acquired a new name midway through World War II. At first officially called Tarrant Field Airdrome, it became Fort Worth Army Air Field (FWAAF) in May 1943, and retained that name for the next four and one-half years. Officials named the training school the Army Air Forces Pilot School. It specialized in four-engine B-24 bombers. About the time Tarrant Field became Fort Worth Army Air Field, the military transferred base commander Colonel James S. Stovall out and Colonel Carlisle I. Ferris took his place.[15]

At this midpoint in the war other changes also occurred. Where once four men had manned the base control tower, by August 1943 three men and a woman from the Women's Army Corps (WAC) directed flight activity. The 900th WAC Company operated at FWAAF. The WACs either worked in the communications office at the base of the tower taking radio and telephone information and logging it on a chart, or they climbed sixty feet up a narrow wooden ladder for tower duty. Four guard dogs the men called "canine soldiers" arrived in August fresh from an eight-week training school at Fort Robinson, Nebraska. Working strictly at night to guard the base, the dogs—Duke, Kelley, Yippie, and Boots—were quite a hit. The men called them WAGS, perhaps an acronym for something, or simply because they were dogs and wagged their tails.[16]

Training officials added a twelve-hour Bomb Approach School to the student officer curriculum in October 1943. The training incorporated teamwork between pilot and bombardier to give the pilot an understanding of the bombardier's task. Reports sent continually to headquarters allowed officials to note that all student trainees logged a total of only 1,983 hours in December 1942, but reached 13,375 hours in April 1944. Instructors followed a policy at FWAAF of asking themselves before permitting a student to solo, "Would you be willing to act as a crew member of any ship this student pilots?" The answers increased the safety rate.[17]

In early January 1944 General Arnold told reporters at the Fort Worth Club on one of his visits to the city: "I want to get this war over with, get these boys back home and then I'm going fishing." The white-haired Arnold had been flying for thirty-three years. He told his audience that when he started, the Air Corps was five men and two airplanes. (Possibly some in the audience remembered a day back in November 1915 when the Air Corps boasted six airplanes, and all flew into Fort Worth under the command of then-Captain Benjamin Foulois.) Regarding the current conflict, Arnold said, "We had to build our air force in one year and fight in the four corners of the world at the same time." By 1944, 2,385,000 people served in the Army Air Forces, and General Arnold commanded them. While his contemporaries still called him Hap (for Happy), his stressful job made the nickname seem sometimes inappropriate. When General Arnold retired from the Army Air Forces on November 8, 1945, after forty-two years of service, he said that the "younger guys should take over." However, he continued to argue the case for a separate air force on various trips to Washington from his new home near Sonoma, California.[18]

Colonel Henry W. Dorr served as commanding officer of the FWAAF on August 1, 1944, when officials held the first open house on the base to celebrate the thirty-seventh anniversary of the air service. Visitors inspected barracks and a B-24 Liberator, and watched a retreat ceremony. Colonel Dorr presented some officers with Distinguished Flying Crosses and Oak Leaf Clusters. By November 1944, the B-24 pilot school had trained 3,370 bomber pilots. From the first class in October 1942 through the twenty-five that followed over the next two years, each grew progressively larger. During that time instructors used seventy-six training bombers. Later when the training classes switched from the B-24 to the B-32, crews needed less instruction because they already qualified on the B-24. Through October 1944 pilots trained at FWAAF flew a total of 217,842 hours in the air and over 40 million miles, with only sixteen fatal accidents.[19]

One accident was particularly memorable, and many Fort Worthians remembered it a half century later. It involved a mid-air crash between two B-24s over what is now North Richland Hills. The accident occurred at 7 a.m. on September 3, 1943. Airplanes and bodies fell to the ground about where a Richland Plaza Shopping Center later was located on East Belknap just east of the present Birdville Independent School District Administration Complex and football field.[20]

Social activities began soon after the base opened. Members of eleven sororities of the Fort Worth Inter-Sorority Council donated $150 in October 1942 to purchase an amplifier for the Special Services that planned theatricals, entertainments, and other events at the Tarrant Field Theater. The Fort Worth Recreation Department announced that men in uniform could play eighteen holes of golf on any municipal course for a fee of thirty cents and could swim in city pools for half price: ten cents for the swim and five cents for a towel. The city encouraged soldiers to attend the free motion pictures shown in city parks and to use the free municipal tennis courts. Wives and children of soldiers could use the gymnasium at the city recreation building and take volleyball classes. City officials invited soldiers to enter teams in the city basketball league.[21]

Hollywood film star William Holden put his career on hold during the war and became a lieutenant in the Army Air Forces attached to the Flying Training Command. He manned a local WBAP radio microphone on February 7, 1943, when the War Department aired its weekly broadcast from Tarrant Field for the second time within two months. More than one hundred NBC stations carried the program every Sunday afternoon. Short wave radios transmitted the program to U.S. forces in various war theaters around the world. The radio communication system at Tarrant Field demonstrated how army planes contacted control towers at landing bases for clearance. On the program Holden and Private Donald Briggs of the base's Headquarters Squadron held a two-way short-wave conversation between a B-24 Liberator and the control tower. Two months later Tarrant Field hosted the Army Hour again. This time the speaker was Major General Barton K. Yount, commanding general of the Fort Worth-based Flying Training Command. A veteran of World War I, he told listeners that pilots in that war received an average of seventy-five hours of training, but some went into combat with as little as seventeen hours. "Today our pilots receive a minimum of three hundred hours of instruction prior to combat," he said.[22]

Not until mid-February 1945 did the base have a camp newspaper. Once the idea developed, promoters held a contest to select a name. One suggestion was *The Lone Star*, and another was *The Scanner*, so the name became *Lone Star Scanner* for the new eight-page weekly. A "scanner" was a crew position on a B-29 for which a training program existed at the field.[23]

Because Fort Worth Army Air Field trained pilots who already were army officers, most men were older than wartime draftees, and many had wives. While the officers remained stateside, they brought their wives to Fort Worth if they could find local accommodations. With the city's growing wartime population these young couples had a difficult time. Those who could rent one room in a private home considered themselves fortunate. If they did not have kitchen privileges, they cooked on a hot plate and washed dishes in a pan in the bathroom. "You don't know how many things I cook in my coffeepot," one military wife said. Sometimes they rented a house from another military family that had been transferred elsewhere.[24]

One of these young military couples, Katherine and Bill Carssow, met in Shreveport, Louisiana, during the war and married June 11, 1943. Second Lieutenant Carssow served as Assistant Trial Judge Advocate at Hondo Army Air Field, forty miles west of San Antonio, before being transferred to FWAAF as a Trial Judge Advocate. Their first child was born in Harris Hospital in downtown Fort Worth in September 1944, but a pediatrician on the base took over the child's care. The Carssows had trouble finding housing and finally rented one room in a private home just off Camp Bowie Boulevard on the west side of Fort Worth. Later they stayed in the Eastwood Apartments on White Settlement Road by subletting from someone else without the owner's permission. When the apartment owner found out, he made them move. Fortunately, a chaplain at FWAAF, Dr. George Neff, invited the Carssows to stay with him and his wife in "an old large camp house on Lake Worth." The two couples remained friends for the next half century. As Trial Judge Advocate at FWAAF, Lieutenant Carssow dealt with soldiers' problems as did Chaplain Neff. The two made tough decisions in order to help various soldiers, and often shared responsibilities and sent their problem cases to each other. Lieutenant Carssow was in his thirties at the time. He remembered being officer of the day on V-J Day and allowing the celebrants "more leeway and tolerance on that V-J night."[25]

If wives were not isolated off base, they provided social activities for each other, such as baby showers. Then as today, a base commander's wife took a leadership role for the women just as her husband did for his officers. Officers often brought their wives on base to the theatre or officers' club functions and married enlisted men did the same at facilities open to them.[26]

Commanders required daily physical training for all officers. Those stationed at Fort Worth Army Air Field enjoyed having a young former pro-golfer named Ben Hogan as their physical trainer (P.T.). They began noticing, however, that he was absent a lot. Word got around that high-ranking officers stationed at the Flying Training Command Headquarters in downtown Fort Worth often "reassigned" Hogan. They wanted to play golf with—and receive instruction from—the famous golfer.[27]

Although their social and physical welfare was important, the FWAAF staff did not overlook religious opportunities for the soldiers. The Protestant chaplain conducted segregated chapel services at separate times for white and black troops on Sundays. He made himself available for counseling, weddings, and assisting the many soldiers who may have been having problems because of their being away from home for the first time.[28]

By late 1944 enough B-24s had been constructed for the war effort and a sufficient number of pilots had been trained to fly them. Thus when Consolidated Vultee began building B-32 Dominators, Army officials activated a B-32 Flight Crew Transition Training School at FWAAF. Specially selected servicemen from FWAAF secretly went over to Consolidated to study the B-32 as it was being built so they could act as instructors once the base received the new airplanes. Unfortunately, a shortage of equipment meant that the training school did not get their first B-32 until the end of January 1945. In the next six months, however, fifty-seven more B-32s arrived. Officials cut back the B-32 training program after V-J Day in August 1945. By November, the Air Force Training Command had turned the field over to the Second Air Force for its Seventeenth Bombardment Wing, and as a peacetime move transferred FWAAF from the Army Air Forces Training Command to the Continental Air Forces.[29]

After the end of the war, Colonel Talma W. Imlay became commanding officer of the FWAAF in October 1945. A 1926 graduate of the University of California and a former professional football player with the New York Giants, Colonel Imlay had served in Britain from January 1943 to October 1944 as Air Inspector of the Eighth Air Force. Colonel Imlay replaced Colonel John T. Sprague who was transferred to San Angelo Army Air Field (later Goodfellow AFB).[30]

Fort Worthians learned in October 1945 that even though the war had ended, the base would not close. Army Air Force headquarters in Washington notified Fort Worth's Congressman Fritz Lanham that the FWAAF "will be retained as a combat unit for the interim air force." Of 450 wartime airfields in the country, only 150 were to be kept open. Fort Worth had been fortunate again. B-32 Dominator classes had ended several weeks earlier and no training occurred at the base after that. The military transferred several lighter aircraft such as B-25s to the field, and planned improvements totaling $2,000,000 to the landing and parking areas.[31]

Even after the war, the FWAAF kept making news. The Fort Worth Chamber of Commerce on May 15, 1946, hosted a banquet at Hotel Texas for pilots of twenty-five P-80 fighter planes—pioneers in jet propulsion—after they made a stop at the FWAAF in a cross-country flight. The 412th Fighter Group, the only jet-propelled group, flew 800 miles in one hour and forty minutes, at a top speed of 575 miles per hour. Four of the airplanes planned to participate in an air show at FWAAF on June 2. The Seventeenth Bombardment Wing left FWAAF in July 1946, and the Fifty-eighth Wing replaced it. On November 1, 1946, the Fifty-eighth reactivated the Eighth Air Force as the nation's postwar global air arm.[32]

Population of FWAAF in November 1946 stood at 4,930, but this increased somewhat when headquarters of the Eighth Air Force and its Seventh Bombardment Wing reached their authorized strength of seven hundred additional personnel. General Roger M. Ramey served as acting commanding general of the Eighth. The Eighth and the Fifteenth, the latter stationed in Colorado Springs, Colorado, comprised the two air forces of the Strategic Air Command, charged with the long-range defense of the continental United States. The Eighth took over five fields of the Fifteenth—Alamogordo, Roswell, and Albuquerque in New Mexico, Tucson, Arizona, and Fort Worth on November 18, 1946. The Eighth also operated Hensley Field at Grand Prairie and airfields at Abilene, Texas, and Deming, New Mexico, on a standby basis.[33]

At the base, officials welcomed the Eighth Air Force, and moved 190 trailers from Fort Hood for families to live in, arranging them in blocks of ten with space between groups set aside as play areas for children. While awaiting housing, some families lived as far away as Weatherford, Mineral Wells, and the U.S. Naval Reservation at Eagle Mountain Lake. Because the base was considered "permanent" the Army authorized expenditures of $800,000 to construct more substantial quarters. Bids were let for the building of one hundred housing units not to exceed $7,500 for each unit.[34]

Flights from FWAAF in the summer of 1947 to places like Japan, Alaska, and Europe became "strictly routine." In fact, General Ramey jokingly called his Eighth Air Force "Ramey's Travel Bureau." Not shying from publicity, his men carried news and radio personnel on a ten-day jaunt to Japan in August.[35]

Approximately 50,000 people attended an open house on Sunday, August 3, 1947, to celebrate the fifth birthday of the field, which would come a few days later. The day proved so sweltering that people stood under the wings of the displayed airplanes for shade. The military also celebrated the fortieth anniversary of the Army Air Forces. Airplanes on display included Mustang fighters, B-25 Billy Mitchells, B-17 Flying Fortresses, B-24 Liberators, A-26 Avenger Attack Bombers, and B-26 Marauders. In addition, the B-36-Al was dedicated as "City of Fort Worth."[36]

When Russia did not relinquish the Eastern European territories it had overrun at the close of World War II (including East Germany), the United States and its allies accepted that a Cold War with the Soviet Union existed; consequently, in the fall of 1947 officials at FWAAF began tightening security, reminding Fort Worth citizens that the Eighth Air Force was "the only air force in the world trained in use of the atomic bomb." Guards gave each visitor to the base a placard stating "Visitor" to hang on car windshields, and carefully checked each vehicle as it left the field. Previously, people could drive in and out the main gate at White Settlement Road and the north gate from the Burger's Lake Road at will.[37]

Unquestionably, the population and the economy of Fort Worth expanded greatly during World War II and the years following because of the "bomber plant" and the "airfield next to the bomber plant," both located on the west side of the city. As of April 1947, the FWAAF represented the second largest payroll in the Fort Worth area with approximately $1 million per month going out to 5,000 officers and enlisted men, plus 452 civilian employees. In 1946 and 1947 the combined monthly payrolls of Convair and the Fort Worth Army Air Field exceeded $4 million for a total of $48 million annually.[38]

After the National Security Act of 1947 created a separate air force—as Billy Mitchell had sacrificed his career trying to achieve—the Eighth Air Force's Seventh Wing formally dropped the word "Army" from Fort Worth Army Air Field as other units did around the country. The local base became simply Fort Worth Air Field. Colonel Allan D. Clark, commander of the Seventh Wing, said, "After all, we're an independent Air Force now, on equal rank with the Army and Navy—no longer merely a branch of the Army." Colonel Clark issued orders for a painter to paint out "Army" from the sign on White Settlement road until a new one replaced it.[39]

Fort Worth newspaper columnist George Dolan wrote that General Arnold was "as proud of his Air Force as a mother is of her first baby." Unlike his mentor Billy Mitchell, General Arnold lived to see the separate Air Force created. In his career he saw the Air Service grow "from almost nothing into the mightiest Air Force the world had ever known." During the war Fort Worth's FWAAF contributed greatly to this reputation. Later, as Carswell Air Force Base it would achieve even more fame.[40]

CHAPTER 7

World War II: Training Command and More

FORT WORTH MILITARY ACTIVITIES DURING WORLD WAR II included much more than what occurred at Consolidated and the Fort Worth Army Air Field. The Fort Worth Chamber of Commerce submitted proposals for many projects to the U.S. government. Although the city did not receive all of them, the ones the military did bestow on it represented an amazing array of opportunities for citizens to serve the war effort, and brought jobs and people into the area. The chamber's executive director and its committees tried to acquire facilities that had a reasonable chance to become permanent after the war ended. It was not luck that brought these things to Fort Worth; the city's business leaders and the area's political representatives worked hard and long for everything the city received.[1]

Officials attracted well over a dozen facilities to the city for the war effort, in addition to the bomber plant and the air base. These included a reopened Saginaw airfield at Hicks Field, a Navy seaplane docking station on Lake Worth, a large Quartermaster Depot on the south side, and a secret Marine glider base on Eagle Mountain Lake. Military officials also selected Fort Worth as the site for the Army Air Forces Training Command national headquarters—a critical facility. Offices for what became the Women Airforce Service Pilots (WASPs) operated in downtown Fort Worth. An Army Records Office (ARO) kept records of personnel of all military camps in Texas. An Army Finance Office (AFO) handled monetary records for the camps in the northern part of Texas. The Fort Worth District Corps of Engineers designed and constructed buildings for both the Army and Air Corps throughout a large part of Texas, and they oversaw projects to control Texas rivers. In addition, a former "narcotics farm" on the south side became a military hospital for rehabilitating traumatized or drug-dependent soldiers and sailors.[2]

Other facilities in Fort Worth included a motor pool located at the former Arlington Downs racetrack and used as a storage and repair center for all motorized military equipment in a five-state area; a fueling, repair, and parts warehouse maintained by the Second Air Service Area Command Headquarters for planes flying in Texas, New Mexico, Oklahoma, Arizona, Arkansas, and Louisiana; and a field office of the Air Materiel Command, which spent $6 million per month in purchases in Fort Worth while supervising nearly $1 billion in contracts in twelve states. Other flight related sites included the Naval Air Training Station built at Municipal Airport (Meacham Field) to train Navy and Marine Corps pilots in the operation of two-motored airplanes; the Navy Ferry Command headquartered at Meacham; an emergency airfield the Army and Navy utilized until 1945 for training and for safe emergency landings located at Singleton Field; and other airports around the county, including Midway Airport in Euless, which provided additional landing capacity if needed.[3]

Fort Worth citizens learned in the spring of 1942 that the control point for all of the Army Air Forces flying training programs for the entire nation would be headquartered in Fort Worth. In July Lieutenant General Barton K. Yount moved the training offices from Washington, D.C. to its new inland central location in Fort Worth. Offices for the staff of 250 officers and 350 civilians were located at the south end of downtown on four floors of the Texas and Pacific Railway (T&P) building near the railroad's busy connection point. Yount oversaw training for all air and ground crews in the Army Air Force across the country with the exception of those in Wyoming; one observer called it "the largest single educational institution in the world today." During the war this command became one of the largest and most important in the Army, the largest single command with its headquarters located outside Washington, D.C.[4]

This training command directed the activities of nearly one-eighth of all men and women in the entire army. Prior to 1943 a Flying Training Command operated in Fort Worth and a Technical Training Command in Knollwood, North Carolina. General Yount combined these two units in July 1943 with the headquarters in Fort Worth, utilizing even more floors of the T&P building. After the merger, General Yount divided the command into western, central, and eastern areas for flying and technical training. As a result it provided direction for three regional training centers: 1) Maxwell Field in Montgomery, Alabama, called the Southeast Air Corps Training Center; 2) Moffett Field in Sunnyvale, California, the West Coast Air Corps Training Center; and 3) Randolph Field in San Antonio, the Gulf Coast Air Corps Training Center. Yount's office officially became Headquarters, Army Air Forces Training Command (AAFTC). From Fort Worth Yount directed a nationwide pilot training program that turned out 80,000 pilots a year. The new combined command supervised and trained aerial gunners, bombardiers, navigators, aerial observers, and

pilots of military aircraft, including gliders. It also operated air forces flying and technical schools and the AAF officer candidate school at Miami
Beach, Florida. The technical training commands nationwide produced
over 500,000 ground and air combat crew technicians from their creation
in 1941 to February 1944. In the last year of the war General Hap Arnold,
commander of the Army Air Forces, praised the training command saying, "The AAF Training Command has done a tremendous job in turning
out large numbers of navigators, bombardiers, pilots, aerial gunners, glider
pilots, liaison pilots, WASPs, and others. It has trained thousands of technicians and specialists essential to air power." Training had slowed by January
1945 when General Yount announced the transfer of thirty major airfields
to other agencies and ended contracts with forty-seven flying schools. Even
so, the AAFTC at the end of 1944 still comprised over 600,000 men and
women working and training.[5]

General Yount announced in April 1945 that he planned to assign prisoners of war to various installations of the AAF Training Command nationwide. The purpose was to protect against personnel shortages in essential
jobs formerly performed by civilians. He conducted surveys to determine
how many prison laborers individual workforces needed. Prisoners were to
perform either skilled or unskilled jobs in categories permitted by the Ge-
neva Convention and approved by the War Department such as laundry,
carpentry, painting, janitor service, plumbing, kitchen police, trash detail,
weed and grass cutting, and stone and brick masonry. General Yount al-
lotted a minimum of one hundred prisoners in April 1945 to each station
such as FWAAF and more if adequate housing was available. A local War
Management Agency in each area had to certify that a shortage of civilian
laborers actually existed for each job before using the prisoners.[6]

Jacqueline Cochran became the first woman staff member of the (then)
Flying Training Command in Fort Worth, heading what became the
Women Airforce Service Pilots (WASPs). Cochran, an outstanding pilot
who held several flying records, worried about U.S. preparedness, so during
the summer of 1941 she had traveled to England to study ferrying activities.
While there, she became the first woman to pilot a bomber in England.
Immediately after the attack on Pearl Harbor she recruited twenty-five U.S.
women pilots and took them to England where they joined the Air Transport Auxiliary Program as contract civilian pilots. Cochran returned to the
United States with the knowledge that many more women volunteer pilots
were needed. In early 1942 as president of the Ninety-Nines International
Organization of Women Pilots, Cochran told the members about the work
of women pilots in England. She wanted American women to do the same,
and some of the Ninety-Nines volunteered.[7]

When Cochran mentioned her idea to General Arnold, he initially rejected it. However, after considering it for a while, he called his former West Point classmate Major General Yount at the Flying Training Command in Fort Worth, and told him to give Cochran what she wanted. Cochran arrived in Fort Worth in October 1942, and she and General Yount got along quite well. Cochran rented an office in downtown Fort Worth and organized the flight school she wanted. She needed airplanes, instructors, a field, and barracks for what might be hundreds of young women. General Yount located a temporary field in Houston at Howard Hughes's airport that Cochran and her women could use. He also located a company whose government contract was about to expire—Aviation Enterprises, Ltd.—and hired them to train Cochran's volunteers to fly military aircraft. Yount even found a few airplanes the women could use for their instruction.[8]

Cochran at first called her school the Women's Flying Training Detachment (WFTD). Original plans called for the women pilots to ferry light trainer airplanes from a factory to a flying base, however, the women also flew larger planes. The first class of twenty-eight women assembled in the Rice Hotel in Houston on November 16, 1942. The average age was twenty-five, but all of the women had been flying airplanes for years. Cochran instructed them to bring enough money for thirty days' expenses until the program's funding arrived. After their training began, Cochran periodically visited the Houston training facilities to ask trainees what they liked and did not like about the program.[9]

At this time another women's flying program existed called Women's Auxiliary Ferrying Squadron (WAFS) for which Nancy Harkness Love had won approval in September 1942. Love earned her pilot's license at age sixteen, and in 1936 she married Robert Love. Together they operated a successful aviation company. After the war began, Robert Love, an Air Corps Reserve Major, was called to active duty in Washington, D.C. where he became Deputy Chief of Staff of the Ferry Command. Nancy Love's proposal to use already experienced women pilots to ferry airplanes within the U.S. was accepted and operated independently of Cochran's WFTD. In August 1943 General Arnold merged the two programs into the Women Airforce Service Pilots (WASPs), placing the merged units under Cochran's direction. As Director of WASP Cochran screened applicants for training and tried to select a geographical balance that represented the entire country. Love continued as Executive Director of all WASP ferrying assignments, overseeing delivery of 12,652 airplanes from factories to their destination bases between October 1942 and December 1944.[10]

Cochran's women trainees had completed only one nine-month course in Houston when she learned of a British training base at Sweetwater, Texas, that no longer was needed. She gained permission to move her women to Avenger Field there, and the second training class soon transferred to the more rural facility. Members of the class flew twenty-six trainers from Houston to Sweetwater on Monday, April 5, 1943. Cochran flew into Sweetwater to visit with the mayor. The two of them planned a day of events so that the town and the young women pilots could get acquainted. Cochran's unit had been the 319th Army Air Force Flying Training Detachment, but at Sweetwater it became the 318th. Avenger Field became the only all female air training site in the country. "Nevertheless, many male-piloted aircraft found their safety on Avenger Field after claiming some sort of flight emergency," one of the women pilots, Dora Dougherty, reminisced later. The WASPs saw through the men's "forced landings," but enjoyed them nevertheless. Because of the strict rules Cochran enforced, some referred to Avenger Field as "Cochran's Convent."[11]

Cochran maintained her office in Fort Worth even after the Sweetwater operation opened. She flew to Avenger Field for graduation ceremonies and other special events. During 1943–44 a total of 1,830 young women participated in the program. Of these, 1,074 graduated and received flight duty. Besides ferrying airplanes, they towed targets; flew student gunnery training; did tracking, smoke laying, searchlighting, strafing, and simulated bombing; drove aircraft missions; flight tested aircraft; gave instrument instruction; piloted weather airplanes; and flew administrative missions. During the eighteen months of military service after the earliest classes completed their training, the WASPs altogether flew sixty million miles in seventy-seven different types of aircraft.[12]

In addition to the training at Avenger Field, WASPs served at Army Air Fields in several Texas communities as well as many others nationwide. They ferried airplanes from factories to England. They also became instructors; some men said they preferred women instructors because they were more patient than the men. WASPs technically came under the Civil Service and earned $250 per month, plus a $6 per diem when away from their assigned station. Their monthly salary was $50 less than that earned by men pilots for ferrying. Thirty-eight of them died in accidents while flying Army Air Force airplanes.[13]

Cochran and her WASPs were severely disappointed when the military deactivated the program on December 20, 1944. By that time General Arnold believed that both enough women and men pilots had been trained. Because male instructors for the men's pilot programs would no longer be needed, some of them requested the ferrying and other responsibilities the WASPs had been performing.[14]

A third of a century elapsed before Congress approved legislation in 1977

Headquarters for the Women Airforce Service Pilots was located in Fort Worth with offices in the same building as the Central Training Command. General H. H. "Hap" Arnold, left, and WASP director Jacqueline Cochran, right, salute. The officer between them is unidentified. *Photo courtesy The Women's Collection, Texas Women's University, Denton, Texas.*

to allow WASPs to be considered a part of the military. Two years later, the Air Force determined that a woman's World War II WASP duty could be considered active military service for the purpose of receiving veteran's benefits. In acknowledgement of their service, about 200 surviving members received the Congressional Gold Medal on March 10, 2010, in an award ceremony in Washington, D.C.[15]

Another important military facility located in Fort Worth during World War II was the Quartermaster Depot activated by the Army Supply Division on May 4, 1942. Located on the city's south side where several railroads and highways converged, the depot was convenient to the large meat supply provided by Fort Worth Stockyards and packing plants. Because of the railroad network with its more than ten major lines, supplies reached Army training camps quickly, the Fort Worth Quartermaster Depot became one of the largest supply centers in the nation during World War II.[16]

Officials broke ground for the new depot on September 8, 1941, on approximately 368 acres due south of downtown on U.S. Highway 81 at

Hemphill Street. A Fort Worth branch of the San Antonio General Depot had operated at 515 Pecan Street downtown since December 3, 1940; however, it closed on May 3, 1942, the day before the new depot opened. Constructed first were two warehouses, guardhouses, and a sewage pumping station. Then workers built six more warehouses (two permanent, four temporary), four sheds, an administration building, a steam engine shelter, utilities, roads, and railroads. The depot eventually included eighty-four buildings and cost $10 million to construct. Every troop train that passed through Fort Worth stopped there.[17]

The chief mission of the new depot was to supply the entire northern half of Texas. Captain Wilfred E. Gerhardt had commanded the branch depot and so became executive officer of the larger Fort Worth Quartermaster Depot; the new commanding officer was Colonel John S. Chambers. On June 4, 1942, the depot notified approximately thirty posts, camps, and stations in that supply area that all requisitions for quartermaster supplies dated July 1, 1942, and thereafter must be prepared by the Fort Worth Quartermaster Depot. At the time of activation 273 civilian employees worked at the depot, and its first shipment departed Fort Worth on May 8, 1942, going to Camp Wolters in Mineral Wells. The depot ranked third in size and importance in the nation during the war with a total storage capacity between 9,000 and 10,000 railroad car loads. By January 1943 it employed over 2,000 civilian workers, and had a monthly payroll of $300,000. Later, twenty prisoners of war became depot workers. Texas housed 10 percent of the nation's 500,000 German and Italian POWs. The ones working at the depot helped stock and assemble supplies for distribution to various military destinations and were paid in canteen vouchers to be used for personal items. Following the close of the war the depot accepted a new mission—"Return and Reburial of World War II Dead"; the depot completed that mission by May 15, 1949, after which it became more a storage than a supply facility.[18]

The Fort Worth Quartermaster Depot was redesignated as the Fort Worth General Depot on September 1, 1954, and the Defense Department directed it to assume the Quartermaster Supply, Signal Supply, and Signal Maintenance Missions of the San Antonio General Depot. The merger saved money as 24,000 tons of supplies and 300 employees moved from San Antonio to Fort Worth. The merger was completed in early April 1955. At that time 1,500 employees (military and civilian) received a total monthly payroll of $560,000. The depot assumed responsibility for supply and storage of quartermaster and signal supplies to posts, camps, and stations in the Fourth Army Area, which included Texas, Arkansas, Louisiana, Oklahoma, and New Mexico.[19]

Yet another important military facility located in Tarrant County during World War II was the U.S. Marine Corps Air Station at Eagle Mountain Lake. Located twenty miles northwest of Fort Worth and south of Newark on the Tarrant-Wise County line, this seaplane base operated on part of the east shore of Eagle Mountain Lake. The 2,477 acres acquired by condemnation cost the government slightly more than $169,000. The original plan called for a secret Marine Corps Glider Pilot Training installation, which the government built at a cost of $4.5 million. A land auxiliary base approximately five miles northwest of the main Marine facility comprised about 1,200 acres. Lake Bridgeport supplied additional water if needed. The base had one large hangar as well as seventy-five other buildings, some brick and others temporary. Three deep wells supplied water, and seventeen temporary apartments housed the Marine and Navy personnel. Very little glider pilot training ever occurred. Instead, during the war the Navy and Marine Corps used the base as a staging area for seaplanes and an emergency inland landing area for both services. Carrier squadrons assembled there for shipping overseas, and fighters used it as a staging area.[20]

Naval Aviator and Senior Grade Lieutenant Joseph Durkin commanded the Eagle Mountain Marine Base, as it was called, beginning in 1943. After graduating from Notre Dame in 1938, Durkin joined the Navy as an aviation cadet, receiving his wings at Pensacola, Florida, in 1943. He flew reconnaissance seaplanes catapulted off ship decks and also missions in the Pacific after Pearl Harbor. Two hundred Navy personnel served under him at the base, along with thirty to forty civilians. Because of the planned secret experiments, personnel kept information about the base relatively quiet, and many Fort Worthians had no idea it existed.[21]

In March 1959, the Department of the Army leased a portion of the former Marine base from the Texas National Guard, and on May 21, 1960, held an official opening and formal dedication of an Eagle Mountain Army Air Field. They used the facility for the aircraft maintenance mission of the U.S. Army Engineers and the Fort Worth General Depot. The Fort Worth General Depot acquired $800,000 to set up the aircraft maintenance depot and to rehabilitate the World War II hangar, shops, and runways.[22]

One important and nearly unique facility located in Fort Worth was the United States Public Health Service Hospital (USPHSH), one of only two in the country to provide facilities and help for psychologically traumatized soldiers. With the nation's twenty-six veterans' hospitals filled with aging World War I vets, it was decided to convert the two large federal narcotics facilities into hospitals where "shell shocked" young men could be sent. One of these narcotics facilities was located in south Fort Worth. The first had opened in Lexington, Kentucky, in 1935, to serve drug addicts east of the Mississippi River, but the U.S. government later decided a second was needed to serve the western half of the country. Consequently, prominent Fort Worth citizens sought to bring the new federal facility to their city.[23]

"We are extremely anxious to obtain the location of the Second Narcotic Farm and want to leave no stone unturned in our efforts in that direction," became the mantra of the Fort Worth Chamber of Commerce in its lobbying efforts for the facility. Publisher Amon Carter even made a visit to the Surgeon General, who passed Carter's concerns on to the chairman of the sub-committee making the decision. "Give him all the information possible about it," he wrote. On June 1, 1931, Fort Worth was announced as the project's chosen location; at that time it was the largest federal building award ever made in Texas. Land purchases and construction occupied the next seven years. Located south of the city on the Missouri Pacific Railroad Line, the hospital's first patient arrived by train on November 8, 1938, from the Lexington facility. When the fifty-one buildings, all connected by tunnels, were completed in 1939, the complex was said to be the largest hospital of its type in the United States.[24]

As World War II neared in November 1941, two Army physicians visited the facility to determine if it could be used as a general Army hospital. Because only 50 percent of its 950-bed capacity was in use at the time, they found it sufficient. Called officially the United States Public Health Service Hospital (USPHSH), the facility would accept mentally ill soldiers from the Army, Navy, or Coast Guard. Dr. Grover A. Kempf, medical officer in charge of the Marine Hospital in Boston, arrived in the spring of 1942 to assume duties in charge of the USPHSH. His staff of 280 included twelve doctors, nineteen registered nurses, five Red Cross psychiatric workers, two occupational therapy directors, two dieticians, a farm manager, an athletic director, and others. In addition, a staff of Navy personnel handled the records of each patient until they were discharged.[25]

The first fifty "mentally traumatized" military personnel arrived in March 1942. After that, about fifty more arrived each month until May 1943 when the monthly arrivals increased to seventy-five. Most of the early patients were young men from either Pearl Harbor or the battles of Midway and the Solomon Islands. One sailor had survived the sinking of three ships—all in one week! Some Marines who arrived from Guadalcanal experienced a combination of malaria, exhaustion, and combat horrors. Most patients arrived in Fort Worth by train; however, on February 3, 1944, the first group of fourteen airlifted soldiers arrived at Fort Worth Army Air Field in a C-47 military plane. Orderlies then transported them by ambulance or bus to the USPHSH. While soldiers coming from the West Coast by train endured seventy-two hours of travel, the airlifted troops were en route only a total of twelve hours from San Francisco. After the successful first flight, plans called for weekly flights of new arrivals. Each patient received free care and stayed until he recovered, although the usual stay was three months. At the time those first airlifted men—sailors or Marines from Pacific battle-fronts—arrived, patients were not being called "shell-shocked" or "mental." Rather, the more sensitive term "neuro-psychiatric patient" came into use. Approximately 70 percent of the war neurosis patients received their discharge after five months, and only 30 percent needed an additional five or six months of care. Methods of medical treatment often either employed electric shock or hypnotherapy, or the use of a hypnotic drug to produce relaxation. Doctors learned that success of treatment often depended on the personality and outlook of the patient before entering the service.[26]

While patients were undergoing treatment, a variety of programs and activities assisted the often depressed soldiers in making the transition to a normal life. Many parents and wives came from all over the country to take advantage of visiting hours every afternoon. Red Cross workers helped patients contact their next of kin, write letters, and even do Christmas shopping for them. Red Cross volunteers called "Gray Ladies"—because of the color of their uniforms—helped the men send greetings on a "recording device." They decorated the hospital for Christmas and other holidays, passed out candy and free cigarettes, planned recreation programs and birthday celebrations, or sometimes just listened.[27]

Craft programs for making pottery, weaving rugs on looms, and painting became serious therapy sessions. Leatherwork became one of the most popular crafts, and patients made items such as wallets and cigarette cases. After a month or more of craft therapy, the average patient generally could move on to work duties such as helping in the wards or working on the hospital farm, either with the animals or in the garden. Cows for dairy products, hogs, and chickens, as well as the vegetable truck farm, provided much of the food for the hospital. Indeed, most of the 1,400 acres of the narcotic farm, and later the federal hospital, was farmland that provided a great deal of work therapy.[28]

Surprisingly perhaps, officials of the hospital complex did not shield the patients from war news. They could read daily newspapers, and at the time Fort Worth possessed two major ones—the *Fort Worth Star-Telegram* and the *Fort Worth Press*. Patients could also listen to the radio as well, and twice a week they viewed current newsreels and movies in the large hospital auditorium.[29]

For those who were up to it, baseball teams and horseshoe pitching contests attracted both participants and observers. When awards such as Purple Hearts and Silver Stars arrived for specific soldiers, the hospital director arranged special ceremonies to present them. On one such occasion a group of soldiers from the Fort Worth Army Air Field came to provide entertainment after the awards presentation.[30]

One particular patient at the USPHSH (which locals persistently called the Narcotics Hospital or Narcotics Farm) was Clayborne Richard Harrison. Harrison had tried to join the service prior to Pearl Harbor, but a bad eye and bad ear caused him to be turned down. After Pearl Harbor the Navy took him. He served as a cook on a destroyer, and later on Florida Island in the Southwest Pacific, where he fixed breakfast for eighteen men before they set out on their daily missions. As he was warming up his griddle at 3 a.m. one morning to make pancakes, it exploded. Although his clothes were burned off, he walked alone down a road to a barracks and woke up someone who took him to a hospital. Harrison believed that a soldier with whom he "had an altercation" put two shells in the stove that exploded. However, his commanding officer could not verify the accusation, and nothing was done. Because of his severe burns, Harrison became addicted to morphine and believed he could not go off it "cold turkey." As a result, the Navy flew him to Fort Worth to be treated at the USPHSH.

Many years later in interviews Harrison described some of his memories from his stay at the hospital. He remembered the male and female nurses as helpful and friendly and that the food was wholesome. Patients all wore white uniforms for easy identification, and guards on horseback rode along the outside of the fence surrounding the hospital to watch for escapees. Harrison worked in a tailor shop during the three months he was there. One moved around using the underground tunnels, but an elevator provided access to ground level and sunshine. He often walked down to the front gate to talk to the guards. Harrison was allowed to have a pass with his picture on it and move about the farm. Even with a pass a patient had to stop periodically at stations where he showed the pass and someone called ahead to the next station, repeating the process until he reached his destination.[31]

Before a patient could be discharged, he had to attend two weeks of Red Cross lectures on what to expect in civilian life. In Harrison's class there were twenty-five to thirty men who were told among other things that they would need to report to the county seat in their home county and record their discharge papers. He and his friends were given three liberties (passes) to go into Fort Worth in the two weeks before being released. On the morning they were discharged, they sat in class again, and Harrison asked a question. The others yelled at him to quit taking up time asking questions. They wanted to hurry up and catch the train for home! After the war Harrison worked building and rebuilding auto batteries and battery chargers, and even went to sea on a Swedish ship.[32]

The USPHSH considered a patient well enough to discharge when he was able to go on three local leaves, return, and then be able to travel to his home alone. The government discharged each soldier from the service after they were released from the hospital, because they did not want to take the chance of sending a mentally ill man back into combat. "The hazard to them and to the service would be too great," was the explanation. Red Cross workers in soldiers' home towns stepped in and assisted them in finding civilian jobs.[33]

Not all patient residents of the USPHSH were U.S. soldiers. A twenty-five-year old prisoner of war named Friedrich Turnow was sent to the hospital from a detention camp (prisoner of war camp, of which Texas had many). Turnow showed signs of a "persecution complex" and thought people were chasing him. One day he wandered away from the milking barn where he had been assigned. The FBI, immigration officials, state police, and local Fort Worth police began searching for him. When seven hours later someone found him wandering along the street at the intersection of Central Avenue and North Main on the city's north side, officials returned him to the hospital.[34]

After World War II officially ended in September 1945, a few patients still remained in the facility. In January 1946 the Navy reassigned the USPHSH in Fort Worth as the center of the nation's neuro-psychiatric program for naval personnel. It became a training center for doctors, nurses, attendants, and corpsmen, and continued to accept military patients. The Fort Worth center accepted the neuro-psychiatric cases from St. Elizabeth's Hospital in Washington, D.C. Perhaps the reason for expansion of the Fort Worth facility was that it achieved an 80 percent cure rate over a six month period.[35]

The very first female patient arrived in January 1947, and the rules changed so that female patients did not have to wear uniforms or perform a work detail. By 1949 all the salaried Red Cross workers left except for the volunteer "Gray Ladies." In 1967 the hospital became part of the National Institute of Mental Health Clinical Research Center, treating neuro-psychiatric cases and narcotics addicts. Treatment philosophy had changed and health professionals believed patients did better when they returned to their own communities instead of enduring institutionalized treatment. Consequently doctors sent patients to community agencies under contract with the National Institute of Health.[36]

In 1971 the government transferred the property to the Federal Bureau of Prisons within the Department of Justice, and most of the drug treatment programs moved to smaller clinics. Officials changed the name to the Federal Correctional Institute at Fort Worth and in 1987 began its conversion to a higher security all-male prison. By 1995 it became the Federal Medical

Center Fort Worth attending to male prisoners' medical needs, especially those of narcotic addicts convicted of federal crimes. At the end of 2005 it lost its medical mission altogether and became the Federal Correctional Institution Fort Worth. Thus, what had been a medical facility for sixty-six years and fulfilled an important mission during World War II became just another federal prison.[37]

In addition to the many military installations other important war-related activities took place in Fort Worth. Civilian training prepared workers for airplane assembly jobs. The program, which changed its name and location several times, gave practical training to thousands of Fort Worth workers looking for jobs in the aircraft and other war-related factories.[38]

The first such classes began July 15, 1940, with six hundred students at Technical High School, on Fort Worth's north side. By December 1941 the Fort Worth School Board allowed program directors to use M.G. Ellis School, also located on the North Side, for classes for seven hundred students. Thirty instructors held classes twenty-four hours a day. The school moved yet again to a three-story building on Commerce Street that could accommodate the 1,200 students and forty instructors then in the program. Within two years 34,396 persons completed pre-employment classes, including those for supervisory positions, and went on to take jobs at Consolidated or other aircraft plants.[39]

Applicants for the school needed to be older than age twenty-eight unless their draft classification showed they had two or more dependents. Classes met every day from 8 a.m. to 5:30 p.m. with a one-half hour for lunch and one hour for supper. Classes resumed again at 7 p.m. and went until 11 p.m. Participants had to pass the test given at the end of the six-week course to be guaranteed jobs. Farmers from local counties who enrolled in the class complained of all the "government red tape" involved in being classified and acquiring social security cards.[40]

In late January 1943 the school moved one more time to the reconditioned horse barn at Will Rogers Memorial Complex west of downtown Fort Worth and was called the Will Rogers Training School. Approximately 1,400 students enrolled, 85 percent of whom were women. Students could take classes in aircraft assembling, riveting, machine tool operation, aircraft lofting, and aircraft inspection. In November, Sidney P. Wilson, a veteran teacher in the Fort Worth school system, became director, holding the title Director of War Industry Training.[41]

City funds financed the school by distributing money through the Fort Worth school system. The Fort Worth City Council rented the horse barn at Will Rogers free to the Fort Worth ISD for the duration of the war. The school board applied for $76,000 in Defense Public Works money to remodel the barn for classes. The government installed $375,000 worth of machinery to use in instruction and furnished instructors. Classes now lasted four months and adult students paid no fees for the training.[42]

People who came to Fort Worth for training and to take jobs in the many war-related factories and institutions needed places to live, and one of them was Liberator Village. Although not an actual incorporated city, it was a community of citizens nevertheless. Liberator Village developed during World War II as a housing complex in White Settlement south of the Consolidated plant. It got its start when the Federal Public Housing Agency announced a $1,250,000 project for Consolidated workers that called for 125 buildings, each with four apartments.[43]

In July 1942 J. J. Bollinger Construction Company of Oklahoma won the contract to build the one- and two-bedroom units. Their bid was a little more than $1 million, and they were to complete the project in four months. Sixty percent of the apartments would be one-bedroom units. Congress passed a bill in October to provide five hundred additional units adjacent to those already under construction. During the early construction process builders referred to the new apartments as the "housing project south of the plant." Acting Chairman of the Fort Worth Housing Authority B. C. Reich Jr. announced on Thursday, November 19, 1942, that they named the new units "Liberator Village" because "it is symbolic of the role the U.S. is to play in relation to the people of Nazi-controlled Europe. Its use may prove a constant reminder to the occupants of the project of the importance of their efforts as workers in the aircraft industry." The workers at Consolidated were, of course, building B-24 Liberators. The apartment units were located on the east and west side of Cherry Lane. Another group of smaller, two-story apartments constructed north of the first ones on Cherry Lane were called "Victory Apartments."[44]

Advertisements for the Liberator Village Apartments stated that preference would be given to Consolidated workers who had not yet been able to bring their families to Fort Worth because of a housing shortage. Applications to rent the apartments could be made at the Fort Worth Housing Authority office. One-bedroom units would rent for $34 per month, and two-bedroom units for $38. Both included utilities. By January 1943 the first one hundred units were almost ready for occupancy and the first families had moved in by the end of the month. By the end of February nearly 225 families had arrived.[45]

Officials announced in November 1943 that for every available apartment, the Liberator Village rental office received ten applications. The Consolidated-Vultee Personnel Department had to certify all applications and rate applicants by job classification. People who held the most vital jobs had a

Liberator Village, located south of the factory, housed workers at Consolidated who assembled B-24 Liberators during World War II. These two-story buildings were the Victory Arms Apartments. *Photo courtesy of the Genealogy, History and Archives Unit, Fort Worth Public Library.*

better chance of getting an apartment. In the beginning, the rental office restricted the units to married couples with no children, as long as one of them worked at Consolidated. Four people could rent a two-bedroom unit, but if they were single, all had to work at the plant. Finally, by December 1943 three-bedroom units became available for families with three or more children. The 1,500 older, smaller apartments were fully occupied. Although originally renters were not supposed to have children, eventually many did. They were also not supposed to have pets, but some also brought those.[46]

The fourth stage of Liberator Village east of Cherry Lane consisted of two- and three-bedroom structures built from long, hollow red tiles; people called the area "The Bricks." These apartments had both a front and back door, which the others did not. Later schoolchildren telling their classmates where they lived, identified themselves as "whites" if they lived in the white apartments, or "reds" if they lived in the red block ones.[47]

Because the apartments did not remain child-free for long, a day care center soon opened for working mothers. There were three Boy Scout troops, a Girl Scout troop, and a Camp Fire group, as well as a Boys' Club. Playgrounds developed in spare space between apartment buildings. The first schools at Liberator Village received so many children they needed two shifts of four hours each, 8 a.m. to noon and 1 to 5 p.m., with children having no recess or lunch at school. One White Settlement teacher in the early days of World War II, Lila B. Race, explained that in 1942 the two first grade teachers each instructed sixty-five students. She often taught double shifts. Fortunately, a new school opened by February 1943 and two more first grade teachers arrived. When school began that first year, no desks were available, so one of the teachers made desks out of apple boxes.[48]

Living in the apartments provided a lasting experience for many families. Because some of them came from rural areas with no electricity, running water, or indoor bathrooms, the apartments seemed luxurious. Each apartment came with a kitchen equipped with an electric refrigerator, a four-burner gas cook stove, a built-in sink, and cabinets. Bathrooms had a dressing table, but curiously cabinets and closets had no doors. The rent included utilities, and apartment managers provided janitorial and garbage service. Renters only needed to provide a bed, a chair or two, a dining table, and a floor lamp. Interior trim consisted of knotty pine wallboard and—before anyone knew better—asbestos shingle exteriors. Either green or brown wood trim decorated building fronts. While apartments had no telephones, within the complex was a little gray flat-roofed building that housed three or four pay phones. New telephone service in Fort Worth during World War II simply was unavailable, but by the late 1940s, occupants finally acquired telephones.[49]

Streets in Liberator Village were paved and named after pilots killed during the war. Apartments had parking areas. Maintenance workers rode small red Cushman motor scooters as they performed free repairs for occupants. Residents who needed to go into downtown Fort Worth, rode in flatbed trucks with wooden benches that made a few Village stops in their run between the courthouse and the bomber plant. Later a bus covered the same route.[50]

Leland Hunter, executive director of the Fort Worth Housing Authority, announced in April 1943 that Thomas S. Byrne, Inc. of Fort Worth won a contract for $90,850 to construct a shopping center for residents of Liberator Village, to be completed in sixty days. The new shopping center included "The Village" movie theatre built of concrete block walls with a concrete floor and no roof. Patrons sat on wooden benches in the open-air building, and in winter a canvas roof attempted to keep out the rain and cold. During summer months Leonard's Department Store showed a free outdoor movie once a week with advertising for the department store's latest sales.[51]

The recreation center, which served both daytime shifts, provided facilities for many different activities. These included a dramatic club, a mixed chorus, dances, and places for numerous clubs and organizations to meet, including Young Men's Christian Association, Young Women's Christian

Association, a Block Leaders' Association, Junior School Patrol, Sunday School, a children's hour, crafts classes, and organized athletics.[52]

Even though World War II ended in 1945, Liberator Village remained occupied for well over a decade. In the late 1950s, the government sold off the four-unit buildings on the west side of Cherry Lane, charging only $100 each for them. Most people who bought them tore them down for the lumber. The units located on the east side were sold by the early 1960s, although the city of White Settlement rented some of them. The government sold the Victory Apartments in 1956. As of the early twenty-first century, only one building of the former Liberator Village remained. On Wyatt Drive, it housed the offices of the local newspaper—the *White Settlement Bomber News*.[53]

Because of the influx of population due to the Consolidated plant and the military installations, communities west of Fort Worth, near proposed sites for the bomber plant and airfield, saw increased interest in housing in their unincorporated areas of the county. In 1941 as the war approached, White Settlement, River Oaks, and Westworth Village all decided it would be in their best interests to incorporate as small cities. In particular, religious members of White Settlement suggested incorporation so the town could pass ordinances against alcohol if it continued to grow. White Settlement citizens were glad they followed their instincts because in only a few months the population boomed to 10,000 residents, most of whom worked at Consolidated or became civilian employees of the new Army Air Field. The school district doubled in 1943, and the number of homes increased from 200 to 1,200.[54]

State Highway 183 connected downtown Fort Worth with Consolidated and the air field. The new highway intersected with White Settlement Road, an old stagecoach road, and by 1942 new houses began developing on both sides of it. These led to two more small cities incorporating—River Oaks and Westworth Village. Property owners in the Castleberry area held an election October 28, 1941, and organized the city of River Oaks in order to keep the district exclusively residential. Citizens worried about newcomers creating trailer camps and tourist courts and "other unsightly installations" that usually followed when a large influx of people settled near military bases. The residents of the community that developed just south of White Settlement road and south of the air field incorporated their town as White Settlement Village in March 1941. Eight months later they held another election and changed the name to Westworth Village. Westworth Village incorporated in order to "preserve their right to remain residential and self-governing." Traffic on the newly completed Highway 183 increased considerably as more people traveled to Consolidated or the Fort Worth Army Air Field, and the new city of Westworth Village had to deal with it.

However, as one citizen wrote to his friend: "the shortage of gasoline and thinness of tires has just about worked out the traffic problem." Following the end of World War II, Westworth Village continued to boom because of growth at the air base (later called Carswell). The government constructed base housing in Westworth Village, whose population increased sixfold in five years from 529 to over 3,000.[55]

Urban historians have coined the phrase "martial metropolis" to describe the situation that caused the three communities of White Settlement, River Oaks, and Westworth Village to become small cities. "Martial metropolis" reflects the large amount of money the federal government spent in the area (at Consolidated and the Army Air Field), which helped spur population growth in the western suburbs of the larger Fort Worth metropolis. For the three "instant" cities, their economic base remained closely tied to military and defense spending; the communities provided no real attraction of their own for growth until the military facilities opened. Later, these three small cities and other nearby suburbs (all characteristic martial metropolis cities) suffered more from funding cuts by the federal government than did the larger city of Fort Worth, which enjoyed more economic diversification.[56]

Although many older citizens of the Dallas-Fort Worth Metroplex in the early twenty-first century may have lived as children in Liberator Village or one of the new suburban communities incorporated during World War II, they were too young at the time to know that U.S. defense and military spending in Fort Worth financed many other things besides Consolidated and the Fort Worth Army Air Field. These included Hicks Field, a Navy seaplane docking station on Lake Worth, the Quartermaster Depot, the Marine Glider Base on Eagle Mountain Lake, headquarters for the Army Air Forces Training Command, offices for the WASPs, an Army Records Office, an Army Finance Office, the United States Public Health Service Hospital, facilities for prisoners of war, and offices for the District Corps of Engineers, the Air Materiel Command, the Second Air Service Command, a Naval Air Training Station, and various emergency landing fields such as Singleton and Midway.

Historians will have to search diligently to find a U.S. city other than Washington, D.C.—and perhaps San Diego and San Antonio—more involved in the war effort than Fort Worth. But many communities, most of them in the West, found themselves the recipients of at least some federal contracts to support the war effort. In addition to the government and related activities outlined in this chapter, many other businesses in the Fort Worth area won defense contracts. One of the most prominent was John Kennedy's Globe Aircraft, whose story fills the next chapter.

CHAPTER 8

Globe Aircraft

FORT WORTHIANS WHOSE PARENTS OR GRANDPARENTS WORKED at the bomber plant during the war may forget that more airplane manufacturing took place in the area than just at the big Consolidated factory west of town. Some people took jobs at the North American plant in Grand Prairie east of Fort Worth in Dallas County. Closer to home, however, was the Globe facility on Blue Mound Road only a half dozen miles north of downtown. The story of John Kennedy and Globe reveals how mandatory wartime aircraft production at first benefited, then adversely affected, an already-existing local company.

John Kennedy, the creator, first of Globe Laboratories, then of Bennett Aircraft prior to World War II, played a major local role in aircraft manufacturing in the war effort with his reorganized Globe Aircraft factory. Kennedy lived in his Scottish-baron-style mansion on Blue Mound Road and often entertained wealthy friends and associates, who included Amon Carter, cattleman W. T. Waggoner, bandleader Paul Whiteman, and cowboy singer Gene Autry. Kennedy maintained his former cattle interests, serving on the board of the Southwestern Exposition and Fat Stock Show held in Fort Worth each year. His memberships included the Fort Worth Club, River Crest Country Club, the Wings Club of Fort Worth, and the Royal Aero Club of London, England. Apparently, Kennedy first became interested in airplane manufacturing when someone pointed out to him that he owned an ideal location for a landing field and factory on the flat land north of Fort Worth. After selling his profitable Globe Laboratories, he also had the money.[1]

Having reorganized his Bennett Aircraft in late 1940 as Globe Aircraft (as discussed in chapter 4), Kennedy planned to build a small monoplane known as the Swift. As of June 1941 Kennedy still was test flying the Swift, having not yet begun production, although he reported orders in excess of $1 million dollars. According to an article in the local Chamber of Commerce magazine, Kennedy was "brimming with enthusiasm when he talks about his new plane." He hoped to turn out three airplanes a day once

John Kennedy, after selling his Globe Laboratories, bought a controlling interest in Bennett Aircraft and renamed it Globe Aircraft. He built a Globe Swift for the civilian market before the war and AT-10 trainers in World War II. *Photo courtesy the National Archives and Records Administration, Southwest Region, Fort Worth, Texas.*

he started production. In the meantime he began negotiating to obtain subcontracts to manufacture parts for companies that already held contracts to build airplanes for the government. Globe qualified as a war plant less than two months after Pearl Harbor, and soon received orders to build Beechcraft twin-engine AT-10 trainer airplanes.[2]

Classes began for future Globe employees just as they had for workers seeking aircraft jobs at Consolidated. In June 1941, Kennedy hired Jim Rivers, a pioneer airplane builder who previously trained workers at North American in Grand Prairie, to teach classes at Globe. The training classes took place in Globe's Plant #3 School of Aircraft. Plans called for 30 to 40 percent of employees (about 1,000) in 1942 to be women who would need to attend the training classes. Also included among the applicants were ten deaf students. They were accompanied by their teacher, Mrs. Marjorie Moore, who relayed in sign language what the instructor said. Kennedy hired knowledgeable aviation experts for his factory. One of these was William G. Fuller, manager of Fort Worth's Municipal Meacham Field, which he had helped establish in the mid-1920s. Fuller resigned from the city in 1942 to become vice president and general manager for Globe.[3]

Fritz G. Lanham, U.S. Congressman for Fort Worth, announced in January 1941 that the U.S. government had awarded a "large" contract to Globe Aircraft to build airplanes for the Army Air Corps. This would necessitate an expansion of the plant, which the government would undertake. Globe became the government's Plancor #898, a cooperative project between the government and private industry as a part of the Defense Plant Corporation (DPC). The DPC entered into a lease agreement with Globe on April 3, 1942, stating the government would fund the plant and Globe would build AT-10 trainer airplanes. With funds from the DPC, Globe began adding onto its facilities in April 1942, and held a brief groundbreaking ceremony during the workers' lunch hour. Kennedy wielded a silver spade in a muddy field to begin the work.[4]

In the midst of all its preparation for war work, Globe received govern-

Globe Aircraft assembled Beechcraft twin-engine AT-10 training airplanes in the north half of the former Bennett factory in Saginaw. *Photo courtesy National Archives and Records Administration, Southwest Region, Fort Worth, Texas.*

Globe Aircraft, located in the growing community of Saginaw north of Fort Worth, employed 2,300 workers during peak production in World War II. *Photo courtesy the University of Texas at Dallas.*

ment approval of its civilian Swift monoplane from the Civil Aeronautics Administration (CAA). The side-by-side two-seater airplane, apparently the first Texas-built airplane to obtain the CAA certificate, could not go into production because Kennedy needed to fulfill the government contracts. In preparing to fill the big government order, Globe stockholders chose an eleven-member board, reelecting John Kennedy, founder of the company, as president. In 1942 Globe also accepted subcontract work from Consolidated. At the peak of production during the war, Globe employed 2,300 workers and carried a monthly payroll of $225,000. Production increased so rapidly that by September 1942 in order to manufacture parts Globe leased 100,000 square feet of space at the Southwestern Exposition and Fat Stock show buildings adjacent to the stockyards on the north side. The city of Fort Worth owned the major stock show exhibit building, having built it in 1936. By leasing the exhibits building and another stock show facility, Globe nearly doubled its factory capacity. Globe called the buildings its Plant 6 and placed an employment office there. Showing their patriotism, some former rodeo performers at the north side stock show took jobs at Globe, including Chester Byers, world champion trick and fancy roper; Tad Lucas, former world champion cowgirl; and Bob Calen, a top trick roper. Globe official Harry M. Katzen, on November 10, 1942, wrote plant superintendent William Fuller, "We're doing everything we can to get our sub-contractors rolling. One of these days you'll be able to see enough assemblies coming in so that you can start building."[5]

Meeting the government's quotas became so important that in May 1943 Globe officials asked for and received permission to increase the workweek for women to seventy hours. This gave the company a six-month exemption to the law that prohibited such long hours for women. The plant operated at full production by July 1, 1943. Kennedy announced in November that for eight months in a row Globe workers had met or exceeded their production schedule. The federal government's Aircraft Production Board responded with a commendation. Things apparently moved so smoothly the following spring that Kennedy allowed a "two-hour family day" to disrupt Globe's routine. On Sunday afternoon, April 16, 1944, Globe officials invited employees and families to tour the plant. Visitors learned that employees had exceeded the War Production Board's requirement for twelve consecutive months. This was not hard to believe because the regular work shift continued during the tour.[6]

Globe pilots tested the AT-10 trainer airplanes that came off the production lines and then transferred them to various training facilities all over the United States. A transport group, perhaps some of Jacqueline Cochran's and Nancy Love's WASPs, flew them to their destinations. In addition to the A-10 trainers, Globe operated a spare parts project in World War II and received a contract to build the nose section for the Curtiss-Wright C-46 Commando, the world's largest twin-engine transport airplane. Globe also acquired a contract for a wing reworking job on the twin-engine AT-17 trainer plane. In July 1944, Globe celebrated the completion of its contract to build AT-10 trainers for the Army Air Forces when the 600th AT-10 trainer rolled off the assembly line on July 30. The contract, worth $25 million, produced the first AT-10 only eighteen months earlier in February 1943.[7]

John Kennedy and Globe officials began as early as December 1944 to plan ahead for the company as a peacetime aircraft manufacturer. The company made application before the Civil Aeronautics Board for authority to operate a feeder airline in Texas. They created a transport division and made plans for feeder airlines originating and ending in Fort Worth. One daytime route would travel west and another east. Kennedy told the Globe board of directors in March 1945 that the company held nearly $8,000,000 in back orders, which included contracts with Curtiss-Wright, North American, and Fairchild Aircraft Corporation for fourteen types of sub-assemblies for the C-82. In addition, in May 1945, Douglas Aircraft of Santa Monica, California, chose Globe as one of four overhaul and conversion centers to be used to turn the Army's C-47 transport and cargo ships into DC-3 commercial carriers. As a result, the company stationed a Douglas representative at Globe. Kennedy reported that the company already had purchased machinery to manufacture a varied line of products in addition to the Globe Swift. He also reported over 60,000 inquiries about the Swift from prospective customers and dealers.[8]

The previous fall Kennedy had announced that the corporation was free of debt, would authorize a 10 percent dividend on April 1, 1945, and that its net worth totaled over $3 million. The board reelected him chairman, president, and general manager. He assured the board that his factory would help provide jobs for "the men coming back from war as well as those who have served faithfully at home." However, according to a March 31, 1945, appraisal requested by the Defense Plant Corporation the Globe facilities, which consisted of an assembly building; three guard houses; a storage reservoir, water tank and tower; a deep well and pump; yard facilities; underground water and sewer lines; parking areas; and fencing, all on 6.38 acres, held a total value of only a little more than $409, 000. The discrepancies between Kennedy's estimation in the fall of 1944 and the government's figures six months later previewed eventual serious problems for Globe.[9]

Globe employees and others expected that the company would do extremely well in the private sector when the war ended. After all, their two-seater Globe Swift was designed, tested, and ready to go. In fact, during the first six weeks of Globe's sales campaign after the war ended, the company received 2,103 orders for the Swift, totaling over $7 million. The first production model came off the assembly line in early September 1945. Called the Swift GC-1A, it was an all-metal private airplane. Kennedy planned to build several thousand within the coming fifteen months. He wanted to be able to retain all of his World War II employees, as he told the board. "We still have some sub-contract work to finish for the Army Air Forces; but when that is done we will be able to turn our full attention to production of the Swift," he told reporters.[10]

By December 1945 Globe counted over $16 million in firm orders for the Swift. To help handle the orders, Globe let a subcontract to the new company that had taken over part of the wartime facilities of North American Aviation in Grand Prairie. Called Texas Engineering and Manufacturing Company, Ltd. (TEMCO), the new company agreed to take on $6 million of Globe's backlog and help produce Swift airplanes. Kennedy already held delivery requests from forty-seven distributors and 361 dealers across the United States. He hoped to produce 4,000 of the airplanes in 1946. In February 1946 stockholders approved a re-capitalization plan offering 150,000 shares of $10 per 5.5 percent convertible preferred stock to common shareholders on a pro rata basis at $9 per share. With proceeds of more than $1 million from the stock offering, Kennedy planned to use $34,000 for reorganization and other expenses; $960,000 for repayment of a Reconstruction Finance Corporation loan; $31,000 for working capital; and $250,000 to purchase the government-owned factory and equipment. By February 1946 Globe held firm purchase orders in excess of $18 million.[11]

That spring Globe sought to purchase for $276,000 from the Reconstruction Finance Corporation (RFC) the building the Defense Plant Corporation had constructed and leased to them during the war. The plant employed 1,000 workers, and officials expected to hire that many more within the year. The purchase agreement called for Globe to make a down payment and receive a ten-year mortgage for the balance. The RFC authorized a loan to Globe on February 11, 1946, for $276,000. By March Globe produced sixty 85-horsepower Swifts and delivered thirty-three of them. Arrangements called for TEMCO to begin manufacturing the 125-horsepower Swifts in April. The maximum speed of the Globe Swift was 145 miles per hour and it had a cruising speed of 130. The company called it "the fastest little plane in the air."[12]

An incident occurred in March 1946 that probably did not alert John Kennedy or any of his Globe officers as it should have, but it was a portent of unfortunate things to come. B. G. Thompson, a dairyman located near the Globe plant, filed a lawsuit in the Sixty-seventh District Court, claim-

The Globe Swift became a civilian favorite after World War II. *Photo courtesy the University of Texas at Dallas.*

ing that waste material of chromium and oil from the plant had poisoned Fossil Creek, which crossed his land. He asked for $13,410 in damages after seventeen of his cattle died. He won the case. Globe officials appealed, and the Fifth Circuit Court found no basis to determine how much damage came from Globe's pollution of the creek and how much from other sources. As a result the appeals court reversed the judgment of the trial court and remanded the case for another trial.[13]

Meanwhile Globe's future prospects still looked bright in April 1946. At the National Aviation Show held in New York, the first big postwar aviation event, journalists paid special attention to Globe's all-metal Swift monoplane. Arriving home from the ego-boosting air show event, Globe officials announced a stock dividend of 13.75 cents per share. That same month the CAA certified the third Swift model—the Swift 125, with a cruising speed of 140 miles per hour, a maximum speed of 150 miles per hour, and a 512-mile range.[14]

By the end of the year, however, the company's fortunes appeared to be shifting. Globe officials announced in November 1946 the cancellation of its contract with TEMCO for the 1,500 Swifts they were to produce. Kennedy cited a seasonal slowdown in orders and a drop in the personal airplane market as the cause. Then the bad news hit. Three creditors, Spencer Thermostat Company of Attleboro, Massachusetts, Eastern Stainless Steel Corporation of Baltimore, Maryland, and Hubert Mitchell's Industries of Hartselle, Alabama, filed an involuntary petition of bankruptcy against Globe in Federal District Court Sixty-Seven in Fort Worth on December 27, 1946. The three companies alleged that Globe was insolvent and owed them a total of $31,730.12. In response, Globe filed a reorganization plan with the federal court, contending that they were not insolvent "within the meaning of the bankruptcy act, though it is unable to pay its debts as they mature." The company asked for an injunction to forestall the prosecution of the suit by the three creditors. Globe asked the court to appoint a trustee to operate the plant so it could continue in operation and fulfill its orders.[15]

The Reconstruction Finance Corporation and TEMCO requested possession of Globe property on which they held liens. Creditors claimed that Globe's petition for reorganization was not filed in good faith and asked that it be dismissed. Their complaint alleged that Globe filed a false and fraudulent registration statement and prospectus on the basis of which stock was issued and sold. The judge told the plaintiff that once it filed an affidavit to the fact of the stock sales he would deny Globe's motion to dismiss the case. Indications were that Globe had used the $1.25 million from the sale of stock for operating expenses rather than retiring the $960,000 RFC loan and purchasing the plant from the government for $250,000. The Securities and Exchange Commission (SEC) held hearings in early April 1947 to determine if the registration statement for the $1.5 million preferred stock issue of 1946 contained any untrue statements. John Kennedy testified on April 9, 1947, "I never withheld any information requested by the attorneys in preparation and sale of the stock issue, and as far as I know all of the information given to them was correct and complete." The government also claimed that Globe had paid a commission of $80,000 to the Production Engineering Company "for the securing of a war contract." The government alleged that the fee payment violated an executive order controlling such payments. On April 15, 1947, Globe trustees Wirt M. Norris and George Newman informed Glenn Smith, the referee in bankruptcy, that the corporation was unable to reorganize. Smith had no choice but to sign an order dismissing the reorganization proceedings and automatically allowing the case to revert back to bankruptcy. On April 20, 1947, adjudication of bankruptcy was completed and a trustee appointed. Thompson, the dairyman neighbor of the Globe plant who had brought the first lawsuit in 1946, lost out. By the time his case came up again in the district court, Globe had filed bankruptcy, and his case was dismissed.[16]

In May, Smith ordered Burton B. Paddock, attorney and newly-appointed trustee for the Globe bankruptcy, to liquidate the assets of Globe Aircraft. Paddock advertised for bids on all assets, subject to prior sales and approval of the Federal District Court. Globe's assets included 143.5 acres of land, 132 Swift airplanes, 27 partially completed airplanes, parts, machinery and equipment, raw materials, office buildings, workshops, cyclone fencing, and landing strip and approaches. Also for sale was the right to manufacture the Swift airplane—the design, patent, trademark, tooling dies, jigs, futures, plaster molds, and an option to purchase planes, parts, and tooling from a previous subcontractor. Although Kennedy and other Globe officials told the SEC they had made no misrepresentations in the stock registration in March 1946, the examiner in June 1947 recommended that SEC revoke the registration. Trustee Burton B. Paddock stated that as of June 1947 the Globe debts were more than $5.3 million. Sale of tangible assets was expected to bring in $800,000. If the RFC claim of $960,000 was allowed, other creditors would receive nothing. The RFC eventually received $10,527.41, and the lease between it and Globe expired June 20, 1947.[17]

Glenn Smith, the referee in bankruptcy, on June 19, 1947, approved the sale of Globe's tangible assets to TEMCO of Grand Prairie for $328,000. Not included were real estate or heavy machinery. The RFC held a lien on the real estate as security for their $960,000 loan. TEMCO acquired not only the Swift airplanes on hand but the patent and manufacturing rights. TEMCO announced that they planned to manufacture the Swift at their Grand Prairie factory. Prior to the bankruptcy TEMCO manufactured 329 Swifts under their subcontract with Globe, and it was ready to reassume production. By November 1947 all of Globe's tangible assets had been sold. John Kennedy on August 28, 1947, wrote the Dallas office of the RFC asking for an opportunity, with some investors, to buy the 143.5 acres of land at $20,000 and to lease the land on which the office building stood. He was still trying six months later. The War Assets Administration announced on November 28, 1947, that the land and building were to be offered for sale "in its entirety."[18]

As of February 19, 1948, the War Assets Administration (WAA) still was trying to sell the Globe property, the land with buildings, and personal property such as machines, tools, and office equipment. Globe files at the National Archives and Records Administration reveal that numerous companies bid for the Globe property, but part was owned by the RFC and part by the WAA, and the two agencies could not agree on a price, making it difficult to sell. The WAA owned the government-built part; when Globe went into bankruptcy, the RFC took title to the real property and personal property owned by Globe. Bids received ranged from $5,000 from a resort owner in Wisconsin to $360,000 from a Fort Worth trading company. Because John Kennedy originally put up his own farm as collateral, he lost it to the government.[19]

From about 1948 to 1950 the General Services Administration (GSA) used the former Globe property as a storage warehouse. On June 30, 1949, the RFC transferred a tract of land with improvements to the Federal Works Agency for the use of the Public Buildings Administration. Later the government transferred it to the General Services Administration. By late 1950 the munitions board asked the GSA to move so that the government could assign it to the Navy Department for probable use by Bell Aircraft Corporation. As of 1953 the official designation of the plant was the Naval Industrial Reserve Plant, Saginaw, Texas. Bell used the facility for over thirty-five years. The building was torn down in 2005, leaving only a tower remaining. Meanwhile TEMCO continued producing the Globe Swift until 1951 when production ceased because of military priorities brought on by the Korean War.[20]

Many years later John Kennedy's son Tom explained that his father had drawn up plans for a new four-seater Globe Swift with a tricycle landing gear, but he was not able to build it because of lawsuits and bankruptcy. In addition, in 1947 the stable that housed his thirty-six prize horses burned, and none of the horses survived. "Dad was completely crushed. He became almost reclusive." One wonders how one man could survive the lawsuits, complete loss of his business and farm, and then his beloved animals, all in about two years. Yet, less than a year after his company collapsed, Kennedy began a campaign to incorporate the small community of 500 people called Saginaw that grew up near his former plant. Law enforcement and a better water supply for residents motivated him. In an election held September 5, 1948, citizens voted 99 to 14 to incorporate. Kennedy won the mayor's race by a vote of 75 to 20 and took office as Saginaw's first mayor on September 27. Voters reelected him in 1951 but he lost in a run-off two years later.[21]

The story of Kennedy's rise from impoverished Scottish teenager working in the Chicago stockyards to wealthy entrepreneur with his Globe Laboratories and successful wartime airplane construction is inspirational. In leading his company to support the war effort of his adopted country, he did not know that circumstances would cause him to lose everything. That he could survive the rapid decline of his fortunes and become a city-builder and first mayor of Saginaw gives testimony to his resiliency and stubborn determination. Despite Kennedy's personal tragedies, his Globe factory provided tangible benefits for Fort Worth. His employment of over 3,000 aircraft workers, both men and women, contributed considerably to the war effort, in local jobs and in the AT-10 trainers produced. After the war, even though he lost the ability to produce his Swift airplane for a civilian market, the appealing design and dependability of the lightweight aircraft assured its continued production. Because of the popularity of his Swift airplane, which people still fly in the twenty-first century, and of Bell Helicopter's lease of the former Globe plant, Kennedy's role in both remained in the news. As mayor of Saginaw he secured his lasting role in the history of northern Tarrant County.

CHAPTER 9

Bell Helicopters

L AWRENCE D. (LARRY) BELL AND BELL HELICOPTER CORPORATION transformed the Dallas-Fort Worth "Mid-Cities" (as the communities between Dallas and Fort Worth are known in the Metroplex) of eastern Tarrant County and added massive defense spending to the area's economy in the last half of the twentieth century. That influence continued undiminished into the new century. The arrival of Bell Helicopter between World War II and the Korean War was one of those unexpected gifts that a city sometimes fortuitously receives. Like the Canadians in World War I and Reuben Fleet with Consolidated at the outbreak of World War II, Larry Bell was just looking for a good place to move. For each of those men and their enterprises, Fort Worth was that place.

Bell Helicopter Company did not begin locally, so when it came to Fort Worth in 1950 it rented the old Globe factory from the U.S. government until it could build its own facility in Hurst. Because the city of Fort Worth incorporated the land on which the Hurst plant would be built, the company is technically located in Fort Worth. Bell was not the first to build helicopters, but the sketchy early development of helicopters in the four decades before Bell, emphasizes the importance of Bell's later success. Although others may have gotten a head start, his company eventually emerged as the giant of the industry.[1]

The word helicopter—meaning spiral wing—dates to 1872. The *idea*, however, can be traced back as far as 1483 when Leonardo da Vinci drew plans for a contraption that looked like a forerunner of the modern helicopter. He wrote, "there shall be wings! If the accomplishment be not for me, 'tis for some other." Experimentation with helicopters began in Europe as early as 1907 with machines capable of lifting a man off the ground. In that year Louis Breguet of France flew his gyroplane two feet off the ground for nearly a minute. A machine designed by George de Bothezat flew at Mc-Cook Field near Dayton, Ohio, on December 18, 1922, six feet above the ground for one minute and forty-two seconds. Six months later, Juan de la Cierva flew at Madrid, Spain, in a rotary wing aircraft, which he called an autogiro. Between 1929 and 1932, the Pitcairn Autogiro Company, established by Harold H. Pitcairn of Willow Grove, Pennsylvania, built a few autogiros, but they were not true helicopters. Although the autogiro could not take off and land vertically, it could take off and land in less distance than a winged airplane. The first successful flight of a true helicopter, a Focke-Achgelis, FA-61, occurred in Germany in 1936. A year later at Bremen, Germany, a woman pilot named Hanna Reitsch flew the same machine for more than one hour. During World War II, a nineteen-year-old American genius named Stanley Hiller built a helicopter that he called the XH-44, "X" for experimental, "H" for Hiller, and "44" for the year 1944.[2]

Russian émigré Igor Sikorsky would spearhead the most successful early American attempts at helicopter manufacture, however. Before he came to the United States, the Imperial Aero Club of Russia had awarded Sikorsky License No. 64 on August 18, 1911, when his 1909 helicopter actually got off the ground. The next year he flew a larger model at the end of a rope. Neither machine could carry a load, however. During World War I he built bombers for Nicholas II, czar of Russia. In March 1918, during the Russian revolution, Sikorsky escaped the country, eventually arriving in New York City. After four years of translating for the Russian Institute and designing aircraft at night, he founded the Sikorsky Aero Engineering Corporation on March 15, 1923, having persuaded fellow Russian immigrants to invest. His first test flight of a direct lift aircraft came on April 20, 1939. On the strength of Sikorsky's work, the U.S. government gave him a contract in 1940 for the world's first production helicopter. Less than 400 helicopters were built in the U.S. during World War II, about half by Sikorsky and the rest by Nash-Kelvinator Corporation in Detroit.[3]

After World War II, Larry Bell soon would challenge Sikorsky, and their two firms became the main helicopter manufacturers in the 1950s. A third important American helicopter designer, Frank Piasecki, built twenty helicopters for the U.S. Navy in 1943. (His Piasecki Aircraft Corporation was renamed the·Vertol Aircraft Corporation, "vertol" for "vertical takeoff and landing," before it was acquired by Boeing in 1960.) It was Bell, however, who would produce more helicopters than all the other helicopter manufacturers combined.[4]

Bell was born in Mentone, Indiana, on April 5, 1894, the youngest of ten children of Isaac and Harriet Bell. Isaac Bell, who worked for a lumber mill, retired in 1907 and decided to move to Santa Monica, California, to be near some of his grown children. Larry Bell, the only child still at home, found the move exciting because several early airplane enthusiasts began their activities in Southern California about the time the Bell family arrived. Young pilots and would-be engineers flew exhibitions to earn money to build their

Lawrence D. Bell began his aircraft career in California working for Glenn Martin and later owned a factory in Buffalo, New York. He moved his helicopter division to Fort Worth in 1950. *Photo courtesy Bell/Textron, Inc.*

own airplane designs. In 1910 Larry Bell watched an air show at Dominguez Field near Long Beach, California, in which Glenn H. Curtiss flew his own airplane. During the ten-day-long show, Bell saw his first airplane, and he and his older brother Grover became so inspired they built a wooden kite model that actually flew.[5]

After that experience Larry read everything he could get his hands on about airplanes. Grover, eleven years older, equally excited, took flying lessons from Glenn L. Martin and became one of his exhibition pilots and instructors. Soon the two Bell brothers decided to buy a used airplane for themselves. Larry took tests to graduate from high school early so that he could work with Grover. After he graduated in 1912, they hired a daredevil pilot named Lincoln Beachey as a mechanic and then following the practice of Curtiss, Martin, and others, put on exhibitions to raise money. Their dreams of an airplane company disappeared on July 4, 1913, when Grover crashed at Petaluma, California, and died the next day. Devastated, Larry Bell temporarily quit aviation.[6]

He caught the aviation bug again soon, for several months later he got a job as a stockroom clerk in Glenn Martin's airplane factory at $9 per week, turning an avocation into a lifelong career. Bell was enthusiastic and hardworking, and Martin soon placed him in charge of the tool room. By age twenty Bell became shop foreman. In 1917 Martin merged his airplane company with Wright interests in Cleveland and moved there to operate a plant. Bell and his wife, Lucille, moved with Martin, and Bell eventually became vice president and general manager. Two future airplane manufacturers who worked for Bell and Martin were Donald W. Douglas, who later created his own company, and J. H. Kindelberger, later of North American

Aviation. Although short, Bell did not allow himself to be intimidated because of his stature. He was more outgoing than Glenn Martin, and did a lot of the selling. Because he was contributing so much to the company, he asked Martin in 1925 if he could buy in as part owner. When Martin said, "No," Bell became so upset that he quit his job and returned to California with no prospects in sight. For a while he sold tools and then became involved in an unsuccessful scheme to find gold. After about three years Bell received a job offer in 1928 from Reuben H. Fleet, president of Consolidated Aircraft Company in Buffalo, New York. Fleet heard Bell's story of his unhappiness with Martin and promised him a stock option arrangement, whereupon Bell promptly accepted a position as sales manager. Within a year he was vice president and general sales manager. Then after Fleet faced a long recuperation after a serious injury from an airplane crash on September 13, 1929, he handed over the operation of Consolidated to Bell as general manager.[7]

In 1935 Fleet decided to move Consolidated to San Diego, California, because of the better climate. At that time Bell had been running the company for six years. Buffalo businessmen learned of the move and did not want to see the factory close, and the many local jobs lost. Consequently, a group of bankers approached Bell and promised financing for a new company if he would remain in the facilities that Fleet would leave empty. Bell asked Fleet about the idea, "What would you think of my resigning from Consolidated and not going with you? I'd like to stay here and capitalize on what you are forced to leave behind." "Well, Larry," Fleet replied, "looking at it from my standpoint, it would force me back into harness. Looking at it from your standpoint, I think it is your opportunity. So, if you want to do it, it is all right with me." Fleet stipulated that he got to take anyone he wanted with him to San Diego. As a result, Fleet paid the way for 311 employees to move. Another one hundred paid their own way to San Diego, with the promise of work once they arrived.[8]

Not everyone in the company made the move to California, though. A number of Consolidated's former employees remained with Bell as well. Two former Consolidated officials who stayed behind with Bell were Ray Whitman and Robert Woods, whom Bell made vice president and chief designer respectively. Larry Bell's new Bell Aircraft Corporation was capitalized at $500,000, and he offered stock at $100 per share. For $1, Fleet sold Bell many miscellaneous items at the factory that would have been unprofitable for him to move to San Diego. Fleet also promised to send Bell some subcontract work worth a couple million dollars "to help get him started."[9]

Bell began his company with about fifty-six employees. Things moved slowly until February 1936, when he received an $800,000 Navy contract to make PBY wings and parts for Consolidated. Fleet had kept his word. However, Bell did not sit still and wait for Fleet's largesse. In 1936 he conceived the idea for a new military airplane, a twin-engine long-range fighter with two 37-millimeter cannons and four 50-caliber machine guns. Called the Airacuda, it used remote control gun turrets. A year later Bell Aircraft Company built the P-39 Airacobra, a smaller, faster fighter. The latter became important in World War II.[10]

In 1938, Bell accepted a remarkable opportunity that would dramatically improve his fortunes as a manufacturer—and eventually change the industrial makeup of Fort Worth as well. At the request of President Franklin D. Roosevelt, he and forty-four other industrialists sailed to Europe on a German ship, the *Europa*. FDR wanted them to see first hand what preparations for war were being made in Europe. While there, Bell took a two-week tour of German aircraft factories. He essentially had been asked to be an industrial spy; however, something important happened that perhaps altered the course of his aviation life. On the inspection tour, Bell saw a helicopter at the Focke-Wulf facility—the FW-61 helicopter that had flown for the first time two years earlier. It had two rotors that turned in opposite directions to offset each other's torque. Bell also liked the plan of a modern German aircraft plant he visited, and he later copied the layout when he built a new assembly plant in Niagara Falls. Bell made an official report of what he saw in Europe to the U.S. Navy on September 12, 1938. Among the things Bell learned on his trip was that Germany was producing 8,000 to 10,000 airplanes a year. By January 1940 Larry Bell employed 1,170 people in his Buffalo plant and plunged the firm wholeheartedly into the war effort, including with the help of the government's Defense Plant Corporation, opening a Bell factory in Marietta, Georgia. At Bell's wartime peak in February 1944, he employed 50,674 workers in four facilities: Buffalo and Niagara Falls in New York, Marietta, and Burlington, Vermont. In the Marietta factory, Bell built about 650 B-29 Superfortresses for the government. The last of 9,588 P-39 Airacobras Bell produced rolled off the assembly line on July 24, 1944. During World War II, Bell turned out a total of 13,600 fighter aircraft.[11]

Innovation remained a priority for Bell; he built, and his company flew, the first American jet propelled aircraft, the P-59 Airacomet on October 2, 1942. His company also developed an airplane, the XC-1, in which Air Force test pilot, Charles E. "Chuck" Yeager, officially became the first to exceed the speed of sound on October 14, 1947. Also, while he was producing all of those B-29s and P-39s for the war effort and experimenting with the X-1, Larry Bell did not forget the helicopter demonstration he witnessed in Germany. He set up a small group of men in a garage to work on a helicopter design.[12]

The helicopter project came to Bell in the person of a thirty-six-year-old Princeton graduate and eccentric inventor named Arthur Young. Young had been working on a helicopter design for over a dozen years at his family's estate in Pennsylvania, where he enjoyed the time and the means to experiment. He had approached several companies with his designs, but they all turned him down. When he came to Bell's Buffalo plant on September 4, 1941, Bell decided to give him a free hand to continue his work. Bell told Young he wanted him to build two man-carrying helicopters within two years. He called the project "Gyro Tests" for security purposes. After housing Young's experiments at the Buffalo plant for a while, on June 24, 1942, Bell moved everything to an old Chrysler agency and garage in the nearby suburb of Gardenville. It was time to build a full-scale model.[13]

People later humorously speculated that Larry Bell moved Young and his helicopter experiments to Gardenville to fool either the Germans or the stockholders! Some called the project "Larry's Folly." The Gardenville site had a big yard that could be used for preliminary testing and even a meadow where short flights would be possible. Workers converted the building into a machine shop, drafting room, office, and workshop; manufacturing the experimental helicopters took place in the garage. Bell sent workers to build a fence around the facility and paint it gray. Then he put up searchlights and hired armed guards. But Young complained that such things would attract too much attention, so Bell sent his men back and removed everything. Only a night watchman remained. In the beginning, Young directed about fifteen people: engineers, body men, tool and pattern makers, flight mechanics, and one welder. More employees arrived, but the total never exceeded thirty-two men before June 1945. Igor Sikorsky once visited the Gardenville site, arriving with the vice presidents of his company in a fleet of Cadillacs. "I zee you use zee vertical engine," he said. "Yes, I use the vertical engine," Young replied. That was all they said to each other. Sikorsky and his vice presidents got back in their Cadillacs and left.[14]

Young took the controls first when in late December 1942 they wheeled their Model 30 out the door. Tethered by cables, the hovering helicopter only got a foot off the ground. Later, Floyd Carlson, first official test pilot, practiced hovering until he could do it with slack in the cable. Then on June 26, 1943, mechanics removed the cable, and Carlson flew very slowly around the meadow behind the garage. By July he was flying at speeds over seventy miles per hour. The craft vibrated at twenty-five miles per hour at first, but after installing a brace on the rotor, it settled down.[15]

Despite the jokes suggesting the contrary, Larry Bell was not keeping his project secret. In March 1944 he released information to the Buffalo newspapers, one of which ran a two-page spread about it. Then two months later on May 10, 1944, at the request of the Civil Air Patrol, Floyd Carlson put on a show to demonstrate the helicopter at the Buffalo Armory. Later on July 4 he put on another demonstration for 42,000 people at the Buffalo Civic Stadium. "The climax of our act was for Floyd to hover the front wheel of the helicopter into my extended hand," Young explained. On March 14, 1945, Ship #2 rescued two men who had been fishing on Lake Erie when the ice began breaking up. Spectators onshore had given the men up for lost because the ice was too heavy for a boat to penetrate, but too weak to risk rescue by sled. The Young-Bell helicopter hovered, retrieved one man and took him to shore, and then returned for the other. Years later Arthur Young reminisced, "I didn't anticipate all the things a helicopter would prove itself capable of doing."[16]

In summer 1945 Bell moved the helicopter crew from Gardenville to his new plant in Niagara Falls. He became convinced that the helicopter would keep his company in business after the war, even though his engineering staff and test pilots disagreed. Bell instructed Floyd Carlson to give free rides to top military brass, foreign visitors, and others who happened to be in the area. Six months after the Gardenville group arrived at the Niagara Falls plant on December 8, 1945, they completed their first Model 47. Soon they produced ten more, using them for demonstrations and training while they applied to be certified by the Civil Aeronautics Administration (later the Federal Aviation Administration) as a commercial helicopter. Bell competed with Sikorsky to receive the first commercial certification, which he did on March 8, 1946. License NC-1H was the world's first for a commercial helicopter. Bell sold the Model 47 for twenty-seven years with more than 5,000 commercial and military versions produced. Bell was fortunate that he had the helicopter, for his company began losing money ($657,000 in 1946) after the government canceled wartime contracts.[17]

Bell invested $10–$12 million on the helicopter before he made a single sale, but once he did, progress came rapidly. His first commercial sale, in November 1946, went to Arizona Helicopter, Inc. and another was sold the following month in Boston to publicize several large department stores. The military made its first helicopter purchase in September 1947, when the Army bought its first Bell Model 47, calling it an H-13. As Larry Bell said of his aircraft, "People must realize that the helicopter is the only vehicle of transportation in the world that's self-contained. If you buy a helicopter, you don't need to build a road, a harbor, a right-of-way, or an airport. You don't need anything. And if you take off in a helicopter, you can go in any direction of the compass, directly to your destination. You don't have to follow a road, you don't have to go to an airport, you just go where you want to go." In 1948, Lyndon B. Johnson used a Bell Model 47D helicopter to campaign in Texas for the Senate, with Bell test pilot Joe Mashman flying it around the state for him. The Waggoner Ranch near Wichita Falls, Texas, purchased a 47-D1 Bell helicopter in 1952 to herd cattle for branding, to find lost animals in dense thickets, and to inspect oil rigs on the ranch. The Bell helicopter had become Texanized.[18]

The Waggoner Ranch purchase was a bit of an anomaly, though. By about 1950 the commercial market slowed and appeared to dry up even though Joe Mashman demonstrated it continuously to attract commercial buyers. As it turned out, the Korean War triggered the beginning of a military success story for Bell. In June 1950 when the war erupted, the Army had before it Bell's proposal for a military product run of five hundred helicopters. Bell eventually got the order. Company officials tell the story that in August 1950 Bell and two colleagues visited Army command headquarters at Fort Monroe, Virginia, to try to convince them to purchase his product. While Bell and Mashman visited offices looking for people to talk to—with no luck—a little girl came by the helicopter with a sticky lollipop and climbed all over it wanting a ride. Sales Engineer Hans Weichsel, who had stayed with the helicopter, told her to go get her daddy and she could have a ride. Meanwhile, he wiped up places the sticky lollipop had touched where he wanted the Army brass to sit. Bell and Mashman came back disgusted, and Bell said, "Let's get out of here!" Weichsel suggested they wait just a bit. Sure enough, the little girl returned with her daddy, a general, and they both took a ride. The general was impressed. After some bargaining, the Army ordered eighty-five Model 47Ds.[19]

Orders began coming in from the Army, which used helicopters almost exclusively for evacuation missions. During the Korean War 80 percent of all frontline evacuations, about 15,000 troops, took place with Bell helicopters. However, Sikorsky H-S helicopters made 75 percent of all air rescues in Korea in 1951. Bell H-13-B helicopters, equipped with .30 caliber machine guns and Bazookas, first engaged in combat in 1950 during the battle for Seoul.[20]

After the company won a competition to build Navy anti-submarine (XHSL-1) helicopters, Bell decided to separate the helicopter activities from airplane manufacturing. He wanted to give the rotary wing division more room to develop a variety of models. From 1946 to 1951 the company built a total of 388 helicopters in Buffalo. Bell continued receiving military orders and did not stop production even while looking for a new site for a helicopter-only plant and his subsequent move to Texas. Hurst was not the only location that Bell considered. He and Bart Kelley visited various cities, including Santa Barbara, California, and Westfield, Massachusetts, during the summer of 1950 before settling on Fort Worth and the Hurst location.

Bell claimed that he surveyed potential sites "from coast to coast and border to border." Fort Worth's good weather and a friendly reception from business leaders proved very attractive, and a Defense Department request to locate inland effectively eliminated the East and West Coast locations.[21]

For several reasons Bell decided to move his helicopter operation out of Buffalo to Fort Worth. He began to see friction between the airplane and helicopter operations and knew he needed to separate them. Bell once explained to his board of directors his thinking in moving the entire helicopter program to Texas: "I want an organization that thinks helicopters morning, noon, and night . . . . We have a great variety of projects in Buffalo. The staff doesn't have time to give more than a lick and a promise to the helicopter." In addition, in order for his new helicopter to compete with several larger companies, like Sikorsky and Piasecki, he needed room to expand. Bell had also experienced a long strike in New York and wanted to move where labor was plentiful with less likelihood of problems. Too, he saw rivalry between the military branches. The Air Force owned his main plant at Niagara Falls. The Navy was not shy in informing Bell that if they ordered his helicopters, they did not want an Air Force-owned factory to build them![22]

Bell transferred six employees in early January 1951 from his Niagara Falls plant then hired ten Texas workers, and started operations at the former Globe plant in April 1951 that he leased from the government. Eventually three hundred families from Buffalo would move to Fort Worth to work in the Hurst Bell plant. Only one worker later decided to return to Buffalo; while a few moved north after retirement, most stayed in Texas. Bell along with company and Fort Worth dignitaries broke ground for the new plant on May 21, 1951. Under a big tent, Fort Worth restaurateur Walter Jetton served Texas barbecue for lunch, and Bell Helicopter pilots gave ten-minute rides to important guests. An audience of three hundred military and business leaders stood in a weed-covered pasture to watch the ceremonies. They learned that a $3.5 million plant would rise on the spot. Because the tiny community of Hurst could not do all the street and utility work that was needed, the city of Fort Worth annexed the land on which the plant would be built and promised to make those improvements.[23]

One could correctly call Hurst a sleepy little town when Larry Bell became interested in it for a new helicopter factory. The community had only acquired a post office in 1949 when Postmaster Bill Souder manned a postal window in a corner of his mother's store. With only thirty-two boxes, the post office earned $875 the first year. Two years later in 1951 when it incorporated, Hurst still possessed only two grocery stores, a service station, and approximately two hundred people in the area. Thanks to the Bell plant, though, the community grew rapidly throughout the 1950s. In 1960, less

An early 1950s aerial view of the Bell Helicopter plant in Hurst shows at front center the house remaining from the fifty-five acre farm bought by Bell from Mrs. W. E. Duskey. The plant later expanded. *Photo courtesy Bell/Textron, Inc.*

than a decade after incorporation, the population reached 10,500. Of the three mid-cities communities—Hurst, Euless, and Bedford—Hurst was the first to grow, and Bell was the reason.[24]

What emerged on that land was the first factory in the world specifically designed to manufacture helicopters. Within a decade the plant spent a quarter of a billion dollars in wages and purchases and boasted the second-largest payroll in Tarrant County. The company then bought more land and expanded. The initial building, however, had a 165,000-square-foot manufacturing area and a 40,000–square-foot, two-story administration building. The company's first projects in Texas included building model 47D helicopters as well as hosting a customer training school and flight-testing. In addition, workers produced the B-36 jet engine cowling pads for Convair in the Globe plant until April 1954. At that time Bell was using Hicks Field for all flight test operations of the HSL-1 helicopter.[25]

When Larry Bell came to Fort Worth on October 26, 1952, to speak at a dinner for management personnel in his Texas Division, he could boast of recent accomplishments by his thriving company. Elton J. Smith of Bell Helicopter had made history on September 17 when he set a new world's record for non-stop distance flight by helicopter flying a Bell Model 47D-1 from the Hurst plant to the front lawn of the Bell Aircraft main plant in Niagara Falls, New York. He made the trip in 12 hours and 57 minutes, covering 1,234 miles and burning 187 gallons of gasoline. In addition to Smith's flight, Bell told his audience that he was celebrating forty years in the aircraft business since those days in Southern California when he had worked for Glenn L. Martin. At the time Bell was the only person still active in the industry who had been an aviation pioneer prior to 1914. He also told his audience that by the end of 1952 the new Texas plant would manufacture 416 rotary-wing aircraft, more than any other company that year. Employment at the local plant at the end of the year grew from 259 to 2,600.[26]

One of Bell's managers in the audience that October night was Joe Fuchs, a German immigrant who had come to the United States in 1925 at age seventeen. After various jobs, including aircraft worker for Consolidated, Sikorsky, and Seversky, he began working for Bell in Buffalo in 1936. After arriving in the United States, he saved money to bring two of his brothers to his new country, and then they all three worked to bring a fourth brother. Within three and a half years, his entire family, including his widowed mother had come to the United States. While Fuchs worked for Bell Aircraft in Buffalo during World War II, he heard a lot of remarks about his German ancestry, but he tolerated them and never changed his name. "We felt the U.S. had done well by us, and none of us ever questioned our duty toward giving all we could to the war effort against Germany in World War II, he said later." Fuchs was one of Bell's employees who moved to Texas in 1952, and Bell did well by him, making Fuchs supervisor of five departments at the Hurst plant. With an entrepreneurial spirit, Fuchs and two fellow Bell employees (John Barfield and Herman Smith) saw a real estate opportunity in the rapid growth of the area around the plant. In 1960 they began building houses while still working at Bell. They did so well that Fuchs resigned in 1968 to keep building houses, and also to keep from being transferred to the night shift. He had worked for Bell for nearly thirty-three years. Buying and selling real estate kept him busy in retirement.[27]

Larry Bell retained personal management of his company until October 1954 when he resigned as general manager, giving the position to Leston P. Faneuf. Bell remained as president, however, and in 1955 the advertising department noted, "There are more Bell helicopters in commercial production than all other makes and models combined."[28]

Larry Bell suffered a stroke in May 1956 but was aware that stockholders voted on July 31 for the Texas Division of Bell Aircraft to become a wholly owned subsidiary corporation—Bell Helicopter Corporation—to be incorporated in Delaware. The new name would take effect on January 1, 1957. On September 18, 1956, Bell asked to be relieved of the presidency, although he remained chairman of the board. He died on October 20 at age sixty-two. He had achieved much during those sixty-two years with only a high school education from Polytechnic High in Santa Monica, California. Bell once said, "No matter where I am, at home or elsewhere, when an airplane flies overhead, I'm going to go outside and look at it; I don't think I'll ever get over that."[29]

The Hurst-Euless-Bedford Independent School district already had decided in January 1956 to name their first high school Lawrence D. Bell High School. When the district dedicated it on March 3, 1957, most of the students of the new high school were sons or daughters of Bell employees. When that building later became Central Junior High, a new Lawrence D. Bell High School opened on Brown Trail. Posthumous honors came for Bell when he was inducted into the Aviation Hall of Fame in Dayton, Ohio, on July 23, 1977, and into the Army Aviation Hall of Fame at Fort Rucker, Alabama, in 1987.[30]

Senator Lyndon B. Johnson came to the Bell plant on December 11, 1957, to cut a big blue ribbon from around a Model 47J helicopter as it rolled off the production line. His visit helped Bell employees celebrate the 2,000th Model 47 produced by Bell. Senator Johnson climbed in the helicopter, tipped his ten-gallon hat, and waved to the crowd. Another politician, President Dwight D. Eisenhower, became the first president to make regular use of a helicopter after two Bell H13J models arrived at the White House in May 1957. Ten years later, one of those two helicopters was placed in the Smithsonian Institution.[31]

During these years a young woman pilot, Dora Dougherty, one of Jackie Cochran's WASPs at Avenger Field, joined Bell Helicopter as a test pilot and human resources expert. Dougherty, a native of St. Paul, Minnesota, enrolled in classes after the war, receiving a doctorate in educational psychology in 1955. She then took a job with the Glenn L. Martin Company in Baltimore in their Human Factors department. In 1958 she accepted a position in Bell Helicopter's Human Factors Group in Fort Worth. Dougherty's job involved aviation psychology—working with flight simulators—but she believed that she needed to be able to fly a helicopter. She received her rating in 1960 and soon began setting women's records and became a "leading figure in the aviation research field." When the Bell company decided to challenge the flight records of two Russian women, it chose Dougherty to make the attempt. During her February 8, 1961, flight she reached an altitude of 19,385 feet, exceeding the Russian's 14,000 feet altitude. Two days later she flew a straight-line distance of 405 miles, breaking the Russian woman's record of 350 miles. Dougherty's records stood until 1966.[32]

Dougherty became Manager of Human Factors Engineering and Cockpit Design for Bell Helicopter in 1962. She and her engineers introduced computers into the cockpit. In 1963 she married journalist Lester Strother, whom she met when he interviewed her. A retired Air Force Reserve Lieutenant Colonel, she appeared before the Senate and House Veterans' Affairs Committees in May 1977 to seek recognition for the World War II WASPs. The women had flown every type of aircraft that the male Army pilots flew and accumulated over sixty million operational miles (equaling 2,000 flights around the world). Dora Dougherty Strother argued that the women deserved recognition as pilots and officers. Congress passed the WASP amendment to the G.I. Bill Improvement Act of 1977, allowing honorable discharges to be issued to all WASPs and World War II Victory Medals. When she retired from Bell in December 1986, President Ronald Reagan wrote her to express "the nation's gratitude" for her contributions as a Women Airforce Service Pilot, as an officer in the Air Force reserve, and as a civilian working in the defense industry.[33]

In 1960 Harvey Gaylord, then president of Bell, wrote a letter to employees telling them that on July 2 the company was sold to Textron, Inc. of Providence, Rhode Island. Textron paid $22 million for Bell Aircraft Corporation's defense business, and Bell became Textron's largest operating division. Textron had started in 1923 when Royal Little borrowed $10,000 to start a yarn processing company. His idea was that stockholders would earn the best return if the company expanded into other industries. Consequently, the company evolved to about thirty divisions operating in five large groups: aerospace, consumer, industrial, metal product, and creative capital.[34]

In purchasing Bell Helicopter, Textron made a wise decision, as the company continued to thrive throughout the 1960s. At its Fort Worth-area plant, Bell produced more than 90 percent of all helicopters flown by U.S. forces in Vietnam by 1966. In fact, October 1, 1966, marked the 120th consecutive month of on-schedule deliveries of UH-1 (Huey) helicopters to the U.S. government. Workers completed a brand new helicopter every two hours. A little over a year later Bell Helicopter officials in a brief ceremony November 8, 1967, presented the U.S. Army with the 5,000th production Huey. By the end of the decade, the Bell plant developed and flew the industry's first attack helicopter, the Model 209 AH-1G HueyCobra. Its first mission in Vietnam took place October 8, 1967.[35]

Bell's continuing success brought the need to expand still further. In the Fort Worth area by late 1965 Bell operated eleven facilities covering 1,421,731 square feet of enclosed space, but this was not enough. At the Amarillo International Airport, site of the former Amarillo Army Air Field in World War II, Bell opened a ninety-acre facility that became a major helicopter modification overhaul and repair center, and an airframe manufacturing plant. In 1979, Bell opened two sales divisions in Canada—Calgary and

Huey helicopters moved off the assembly line in 1964 when the Hurst plant produced at full capacity during the Vietnam War. *Photo courtesy Bell/Textron, Inc.*

Ottawa—as well as three in the United States, in Fort Worth, Philadelphia, and Van Nuys. Three more followed quickly in Atlanta, Chicago, and Denver.[36]

Helicopter sales to foreign countries soon brought in added revenue, which while welcome, sometimes presented problems. The Shah of Iran purchased five hundred helicopters in the late 1970s and hired Bell to send people to train Iranian pilots to fly them. When the 1979 Iranian revolution took place, Bell official Jim Atkins made the decision to pull all U.S. Bell employees out of the country. As the company expanded sales worldwide, Bell Helicopter Textron's motto became "People the World Over Depend on Bell Helicopter." International sales in 1980 topped $300 million, and officials began talking of a "three-pronged" business with $300 million in sales in each of the categories: commercial sales in the United States and Canada, foreign sales, and U.S. military sales. These figures turned out to be overly optimistic as sales in all three categories in 1984 totaled $672 million. However, when Bell delivered its 25,000th helicopter, a Model 222 on January 18,

1981, company officials noted that Bell had manufactured more helicopters than all other companies in the free world combined. The company created Bell Helicopter Asia in 1983 as a new branch to sell to Southeast Asia. Facilities consisted of a headquarters, marketing office, warehouse, and parts distribution center. Press releases noted that two-thirds of all helicopters in Southeast Asia were Bells. Bell also signed an agreement to create Korea Bell Helicopter Company in mid-1986. Also in 1986, the company agreed to move production of its 206B Jet Ranger and 206L Long Ranger production lines to Mirabel, Quebec, north of Montreal.[37]

Local growth continued alongside foreign expansion. Bell gave up the Globe facility in Saginaw in January 1989 and moved its operations to a 256,410 square foot building at 2900 West Seminary Drive in South Fort Worth. The plant was 40,000 square feet larger than the Globe plant.[38]

Bell's first twenty-first-century project—the V-22 Osprey that lifts like a helicopter and flies like an airplane—was a long time coming. Early in 1951 the Navy named Lockheed and Convair co-winners of a competition for a prop jet, vertical rising airplane, the dream of aviation engineers for some time. Lockheed's design was the XFV-1, which could fly straight up, level off for a high-speed flight and come back down vertically. When their experimental model was tested, however, it never flew vertically. The Lockheed-Convair project never got beyond their prototype. Bell, however, was working on what they called a "convertiplane" as early as 1953. A later Convair model, the XYF-1, took off on November 2, 1954, as test pilot J. F. Coleman in San Diego, California, flew vertically, shifted to horizontal, and then changed back to vertical to land. Three months later, Bell unveiled its XV-3 Convertiplane in February 1955, tested it in its first official flight in August, but announced no target date for being able to convert from helicopter to airplane in flight. Not until 1958 was Bell's Army XV-3 able to achieve full conversion by tilting rotors while in flight, the first aircraft of its type to do so.[39]

Bell never gave up, but other aviation manufacturers continued experimenting as well. The Curtiss-Wright X-19 VTOL transport flew successfully for the first time on June 26, 1964, in a series of short-duration tests. Dallas's Ling-Temco-Vought (LTV) on December 29, 1964, conducted successful first-flight tests of their XC-142A V/STOL transport aircraft that could take off and land vertically. Hawker Siddeley's operational VTOL jet aircraft became the British Royal Air Force's Harrier airplane in the 1970s. However, with no competition, the Navy awarded a Bell-Boeing consortium a preliminary design contract in April 1983 for an experimental plane-helicopter, the V-22. Then on May 2, 1986, the Navy approved a $1.714 billion fixed-price incentive award for a seven-year full scale development of the V-22 in a joint project between Bell Helicopter Textron Fort Worth and Boeing Vertol Company, Philadelphia. Including government-furnished equipment and support, the price tag would total $2.5 billion. The V-22 was to be called the Osprey. The two companies' presidents, Leonard M. (Jack) Horner of Bell and Joseph Mallen of Boeing Vertol, issued a joint statement: "The V-22 establishes American preeminence and leadership in a new and extremely valuable aviation technology that combines the vertical life efficiency of a helicopter, with the high-altitude, high-speed cruise of a turbo prop airplane." The V-22 could carry twenty-four combat-equipped troops in the world's first production tilt-rotor aircraft.[40]

The two companies divided production duties with Bell responsible for the V-22's wings, nacelles, transmissions, rotor and hub assemblies, and integration of the government-furnished engines. Boeing Vertol would develop the aircraft's empennage, overwing fairings, fuselage, and avionics integration. Put simply, Bell built the wings and Boeing the fuselage. Subcontractors Allison and Grumman provided the engine and the tail, respectively. Each would assemble three prototypes, with the first flight planned for June 1988.[41]

The first V-22 Osprey flew on March 19, 1989, in its helicopter mode for a fifteen-minute flight at Bell's Flight Research Center in Arlington. Bell President Jack Horner called the flight "one of the greatest aeronautical accomplishments in the last 40 years." The V-22 flew in airplane mode six months later on September 14, 1989, changing from helicopter mode to airplane mode while in flight. Then on April 25, 1990, a smaller version, the XV-15 prototype, gained approval to fly to Washington, D.C., to allow members of the Aviation Subcommittee of the House Public Works and Transportation Committee to view its performance. The committee was interested in civil applications of tilt rotor technology. Officials from NASA, the FAA, and Bell and Boeing testified before the subcommittee hearings. Congressman Jim Wright, who had worked with Bell/Boeing and the Navy to help get the V-22 contract, enjoyed being present that day at Bolling Field in Washington, D.C., when the first test model of the Osprey arrived from New York, flying across the Potomac River. "What we were establishing was that the Osprey was a revolutionary concept and could fly from New York to Washington, D.C. in forty minutes for commercial application. To fly, you spend a lot of time in traffic to get to the airport. It takes too much time. The Osprey would save time because it could land in a small space," Wright said.[42]

Since the first tilt-rotor helicopter in 1957—the XV-3—it had taken nearly four decades to develop the successful V-22. What took so long? Bell President Webb Joiner in 1997 explained:

A low weight engine with enough power was needed. Weight is so sensitive. No engine with low enough weight could give the power. Finally, composite technology allowed us to build a lighter plane. . . . .It is difficult to express how far the technology [of the helicopter] has gone in the thirty-five years I have been here. It has gone almost from the Model T to the space age since the 1950s. . . . Helicopters had one little radio on board. Half a century later, half the cost consists of sensors. The helicopter is a flying laboratory. We started fifty years after the airplane, but we are on a par with the aircraft industry. . . . Compared to airplanes, helicopters are a tiny little company. . . . The V-22 will change the industry. There will be a few [people who] still will want old helicopters, like on a ranch.[43]

A Marine Air Station near Jacksonville, North Carolina, deployed the first combat squadron of Bell tilt-rotor V-22 Ospreys, called MV-22s, in September 2007. After twenty-five years of development, Bell, in the spring of 2008 received a $10.4 billion contract for 167 V-22 Ospreys at a cost of $80 million each. An Air Force version also would be built. Military orders promised the company production until 2012. (Military contracts always become subject to cuts and changes, however.) The Bell Osprey took part in major combat operations for the first time on December 4, 2009, in Afghanistan.[44]

Other than the work on the V-22 Osprey, by the 1990s four major helicopter manufacturers in the U.S. competed for government contracts— Bell, Boeing, McDonnell Douglas, and Sikorsky. "Teaming" became the future of the industry. Joiner explained that even further than teaming with other U.S. companies, "Today you have to have relationships with other countries, Korea, etc. and let them build part of it. You have to help finance. It is the future. It's very complicated, very complex."[45]

Attempts to analyze the economic and social impact of Bell Helicopter on the Fort Worth-Mid-Cities community are limited here to snapshots of particular times. By September 1954, Bell's annual Texas payroll was $17 million. A Bell publication at the time estimated that the company's 4,000 employees could support 568 businesses (including 273 retail), twenty-seven physicians, four clinics and a hospital, twelve dentists, forty-one attorneys, twelve cleaners, five laundries and washaterias, two dairies, thirty-five churches, eleven public schools, a liberal arts college and a business college, twenty insurance offices, seven contractors, nine plumbers, four bakeries, two banks, four optometrists, thirteen parks, a newspaper, three radio stations, six theaters, and nineteen beauty and barber shops.[46]

Over its first five years in Texas the company reported paying a total of

Two Air Force CV-22s Ospreys fly over downtown Fort Worth in 2008. *Photo courtesy Bell/Textron, Inc.*

$75 million to its employees and $20 million annually to various vendors and subcontractors, many locally. In Texas, 750 companies were doing business with Bell, with 380 of them in the immediate area. Also in its first five years, the company sold $188 million in aircraft and parts. The company quickly emerged as Tarrant County's second-largest employer.[47]

In the next two decades Bell grew to prominence in the field. By 1960 over a dozen companies with a combined payroll of over $26 million had followed Bell into the Hurst area. With Bell's $18 million a year payroll, that was a combined total of $44 million going into the local economy. In Bell's first decade in active production in Texas, 1951–61, the company spent more than a quarter of a billion dollars for wages and purchases. More than 3,000 persons were on the company payroll in 1961, and by 1967 payroll totaled $80 million a year and an additional $110 million was paid to local subcontractors. Bell, in the mid-1970s, briefly became the biggest employer in the county; the rest of the time its rank usually remained second to the defense plant west of the city.[48]

In the early twenty-first century, Bell completed its "first new helicopter designed for the civil[ian] market . . . . since the mid-1970s." The Bell 429 twin engine made its flying debut in February 2009 with sales beginning a few months later. It is aimed at "air ambulance users, law enforcement, and corporate and off-shore transportation services." Consequently, in the new century the company has employed 10,000 people, with as many as 6,600 in Tarrant County.[49]

Local pride in Bell Helicopter's accomplishments came early. In a speech on the floor of the U.S. House of Representatives in November 1971, Fort Worth's congressman at the time, Jim Wright, pointed out that on more than $1 billion worth of military contracts, Bell had fulfilled its obligation each time "below negotiated cost." More bragging rights came when Australian Dick Smith left Bell's Hurst plant on August 5, 1982, on a leisurely solo flight around the world by helicopter. He stopped at many places on anniversaries of famous flights. When he arrived back in Hurst on July 22, 1983—the fiftieth anniversary of Wiley Post's completion of the first around-the-world flight by fixed wing aircraft—Smith became the first pilot to make a solo flight around the world by helicopter and the first to fly a helicopter solo across the Atlantic. He flew a Bell Jet Ranger III single-engine on his 35,258-mile flight. Nor did reasons for pride end there. Bell CEO Webb Joiner in the mid-1990s explained that the number of helicopters produced by Bell was about equal to the number produced by the rest of the world combined. At that time he noted that Bell sales to non-U.S. government customers represented about 57 percent of those helicopter sales. "As an aerospace producer in the metroplex, Bell has generally always been the second largest defense contractor in the county," he said. (Lockheed-Martin and its previous owners have consistently ranked first).[50]

A few cities across the United States have enjoyed the economic boost of a large defense plant: Marietta, Seattle, San Diego, and Wichita, among others. By hosting both Bell and Lockheed Martin, Fort Worth joins with Los Angeles in having more than one major installation. More than half a century after Larry Bell chose the Fort Worth area for his helicopter plant, local job holders can be grateful that the young airplane enthusiast did not give up aviation as he once intended. Fort Worth's aviation history would have been very different without Larry Bell and Bell Helicopter.

CHAPTER 10

The Sound of Freedom: Carswell and Beyond

ORT WORTH ARMY AIR FIELD (FWAAF) ENJOYED AN opportunity available to few others: remaining open during the years immediately following World War II. FWAAF, which became Carswell Air Force Base in 1948, continued as an important part of the front line of defense during the Cold War. Pilots and airmen of Carswell distinguished themselves by breaking records and accomplishing several flight firsts. By the time FWAAF became Carswell, local citizens were accustomed to noisy airplane take offs. The B-36s and B-32s left from World War II soon became B-58s, F-111s, and F-16s. Locals equated those roaring exhausts to sounds of freedom, because, while still FWAAF, the base became part of the Eighth Air Force in the new Strategic Air Command (SAC) created on March 21, 1946.[1]

The military brought General Curtis E. Le May back from Europe to head SAC at Andrews Army Air Force Base in Maryland for two years, and then in November 1948 moved the command and Le May to Offutt Air Force Base (AFB), Nebraska. Le May explained the purpose of the Strategic Air Command: "Its mission was to serve as a deterrent against the enemy—a deterrent against nuclear warfare—a striking force so efficient and so powerful that no enemy could, in justice to his own present and future, attack us—through a sneak assault, or any other way." The idea of SAC became so well known that Paramount movie producers brought eighty members of a film crew to Fort Worth for two weeks in April 1954 to make a movie called *Strategic Air Command*. The movie, starring Jimmy Stewart and June Allison, featured the B-36. The movie's story concerned reserve officers called back into service during the Korean War. Stewart, himself an Air Force colonel in World War II, played a highly paid baseball player recalled to active duty.[2]

Many other military changes took place after World War II that affected the air base west of Fort Worth. Career officers from the Billy Mitchell days of the 1920s and 1930s still were using their influence to push for a separate branch for the Air Force. They wanted one department of defense with three separate, but equal branches: Army, Navy, Air Force; the Navy, however, especially opposed the idea. After the war President Harry Truman showed that he had been listening. In a special message to Congress on December 19, 1945, he proposed a single department of defense, explaining that "strategy, program and budget are all aspects of the same basic decision." A month later in his State of the Union address Truman repeated his request.[3]

One of the long-time backers of a separate air force, Lieutenant General Ira C. Eaker, a native Texan and the deputy chief of staff of the Army Air Force, was visiting Fort Worth Army Air Field on July 26, 1947, when news came that President Truman had signed the National Security Act of 1947, creating the National Security Council, the Central Intelligence Agency, the Department of Defense, a permanent Joint Chiefs of Staff, and a Department of the Air Force. General Eaker commented to the local press: "that's the wisest measure to pass Congress since colonial times," adding that unification of the military branches would "greatly promote efficiency and economy of national defense." President Truman appointed W. Stuart Symington as the first secretary of the Air Force and named General Carl A. Spaatz to be the first chief of staff of the Air Force. James V. Forrestal became the first secretary of defense.[4]

The official separation of the Army Air Forces from the Army came on September 18, 1947, subsequently proclaimed as Air Force Day. For the first time, President Truman presented a consolidated budget for the entire defense organization. However, as the new system developed, each of the three military branches insisted on having its own aircraft under its own command. Rivalry and budget requests continued to create problems. The new Air Force immediately changed the airplane letter designations the Army Air Forces had used in World War II from *P* for pursuit to *F* for fighter. Then in 1949 Air Force personnel, including of course those in Fort Worth, took off their army uniforms and adopted the new Air Force blue.[5]

As a direct result of the National Security Act's passage and creation of the separate Air Force, all Army Air Fields that remained open changed their names. Fort Worth Army Air Field became Fort Worth Air Field after the separation became official. The new Air Force quickly decided to name its air bases after heroes of World War II who had died in airplane accidents. Consequently, Brigadier General Roger Ramey, commander of the Eighth Air Force at Fort Worth Air Field, learned on January 19, 1948, that the field's new name would be Griffiss Air Force Base in honor of Lieutenant Colonel Townsend Griffiss. Colonel Griffiss, a member the Eighth Air Force, had been one of the first U.S. airmen to die abroad in

World War II. British forces accidentally shot down his plane over southern England on February 15, 1942, as he was returning from an important mission to Russia. The military posthumously awarded Griffiss the Distinguished Service Medal. Many longtime Fort Worth residents may be unaware that the base once bore the name of Griffiss AFB, since the name lasted only two weeks.[6]

Local citizens along with their congressman, Wingate Lucas, contacted Washington with the plea: "change the name to Carswell; we have our own World War II hero." Born July 18, 1916, in Fort Worth, Horace S. Carswell Jr. grew up in the north side where his father worked at the Fort Worth Stockyards. At North Side High School the popular young man played football, worked on the annual staff, and dated lots of girls. After attending Texas A&M for a year,

Major Horace S. Carswell, who grew up in Fort Worth, flew B-24s in the China theater in World War II. He received the Congressional Medal of Honor for his selfless action on October 26, 1944, which resulted in his death. *Photo courtesy of Dalton Hoffman Local History Collection.*

Carswell returned to Fort Worth where he worked part time while taking classes at Texas Christian University (TCU), majoring in physical education, and again played football. He graduated in 1939, and in March 1940 enrolled in pilot training school. He became an instructor at Randolph Field, San Antonio, and was one of the first officers sent to San Angelo in January 1941 as a flight instructor when the Army Air Field was activated. In San Angelo Carswell dated a girl he met earlier at TCU, Virginia Ede. They married in October 1942 and their only child, Robert Ede Carswell, was born the following September. Carswell became a captain in January 1943 and in April a major. He left for the Pacific Theater early in 1944 as operating officer of the 508th Bomb Group in the Fourteenth Air Force.[7]

Two particular flying missions highlighted his distinguished career. On October 16, 1944, he flew a B-24 Liberator—perhaps built in Fort Worth—and located a convoy of Japanese ships in the China Sea, moving toward Formosa (now called Taiwan). His crew dropped bombs that blew up a

5,170-ton cruiser, which folded in the middle and sank in just a few minutes, after the bomb apparently hit the cruiser's powder magazine. After the cruiser sank, Carswell turned back for a final run over a destroyer, and the bombardier dropped three more bombs. As Carswell headed the B-24 home, the men saw the destroyer sinking. The military called this "one of the notable bombing exploits of the war."[8]

Having had such tremendous success on October 16, Major Carswell was anxious to repeat the experience. Thus, eleven nights later on October 26, 1944, he and a different crew made a one-airplane strike against a twelve-ship convoy in the South China Sea on a bombing run at six hundred feet. On a second low-level run thirty minutes later, Major Carswell's crew scored two direct hits, but a hail of steel from the Japanese ships struck the four-engine B-24. The resulting flak knocked out two engines completely, damaged a third, punctured one fuel tank, and crippled the hydraulic system. The hits wounded the copilot and destroyed the bombardiers' parachute. Because the B-24 barely could make 125 miles per hour, the men threw out their remaining ordnance to lighten the load. Major Carswell guided the crippled airplane toward land, but the third engine failed as he reached solid ground. He ordered eight of the crew to bail out and hoped to limp home with his two remaining crew members. However, he did not have the power to get over the mountains; the B-24 crashed and burned as it struck a mountainside. The crew members who had just bailed out heard the explosion and saw the flames. Carswell and his wounded copilot perhaps could have bailed out, but they were trying to get the B-24 back to base for the bombardier, Second Lieutenant Walter W. Hillier who, without his parachute, could not jump. Charles F. Thompson, an Army Air Corps second lieutenant who once flew with Major Carswell in the China theatre, later commented on the flight that took his friend's life:

> In my opinion, there were not more than a handful of pilots that could have kept a B-24 from crashing into the water after losing two engines at only a 400-foot altitude. Carswell gained altitude by feeding in the throttles to the maximum point of the engines, all the time working the flaps up and down to gain lift and air speed, level out and repeat the procedure time and time again, sometimes gaining as little as 20 feet at a time," he said. "The procedure must have been exhausting—but the man could really fly.[9]

The government posthumously awarded Major Carswell the Congressional Medal of Honor, Distinguished Flying Cross, Distinguished Service Cross, Air Medal, and Purple Heart. His Medal of Honor citation read: "With consummate gallantry and intrepidity, Major Carswell gave his life in a supreme effort to save all members of his crew. His sacrifice, far beyond that required of him, was in keeping with the traditional bravery of America's war heroes." Carswell became the first Fort Worth man to receive the Medal of Honor, the nation's highest military award; and, in fact, he was the only Congressional Medal of Honor winner in the entire Fourteenth Air Force during the war.[10]

Years later at Memorial Day ceremonies in 1951 at Carswell's gravesite in Rose Hill Cemetery in Fort Worth, Amon G. Carter said, "He sacrificed his life rather than abandon a helpless comrade." Local Congressman Wingate Lucas said, "we borrow from his fame, that we may be reminded and that succeeding generations may know of his valor, so our children will learn of the heroism exhibited by one who had lived here in this city." Yes, Fort Worth had its own World War II hero.[11]

The Air Force announced on Thursday, January 29, 1948, in Washington, D.C. that the name of the Fort Worth base would be changed from Griffiss AFB to Carswell AFB. The city of Fort Worth needed about a month to plan a dedication and invite Major Carswell's widow and four-year-old child to Fort Worth for ceremonies held Friday, February 27, 1948, at the newly renamed base. Congressman Lucas flew in from Washington, D.C. to attend. The Air Force transferred the name Griffiss AFB to the Rome Air Depot at Rome, New York, to honor Lieutenant Colonel Griffiss, who actually was from New York State.[12]

The very first B-36 bomber for the Strategic Air Command rolled off the Convair assembly line in June 1948. Colonel Alan D. Clark, Seventh Bombardment Wing Commander, and Major General Roger M. Ramey, Eighth Air Force Commander, accepted it for Carswell on June 26. That particular airplane later was designated *City of Fort Worth* on July 22, 1949, and a plaque was placed on its nose to that effect. Carswell extended its main north-south runways to make them two miles long to handle the massive B-36s that kept arriving. Only two groups—the Seventh and Eleventh Bombardment Groups of the Eighth Air Force—could fly the big bombers known to be able to go "anywhere, at anytime," and both groups were based at Carswell. The B-36 truly became Fort Worth's airplane. The Eighth Air Force in 1949 was the only military organization in the world capable of dropping the atomic bomb. Its presence in Fort Worth brought a great deal of publicity to the city—as well as money. Payroll for the 5,000 officers, airmen, and civilians, as well as other local expenditures, brought the local economy more than $1 million per month.[13]

The U.S.A.F. Seventh Bombardment Wing at Carswell flew and maintained the B-36s during the Cold War. Created October 1, 1919, as the First Army Observation Group, the designation changed to the Seventh Bombardment Group on March 26, 1921. They served in three theaters in World War II—Asia, the Pacific, and the Middle East. After the war the military reactivated them at Fort Worth Army Air Field on October 1, 1946, and the unit became the Seventh Bombardment Wing on November 10, 1947. The men in the wing and their families remained on a continuous twenty-four-hour alert from 1948 to 1958.[14]

As part of training, B-36 crews periodically launched practice attacks on various unsuspecting U.S. cities. They also made training flights to overseas locations. To provide a larger area for Cold War training, SAC authorized a search for over 80,000 acres in Crockett and Val Verde counties in the Big Bend area of Texas to lease for a bombing range for the Eighth Air Force based at Carswell.[15]

Despite the unification of the military branches under the Department of Defense, rivalry between them continued. Battles in Congress over appropriations affected the B-36 airplanes that the Carswell crews flew. The Navy wanted money for a new aircraft carrier, and the Air Force requested expansion of the B-36 Peacemaker, the long-range bomber that had been planned early in World War II. The Navy claimed that the B-36 could never fly 10,000 miles without being refueled, and it also said that the B-36 was too big, too slow, and an easy target, calling it a "billion dollar blunder." Of course, the Air Force answered back that a huge aircraft carrier was like a "sitting duck" and only air power could protect the United States during the Cold War. Meanwhile, the Navy began lobbying Congress to cut funding for the B-36. In light of this controversy, Major John D. Bartlett, commander of the 436th Bomb Squadron at Carswell, had an idea late in 1948 as the seventh anniversary of the Pearl Harbor attack neared. He hoped his plan would assist the Air Force in their battle with the Navy. Why not fly one of Carswell's new long-range B-36s to Pearl Harbor and back on a secret trip to prove that it really could fly to a far away target and return to Carswell without refueling? Also, he wanted to see if they could sneak up on the Navy, which would require flying at 25,000 feet, above the Navy's radar, once they reached Hawaii.[16]

Through classified communications up the chain of command, Bartlett contacted SAC commander General Le May at Offutt AFB, and Le May gave his permission. "The Mission: To carry a simulated bomb load to Pearl Harbor on 7 December 1948 and be overhead at approximately the same time that the Japanese bombers had struck 7 years earlier." Major Bartlett and others wanted to prove the capability of the B-36 in order to boost the Air Force's position in requesting more long-range bombers.[17]

Captain John A. Harrington of the Seventh Bomb Group piloted the B-36 on its secret mission. Knowing the gasoline supply would be very

In May 1958 Carswell celebrated ten years of service for the B-36 while at the same time welcoming the new B-58s that were replacing it. The B-36 Peacemaker never dropped a bomb in anger, but rather "kept the peace." *Photo courtesy Lockheed Martin.*

tight, he fueled the airplane at the end of the runway—rather than near the hangar—to save gas. Three men—Major Bartlett, Captain John A. Harrington, and Lieutenant Colonel Howard Hugos—took turns flying three hours on and two hours off. It would be the first time the B-36 flew with its maximum designed gross weight of 329,000 pounds. In fact, the B-36 was a ton and a half over limit, but the crew did not realize this until the trip was all over. They added a fuel bladder with 3,000 gallons of gas in the number three bomb bay, but they also carried 10,000 pounds of bombs. They took life vests and rubber rafts as well. The crew worried whether the tires would hold up with the heavy load and how takeoff would proceed. Leaving on December 6, 1948, they filed no flight plans, did not notify Air-Sea Rescue teams, and cut radio contact. They did not want to give the island an advance notice of their intentions. When the B-36 reached Pearl Harbor on December 7 undetected, the crew took radar photographs to prove that they were there. After dropping their bomb load in the ocean, they headed home, but one engine went out. The pilots could not sleep on the two hours they were supposed to be resting because of the noisy engine. The sixteen-man crew returned to Carswell after flying 8,000 miles in thirty-five and a half hours without landing.[18]

Other Carswell personnel had no idea about the mission until it was all over. When the airmen returned, however, the news spread rapidly throughout the base as residents celebrated having caught the Navy napping. The radio operator kept logs of the trip and recopied them neatly to turn over to General Le May at SAC headquarters. The Air Force Public Affairs people let the Navy and local Hawaiian newspapers know what the Fort Worth-based crew had done; however, because the B-36 trip embarrassed the Navy, the latter squelched news of the trip, and it did not receive much media coverage. "It raised a few eyebrows in Washington, but it did not get as much publicity as we wanted because it embarrassed too many people," became the disgusted conclusion at Carswell. Perhaps the trip brought good results for Carswell and the Air Force, however, because the secretary of defense canceled the Navy's plans for their super carrier in favor of funding the B-36. The Air Force won that round. The battle was not over, however. A group of Navy officers defied regulations and precipitated some well-planned and well-publicized Congressional hearings. Called the "revolt of the Admirals," the Navy officers' tactics attacked the B-36 program, calling it worse than worthless. The Navy felt slighted. Their "revolt" eventually paid off, when naval aviation gained funds for a carrier program.[19]

Postwar cuts and retirements left many crews and maintenance teams shorthanded, so the Air Force began transferring airmen among units. Racial segregation, however, remained the standard practice. Because the Air Force was a separate branch, they believed they could act on their own. Therefore, three months before President Harry Truman, issued his Executive Order 9981 on July 26, 1948, directing desegregation in the Armed Forces, the Air Force announced its intention to integrate. Their plan took a year to implement, so it was in May 1949 when the 332nd Wing, an African American group under Colonel Benjamin Davis Jr., disbanded, and the men were reassigned to white Air Force units.[20]

Within SAC, General Le May instituted a new rule: Each time a commander suffered a major accident in his wing, he had to make a trip to

Offutt AFB to see Le May about it. When news spread that each commander so "invited" received the stripping down of his life, accidents dropped from sixty-five per 100,000 hours in 1948 to three per 100,000 hours nine years later.[21]

Strict measures and success created pride. Airmen in SAC, including those at Carswell, knew that they were winning the "Big War—the One Which Didn't Have to Be Fought—purely because of the existence and might of SAC." Carswell's B-36 obviously was not called the Peacemaker lightly and proved to be a major part of SAC's success. In the early postwar era, bombers in the Strategic Air Command possessed the capability "to obliterate" the most remote spot on earth within hours. One SAC crewman remarked, "You can get the feeling that you're playing games for real, Hide-and-Seek, I Spy, Red-Rover-Come-Over, King-of-the Mountain, Monopoly, any one or all of them." Each B-36 crew was assigned secret targets behind the Iron Curtain, usually an industrial complex or a military base. Airmen studied pictures of their designated marks. "We know more about our targets than we do about our own home towns," one pilot said. Such crews trained at Carswell and two other U.S. bases.[22]

Most Fort Worthians did not realize that included in Carswell's serious war games were thirteen concrete boxes holding nuclear bombs that sat in a field due west of Carswell and Convair. On 445 acres, at a cost of $175,000, workers constructed concrete bunkers, or igloos, for the nuclear bombs that a B-36 carried. Moving the bomb loads to the bunkers through approximately half a mile of residential subdivisions presented a problem that personnel successfully managed. Residents may have wondered at the contents of closed trucks, but they had become accustomed to much military activity, and thus paid little attention. Other ammunition storage also conformed to the safety requirements of the Armed Forces Explosive Safety Board for ordnance storage. How Fort Worthians might have reacted to having such instruments of mass destruction in their midst can only be imagined.[23]

During the Cold War, SAC officials intended to be ready. Perhaps they remembered a statement by General George Kenney, the first commander of SAC and the Air Commander in the southwest Pacific in World War II. Kenney had said, "Having a second-best Air Force is like having a second-best poker hand. It was fine for bluffing, but no good if called." Through the efforts of the Strategic Air Command crews at Carswell, and elsewhere, the United States had no intention of being second best.[24]

Several famous SAC flights, besides the trip to Pearl Harbor, originated at Carswell consisting of crews stationed there. None was more celebrated than the flight of the *Lucky Lady II*, a B-50 Superbomber—an overgrown B-29—of the Forty-third Bomb Group. The propeller-driven, medium bomber made the first ever nonstop around-the-world flight. Captain James Gallagher headed a fourteen-man crew that left on February 26, 1949, and returned on March 2 after covering 23,452 miles in ninety-four hours and one minute. KB-29 tankers of the Forty-third Air Refueling Squadron refueled the B-50 four times in the air—over the Azores, Saudi Arabia, the Philippines, and Hawaii. The speed during the flight averaged 249 miles per hour. Two men held each crew position so that they could relieve each other at the controls. The Air Force called it "a training maneuver designed to test the capabilities of the aircraft from an engineering standpoint, the feasibility of air-to-air refueling, and the efficiency of the Air Force communications network." Waiting at Carswell to greet the crew when the B-50 touched down on its return were Secretary of the Air Force W. Stuart Symington, Chief of Staff Hoyt S. Vandenburg, and SAC Commander General Le May. Each crew member later received the Distinguished Flying Cross for being part of the first combat aircraft flight to make a nonstop trip around the world. Symington praised the flight as a means to ensure "against the contingency that suitable overseas bases might not be available at the outset of any future hostilities."[25]

Only a few days after the successful flight of the *Lucky Lady II* —and while its crew were still bragging—another crew flew a B-36 on a trip of 9,600 miles without refueling. Even longer than the secret trip the previous December to Hawaii and back, the B-36 made a big circle across the United States from coast to coast a couple of times. Their route went from Carswell to Minneapolis; Great Falls, Montana; Key West, Florida; Houston; Fort Worth; Denver; back to Great Falls; Spokane; back to Denver; and then returned to Fort Worth. Captain Roy Showalter piloted the B-36 with a crew of twelve. The first time B-36s actually landed on foreign soil came in January 1951 when six of the huge Peacemakers flew to England and then returned to Carswell.[26]

All was not record flights and clear skies at Carswell, however. Bad weather created problems on at least two occasions, and accidents occurred. Major General Roger Ramey and his base saw floodwaters isolate Carswell from the city of Fort Worth in April 1949 as the Clear Fork and West Fork of the Trinity River both overflowed their banks. Muddy floodwaters compromised their base water supply, and General Ramey rationed what they had stored in overhead storage tanks. He ordered several hundred airmen to help evacuate Liberator Village residents using a crash boat and several rubber life rafts. He sent trucks from the base to help pull partly submerged trailers from the Lazy Land Trailer Court on White Settlement Road, and placed thirty or forty civilians in the base hospital. Carswell personnel also provided blankets, cots, food, and shelter for those left homeless by the floodwaters.[27]

A serious accident involving a B-36 occurred on September 15, 1949, when one of the big airplanes lost power as it roared down the runway at 100 miles per hour preparing for takeoff. Ground personnel noticed flames shooting from one engine and the B-36 lifted off but then dropped back to the ground. The pilot tried to brake, could not stop in time, and the huge aircraft splashed into Lake Worth. "The thing looked like a huge winged fish slithering into the lake," related J. M. Crump who lived on the lake across from Carswell. Others described it as a "dying whale with its mouth open, gasping for air." The tail was four stories high, but after the B-36 sank, only a tip of several feet stuck up out of the lake. Five men died in the crash. Navy divers and an Eighth Air Force salvage crew towed the bulk of the main hull and the broken left wing to shore with tractors and winches. They did not locate the nose section until a month after the crash.[28]

Carswell and the Strategic Air Command B-36s remained so important to the security of the United States that damages from a severe tornado at the base placed the entire country in danger. Newsman Bob Considine later reported that the Labor Day tornado at 6:42 p.m. on September 1, 1952, made the United States "vulnerable." He wrote: "If Russia had opened the active end of its oblique war against us, with atomic attacks on U.S. cities, we could not have retaliated with enough of our intercontinental B-36s, a premise on which a great deal of the security of the 155 million Americans (and the rest of the free world) is based. We had no B-36s to speak of." Considine may have exaggerated the situation somewhat, but the tornado damages were serious. Another writer described the effects of the 91–125 mile per hour winds when the giant airplanes were "lifted like toys and hurled into each other." The winds destroyed one $3.5 million B-36, damaged 76 others at Carswell and 35 more at Convair. The air base and the defense plant shared the same runway, so the huge Peacemakers were parked near each facility. The tornado destroyed or damaged other smaller aircraft, and one hangar collapsed at Carswell. The government released no information about the damage until workers completed enough repairs to make the United States safe again. The Air Force flew six hundred technicians to Carswell to reconstruct the damaged B-36s, and Convair hurried up its next deliveries to the government. Authorities placed Air Force personnel on seven-day workweeks and twelve-hour workdays to begin the clean up and repair. Within thirty-three days after the tornado, fifty-one of the damaged airplanes were operational, and some new deliveries had arrived. Secretary of the Air Force Thomas K. Finletter called it a "remarkable achievement."

Early estimates of damage totaled $50 million, but actual damages came in at only somewhat more than $23 million. Some Air Force personnel wondered why Russia had not attacked and assumed the Russians lacked either the atomic bombs to drop or the bombers to carry them such a distance, or else their spy system was so weak around Carswell that they had never really known the severity of the damage. The general public had no idea how many B-36s the Air Force owned so did not know that the tornado rendered almost half of the Strategic Air Command's B-36s out of service, if only temporarily. Thankfully, only one person was injured severely enough during the tornado to require treatment at the base hospital. By May 1953 the military reported seventy-five of the seventy-six damaged B-36s back in service. Thereafter, when severe weather threatened, commanders at Carswell ordered pilots—well ahead of any storm—to fly the airplanes to safer bases such as Biggs AFB at El Paso or Davis-Monthan AFB near Tucson, Arizona.[29]

Occasionally security-related excitement caused extra activity at Carswell. One day a report came in to the Fort Worth police and base security that an unidentified person took pictures outside the wire fence near the restricted aircraft and maintenance areas. Authorities sent bulletins with the man's description across Texas and to four other states asking security personnel to be on the lookout for him. Later, the scare died down when the photographer turned out to be a soldier on the base who said he was new to Carswell and was just taking pictures to send home to his family. One area of Carswell, called the "white area," was so secret that it was censored out of all photographs, thus the name. It was inside a third barbed-wire fence where the crews trained to fly B-36s. No one could enter the "white area" without top-secret clearance. To get inside, an airman had to pass through three guard gates and be physically recognized by the Air Police. A corporal on duty once refused to admit the base commander because he had never seen him. He called another guard who knew the commander and let him in.[30]

Some classified events at the base happened weeks before news leaked out to the public. A B-36 from Carswell flew to Eniwetok Island in the South Pacific for a test of a real hydrogen bomb, dropping it on November 1, 1952. A B-36 with a "specially selected" maintenance crew and flown by a "super-selected" team made the "top-secret mission." Although the bomb bay doors received a fresh coat of paint before leaving Carswell, when the B-36 returned from its non-stop flight, the bays were "blackened, scarred, and blistered." The Atomic Energy Commission announced the tests on November 16, but gave little information. A *Fort Worth Star-Telegram* reporter, late in January 1953, learned of the flight and that the B-36 had picked up the bomb in a western state at the start of the mission.[31]

A bit less dramatic, but secretive and important nevertheless, was a scenario the Strategic Air Command initiated in October 1953 to test base security. SAC Headquarters at Offutt AFB in Omaha, Nebraska, sent a team of one officer and four airmen to Carswell pretending to be enemy agents. Once at Carswell they were to try to reach a B-36 and "theoretically" sabotage it. One of the men swam from a location on the civilian side of the base to try to reach a Carswell site on Lake Worth, but security guards frightened him off. Only one "agent" managed to get inside the base, but guards apprehended him just as he reached the flight line. The pretend agents' instructions were simply to leave a prearranged mark on a B-36 to show that someone could get close enough to sabotage it. The security personnel passed the SAC test because they caught all five of the interlopers. Actually, SAC ran such tests periodically, so Carswell personnel always had to be prepared.[32]

A dog patrol helped guard Carswell and protect its Strategic Air Command secrets. Called the Sentry Dog Section, the German Shepherds, each with their own human handler, began guarding Carswell in October 1955. After eight weeks of training at Camp Carson, Colorado, the dogs learned to attack at their handler's order. If possible, the dogs remained with the same handler until retirement and trusted only that handler. In 1960, three six-dog squads patrolled restricted areas. "When I am on guard duty at night, I would rather have my dog with me than a .45," stated Airman Second Class Vernon Guy, whose five-year-old dog was named Rex. The dogs, always on leash while on patrol, responded to hand signals as well as verbal ones.[33]

A new security program installed in 1954 involved considerably more expense than a dog patrol. Over 10 percent of the $5 million the Air Force spent that year went for a contract with Paschall-Sanders Construction Company to install radar gun sites to protect Carswell. An antiaircraft battalion armed with 75-millimeter radar-controlled Skysweeper rifles sent nearly 400 men from Colorado Springs to Fort Worth to operate fifteen of the radar guns. A new program called the USAF Continental Air Defense Command (CONAD) began on September 1, 1954, as a joint effort between the Air Force, Army, Navy, and Marine Corps. With this new equipment made up of five towers, Fort Worth housed the only installation in the Southwest capable of destroying an enemy bomber if it approached. The equipment could detect low-flying enemy aircraft fourteen miles away and get its gun into position. After the alarm sounded the gun crews could quickly begin firing radar-aimed 75-millimeter shells every one and a half seconds. The antiaircraft radar protection, located seven miles northwest of Fort Worth, scanned the sky constantly. Called the Five Texas Towers, the equipment completely encircled Carswell and gave Fort Worth and Convair protection with their full strength of fifteen guns. A crew of eighteen officers, 333 enlisted men, and four warrant officers made up the personnel of the 546th Antiaircraft Artillery Battalion, the Skysweeper Battalion, under the supervision of Lieutenant Colonel William A. Brinkerhoff. Many local Fort Worth residents remained completely unaware that this system existed, although local landowners had to provide sites for the guns. The military deactivated the 1954 system three years later when a Nike Missile protection system replaced it.[34]

In June 1955 a major change took place when military officials transferred the Eighth Air Force headquarters away from Carswell, where it had been located since 1946, to Westover AFB in Massachusetts. The Air Force reasoned that bombers needed to defend Europe could reach their targets more quickly from New England than from Texas. Thereafter Carswell came under command of the Second Air Force with headquarters at Barksdale AFB near Shreveport and Bossier City, Louisiana. Also in June 1955 the new B-52 made its first appearance on SAC bases, including Carswell, eventually replacing the B-36 and B-47 as the Air Force's mainstay bomber. B-52s were refueled in the air and could circle the globe without stopping, making it the workhorse of the Strategic Air Command. Eighteen KC-135 Stratotankers called "flying gas stations" based at Carswell serviced the B-52s. After over thirty years of service thirty-one B-52s resided at Carswell in 1987, and the airplane "remains the world's foremost strategic bomber."[35]

A special Memorial Day ceremony and Open House on May 30, 1958, honored the last Fort Worth-built B-36 with the announcement that the B-36 was being retired after exactly ten years of flying at Carswell. The new B-52s had been arriving all spring. At the B-36's retirement ceremony Lieutenant General C. S. Irvine, Deputy Chief of Staff for Materiel, USAF headquarters, said, "The B-36 is the first major weapon system of our time to accomplish its purpose and be retired—without having fired a shot in anger. It kept the peace." Pundits enjoyed telling the story that even though the B-36 never dropped a bomb in anger, it did drop something by accident. A fifty-pound airspeed calibration instrument dangling from a long cable came loose during a 1946 test flight of the original XB-36. It crashed through the roof of a Fort Worth elementary school and destroyed a toilet in the boys' rest room![36]

While the transition from B-36s to B-52s at Carswell seemed to go smoothly, at least one crew told quite a bumpy story. Six crewmen and three instructors left the base at 2 p.m. on October 21, 1958, and the giant, eight-jet B-52 bomber radioed "Mayday, Mayday" seven minutes and forty-seven seconds later. Although only a light rain had been falling in Fort Worth when the airplane left the base, the B-52 flew into a severe hailstorm

YB-52. *Photo courtesy United States Air Force via Don Pyeatt.*

twenty-five miles southwest of Carswell at 8,000 feet. Thunderstorms had been predicted for areas south of Fort Worth, but the men planned to turn west and then north to avoid them. However, just ten miles south of Carswell they encountered baseball-sized hail that smashed the windshields, knocked away the protective radar housings, punctured the wings and engine nacelles, and knocked out their airspeed indicator. The crew saw aluminum flying off the battered engine nacelles and did not know how long the engines would continue to function. They prepared to bail out. The battering lasted only forty-seven seconds before they found an opening in the clouds and climbed to 23,000 feet to assess the damage. The control tower located a KC-135 jet tanker returning from Waco and radioed it to find the B-52 over Mineral Wells and check out the damage. Later, back at Carswell, the B-52 circled for a time to burn up excess fuel to lighten the airplane before attempting a landing. The KC-135 flew in tight formation with it and continually reported its airspeed. At one point the B-52 flew low on the ground so that ground crews could look for damage to the underside. They found none, and the B-52 landed safely.[37]

In 1958 a new airplane arrived on the scene to challenge the B-52. The B-58, known as the Hustler, was the world's first supersonic bomber and capable of flying at twice the speed of sound. It began rolling off the runway at the General Dynamics (formerly Convair) aircraft plant next door and arrived on the flight line at Carswell August 29, 1958, to begin testing and evaluation. Eventually Carswell pilots would be trained to fly it. The Air Force requested a $29.6 million appropriation for ground support equipment at Carswell because of the new B-58. The Air Force had asked for forty-seven Hustlers, but Congress cut the initial number to thirty-six because of design changes that increased the cost.[38]

Just as with the B-36s and B-50s, a Carswell crew set a new record in the B-58 when a crew from the Forty-third Bomb Wing flew a B-58 from New York to Paris on May 26, 1961, in three hours, nineteen minutes, and eighteen seconds, cutting the existing world record in half. The flight commemorated the thirty-fourth anniversary of Charles Lindbergh's solo flight over the same route, which took thirty-three hours and thirty-two minutes. The Carswell crew averaged just over 1,089 miles per hour, and called their plane *Spirit of St. Louis II*. They won the MacKay Trophy awarded annually by the Air Force Chief of Staff for the "most meritorious" flight during the year. During its decade of operational service with SAC, B-58 crews established nineteen world speed and altitude records and won five of aviation's major trophies, two of them twice.[39]

Surprisingly, General Le May did not like the B-58. Apparently Le May was very pro-Boeing and favored keeping the B-52 rather than switching to the B-58. In fact, a worker in Fort Worth's General Dynamics plant said that people who worked in Fort Worth nicknamed the Boeing factory in Hutchinson, Kansas, "Le May's Barn" because it built the B-52 and he so favored it. One stated objection to the B-58 was that it was "the most costly and complex airplane which had ever been produced in quantity." Its three-man, tandem crew consisted of the pilot, navigator-bombardier, and defense system operator; there was no copilot. Another complaint was that it could not carry enough fuel to be long range like the B-36. "People who flew the plane, though, liked it," said Convair's long-time test pilot B. A.

YB-58. *Photo courtesy United States Air Force via Don Pyeatt.*

Erickson. "It was absolute pure joy to fly." The cabin noise level was low. The cabin stayed at room temperature and was free of noticeable vibration, riding smoothly even in turbulence. Despite the fact that General Le May did not like the B-58, Fort Worth's new congressman, Jim Wright, helped get legislation approved for more of them. However, even after Congress appropriated $525 million, Le May refused to spend it.[40]

In order to challenge Le May's dislike Wright decided to take a ride in it himself. He obtained permission from the Secretary of the Air Force, Eugene M. Zuckert, and declared his ride to be the most exciting thing that happened to him at Carswell, all the generals he met there notwithstanding. As a two-star general in the Air Force Reserve himself, he apparently was more impressed by airplanes than by generals.[41]

Carswell's pilots flew the B-58 for nine years, from 1961 to 1970. Like the B-36 and B-47 before it, it never saw combat duty. Teamwork between Carswell and the airplane factory to the west of the runway worked well through the years. The plant built B-24s, B-32s, B-36s, and B-58s up through the 1960s, and the military base next door taught young men to fly them. Three to four hundred Convair employees worked fulltime at Carswell in the early 1960s, jointly studying problems and making suggestions to the base personnel who kept the various airplanes flight ready. A new airplane came on the scene by the end of the 1960s, the FɪɪɪA that General

Dynamics built and Carswell personnel flew. The 240th Bomb Group received their first F111A in 1969.[42]

Carswell crews participated fully in the Vietnam War as the Seventh Bombardment Wing with its B-52Fs carried out many flying missions against targets in Southeast Asia. From September 1963 to March 1964 Carswell crews launched consecutively nearly 400 B-52s on time in Vietnam without a delay of more than five minutes. The Seventh Bomb Wing maintenance crews averaged seventy-two hours per week on the flight line regardless of the weather. A fleet of KC aircraft also had to be kept at the ready to handle refueling operations for the B-52s. The base remained prepared at any moment for an Operational Readiness Inspection (ORI), and the object, of course, was capability to go to war at any moment. Five crew members of a Carswell B-52 downed in Vietnam were held captive in Hanoi for a time. When all bombing in Vietnam ceased in August 1973, Carswell's crews returned home the next month. Although the end of the war meant less activity for the base, it still did have to cope with the conservation alert in place because of the 1973 oil crisis.[43]

Toward the end of the decade, in 1977, another new airplane rolled off the assembly line next door at General Dynamics; Carswell pilots began flying the F-16. General Dynamics had built, and the Air Force now flew, an airplane that would last them well into the twenty-first century.[44]

Despite challenges such as the oil embargo, building and expansion remained a constant through the years at the military base. Texas's congressional representatives fought for appropriations that would favor Fort Worth and Carswell. On April 15, 1950, Senator Lyndon B. Johnson of Texas and Fort Worth's local congressman, Wingate Lucas, each telephoned Raymond Buck, president of the Bucco Corporation, to inform him that the U.S. government had certified his company to receive a $5.2 million contract to construct six hundred units of rental housing on Highway 183 near Carswell. The units would include two- and three-bedroom houses for officers and enlisted men's families, with rents ranging from $62 to $115 per month.[45]

A major expansion program began at Carswell in late 1952 that included a 3,300-foot extension to the runway and a large hospital. The Army planned a hospital on the West Coast, the Navy on the East Coast, and Carswell's in Texas would belong to the Air Force; personnel from all three branches could use any of them. The military planned other construction projects, including a hangar large enough to hold six B-36s, dormitories, dining halls, a service club, and a warehouse, but when Congress cut back the appropriations, some projects had to be postponed. The runway extension was a priority, however, because the B-36s needed more space. Carswell's 7,200-foot

The top of this photo is west. Lake Worth lies to the north of Carswell on the right edge of this picture. *Photo courtesy United States Air Force via Don Pyeatt.*

runway received a 3,300-foot extension to the south, giving the big bombers two miles of 300 feet wide of heavy concrete on which to take off and land. Unfortunately, for those in its path the extension would take over a dozen homes, force the closing of a portion of White Settlement Road, and require the moving of White Settlement Cemetery.[46]

Base expansions anywhere have their critics and Carswell was no exception, and owners of private land sometimes lost out. The eminent domain provision in the U.S. Constitution allows the government to take over private property, often bringing complaints like the one of a man whose one-half acre of land fell in the path of Carswell's runway extension. The farmer was so unhappy that he wrote a letter to President Dwight D. Eisenhower. He complained that he made his living off the land and had already lost $1,000 by not planting his crop after getting a letter that the government wanted his land. "I served my time in world war two and got a disab[ility]. I don't think it is right the way the government is doing us people."[47]

Ultimately, Congress restored enough appropriations for $10 million worth of construction and expansion to be completed at Carswell by the end of 1954. The Corps of Engineers spent $7.26 million on runway aprons, increasing the thickness of the concrete, an additional runway extension to

11,500 feet, and on a large maintenance hangar that could hold four B-36s. The rest of the money was used to build two barracks, a mess hall, a vehicle maintenance shed, five dormitories, and two combination dining hall and administration buildings.[48]

Construction at the base continued throughout the later decades of the twentieth century. Groundbreaking took place on March 22, 1983, for a new $8.2 million 116,000 square foot commissary building that would have retail grocery space, offices, and a warehouse. Plans called for the new commissary to be completed by August 1984. Military spokesmen wisely advised the public that the money would come from a surcharge paid by patrons and other non-appropriated funds, and would not require additional money from taxpayers. Support facilities for Carswell in 1988 included living quarters of various styles for military personnel, with long waiting lists for airmen to get into them. No guest housing was available. There was a day-care center for small children, and school-age children attended classes in nearby local schools. Twenty-five colleges and universities operated within reasonable commuting distance from Carswell. The Robert L. Thompson Strategic Hospital served over 300,000 outpatients annually as it cared for active duty and retired personnel and their families. Only San Antonio supported more Air Force retirees living in its area than Fort Worth. Congressman Jim Wright believed that many retired locally because Fort Worth fully welcomed the military.[49]

Carswell personnel and their families found many activities available when off duty. The base football team, the Bombers, organized games with other air force bases, and there was a horseback riding club. Service men and women also enjoyed enlisted and officers clubs, an eighteen-hole golf course, a twenty-lane bowling alley, and a recreation center with arts and crafts areas.[50]

Although the *Carswell Sentinel*, a local weekly newspaper, was unofficial and not published on the base, it supplied news of activities to base personnel and retirees. The newspaper listed social events, touring performers, softball games, bowling, photography contests, a "Miss Carswell" contest, basketball, hunting leases, as well as providing classified ads, other advertising, and a forum for comments from Carswell's commander when he wanted to communicate with everyone.

An Air Force base like Carswell made up a close-knit community with common goals. The Air Force planned it that way. An airman's wife received instruction on making a congenial home, raising a family her husband would be proud of, and generally doing things to strengthen her husband's morale. She was urged to volunteer her time in projects for the benefit of her husband's unit and in youth activities. A book written espe-

Carswell's large hospital was constructed in the early 1950s. After the base closed temporarily in 1993, the hospital later became a federal facility for women prisoners. *Photo courtesy Naomi Stewart.*

cially for wives cautioned, "It is said that domestic troubles have killed more aviators than technical or mechanical failures or low ceilings, so as an Air Force wife your responsibility is great." Of course, these instructions had to be modified as more and more women entered the military. In the twenty-first century Air Force a voluntary "orientation for spouses" offers counseling and other services available.[51]

In 1988 Carswell was home to the Nineteenth Air Division, the Seventh Bombardment Wing, the Seventh Combat Support Group, and an Air Force Reserve unit—the 301st Tactical Fighter Wing. In addition, there were other tenants. As the 1990s began at Carswell, base personnel cooperated in the Persian Gulf War (comprising military operations Desert Storm and Desert Shield). At the time Carswell still housed the largest B-52 wing in SAC. Virtually every wing unit deployed personnel in support of Desert Shield and then, as of January 1991, Desert Storm, with a total involvement of 800 airmen (or women) who played an important role in the war's battles. Wing maintenance and personnel remaining at Carswell supported the Seventh Bomb Wing's efforts.[52]

Little did Fort Worthians and Carswell personnel suspect that all this activity was about to change. A base closing commission that Congressman Dick Armey of Denton, Texas, helped create began studying how to operate the military more efficiently. Texas Senator Phil Gramm also supported the idea of base closures, arguing that it was difficult to have enough money to train troops properly while maintaining excess military bases. Gramm said the choice was between "technology and military personnel" and that we could not keep putting "our money into mowing the grass and guarding the fences at outdated facilities." When Secretary of Defense Dick Cheney began announcing bases that were candidates for closure, North Texans really did not expect to see Carswell on that "outdated facilities" list. After all, a lot of money had just been spent to completely renovate the off-base housing; the base complemented the production of airplanes at the plant next door—General Dynamics, and Carswell still had a job to do training pilots to fly the airplanes General Dynamics built. Nevertheless, on April 12, 1991, Carswell made the list of the fourteen bases initially cited for closure.[53]

The Base Realignment and Closure Commission (BRAC) final report recommended that thirty-four bases be closed and forty-eight realigned. The president and Congress accepted its recommendations with the Base Realignment and Closure Act of 1990. Other Texas closures included Bergstrom AFB in Austin and Chase Field Naval Air Station in Beeville. The Naval Air Station at Grand Prairie in Dallas County later closed as well. From 1988 to 2001, the Base Realignment and Closure commission reduced the total military personnel by 35 percent, saving $3–4 billion a year. The closing of Carswell represented the end of an era for Fort Worth. Considering the many name changes, a military base existed on that site since 1942.[54]

While the Ninth Bomb Squadron celebrated seventy-five years of history in June 1992, their contingent at Carswell expected the group to deactivate when the B-52s left Carswell at the end of the year. In conjunction with the reorganization and consolidation efforts the Department of Defense decided to "disestablish" the Strategic Air Command. After thirty-four years SAC was "standing down" because the Cold War was over. "We realized we are one of the reasons why the world is now a safer place,"

Captain Chris Potter, a Seventh Air Refueling Squadron aircraft commander, said on hearing the news. Changes in the Soviet Union were one of the reasons for ending SAC, the rest were economic, according to Secretary of Defense Cheney.[55]

The Seventh Bomb Wing, which had been stationed in Fort Worth since 1946, lowered its command flag on September 30, 1993, ready to move to Dyess AFB in Abilene. Their B-52s already were operating there. The airmen did not all move to Dyess, however, but were dispersed to various assignments. Carswell thus officially closed on September 30, 1993. This meant that the community lost the jobs of 4,660 military personnel and 880 civilian positions. On October 1, 1993, the Air Force Reserve's 301st Fighter Wing assumed base protection and responsibilities. When Carswell closed, federal and city officials scrambled to find an alternate use for the base's large hospital. The federal government ultimately chose to transform it into a prison hospital for women beginning in July 1994.[56]

Carswell's closing made a tremendous economic impact on the local area. The base held land in three communities as 58 percent of the base was in Fort Worth, 34 percent in Westworth Village, and 8 percent in White Settlement. In addition, other nearby communities—Benbrook, Lake Worth, River Oaks, Sansom Park, and Westover Hills—experienced decreased retail and housing sales. As devastating to the community as the loss of more than 5,000 personnel was the domino effect of those losses on businesses such as grocery stores, restaurants, movie theaters, car dealerships, and department stores. Ridgmar Mall just south of Carswell saw a drastic drop in shoppers, and several smaller stores closed. Spending in the zip code that included Ridgmar Mall dropped dramatically in 1991, 1992, and 1993 because of the transfer of so many Carswell personnel.[57]

The impact of the closure on the larger Dallas-Fort Worth Metroplex was not as devastating as it would have been in the 1950s or 1960s when the city depended more on military expenditures. A great deal of economic diversification had taken place in the more than three decades since then. The closing of Carswell and the knowledge that it was gone saddened many residents who had been closely involved with the base or its people. An entire generation matured in Fort Worth, especially on the west side, with the idea of Carswell's pilots and crews protecting the skies. They attended school with children of Air Force families. Residents of other parts of the city, however, experienced little change in their lives. Although the situation in Fort Worth was disappointing, the city fared better than others like San Antonio, where multiple base closings would have a larger impact.[58]

Consumer spending in the western suburbs of Fort Worth increased for a bit in 1994–95 but dropped again from 1996 to 1998. To attract more customers, Ridgmar Mall's owners spent $470 million on a facelift unveiled in 1999. Local residents soon flocked back to the mall. Studies revealed that in 1996–97 137,000 retirees and dependents, representing 37 percent of all retired military in the United States, lived in western Fort Worth, and it was one of the top three military-retirement cities in the nation, all of which were in the Sun Belt. As a sign of the aging population in the areas of Tarrant County once dominated by the military, United States Census records for 2000 revealed that fewer families in White Settlement had children than just a decade earlier. In 1990, 29 percent of families had children, but by 2000 that figure had dropped to 21.5 percent. The percentage of residents 65 or older increased from 11.6 percent to 12.4 percent during those years. The total population of White Settlement in 2000 stood at 14,831, down from 17,801 a decade earlier. Obviously, the closing of Carswell in 1993 produced a profound effect.[59]

After Carswell closed, local leaders, including Fort Worth Mayor Kay Granger and Congressman Pete Geren, who had replaced Jim Wright, had an idea based on a late 1980s Pentagon report on developing a military reserve base. In 1993 Granger and Geren pitched the idea to Defense Secretary Les Aspin that a reserve base could help with preparedness for future wars. In late 1993 and 1994 the Air Force Reserve's 301st Fighter Wing remained the only unit occupying the base. Geren and Granger at least hoped to persuade the Base Realignment and Closure Commission to keep the wing in Fort Worth. Under BRAC authority Congress later directed that the nation's first joint reserve base, a base for all military reserve branches, be established at the former Carswell AFB. The efforts of the two politicians had paid off.[60]

In 1994 Carswell made history as the only military base closed by the BRAC cutbacks to reopen, although under different jurisdiction. Because of the closing of the Grand Prairie Naval Air Station southwest of Dallas, the military decided to relocate some of its personnel to Fort Worth and reconstitute the former Carswell as a Naval Air Station. The official name became Naval Air Station Fort Worth Joint Reserve Base. An abbreviated form of the new name, NAS Fort Worth JRB, appeared on new signs and the reorganized base officially opened October 1, 1994. The 301st maintained jurisdiction until September 30, and the base officially had been closed for only one year. The 1,800-acre base became the center for training 8,000 reservists from the Navy, Marine Corps, Army, Air Force, and Texas Air National Guard, providing the military's first experiment in such a joint facility. More than 3,000 people acquired fulltime jobs, representing less than half of the 7,200 active duty personnel stationed at Carswell in the late

1980s. However, over $75 million in needed construction projects revitalized the new joint reserve base in the following months.[61]

Congressman Geren persuaded local people and military officials to retain the name Carswell Field for the airstrip at the base to preserve the memory of Major Horace Carswell. Commander Mark Danielson designed a memorial—an eagle with its wings extended, standing on the center section of a three-blade B-24 Liberator propeller in a concrete pedestal. Deran Wright sculpted it, and a marble plaque on it honors Carswell. Geren spoke at the dedication ceremony in February 1995 when officials unveiled the memorial at the main operations building and tower. Major Carswell's son Robert Carswell, who lived out of state, saddened that the base named to honor his father had closed and then reopened with a new name, did not attend the dedication of the memorial.[62]

Once the Navy assumed control of the base, they worked carefully to make it a joint base. The former Carswell Club became Desert Storm because all branches of the service had participated in the 1991 Gulf conflict. Later the name was changed to Lone Star Center and Western decor added to stress the base's Texas location. The commander invited retirees of all branches to come and eat at the club. The base's renamed streets represented all service branches as did static airplane and helicopter displays along the main entrance roadway. Many local Fort Worthians remained disappointed that Carswell closed and were not reassured initially when NAS Fort Worth JRB took its place one year later. Finally, by the early twenty-first century they could hope that the base's joint responsibilities would make future closures less likely. The Joint Reserve Base drew reservists from the thickly populated fourteen-county North Texas area, including the Dallas-Fort Worth Metroplex with its population of 6.5 million people a decade into the twenty-first century. In addition, reservists traveled to the Joint Reserve Base for maneuvers from as far west as Midland-Odessa and as far south as Houston.[63]

Environmental issues became a new concern at the base toward the end of the twentieth century. In the 1940s both the air base and the aircraft manufacturing plant had allowed toxic chemicals to soak into the ground indiscriminately. Maintenance crews at Fort Worth Army Air Field during World War II, and early crews at the Carswell base did not realize that oil, cleaning solutions, and other toxic chemicals would harm underground water systems if routinely dumped. Carswell officials learned as early as June 1954 that they needed to be careful of the "hazards arising from the disposal of volatile liquids" and began to be a bit more careful, but damage to the ground environment already had been done.[64]

Because the Air Force was the service in charge of Carswell when the damage took place, the Air Force became responsible for the cleanup, even after the Navy assumed jurisdiction of the base. With additional appropriations the Air Force hired private contractors to use the latest techniques to extract the chemicals from the soil and monitor progress. An Air Force Commission on Environmental Excellence (AFCEE) handled the cleanup and in 1995 created two citizens groups in the local community so they could communicate the progress of the cleanup. These committees were called Restoration Advisory Boards (RAB), and one was created for Air Force Plant 4 (the manufacturing plant) and one for the former Carswell. Almost immediately the two separate RABs were combined into one, and its citizen-members met quarterly with AFCEE officials and the contractors who were doing the environmental cleanup. Toward the end of the first decade of the twenty-first century, the cleanup was progressing smoothly, and some areas became safe for use again. As crews completed cleaning an area, the Environmental Protection Agency signed off on them as safe. For example, the area west of Carswell and Plant 4, where huge concrete bunkers had stored nuclear weapons, eventually was sold to builders for a housing development. By the end of 2009, most areas had been cleared, and RAB activities began winding down.[65]

After the attack on the World Trade Center and the Pentagon on September 11, 2001, and America's war on terrorism began, NAS Fort Worth JRB for a time was practically locked down. Even retirees could not reach the commissary, pharmacy, and post exchange, and these operations soon opened off base. Some complained that the base enforced security "tougher than at most other bases across the country," but base commander Captain Stephen McMullen said he was following instructions "to the letter."[66]

Local citizens gradually became aware that the reopened military base in Fort Worth represented one of the most important in the nation as a combined reserve base for all the services as well as for the Texas Air National Guard. The roar of airplanes flying overhead represented no less the sounds of freedom than when B-36s, B-52s, and F-111s flew over Carswell, although the Navy pilots flew F-14 Tomcats, an airplane designed in the 1960s, and later, F-18s. NAS Fort Worth JRB, in addition to its reservist activities, fulfilled functions that Carswell once performed such as providing a runway for test flights of aircraft produced next door at Lockheed Martin.[67]

Obviously, a military base, whether it supported the Air Force or the Navy, located adjacent to the factory that built the airplanes it flew brought a great deal of revenue to the city of Fort Worth and its suburbs. However, analyzing the specific economic impact of Carswell and the Naval Air Station on the area is difficult. One broad observation that may be made with certainty is that military and defense spending became the largest industry and together employed the most people in Fort Worth and Tarrant County during the last half of the twentieth century. While Fort Worth remained Cowtown, all those cattle over at the stockyards began dwindling; the yards finally closed in 1992.[68]

Carswell's early statistics offer a good idea of what such installations can mean to the areas around them. At a time when privates made $100 per month and generals $1,000, the monthly payday at Carswell in October 1950 put approximately $1.5 million into the local economy. In addition, a purchasing agent for the base buying only necessary items, such as medicine, paint, office supplies, vehicle parts, and food spent $3 million per year. The Fort Worth Chamber of Commerce in December 1953 estimated that "at least 70 percent" of the $33 million local military payroll would be spent in Fort Worth. The monthly payroll for Carswell in 1956 was $2.25–2.5 million, which supported 7,700 officers and airmen with their wives and children as well as civilian employees—more than 19,500 people all told. By June 1960 conservative estimates revealed that Carswell put $42.6 million into the local economy annually, including salaries and operational costs. Approximately 350 Fort Worth firms did business with the base or its personnel or families that year. The base spent $216,455 monthly for goods and services. At that time Carswell had a total population of just more than 26,000. In 1978 the Defense Department reviewed Carswell's operations as a part of its Air Installation Compatibility Use Zone (AICUZ) program. At that time the base employed about 15,000 military or civilians and generated a $68.1 million annual payroll and more than $200 million impact on Tarrant County. Both inflation and salaries had increased.[69]

A 1983 *Guide to Military Installations* again reminded readers of benefits beyond the financial. It emphasized that the history of the Strategic Air Command and its accomplishments paralleled the history of Carswell Air Force Base with its famous record-breaking flights and important defense mission. In that year Texas ranked second among the states with the most military bases, Carswell being one of the most important. In 1984 the *Carswell Sentinel* estimated that active duty and civilian employees at the base, plus retired military and U.S. Air Force Reserves at Carswell spent $15 million each month in the local economy. The monthly payroll in these four categories was nearly $22 million. A decade later the newspaper estimated that the 26,732 military retirees in the area brought $1.4 billion into the Metroplex economy with their jobs, purchasing power, taxes paid, and the domino effect of their presence. The number of military retirees equaled the number of employees at Lockheed. Because the commissary reopened in March 2008 after being closed for fifteen years, more economic activity took place on base. The North Central Texas Counsel of Governments in its ranking of its sixteen-county region cited the three top employers as Lockheed Martin, 13,500; American Airlines, DFW, 11,709; and NAS Fort Worth JRB, 11,350 in the first decade of the twenty-first century.[70]

After Captain T. D. Smyers became the eighth commander of NAS Fort Worth JRB in 2008, the North Texas native pointed out that the total population again reached the number stationed at Carswell when it closed. He oversaw about 11,000 people, who at various times worked at NAS Fort Worth JRB, civilian employees, 2,200 active and 6,200 part time reservists. The current base of 1,800 acres, however, is only two-thirds the size of Carswell because the government disposed of property before the military made the decision to create the naval air station. During his tenure Captain Smyers has seen steady growth in new buildings and renovations, added military units, and active participation in the wars in Iraq and Afghanistan. Although NAS Fort Worth became the first joint reserve base, it presently is one of several nationwide. Captain Smyers planned and hosted a two-day Air Power Expo at the base April 16-17, 2011 celebrating the centennial of U.S. naval aviation, the biggest air show ever held there. In the base newspaper the *Sky Ranger* after the show he reported that "It exceeded my expectations in terms of both attendance and awesomeness." Captain Robert Bennett became the ninth commander of NAS Fort Worth JRB in a change of command ceremony July 15, 2011.[71]

The west side military installation provides protection against its foes for Fort Worth and America with its continuous military training. The thundering roar of airplanes taking off from the Naval Air Station's Carswell Field, heading across Lake Worth and circling the city, reminds residents daily that the sound of freedom owns the skies over Fort Worth.

CHAPTER 11

Air Force Plant 4: General Dynamics to Lockheed Martin

ONTINUOUS OPERATIONS AT THE AIRCRAFT MANUFACTURING
facility west of Fort Worth that began as the "bomber plant" in
1942 meant stability and jobs for the area; however, the tenants
leasing the Air Force's Plant 4 changed several times. For the first twelve
years it was Consolidated Aircraft Corporation, which became Consolidated Vultee and later Convair. Then the newly renamed General Dynamics
acquired Convair in 1954. With $371 million in sales in 1953, the purchased
company actually was a larger business than its purchaser, which acquired
only $206 million in sales the previous year. Company officials decided that
the name Convair would be retained, at least for a time.[1]

A year earlier, General Dynamics had been known as Electric Boat.
Founder John Phillip Holland in 1900 sold the U.S. Navy its first work-
able submarine, an odd-looking vessel fifty-three feet long that became the
world's first successful submarine. Electric Boat then sold many submarines to the U.S. Navy through two world wars. Lawyer and financier John
Jay Hopkins, head of Electric Boat in 1947, realized that a permanent defense industry could be profitable after World War II, and he convinced the
board of directors to acquire Canadair Ltd., of Montreal, the largest aircraft
manufacturer in Canada. The company changed its name to General Dynamics Corporation in April 1952 because Electric Boat no longer applied
to a company that also built airplanes. In 1954 after the Convair purchase,
General Dynamics consisted of the Electric Boat Division in Groton, Connecticut, with 6,500 employees; Canadair Ltd. of Montreal, with 11,000;
Electro Dynamic Division of Bayonne, New Jersey, with 400; and Convair
with 45,000 in San Diego and Fort Worth.[2]

With the acquisition of Convair, General Dynamics could do research
and develop products for all the related fields of the U.S. defense program.
Hopkins called it "Dynamics for Defense" and reorganized the company's
areas into hydrodynamics (submarines), aerodynamics (airplanes), and nu-

cleodynamics (missiles.) General Dynamics even launched a program in 1955 to build the *Nautilus*—the world's first nuclear-powered submarine. Even before General Dynamics (GD) bought Convair, the Fort Worth factory had won out over Lockheed to become the first aircraft plant in the nation to do research for a nuclear-powered bomber. One-third of Convair's employees worked on the nuclear airplane program from 1951 to 1952, but they got nowhere. Then in the summer of 1955 Convair officials announced that a new special department would direct research and development of an atomic-powered aircraft. Two years later the company constructed a 578,000 square foot off-site engineering building on Montgomery Street on Fort Worth's near west side.[3] When Hopkins died in 1957 Frank Pace Jr., executive vice president and vice chairman of the board, and a former secretary of the army in the Truman Administration, took over as head of General Dynamics.[4]

The Air Force's Air Materiel Command at Wright-Patterson AFB in Dayton, Ohio, announced in November 1958 that GD had won a $2.5 million contract for the ongoing nuclear-powered aircraft program. A fenced-in area to the north of the actual plant building on the shore of Lake Worth became the new site for the program. Known as the Nuclear Aerospace Research Facility (NARF), the Air Force called it "the only facility of its kind." The program used a B-36H as the test airplane for which it attempted to develop the ability for an airplane to operate with nuclear power and to become a command post able to stay aloft for two weeks or more. The first test flight was on September 17, 1955. In all, forty-seven test flights took place, but only twenty-one with the nuclear reactor critical, meaning that a chain reaction was occurring. The flight crew did not activate the nuclear-powered turbine engines until the B-36H was well away from populated areas. By the late 1950s officials determined that the program was both too dangerous and impractical, and President John F. Kennedy officially canceled it in 1961.[5]

The Fort Worth plant of Convair/GD became a full-fledged operating division of the General Dynamics Corporation in May 1961, and at that time officially dropped Convair as part of its name. By then GD had nine divisions, building everything from submarines to missiles, rockets, and military and commercial airplanes. Very little aircraft manufacturing took place in San Diego anymore. In 1961 seven other aircraft companies competed with General Dynamics for military dollars: Lockheed, Republic, and North American, which were building airplanes for the Navy; Douglas, Chance Vought, and Grumman, also mostly Navy suppliers; and Boeing, almost exclusively an Air Force airplane supplier. General Dynamics and

Boeing soon began competing strenuously for a government contract for a new fighter airplane for the Air Force.[6]

President John F. Kennedy's Secretary of Defense, former Ford Motor Company executive Robert S. McNamara, wanted to use the cost-efficiency measures of private industry in the procurement of defense aircraft. He requested that the Fort Worth branch of General Dynamics and Boeing in Seattle design an airplane that both the Air Force and the Navy could use. Immediately, officials in both services balked. The Navy and Air Force had been competing for years for scarce defense dollars. A Navy airplane needed to be lighter and able to take off and land on the short distance of an aircraft carrier. An Air Force fighter bomber could be heavier, carry more equipment and bombs, and enjoy the luxury of a longer runway. A group called the Defense Systems Acquisition Review Council (DSARC, pronounced dee-sark), composed of assistant secretaries of defense of the various services, generally made decisions about which company's plans to accept. Before it did so, however, top military officers had an opportunity to argue their case before the council.[7]

Aircraft companies quickly learned that if they wanted to get contracts, it was in their best interests to hire lobbyists who were retired officers of the particular service branch whose contract the company wanted. A 1962 investigation demonstrated that the companies receiving 80 percent of Defense Department contracts collectively employed 476 retired officers above the rank of colonel or Navy captain. General Dynamics headed the list with 186 military retirees. If anyone was taking former President Dwight D. Eisenhower's 1961 warning of a military-industrial complex seriously, this situation might have warranted some intense evaluation.[8]

Both GD/Fort Worth and Boeing drew up plans for the airplane that was being called the TFX, for experimental tactical fighter. Three times during 1962 the top military officers recommended that Boeing be awarded the TFX contract. However, on November 24, 1962, the Department of Defense announced that GD/Fort Worth was being awarded the $439 million TFX contract. GD/Fort Worth was to work with Grumman Aircraft Engineering Corporation of Bethpage, New York, as principal subcontractor. The airplane would be the F-111.[9]

Boeing actually had submitted a lower bid, but Secretary McNamara overruled the Evaluation Group, the Source Selection Board, the Air Force Council, and the most influential officers of the Navy and Air Force when he gave the contract to GD/Fort Worth. The Secretary of Defense certainly possessed the authority to overrule and choose contractors, but it was unprecedented. Boeing officials immediately cried foul. Senator

F-III. *Photo courtesy United States Air Force via Don Pyeatt.*

Henry "Scoop" Jackson of Washington, where Boeing was based, asked for a Congressional investigation of the awarding of the contract. Idaho Senator James McClellan headed the subcommittee that handled the investigation. The committee continued in existence in two phases for seven years. Its final report attacked the foresight, motives, and integrity of officials high in the Kennedy Administration and the management of General Dynamics. The report condemned the program and disagreed with the entire concept of a common airplane for both service branches to use.[10]

McNamara in the beginning told Boeing and GD that commonality would be a factor. In the fourth evaluation of designs GD/Grumman presented one with 14,423 common parts that was 83.3 percent identical in Navy and Air Force planes. Boeing's plan possessed 18,653 parts and only 60.4 percent commonality between the two aircraft. Boeing also added some innovations to appeal to the military that the civilian service secretaries and McNamara viewed as untested and possibly a slowdown to the program. An example of this was titanium in the wing, whereas GD used aluminum and steel, tried and true metals. Boeing pleased the military, but their design offered risks. Analysts concluded that Boeing probably designed the best airplane, and so even though risky, the armed services favored it. General Dynamics/Grumman planned a safer, more cost-effective airplane, and McNamara's stress on thriftiness won. McNamara said, "I decided to select General Dynamics as the developer since I concluded that it was the best qualified to design the most effective airplane that could be produced at the least cost in the least time to meet our military requirements."[11]

Winning the contract to build the F-111 brought employment in Fort Worth's plant in 1967 to 28,000, its highest level in a decade. Two versions of the airplane were to be constructed: the Air Force's F-111A and the Navy's F-111B. However, with the controversy surrounding the program, the government cut back on orders, and it did not become the boon that GD had hoped it would. Some GD officials believed the company had not defended itself properly during the F-111 controversy. In 1968 the Navy opted out of the F-111B program and went with the F-14, which meant an abandonment of McNamara's major criteria of commonality. Despite the

The KC-135 above is refueling the F-22 below it in the air. *Photo courtesy United States Air Force via Don Pyeatt.*

F-16. *Photo courtesy United States Air Force via Don Pyeatt.*

long controversy over its selection, the 564 F-111As that General Dynamics produced served the U.S. Air Force nearly three decades, three times longer than either the B-36 or the B-58. The military officially retired the F-111 in August 1996.[12]

By 1968 several GD divisions besides Fort Worth and its F-111 faced financial difficulties. Electric Boat suffered cash flow problems; Canadair lost $10 million on cost overruns, and Bethlehem Steel—which GD had purchased in 1963—lost $240 million on fourteen ships for the U.S. Navy. When David Lewis arrived in 1970 as the new president and CEO of GD, he fired all but one of the eleven vice presidents and tightened operations. Those who knew Lewis well said that he did his homework and knew more about his managers' programs than they did themselves. He did not tolerate superficial preparation by his subordinates, intimidating employees by waiting silently for them to speak. He soon got busy acquiring contracts for each of GD's divisions. Then on February 10, 1971, Lewis announced that he was moving GD corporate headquarters from New York to St. Louis to provide easier access to major operating locations. (Apparently, Lewis agreed to leave McDonnell Douglas and assume control of GD if he could move the headquarters to St. Louis where he had lived since 1946.)[13]

Production of the F-111 declined in the early 1970s, with accompanying layoffs. Many people feared that the Fort Worth facility would close. Fortunately, building a prototype for a new airplane project promised more activity for the plant. The year 1975 was a turning point for GD's Fort Worth Division. A contest took place for a new fighter airplane for the Air Force that involved GD's YF-16 prototype and Northrop's YF-17 prototype that generated much competition during the "fly off" period involving test flights of each company's experimental model. An aeronautical engineer at General Dynamics, Harry J. Hillaker, has been called the "father of the F-16." He went to work for Consolidated in 1941 in San Diego, and the company transferred him to Fort Worth in 1942. He did engineering work on the B-36, B-58, and F-111 before tackling the YF-16 project. He got ideas from Air Force pilot Major John Boyd for the lightweight, highly maneuverable, and affordable fighter that the Air Force wanted. Boyd and other pilots secretly passed design concepts they preferred to Hillaker. A flyoff in 1974 between the two companies' models proved that Hillaker's was the better design. On January 14, 1975, the Air Force announced their choice of GD's lightweight fighter airplane, the F-16. Only five months later General Dynamics, with the support of the government, negotiated what they called the "Deal of the Century" when four NATO countries—Norway, the Netherlands, Belgium, and Denmark—agreed to purchase for their own air forces the F-16 rather than France's Mirage. Military analysts have called the F-16 "arguably the best military airplane of the jet age."[14]

President Eisenhower's 1961 comments about a "military-industrial-complex" apparently remained on some people's minds two decades later, for in February 1982 a *Chicago Sun-Times* article declared, "General Dynamics stands to become the military-industrial-complex's super contractor of the decade, dwarfing McDonnell Douglas Corporation, United Technologies Corporation, Boeing Company, General Electric Company, and Lockheed Company." The occasion for the comment apparently was General Dynamics' purchase of Chrysler Defense, Inc. (CDI) from Chrysler Corporation, making it GD's Land Systems Division. With that purchase GD became America's most important defense contractor, the only company to hold major, long-running multi-billion-dollar weapons contracts with *each* of the three military services: F-16 fighter planes for the Air Force, nuclear-powered submarines or sea-launched cruise missiles for the Navy, and M-1 tanks for the Army. Of all the GD divisions, however, Fort Worth consistently led the others in sales and profits.[15]

General Dynamics' competitors and those who wanted to cut government defense spending certainly could have labeled Fort Worth's Carswell Air Force Base and the adjacent aircraft manufacturing facilities as a military-industrial-complex. One definition of a military-industrial-complex is "an interwoven system of production comprising the Pentagon, the armed services, private firms, and political players." However, because of the economic boost to the economy and the numerous jobs provided, most Fort Worthians were unlikely to hold negative views of such an entity, nor complain to their elected representatives who had helped obtain the lucrative government contracts.[16]

Although the Fort Worth Division was not involved, fraud, perjury, and racketeering charges brought bad publicity for the entire company. In the 1980s the Justice Department and Congress began investigations of the submarine division of General Dynamics. Prosecutors argued that the head of the Electric Boat Division bid too low to get a government contract and that Electric Boat defrauded the Navy out of billions of dollars. The government dropped its case after four years when it could not prove the charges. Eventually the Pentagon recouped $244 million in disputed overhead by withholding progress payments on ongoing Navy defense contracts, fining General Dynamics $700,000, and suspending it from bidding on further Pentagon contracts. They lifted the suspension within six months. The company announced later that year that all further growth would be in the defense industry; they then sold some non-related divisions.[17]

By 1990 annual sales in all ten remaining divisions neared $10 billion, with 106,000 persons on the payroll. General Dynamics remained one of the largest defense contractors in the United States, and military aircraft accounted for one-third of its total sales. Fort Worth in 1990 was the only division still building complete aircraft and was in the second decade of its huge F-16 program. As of that year, sixteen nations had ordered F-16s, and three were assembling them on production lines, with others expected to do so in the future. Confirmed orders of F-16s as of 1990 totaled 4,163. With the F-16 GD finally found a winner. After thirty years of production, over $100 billion in sales, and more than 4,000 built, the F-16 remained in demand in the first decade of the twenty-first century as the mainstay of twenty-five nations' militaries. Orders of F-16 jets from foreign governments have kept coming in, extending production into 2015 or beyond.[18]

William A. Anders, a former astronaut, became CEO of the huge General Dynamics Corporation on January 1, 1991. Because the Cold War had ended, he believed military contracts would be more difficult to acquire in the future. Therefore, in 1993, he decided to break up the company and sell its individual components, which would increase the value of the stock. After learning of Anders's plans, Gordon England, head of GD's Fort Worth operation, called Ken Cannestra, head of Lockheed's Aeronautical Systems Group, and proposed that Lockheed purchase the GD fighter operation. Cannestra in turn recommended the idea to Lockheed's chairman Daniel N. Tellep.[19]

General Dynamics was already partnered with Lockheed in a proposed F-22 contract, so the purchase of GD's fighter would give Lockheed a two-thirds interest in the project. The F-22 Raptor was a stealth fighter that would replace the F-15 already in use. Cannestra and Tellep knew that GD's Fort Worth management and production methods were similar to Lockheed's. It possessed six hundred backorders for the popular F-16, and had the contracts to service and maintain the thousands of F-16s already in operation. Despite being near bankruptcy in the 1970s, in 1993 Lockheed was in a position of strength because of new government contracts, especially for the F-22, and it purchased GD's fighter aircraft division on February 28, 1993, for $1.2 billion. Lockheed was so meticulous about its integration into the Fort Worth operations that within six months the division was operating as if it had always been a part of Lockheed, according to Cannestra.[20]

Lockheed Aircraft Corporation was another one of the historic aircraft companies that began on the West Coast in the second decade of the twentieth century with young airplane enthusiasts. Two brothers, Allan and Malcolm Loughead—pronounced Lockheed—were born in Niles, California (now part of Fremont). Like Larry Bell, Glenn L. Martin, the Wright brothers, and many other young men at the time, the Loughead brothers became interested in airplanes. They built their first airplane in 1913, a hydroplane that flew sixty miles per hour on its first trial over San Francisco Bay.[21]

In 1916 when Malcolm was twenty-nine years old, and Allan twenty-seven, the two young men moved to Santa Barbara, California, and established the Loughead Aircraft Manufacturing Company in the back of a garage near the waterfront. Anthony Stallman became factory superintendent. They hired a quiet young man named John (Jack) Knudsen Northrop, a garage mechanic and architectural draftsman whose highest educational achievement was his graduation a few years earlier from Santa Barbara High School. Malcolm Loughead got a patent in 1919 on a four-wheel hydraulic brake and left the company. Jack Northrop left in 1923 to take a job with Donald Douglas, and eventually to start his own aircraft business.[22]

Left alone, Allan Loughead changed the spelling of his name to reflect how it was pronounced and in 1926 formed the Lockheed Aircraft Corporation with some new capital. In 1928 Allan moved the company to larger quarters in Burbank, California, but the company went broke in 1931. This ended the involvement of a Lockheed with the company. However, in 1932 a syndicate of young investors headed by Robert Gross, a thirty-five-year-old Boston banker, purchased the Burbank company, kept the Lockheed name, and began production. Their first airplane was a two-engine model called an Electra. Fortunately for Gross and his investors, aviation was an industry that not only did well but expanded during the Great Depression. In 1938, the Lockheed Company converted a Super-Electra into a bomber and sold two hundred of them to the British, who called them Hudsons. At the time this was the largest single order ever received by an American aircraft manufacturer. By 1939 the Lockheed Company earned an annual profit of $3 million, with 329 of their 356 total orders for military customers. As a portent of the future, the Lockheed Company became dependent on military contracts.[23]

In 1960 the four major aerospace companies that obtained government contracts worth one billion dollars or more were Lockheed, Boeing, North American, and General Dynamics (Convair's Fort Worth Division being a part of GD at that time). However, for most of the 1960s, Lockheed was the largest of the four. By the late 1970s U.S. aerospace companies were responsible for half the world's arms trade. Lockheed remained a part of this, as did General Dynamics' Fort Worth Division with its F-16. By the 1980s the four major aerospace companies were McDonnell Douglas, General Dynamics, Lockheed, and Northrop. They continued to be very dependent on Department of Defense contracts, and by the end of the decade most faced financial problems. It is no wonder, then, that they sought buyouts or mergers in the 1990s.[24]

After Lockheed's purchase of the fighter division of General Dynamics, Dan Tellep of Lockheed began planning a merger with Martin Marietta in 1994. He decided to present the offer to them as a "merger of equals." He realized that future government contracts would be fewer in number because of the end of the Cold War, and competition would be keener. This time, he chose to eliminate another competitor by merging with it. He believed his plan was necessary "to ensure preservation of critical defense assets and to insure the growth and prosperity of Lockheed shareholders and employees."[25]

Glenn L. Martin, original founder of the company that Tellep decided to court, had borrowed $800 in 1906 from a local bank to start his own garage. The next year he began to think about building airplanes with his mechanics at his garage doing the work. His first effort, a twelve-horsepower Model N Ford automobile engine bolted onto a glider, crashed on its first flight. Nevertheless Martin persuaded Santa Ana investors to put $100,000 into the Glenn L. Martin Company, which he incorporated on August 16,

1912, intending to manufacture and sell airplanes and hydroplanes. "The United States is far behind in military aeroplanes, but one of these days we will wake up and lead the other countries," Martin told the *Los Angeles Express* at the time. By 1914 one of Martin's employees was young Larry Bell. In 1916 the Wright Company of Dayton, Ohio, acquired Martin's entire California operation, forming the Wright-Martin Aircraft Corporation, with a capitalization of $5 million. Martin moved to Ohio and became vice-president in charge of all airplane production. In 1958 the company became the Martin Company, although Martin had died in 1955. In 1961 the Martin Company merged with the American Marietta Company, a cement and chemicals firm, resulting in the Martin Marietta Corporation, which phased out airplanes and concentrated on missiles and electronics.[26]

It was this Martin firm that Lockheed CEO Dan Tellep courted over thirty years later. Once Tellep contacted Martin Marietta's CEO, Norman R. Augustine, they kept their negotiations secret, although both agreed the merger would create a stronger company that could compete better for both U.S. and international business. The merger became official March 16, 1995. The two partners agreed to move the headquarters to Martin Marietta's fairly new building in Bethesda, Maryland, and to call the company Lockheed Martin. At the conclusion of the merger they terminated only 1,600 employees out of a total of 177,500. Another acquisition took place when Lockheed Martin added the defense electronics and systems integration of the Loral Corporation in January 1996.[27]

Lockheed Martin's first major project after the merger became the F-22 Advanced Tactical Fighter program. The Fort Worth plant manufactured the center fuselage section, partner Boeing in Seattle constructed the tail and rear section, and the Marietta, Georgia, plant completed the final assembly. The cost of each F-22 Raptor stealth-capable airplane was $99.7 million. Company publicity bragged that the speed, stealth, and agility of the F-22 would make it "dominant over every fighter in the world." The government intended the Raptor to be the "definitive fighter aircraft in the world for most of the twenty-first century. However, a new fighter program in which Lockheed became a major player threatened to replace its own F-22."[28]

A big defense contract competition in the closing years of the twentieth century came when the government wanted an airplane, called the Joint Strike Fighter, to replace the very successful F-16. At first, Lockheed Martin, Boeing, and McDonnell Douglas competed. However, Boeing merged with McDonnell Douglas on July 25, 1997, making the new company even bigger than Lockheed Martin. Only three big companies remained in the defense industry at the end of the twentieth century: Lockheed Martin,

Boeing McDonnell Douglas, and Raytheon. Each of the two competing companies was to build and fly a prototype of what was being called the JSF. Boeing McDonnell Douglas's experimental airplane was the X-32 and Lockheed Martin's the X-35. Lockheed Martin's design borrowed heavily from the F-22. To cut costs they designed the airplane with as many common parts as possible in each of its three models to show theirs the most economical—shades of the 1960s F-111 controversy. In this venture Lockheed Martin was, in a sense, competing against itself for scarce defense dollars that they also needed for the F-22. In addition, Lockheed Martin remained engaged in other new projects in the missile and attack submarine field.[29]

After a five-year competition Air Force Secretary James Roche announced for the Pentagon on October 26, 2001, that the Defense Department had selected Lockheed Martin over Boeing McDonnell Douglas for the $200 billion Joint Strike Fighter contract. He called Lockheed Martin the top performer. Texas Senator Kay Bailey Hutchison who was present in Fort Worth at Lockheed for the announcement said, "it's only the biggest military contract in the history of the world." Secretary Roche explained the government's reasoning: "It became clear, as we went through the process, that the Lockheed Martin team was a clear winner from the point of view of best value for the government. I would not characterize [the decision] as a squeaker at all, nor would I say by a mile."[30]

The JSF or F-35, as Lockheed Martin's product is now called, is a family of three aircraft to serve three military services. The F-35A, for the Air Force, will use conventional runways and can drop bombs. The F-35B for the Marines is the most technically complex because it must do a short take off and vertical landing (STOVL). The F-35C for the Navy needs a larger wing and tail for control to land on carriers. Delays and cost overruns plagued the F-35 program, but despite cuts in the defense budget the three models remained the highest priority. Lockheed projected that revenues from its aeronautics division would total $20 billion by 2015. Analysts predicted that the F-35 would be the "single most important defense program of the next decade."[31]

Secretary of Defense Robert Gates, a holdover from the George W. Bush Administration, reported shortly after President Barack Obama took office that Pentagon officials were considering cuts in the F-35 program. Instead, in April 2009 Gates announced that the administration planned to stop production of the F-22 fighter jet after it completed its initial order. On the other hand, the Pentagon intended to continue and even to speed up production of the F-35, the nation's biggest weapons program. In fact, Gates visited Fort Worth and the Lockheed Martin plant on August 31, 2009,

F-35. *Photo courtesy Lockheed Martin.*

and told assembled employees, "The F-35 is the core of our combat tactical aircraft in the future. My view is we cannot afford as a nation *not* to have this airplane." A total of 1,800 Fort Worth Lockheed Martin employees worked in the F-22 program, but most of them would shift to the F-35 as it accelerated. When Gates visited, the F-35 joint strike fighter program had three airplanes in flight testing and eight more nearing completion. Norway became the first foreign country to select the F-35 Lightning for its own air force, placing an advance order.[32]

One must look back seven decades to review the story of the aircraft manufacturing plant next to the Fort Worth air base and the many economic fluctuations it faced before finally acquiring the largest military contract ever. Politics no doubt played a pivotal role in contract selection at the "bomber plant" through the years, and Fort Worth citizens did not complain if they believed more jobs came their way because of favorable influence. Fort Worth and surrounding suburbs supplied the workers for the plant whether it was Consolidated, Consolidated Vultee, Convair, General Dynamics, Lockheed, or Lockheed Martin.

Arguably, workers have changed just as much since the factory opened in 1942, as have the names of the company and its ever-advancing technological aeronautical products. The aerospace industry in the twenty-first century is too complex to be able to hire bright high school graduates like Jack Northrop or energetic hard workers like Larry Bell and promise much advancement. Even a person like Glenn L. Martin, who had two years of college, probably would not get a job today as an engineer designing airplanes in the huge aerospace firm that today partly bears his name. These early twentieth-century giants and others like them could not have imagined the sophistication of the technological projects being built in the factories still bearing their names. An older employee during the 1990s made the following observation:

> Management now is not the old aircraft engineer who worked hard and worked his way up and knew the aircraft industry. Now company officials use 'management style.' If Timex used some new cost cutting measure, then Lockheed Martin management expects to be able to employ the same tactic here. They forget that our product is unique, has a small market, and even takes a great deal of diplomacy with foreign governments just to sell it. Everything is cost cutting.[33]

When historians examine the overall economic and social impact of Lockheed Martin and its predecessors on the city of Fort Worth and adjoining areas, they must look back to population and financial figures for the 1940s when the defense plant started. Fort Worth's population in 1940 was 177,692 before the earliest tenant, Consolidated, arrived. A decade later the city's population had grown to 277,047 due to Consolidated and other World War II-related activities. Native Texan Loyd L. Turner, with bachelor's and master's degrees from Baylor University, began work for Convair in San Diego in 1946 after serving as an Army Air Corps Intelligence Officer in World War II. In 1948 he transferred to the Fort Worth plant as Director of Public Relations, and in 1952 became Special Assistant to the Fort Worth Division General Manager. In 1953 while campaigning for the Fort Worth School Board, of which he later became president, Turner spoke of the importance of Convair: "an estimated one-fourth of the 48,000 children in the Fort Worth Public Schools are Convair children." Turner had a child at South High Mount Elementary School at the time. Indeed, as more families moved to Fort Worth during and after the war, employment more than doubled. Certainly more children attended Fort Worth schools. Between 1940 and 1950 the Arlington Heights area in west Fort Worth grew from 17,844 to 62,301, a 248 percent growth in population. The Fort Worth Chamber of Commerce estimated in October 1951 that for each of the 30,000 Convair employees, there was a family of 3.5 persons. Thus, Convair's payroll supported 105,000 persons, most of whom lived in Fort Worth. In 1952 the Convair plant was the "largest single industrial operation in the Southwest" and had "the largest working force in the nation's aircraft history." These population gains also led to economic gains for Fort Worth. In 1947 the Consolidated Vultee (Convair) plant accounted for approximately $30 million dollars of the community payroll of $78 million, a percentage of 38.4. Since the plant began operation in 1942, a decade later it could count over 3,000 bombers—or 75,000,000 pounds of air frames— constructed. Employees received "more than $390 million in paychecks during that first decade." In 1958 Convair subcontracted with 571 Fort Worth firms and spent $7,686,716 with them. That outside forces often controlled the fate of military manufacturing cities like Fort Worth was something area citizens learned to accept. Industry cannot always get its way, but must rely on the government's lead even sometimes "at the expense of the industry's long-term well-being." Even so, Fort Worth's military industries have fared quite well. Consolidated-Convair-General Dynamics in the 1942–1968 time period enjoyed an average employment of 18,179 with a total payroll for that period of more than $2.7 billion.[34]

The defense industry, including activities in Fort Worth, was by the end of the twentieth century becoming economically inefficient, which would create a problem in a national emergency. The industry became more and more dependent on foreign aircraft sales as well as foreign parts and materials. Nationwide, manufacturing became concentrated in fewer and fewer large firms. Costs kept going up for the manufacturer, so they increased for the taxpayers as well. One generation of military equipment could cost three to five times as much as the prior one, resulting in less military equipment produced. In contrast, commercial equipment such as televisions, cameras, and other devices decreased in price as their performance capabilities increased. There was no doubt that military aircraft constructed in Fort Worth and elsewhere reached astounding performance goals, but continually cost the taxpayers more. In fact, by the late 1970s the U.S. government provided funds to bail out aircraft companies such as McDonnell Douglas, General Dynamics, and Lockheed.[35]

A look back at aircraft production in the 1950s and 1960s provides an expensive contrast. U.S. government aircraft contractors produced 3,000 relatively inexpensive aircraft per year during the Korean War. In the mid-1960s during the Vietnam War, production dropped to 1,000 airplanes per year. By 1980, the industry provided about 300 very complex aircraft for the U.S. government, and only a little more than that figure to satisfy foreign military sales. As a result of this scenario, as many as 80,000 firms quickly left the defense industry if they could find alternative products to make and markets for them. Because the Fort Worth plant retained its production demand, even through changing names and mergers, it grew in importance as the competitive atmosphere began to shrink. By 1989, nearly 80 percent of business performed for the Department of Defense was on a fixed price basis rather than the previous cost-plus basis. Fixed price contracts presented a problem for companies doing research and development, and as a result many such firms simply quit bidding on defense contracts.[36]

While the Fort Worth plant certainly experienced fluctuations in contracts that necessitated layoffs, at least it managed to remain open. Many Fort Worthians have stories to tell about being laid off, working another job at lower pay, and then being called back and accepting the risk of another layoff because of the higher wages the plant offered. Other workers decided they did not like the uncertainty of layoffs. One of these workers, Azle resident B. J. Clark, worked for Convair and then took a job at Bell when he was laid off. Bell let him go, too. Then he worked at Howell Instruments for a number of years, but he finally decided to start his own business and became a subcontractor for General Dynamics/Lockheed and Boeing. While he has done quite well and has employed as many as fifty people at his Clark's Precision Machine and Tool, he still depends on the uncertainty of government contracts. A decision can be made to stop a program very suddenly, or Congress can cut off funding. Consequently, Clark's wife, Betty, who worked as his secretary for many years, kept up her nurse's license in the early days—just in case. Numerous stories like the Clarks' took place throughout the Metroplex over the years, but most of the layoffs did not result in the dismissed employee beginning his own business and prospering. Many just took other, often lower paying, jobs and hoped to be called back when new contracts arrived.[37]

Over its first three decades the Fort Worth defense plant produced B-24s, C-87s, B-32s, B-36s, the experimental XB-60 (jet version of the B-36), and the B-58, the latter the world's first supersonic bomber. In the last three decades of the twentieth century the F-111 and the F-16 kept the local plant operating until the "biggest" contract ever, the F-35, came along. In addition, Fort Worth produced space projects such as the Centaur and Surveyor nose cover and booster sections for the Atlas missile. The "only nuclear facility of its type" in the nation at the time, Nuclear Aerospace Research Facility employees performed data-gathering operations. The facility evolved from what locals first called the "bomber plant" to be the "world's largest defense company" with its F-16s flying the world and its F-35s in three models preparing to soar.[38]

Despite the fluctuations of layoffs, the defense corporations housed in the building called Air Force Plant 4 have boosted the Fort Worth economy greatly over the decades. When the Chamber of Commerce worked hard to attract a "bomber plant" in the early years of World War II, they probably had no idea that the Consolidated company they welcomed would be the forerunner of a continuous aircraft manufacturing operation that would last well into the next century. Indeed, a decade into the twenty-first century Lockheed Martin ranked as the nation's largest defense contractor.[39] The city of Fort Worth and its suburbs continue to benefit from that distinction. The importance of the aircraft manufacturing plant in the west part of Fort Worth over its seven decades of operation can be seen in how it changed Fort Worth's economic focus from cows to airplanes. No longer was livestock the biggest business in Cowtown, because military aircraft came to hold that distinction.

CHAPTER 12

Military Impact

ORT WORTH LIKES TO CALL ITSELF "THE CITY WHERE THE WEST begins." Indeed, it began as a military fort on the fringes of the western frontier, but cattle drives and livestock sales dominated the economy until the mid-twentieth century when military interests again ruled. It seems appropriate that other communities like Cowtown with a similar defense-military emphasis also are located west of the ninety-eighth meridian—that line dividing the country east and west. Military installations, even in twentieth- and twenty-first century America, are predominantly a western phenomenon. To comprehend fully the impact of the military on Fort Worth, and the nation, it is necessary to look at some of these other cities and compare their experiences. Fort Worth's substantial military contribution represents only a part of a much larger whole. This chapter will examine that broader picture to help place the Fort Worth experience in context.

First, however, a quick review of Fort Worth's past, population growth, economic gains, and how they benefited through the city's partnership with the military will help explain the latter's tremendous impact. Military-defense concerns have been nearly a constant from the days of Bird's Fort and the establishment of Fort Worth itself up to the present. Many cities throughout the United States have the word fort in their name, reflecting their beginnings as a home for military troops. Although Fort Worth only operated as a fort for the four years from 1849 to 1853, for nearly half its existence the city has housed military troops.

In addition, for nearly the same period the city has supplied defense materials for the nation's use. The largest defense plant built in the United States during World War II still operates, although the companies leasing the government-owned Plant 4 went through a series of owners: Consolidated, Consolidated Vultee, Convair, General Dynamics, Lockheed, and Lockheed Martin. Bell Helicopter, which located to Fort Worth in 1950, still survives after more than half a century. These two manufacturing plants each have been building major aircraft for the nation's defense for well over half a century as well.

Numerous small businesses through the years have accepted government defense contracts in support of Fort Worth's larger factories. Ralph Heath, president of Fort Worth-based Lockheed Martin Aeronautics, wrote in a 2010 *Fort Worth Star-Telegram* guest column that "more than 900 aerospace and defense related businesses" existed in North Texas and provided "an estimated 60,000 direct jobs." It would be impossible to mention all the nine hundred or more subcontractors of various sizes that at any one time are working with Lockheed Martin, Bell, or other large manufacturers. Among the more prominent, which may be used here to represent all the others, was Menasco. A lot of people in Fort Worth, on first hearing the name perhaps thought that Menasco was an acronym, like TEMCO (Texas Engineering and Manufacturing Company). No so, as Al Menasco would explain if he could. Menasco Texas, a division of the older, larger Burbank, California, based company, opened its new 100,000 square foot, $5 million manufacturing facility in Fort Worth in October 1956 on forty-five acres near Highway 157 and Pipeline Road, southwest of Euless. Later, the company, which provided landing gear to major airplane manufacturers, expanded to three Metroplex locations for a total of 350,000 square feet, in addition to facilities in Arlington.[1]

Military aviation provided half the manufacturing employment for Fort Worth in the early 1960s in a city that depended on manufacturing as its main economic source. In fact, the entire Dallas-Fort Worth Metroplex ranked second only to Los Angeles in U.S. aircraft manufacturing by the mid-1950s. Total Fort Worth area employment in aircraft manufacturing was 46,000, and Convair provided nearly half of that at 21,000. Early in 1952 the Fort Worth Chamber of Commerce calculated the impact of the Flying Machine Industry—as they called it—on the area. At that time a total of 65,000 people worked directly in the aircraft industry at: Convair (30,000), Marine (6,000), Bell (2,000), General Motors (6,000), and Chance Vought and TEMCO (21,400). Convair's 30,000 employees represented one-tenth of the population of Fort Worth. Thousands more worked for subcontractors like Menasco. Writing in 1953, Loyd Turner, special assistant to Convair's division manager, agreed that the Dallas-Fort Worth Metroplex represented the second largest aircraft manufacturing center in the United States, behind only the Los Angeles area. At that time the Metroplex's airplane factories employed 45,000 people and had an annual payroll of at least $185 million. In addition, they paid out more than $81 million for services and supplies bought in Texas.[2]

Business analysts have reasoned that for every person employed in industry, it takes another "composite person" to provide goods and services. That composite person would be part grocer, housing contractor or landlord, dry cleaner, doctor, lawyer, preacher, schoolteacher, and all the other service providers wage earners need and want. Thus, if 20,000 persons in Fort Worth worked in military aviation, another 20,000 would be serving them or their families in some way. A United States Chamber of Commerce study in 1960 showed that for each one hundred factory workers a city realized $590,000 in personal income, $270,000 in bank deposits, and $360,000 in retail sales.[3]

In 1959 Texas's Big Four aircraft manufacturers—Convair, Bell Helicopter, Chance Vought, and TEMCO—accounted for an estimated 95 percent of the state's employment in the aircraft industry. The first two were the largest and were located in Fort Worth (Tarrant County). The latter two operated in the Mid-Cities area (between Dallas and Fort Worth), employing some Tarrant County workers even though they were in Dallas County.[4]

Historian Roger W. Lotchin edited a book presenting the argument that cities with either defense or military installations become a "martial metropolis." The growth of the military in those cities contributes greatly to urbanization, the "process by which population becomes concentrated." Cities like Fort Worth grow, but also more cities develop in the suburbs. Lotchin contends that in a martial metropolis growth is influenced by "military money, patronage, and prestige." This appears to be the case with Fort Worth and its suburbs on the west side near Lockheed Martin and the Naval Air Station and to the east in the Hurst-Euless-Bedford area near Bell Helicopter.[5]

Tarrant County's population nearly tripled between 1940 and 1960 due to World War II and the build up of the defense industry that replaced livestock marketing as the biggest business in town. In the decade leading up to 1950 the population increased from 225,521 to 361,253, a growth rate of 60 percent, and it increased another 49 percent between 1950 and 1960 to 538,267, almost triple what it had been twenty years earlier. Between 1940 and 1960 Fort Worth's population increased from 177,662 to 356,149. In 1960 the population of six suburban cities west of Fort Worth near the major defense plant and the Air Force base was: Benbrook, 3,252; Lake Worth, 3,846; River Oaks, 8,419; Sansom Park, 4,622; Westworth Village 3,229; and White Settlement, 11,377. Yet, each of these cities had populations of less than 500 before World War II, some less than 200, and others had not existed at all.

Surrounding the Bell Helicopter plant east of Fort Worth are three Mid-Cities communities that developed as a direct result of Bell. Hurst came first, then Euless, and the last to grow was Bedford. Collectively called H-E-B, each town possessed a population of less than one hundred in 1940. Two decades later Hurst had 10,520 people; Euless, 4,236; and Bedford 2,706. Other northeast Tarrant County communities that benefitted include Colleyville, Grapevine, Haltom City, Keller, North Richland Hills, Richland Hills, Southlake, and Watauga.[6]

The increase in the area's population created a demand for more housing and services, and stimulated an increase in wholesale and retail trade. David Larry Thomasson, writing in 1964, made a study of the Metroplex for his master's thesis at Texas Christian University. He noted that "Since the establishment of the defense plants in the early years of World War II, the area's population growth rate had exceeded that of the nation. The population of the Fort Worth Metropolitan area has increased approximately fifty-five percent since 1940, compared to fifty percent for the state, and 28.5 percent for the nation." By 1980 the population of H-E-B had increased tremendously with Hurst at 31,420, Euless at 24,002, and Bedford, 20,821. However, population in the communities nearest the airplane factory in west Fort Worth—River Oaks, Westworth Village, and White Settlement—remained almost constant at 6,890, 3,651 and 13,508, respectively; Fort Worth's population, however, grew to 385,141. In the first decade of the twenty-first century, with a population surpassing six and a half million, the Dallas-Fort Worth Metroplex was the fourth largest in the nation. Fort Worth's population alone was over 700,000 thousand. Military spending in North Texas contributed tremendously to that population growth by providing jobs and attracting families.[7]

Salaries and manufacturing totals relate to the increasing federal dollars being spent locally on military goods and services. Total Tarrant County income in 1940 was more than $171 million, but a decade later tripled to over $568 million. Aircraft manufacturing, the largest single industry in Fort Worth, paid over $152 million in salaries in the year preceding March 1959, and Convair's share of this was $133 million. Fort Worth city officials bragged in April 1965 that the city was the "aviation capital of the world" because the F-111 was "king of the skies" with Great Britain and the U.S. Defense Department placing billion dollar orders and Bell Helicopter's sale of 406 UH-1D Iroquois helicopters to Germany that year.[8]

Similar figures and statistics could be cited for each decade in the last half of the twentieth century. For example, in 1990 Tarrant County reported over $3.6 billion in defense spending, approximately 25 percent of defense spending in Texas, and the largest allocation to any single region in the United States. Contracts for manufactured aircraft and aircraft parts totaled more than 77 percent ($2.8 billion) of all Tarrant County defense spending. Missile and space programs provided competition for defense dollars for

Fort Worth's airplane projects, as well as other aircraft manufacturers, so the city has fared well. In the two decades between 1980 and 2000 total wages paid in all categories in Tarrant County increased from $4.9 billion to $5.9 billion. Proposed defense spending for 2009 in the Fort Worth area totaled nearly $19 billion, but the continuation of funding at that level remained uncertain due to a tighter defense budget and canceled projects.[9]

In 1952 Raymond V. Lesikar, of the University of Texas Bureau of Business Research, explained the reasons for the concentration of aircraft production activities in the Dallas-Fort Worth Metroplex. These included the government's desire to decentralize its military contracts, ideal flying weather with adequate land for plants and runways, and a high enough population concentration to provide an excellent labor supply. Efforts by the Fort Worth Chamber of Commerce to recruit business by using its influence with the government was also a major factor in acquiring contracts, and government officials themselves have delivered for Fort Worth.[10]

Local citizens perhaps hated to admit it, but they realized politics played a role in Carswell receiving important assignments and Air Force Plant 4 in all its ownership changes, obtaining million- or billion-dollar contracts. Lyndon Baines Johnson, first as senator and then as vice president and president, used his considerable talents at arm twisting to bring home huge benefits for Texas. Fort Worth's congressman Wingate Lucas of Grapevine early on fought for Major Horace Carswell's name to grace the previous Fort Worth Army Air Field and for contracts for the defense plant. Then when Congressman Jim Wright began representing the local congressional district in 1955, his thirty-four year tenure and positions as Majority Leader and Speaker of the House of Representatives gave him opportunities to fund many programs for Fort Worth, both for the stockyards and for defense-related facilities. After political shifts in Congress forced Wright out and a Base Realignment and Closure Commission (BRAC) shut down Carswell, many local citizens often complained, "If Jim Wright had still been there, Carswell wouldn't have closed."[11]

Fort Worth became part of a broad expansion of the military during and after World War II that developed more in the western half of the United States than elsewhere. Not surprisingly, with its long-standing claim as the "city where the West begins," Fort Worth became a large and important part of this western demographic. Fort Worth and Tarrant County have been fortunate in their connection to the military, and the area developed significantly because of it.[12]

The years during and after World War II fit a pattern that saw a military emphasis throughout the trans-Mississippi West. During the war American tax dollars funded the Defense Plant Corporation (DPC), that provided financing for 71 percent of the aircraft factories in the country, including the Consolidated plant in Fort Worth and the expansion of Globe. Almost all of these new DPC factories were located west of the Mississippi River in places like Tulsa, Wichita, St. Louis, Dallas-Fort Worth, Seattle, and Los Angeles.[13]

The war transformed the American West by creating manufacturing jobs, aerospace and electronics industries, and even a large service economy to support the substantial influx of people from Oklahoma and Arkansas, and the mostly rural workers who flocked to the western cities. Southern California in particular expanded, building on its early start with the first aviation pioneers like Glenn L. Martin, the Loughead (Lockheed) brothers, Jack Northrop, Larry Bell, Donald Douglas, and others who got their starts in the second decade of the twentieth century. In contrast, Fort Worth's first venture into aircraft manufacturing came nearly two decades later than California's with the Bennett/Globe operation on the north side. Not until World War II did the large defense plant open on the west side of Fort Worth.

The federal government invested at least $40 billion in the West during World War II, creating hundreds of thousands of new jobs. What once had been an agricultural economy based on raw materials became a diversified job market including military industries and their technological support systems. The West became more self-sufficient with its increased population and the expansion of its cities. In addition, the racial composition of the area became more integrated. Had the war not accelerated the process, many years might have been necessary to complete the racial and cultural transformation of the American West that actually occurred because of population shifts. Questions still exist as to how thoroughly America's "melting pot" brought racial and ethnic groups into the mainstream. Evidence from the metropolitan-military-complexes suggest that ethno-cultural groups behaved similarly to the Anglo-Americans in their area—they obtained industrial jobs or joined the military.[14]

Historian Gerald Nash affirms that "the westward flow of population in the twentieth century was more significant in terms of numbers than it had been in the nineteenth century." World War II "transformed the West and made it the pace-setting region of the nation." Others also believed that no other event in western history did more to "transform" the region than the war. Of seventeen western states that experienced this phenomenon, Texas ranked second only to California in the number of military bases created during the war. However, had the Cold War not followed on its heels, growth might have been stunted.[15]

A quartet of writers with two National Science Foundation grants made a study in the late 1980s of what they call the "Gunbelt"—a line of states stretching from Washington State, down through Southern California, through the Southwest and Texas, up to the lower Great Plains, across to Georgia, Florida, and then up the East Coast through New York to New England. The four authors, in their book *The Rise of the Gunbelt*, argue that during World War II and the decades that followed, the government's defense contracts created a new economic map of the country. Major manufacturing jobs shifted from the upper Midwest (states like Illinois, Michigan, Indiana, and Pennsylvania) to the South and West. Manufacturing lost ground in the upper Midwest, per capita income dropped, and population shifted to the Gunbelt states.[16]

They consider California and New England to be the first areas in the country where military-defense projects began—the Electric Boat submarines in Connecticut and the original pioneers who began their airplane construction in Southern California in the second decade of the twentieth century. Since the 1970s the top three Gunbelt states consistently have been California, New York, and Texas in that order, with the Dallas-Fort Worth Metroplex sometimes ranking second, but with Los Angeles always the "aerospace capital of the nation." Los Angeles and Orange Counties possess the "greatest concentration of ultra-high-tech weapons-making capacity in the world," and some people call Los Angeles the "capital city of the military-industrial-complex."[17]

Los Angeles and Fort Worth have at least one similarity. *Los Angeles Times* owner Harry Chandler and *Fort Worth Star-Telegram* owner Amon G. Carter were contemporaries who began promoting their cities after World War I. Each worked successfully for four decades to attract industrial business and aviation to their areas.[18]

Other locations in the Gunbelt are of interest as well. These include Seattle, where Boeing dominates the city's economy, making it an "aerospace company city." Fortunately for Seattle, Boeing has succeeded in commercial aviation, which helps preserve jobs when defense contracts fail. In the early twenty-first century Boeing lost a couple of hard-fought contracts to Fort Worth's Lockheed Martin. Also in the Seattle area is the Puget Sound Naval Shipyard and a Trident submarine base, but Boeing is the big defense-related employer. Boeing also has branch plants in Wichita and Philadelphia. Wichita is similar to Fort Worth in that it was first a cowtown and then later a manufacturing center for aircraft.[19]

Thought of more as a vacation area, perhaps an unlikely Gunbelt city is Colorado Springs, south of Denver. As in many successful military communities, including Fort Worth, Chamber of Commerce boosterism won the day for Colorado Springs. City fathers attracted Fort Carson, a Space and

Operations Center, the North America Air Defense Command (NORAD), and some defense plants. An achievement that Fort Worth had hoped to win—the Air Force Academy—went to Colorado Springs.[20]

San Diego, St. Louis, Wichita, central Utah, and Dallas-Fort Worth all figure into the Gunbelt map. Each relies on one or two major companies with large contracts from the U.S. government for aerospace technology. Not totally, but for the most part the Gunbelt story is a western one, perhaps explaining why the authors of *The Rise of the Gunbelt* chose that metaphor. The West has wide-open spaces, and many of the Air Force generals who play an important role in allocating defense dollars spent their early career assignments on bases in western states. Most military bases during World War II were in the West and some survived closing after the war. Some existing western bases such as Fort Bliss in El Paso and Fort Sam Houston in San Antonio, however, had been established during the Indian wars or at some other point during the nineteenth century. The southern and western emphasis in Sunbelt and Gunbelt cities as opposed to those in the Midwest and Northeast reflects a logical choice to get away from snow, grime, high labor costs, unions, unemployment, older infrastructure, a shrinking tax base, and cramped conditions and capitalize on the West's wide open spaces. *Gunbelt* authors see the rise of the aerospace industry in the West as an "American phenomenon" and a part of the frontier mentality of innovation. Westerners were more likely to accept new ideas and more willing to strike out for new places and new aerospace jobs.[21]

Only the Soviet Union had as much wide-open space as the United States for military bases, missiles, and bomb testing. America's Western cities possessed more cheap land on their outskirts available for industrial expansion than did eastern cities. Old West boosterism of the late nineteenth and early twentieth centuries found a new purpose in the latter half of the twentieth as cities sought either to acquire defense plants or retain military bases. Federal money to provide roads, water supplies, even to buy the land, proved easy to obtain after World War II as the Cold War developed. In fact, the authors call the increased aerospace industries in the Gunbelt a product of the Cold War. They even hint that the Gunbelt states may have prolonged the Cold War by exaggerating the threat and continually pressuring their congressional representatives for defense appropriations. Gunbelt citizens likely would disagree with that analysis and point to the U.S. military buildup and weaknesses in the Soviet economic system that in the long run forced the decline of the Soviet Union. Other consequences according to the Gunbelt theory include expensive infrastructure projects with taxpayer money that benefitted some regions of the country over others, a shift of the labor force from the industrial Midwest to the Gunbelt, and an emphasis on white collar aerospace engineers over the blue collar workers of the older industrial plants. Employees of the aerospace industries saw the Gunbelt as a good thing, new cities created with upper middle class lifestyles, and good real estate markets.[22]

Historian Roger Lotchin writes that "Whether as forts in the nineteenth century or metropolitan-military complexes in the twentieth, American cities have been firmly touched by the phenomenon of war and defense." Power and wealth shifted somewhat from the East and Midwest to the South and West partly because of defense contracts that went to businesses in those areas. Fort Worth, of course, played a large role and benefited greatly. Americans in these areas saw the defense budget "as much a matter of urban welfare—jobs!—as of warfare." The explanation many give for the uneven distribution of government military appropriations among the various states is politics. The state whose congressional delegation fights harder for defense dollars generally wins. The experience of Fort Worth, the city on the ninety-eighth meridian where the West begins, illustrates the impact. As early as January 1942 the hardworking Fort Worth Chamber of Commerce that continually sought congressional help revealed that 350 local businesses already had performed defense work at an estimated value to the community of $45 million.[23]

Always mentioned first around Fort Worth are the large concerns like Consolidated, but many other businesses provided needed wartime supplies. During World War II, Fort Worth became the largest shell-producing center west of the Mississippi River. Texas Steel Manufacturing Company delivered its three millionth 81-millimeter mortar shell on December 1, 1944, and by that time had manufactured over five million shells and projectiles of all sizes. In addition, American Manufacturing Company delivered its five millionth shell to the Navy and Army Ordnance Departments in July 1944. During the war American Manufacturing Company "turned out more different sizes of Army and Navy shells than any other plant in the nation." Also producing shells were the local Crown Machine and Tool Company and Mechanical Manufacturing Company.[24]

Clifford Cummings, an engineer at the Jet Propulsion Laboratory in Pasadena, California, in the 1950s said, "inefficient production such [as] is generated by making planes and missiles that will in all probability never be used is essential to economic stability." Fort Worthians enjoyed the benefits of Cummings' philosophy, for the local B-36 program featured the big Peacemaker "that never dropped a bomb in anger." As a result of that program and others, however, local high school graduates could skip college, earn high wages at Convair/General Dynamics or Bell Helicopter, work thirty-five to forty years, and retire with good benefits. College graduate engineers fared even better. These two plants boosted blue-collar, middle class wages and local opportunities tremendously.[25]

Not only did local citizens benefit in the late 1900s and early twenty-first century from defense plants, the military base (Carswell and then NAS Fort Worth JRB), provided and continues to provide economic support to the area. Fort Worth's military-defense budget is balanced between actual military personnel in the city and manufacturing facilities for the airplanes and helicopters the government builds, maintains, and flies. Numerous cities throughout the West host a military base. Others enjoy the economic boost of defense manufacturing facilities, but not all have both, like Fort Worth, San Diego, and Colorado Springs.

Los Angeles concentrates on high tech manufacturing and leads the nation in that effort. A Gunbelt-Sunbelt city that takes the opposite approach and probably possesses more military personnel than any other community in the country, but with no defense plants, is San Antonio. It has been called the "West Point of the Air" because at various times all basic training for Air Force personnel has taken place there, at Randolph AFB or Lackland AFB. While Kelly AFB closed in 2001, and Brooks AFB became a major medical research facility, three bases remain: Lackland and Randolph for the Air Force, and Fort Sam Houston for the Army.[26]

Beginning as an agricultural area west of Dallas in the mid-nineteenth century, Fort Worth's very first military post, Bird's Fort, disbanded and its residents moved to Dallas. Then as a tiny fort on the frontier in 1849, defending itself against a nearby native foe, Fort Worth and Tarrant County fared extremely well through the years. Prominent citizens who worked hard to bring business to the settlement on the bluff overlooking the West and Clear Forks of the Trinity River deserve the credit. First they encouraged cattle drives; then they built railroads and attracted meat packing plants and stockyards, eventually becoming a wealthy cowtown. Chamber of Commerce efforts to lure early pioneer flyers to town and their successful bid to attract three Canadian airfields and a military camp in World War I began a pattern that continued. World War II and its massive defense expansion cemented Fort Worth's future course as a military city. Local citizens worked hard to acquire the facilities to do their part in the war effort. Then, the Cold War necessitated continued defense procurement. Fortunately for Fort Worth, the contracts and the jobs continued for the remainder of the twentieth century and into the next. Early Fort Worth citizens in the mid-1800s could not have known that a century and a half later their community would develop into a major supplier of military materials for the entire nation, and in many cases, the world.

Of the three legs supporting Fort Worth's economy over the last century and a half—livestock, oil, and military—all have been vital in creating the city that Fort Worth has become. However, the military leg goes to the core of the city's very being, since its beginning as a fort for defense those many years ago. Is it any surprise then that Fort Worth flies boldly into the twenty-first century as an arsenal of defense on the wings of Lockheed Martin F-16s, F-35s, and Bell Helicopter Ospreys?

Notes

PREFACE

1. Jackie L. Marsh, "Community pays tribute to Carswell," *Carswell Sentinel*, May 29, 1992, 9.

2. Don Tipps, *The Story of Bird's Fort: Birthplace of the Metroplex* (Fort Worth: Privately printed, 2003), 11–12.

3. Ty Cashion, *The New Frontier: A Contemporary History of Fort Worth and Tarrant County* (San Antonio: Historical Publishing, 2006); Mike Patterson, *Fort Worth: New Frontiers in Excellence* (Chatsworth, Calif: Windsor Publications, 1990).

4. "World Spotlight on City Aviation," *Fort Worth Star-Telegram*, Oct. 30, 1949, *Fort Worth Star-Telegram* Collection, Carswell Folder, Special Collections Library, University of Texas at Arlington, Arlington, Texas, cited hereafter as UTA.

5. Chris Vaughn, "Military gets positive marks in Texas poll," *Fort Worth Star-Telegram*, May 20, 2001, sec. B, 7.

6. Patterson, *Fort Worth*, 46.

7. Fort Worth Chamber of Commerce, "Fort Worth Industries Geared Into Arsenal of Defense," *Fort Worth* (October 1951): 7.

CHAPTER ONE

1. Tipps, *The Story of Bird's Fort*, 10–12; Michael Walter Farrington, "Middleton Tate Johnson: Texas' Would Be Governor, General and Railroad Entrepreneur," (M.A. thesis, University of Texas at Arlington, 1980), 35–37; *The Texas Almanac for 1857* (Galveston: Richardson, 1857), 70.

2. Farrrington, "Middleton Tate Johnson," 35–38; Tipps, *The Story of Bird's Fort*, 11–12, 14; Dee Barker, "Bird's Fort As Recorded in Official Documents and Letters from Jonathan Bird," (1990, three typewritten pages, in possession of author), 1; The Clear Fork and the West Fork are already merged at this location.

3. Barker, "Bird's Fort as Recorded in Official Documents," 2–3.

4. Tipps, *The Story of Bird's Fort*, 22–23, 27–28.

5. "No. 203 Proclamation by Sam Houston [Bird's Fort Treaty, September 29, 1843]" in Dorman H. Winfrey and James M. Day (eds.) *The Indian Papers of Texas and the Southwest, 1825–1916* (Austin: Texas State Historical Association, 1995), 242–45; Richard F. Selcer and William B. Potter, *The Fort That Became A City: An Illustrated Reconstruction of Fort Worth, Texas, 1849–1853* (Fort Worth: Texas Christian University Press, 1995), 126.

6. Farrington, "Middleton Tate Johnson," 24–25, 42–43, 46–47.

7. Ibid., 48–50.

8. Farrington, "Middleton Tate Johnson," 1, 54; Mack Williams, *In Old Fort Worth* (Fort Worth: The News Tribune, 1977), 26.

9. Randolph B. Campbell, *Gone To Texas: A History of the Lone Star State* (New York: Ox-

ford University Press, 2003), 196–97; Farrington, "Middleton Tate Johnson," 54–55; Edward S. Wallace, *General William Jenkins Worth: Monterrey's Forgotten Hero* (Dallas: Southern Methodist University Press, 1953), 12, 14–17; "Major General William J. Worth," *U. S. Veterans Memorial Institute News* 9, No. 8 (1985): 1.

    10. S. B. [Simon Bowden] Farrar to C.C. Cummings, Sept. 23, 1893, in *Fort Worth Genealogical Society Footprints* 41 (November 1998): n.p.

    11. Ibid., also cited as "Letter Describing Founding of Fort Worth Tells of Wild Beauty, Indians and Game," *Fort Worth Star-Telegram*, June 6, 1940, *Fort Worth Star-Telegram* Collection, Fort Worth History Folder, UTA; Farrington, "Middleton Tate Johnson," 55.

    12. Selcer and Potter, *The Fort That Became a City*, 7–10 (quotation, 8), 18, 26, 31.

    13. Ibid., 35–36, 43.

    14. Thomas T. Smith, *The U.S. Army and the Texas Frontier Economy, 1845–1900* (College Station: Texas A&M University Press, 1999), 28–29, 35–36.

    15. Selcer and Potter, 102.

    16. Ibid.

    17. "Survivors Told of Fort Worth Battle," *Fort Worth Star-Telegram*, Oct. 30, 1949, *Fort Worth Star-Telegram* Collection, Fort Worth History Folder, UTA; Selcer and Potter, *The Fort That Became A City*, 128, 132–33.

    18. Selcer and Potter, *The Fort That Became a City*, 120; *The Texas Almanac for 1857*, 70.

    19. Leonard Sanders and Ronnie C. Tyler, *How Fort Worth Became the Texasmost City* (Fort Worth: Amon Carter Museum of Western Art, 1973), 11.

    20. Bascom Timmons, "Army Inspecting Officer, Here in 1853, Found Guardhouse Empty of Dragoons," *Fort Worth Star-Telegram*, Oct. 30, 1949, *Fort Worth Star-Telegram* Collection, Fort Worth History Folder, UTA.

    21. Selcer and Potter, *The Fort That Became A City*, 147.

    22. Sanders and Tyler, *How Fort Worth Became the Texasmost City*, 9.

    23. Sanders and Tyler, 18; James Farber, *Fort Worth in the Civil War* (Belton, Tex.: Peter Hansbrough Bell Press, 1960), 26.

    24. Sanders and Tyler, 18–19; Farber, *Fort Worth in the Civil War*, 15, 20–21, 26; Robert H. Talbert, *Cowtown-Metropolis: Case Study of A City's Growth and Structure* (Fort Worth: Texas Christian University Press, 1956), 119.

    25. K. M. Van Zandt, *Force without Fanfare: The Autobiography of K.M. Van Zandt*, Edited and with an Introduction by Sandra L. Myres (Fort Worth: Texas Christian University Press, 1968), 111, 114 (quotation).

    26. Ibid., 125.

    27. Robert A. Calvert and Arnoldo DeLeón, *The History of Texas* (2nd ed.; Wheeling, Ill.: Harlan Davidson, 1996), 172; Smith, *The U.S. Army and the Texas Frontier Economy, 1845–1900*, 4, 174 (quotation).

    28. Sanders and Tyler, *How Fort Worth Became the Texasmost City*, 108.

    29. Williams, *In Old Fort Worth*, 15; Quentin McGown to J'Nell Pate, June 4, 2007, email (printed copy in possession of the author).

    30. "Survivors Told of Fort Worth Battle," *Fort Worth Star-Telegram*, Oct. 30, 1949, *Fort Worth Star-Telegram* Collection, UTA.

    31. Bill Potts, "1911 Sees First Plane Flown to Fort Worth," *Fort Worth Star-Telegram*, June 22, 1937, *Fort Worth Star-Telegram* Collection, Air History Folder, UTA.

    32. "1911 Brought First Flight at Fort Worth," *Fort Worth Star-Telegram*, Oct. 30, 1949, *Fort Worth Star-Telegram* Collection, Aviation History Folder, UTA.

    33. Bill Potts, "Fort Worth Saw Its First Airplanes in 1911," *Fort Worth Star-Telegram*, June 20, 1937, *Fort Worth Star-Telegram* Collection, Aviation History Folder, UTA; Harry Connelly, "The Silver Anniversary of Aviation," *Fort Worth Star-Telegram and Sunday Record Magazine Section*, Dec. 16, 1928, 4–5; "1911 Brought First Flight At Ft. Worth," *Fort Worth*

Star-Telegram, Oct. 30, 1949; "'Thrillers' Promised By Flyers on Closing Day of Aviation Meet," *Fort Worth Star-Telegram*, Jan. 13, 1911, *Fort Worth Star-Telegram* Collection, Aviation History Folder, UTA.

34. Robert E. Cunningham, *Aces High* (St. Louis: General Dynamics, 1977), 3; "1911 Brought First Flight At Ft. Worth"; [First name missing] Heinecke, "Fort Worth Aviation," copy of five pages typed notes dated October 1950, *Fort Worth Star-Telegram* Collection, UTA; "Airmen Will Open Meet In Brilliant Flights; High Wind Sweeps Field," *Fort Worth Star-Telegram*, Jan. 12, 1911, typewritten text of 1911 story, Aviation Folder, *Fort Worth Star-Telegram* Collection, UTA; "'Thrillers' Promised By Flyers on Closing Day of Aviation Meet," *Fort Worth Star-Telegram*, Jan. 13, 1911, *Fort Worth Star-Telegram* Collection, Aviation Folder, UTA (quotation).

35. "Simon Plays Hide and Seek in Wind: Fool Flyer Thrills Crowd on Closing Day of Aviation Meet," *Fort Worth Star-Telegram*, Jan. 14, 1911, *Fort Worth Star-Telegram* Collection, Aviation Folder, UTA.

36. E. P. Stein, *Flight of the Vin Fiz* (New York: Arbor House, 1985), 8–9; Henry H. Arnold, *Airmen and Aircraft: An Introduction to Aeronautics* (New York: Ronald Press, 1926), 93, 264–65. (quotation, common expression)

37. Eileen F. Lebow, *Cal Rodgers and the Vin Fiz: The First Transcontinental Flight* (Washington, D.C.: Smithsonian Institution Press, 1989), 27, 36–37.

38. Lebow, *Cal Rodgers and the Vin Fiz*, 27, 36–37, 82; Sherwood Harris, *"Coast to Coast in 12 Crashes,"* *American Heritage* (October 1964): 47.

39. Sherwood Harris, *The First To Fly: Aviation's Pioneer Days* (New York: Simon & Schuster, 1970), 256; Lebow, *Cal Rodgers and the Vin Fiz*, 182.

40. Stein, *Flight of the Vin Fiz*, 210.

41. Potts, "1911 Sees First Plane Flown to Fort Worth"; Stein, *Flight of the Vin Fiz*, 210, 212; Lebow, *Cal Rodgers and the Vin Fiz*, 162.

42. Stein, *Flight of the Vin Fiz*, 316, 322-323, 337; Henry Serrano Villard, *Contact! The Story of the Early Birds* (New York: Thomas Y. Crowell Company, 1968), 135; Roger E. Bilstein, *Flight in America 1900–1983: From the Wrights to the Astronauts* (Baltimore: The Johns Hopkins University Press, 1984), 25; Harris, *The First To Fly*, 10; Art Ronnie, *Locklear: The Man Who Walked on Wings* (New York: A.S. Barnes, 1973), 22.

43. Potts, "1911 Sees First Plane Flown to Ft. Worth"; Bess Stephenson, "Wise Cou . . . .When Pla. . ." (headline partially missing) *Fort Worth Star-Telegram*, June 7, 1942, *Fort Worth Star-Telegram* Collection, Aviation History Folder, UTA; Connelly, "The Silver Anniversary of Aviation," *Fort Worth Star-Telegram and Sunday Record Magazine* Dec. 16, 1928, *Fort Worth Star-Telegram* Collection, Aviation History Folder, UTA; Heinecke, "Fort Worth Aviation," and Dick Collins, "When Decatur Was Put On The Map of the Air," *Fort Worth Star-Telegram and Sunday Record Magazine Section*, Dec. 16, 1928; Reprint of a news article that appeared in the *Wise County Messenger*, June 4, 1915, *Fort Worth Star-Telegram*, Aviation History Folder, UTA.

44. Sanders, *How Fort Worth Became the Texasmost City*, 165–66; Connelly, "The Silver Anniversary of Aviation,"; Jerold Edward Brown, "Where Eagles Roost: A History of Army Airfields Before World War II" (Ph.D. diss., Duke University, 1977), 57; Gene Gurney, *A Chronology of World Aviation* (New York: Franklin Watts, 1965), 21; "Military Hops First in Texas," *Fort Worth Star-Telegram*, Oct. 30, 1949, *Fort Worth Star-Telegram* Collection, Aviation History Folder, UTA.

45. Gurney, *A Chronology of World Aviation*, 21; Heinecke, "Fort Worth Aviation," 2; "Military Hops First in Texas"; Mack Williams, "In Old Fort Worth Growth of West Side Dates Back to WWI Camp Bowie," *Fort Worth News-Tribune*, Sept. 19, 1986, sec. C, 1; Sanders, *How Fort Worth Became the Texasmost City*, 165–66, 171.

46. Harris, *The First to Fly*, 16.

CHAPTER TWO

1. Charles C. Bandy, "Camp Bowie: Shaper of Destiny," (research paper, Retrofest Competition, Tarrant County Junior College, Northeast Campus, 1996).

2. "Building a Business," Ben E. Keith Co., <http://www.benekeith.com> [Accessed February 2, 2007].

3. Williams, "In Old Fort Worth Growth of West Side Dates Back to WWI Camp Bowie," *Fort Worth News-Tribune*, Sept. 19, 1986 (quotation); Bill Leary, *Flyers of Barron Field: Chronicle of the Wild Antics of Flyers Stationed Around Fort Worth in World War I* (Fort Worth: Yrael Publishing Co., 2003), 117–19; Hugh Morgan, "Royal Flying Corps in Texas," Part I, *Aeroplane* (November 1992): 48, 50; Program, Veteran's Day, Nov. 11, 1966, Carswell Air Force Base (in possession of Gretchen Barrett, daughter of Harry Brants); S. F. Wise, *Canadian Airmen and the First World War. The Official History of the Royal Canadian Air Force* (3 vols.; Toronto: University of Toronto Press, 1980), I, 89–92.

4. Ronald D. Russell, "Canada's Airmen and Airwomen in the First World War," *Airforce: The Magazine of Canada's Air Force Heritage* 28 (Summer 2004): 34.

5. Alan Sullivan, "The R.F.C. in Texas," in *Aviation in Canada 1917–1918* (Toronto: Rous & Mann, 1919), 233–34; "Brief History of Benbrook, Texas," Benbrook Comprehensive Plan, June 2, 1994 (in possession of author); Leary, *Flyers of Barron Field*, 120–21; Wise, *Canadian Airmen and the First World War*, I, 92–93 (quotation, 93).

6. *Selected Tarrant County Communities Tarrant County Historic Resources Survey* Fort Worth: Historic Preservation Council for Tarrant County, Texas, 1990), 167; Robert H. Talbert, *Cowtown-Metropolis*, 127; Jim McMullen, "Old World War Airfields in Fair Shape to Use Again," *Fort Worth Star-Telegram*, May 25, 1940, *Fort Worth Star-Telegram* Collection, Air Fields Folder, UTA.

7. John B. Rae, *Climb To Greatness: The American Aircraft Industry, 1920–1960* (Cambridge, Mass.: MIT Press, 1968), 15; Alan Skinner, "Concrete Fokker in Tarrant County," (paper, Texas State Historical Association Annual Meeting, Fort Worth, Texas, March 3, 2005).

8. Jack B. Jaynes, *Eagles Must Fly*, ed. Charles H. Young (Dallas: Taylor Publishing, 1982), 46; Leary, *Flyers of Barron Field*, 206; in 2004 construction workers discovered a buried concrete Fokker when a new housing development was being built on the site of the former gunnery range. They left the Fokker in place and a local historical group obtained a historical marker for the site. Skinner, "Concrete Fokker in Tarrant County."

9. Cecil J. Holms, "Tale of an Early Bird," *Airforce: The Magazine of Canada's Air Force Heritage* 26 (Fall 2002): 40.

10. "History of Barron Field," 1–2; *Barron Field Review*, 7; Fort Sam Houston to Barron Field, June 29, 1918, and Barron Field to Fort Sam Houston, July 4, 1918, Telegrams, Barron Field General Correspondence Folder, Army Air Forces World War I Organization Records Air Service Aviation Fields, Barron Field, Everman, Texas, Box 32, RG 18, National Archives Records Administration, SW Region, Fort Worth, Texas (cited hereafter as National Archives SW); "Claim for Damages to Barron Field," case brought by Mrs. J. Martin Scott, Dec. 31, 1920, Waxahachie, Texas, Army Air Forces World War I Organization Records Air Service Aviation Fields, Barron Field, Everman, Texas, RG 18, Box 39, Decimal 154 to 200.5, National Archives SW; "History of Barron Field," 3 (typewritten history copied from *Barron Field Review*, a yearbook published in the latter part of 1918), *Fort Worth Star-Telegram* Collection, Barron Field Folder, UTA; *Barron Field Review* (1919), copy in Tarrant County Archives, Tarrant County Historical Commission, Fort Worth, Texas.

11. Chad Slate, "Benbrook's Name: What's in a Name!" one-page article copied from scrapbook on history of Benbrook in Benbrook Public Library, Benbrook, Texas; "Brief History of Benbrook, Texas," excerpts from the Benbrook Comprehensive Plan, 5 article dated June 2, 1994, obtained from Benbrook Public Library.

12. Jason Coward and Mark Robertson, "Carruthers Field," one-page item in notebook on Benbrook history in Benbrook Public Library, copy in possession of author.

13. Russell, "Canada's Airmen and Airwomen in the First World War," 34–35; Morgan, "Royal Flying Corps in Texas," Part I, 48; Wise, *Canadian Airmen and the First World War*, I, 93–94; Sullivan, "The R.F.C. in Texas," 237; Hans Neubroch, "The Extraordinary Life of Wing Commander Dermott Allen, Late Royal Irish Fuseliers" (typescript article in author's files, acquired from Dr. Griffin Murphey), 4–5, 9, 15; Speech on Dermott Allen by Royal Air Force Group Captain Hans Neubroch at Elks Lodge, May 28, 2007, after a ceremony at Greenwood Cemetery honoring the Canadian pilots buried there (author's notes).

14. David C. Cooke, *Sky Battle, 1914–1918: The Story of Aviation in World War I* (New York: W. W. Norton, 1970), 189; James W. Atkinson, *The Soldier's Chronology* (New York: Garland, 1993), 299; Gurney, *A Chronology of World Aviation*, 25; C. J. H. Holms, "Tale of an Early Bird" (excerpt from longer manuscript that later appeared under same title in *Airforce* magazine, copy in author's possession), 9.

15. Wise, *Canadian Airmen and the First World War*, 94; Stephen F. Tillman, *Man Unafraid* (Washington, D.C.: Army Times Publishing, 1958), 207; "Field Named for Gallant Air Officer," *Taliaferro Target*, Nov. 1, 1918, 1.

16. Don Clark, "The Birds Fly South," in *Wild Blue Yonder: An Air Epic* (Seattle: Superior Publishing Company), 66; Leary, *Flyers of Barron Field*, 24.

17. Wise, *Canadian Airmen and the First World War*, 95; Sullivan, *Aviation in Canada 1917–1918*, 244; C. W. Hunt, *Dancing in the Sky: The Royal Flying Corps in Canada* (Toronto: Dundurn, 2009), 189.

18. Wise, *Canadian Airmen and the First World War*, 95 (first quotation); Peter Kilduff, "Prairie Pilots," *Airextra* Incorporating Aircraft Illustrated Extra (n.p., n.d.; Copy in author's possession, courtesy Dr. Griffin T. Murphey), 32 (second quotation).

19. Cecil J. H. Holms, "Tale of an Early Bird," 12–14. Manuscript provided to author by Dr. Griffin Murphey.

20. Sullivan, *Aviation in Canada 1917–1918*, 243; Clark, *Wild Blue Yonder*, 87, 91 (quotations).

21. W. L. Kenly, May 17, 1918, cited in Neubroch, "The Extraordinary Life of Wing Commander Dermott Allen, Late Royal Irish Fuseliers," 8.

22. "Barron Field 'Birds' To Meet," *Fort Worth Star-Telegram*, Sept. 20, 1931, *Fort Worth Star-Telegram* Collection, Barron Field Folder, UTA; Leary, *Flyers of Barron Field*, 22; Morgan, "Royal Flying Corps in Texas," 51; Memo War Department Office of the Chief Signal Officer, April 16, 1918, on Naming of Three Fields, Army Air Forces World War I Organization Records, Air Service, Aviation Fields Barron Field, Everman, Texas, Box 24, RG 18, Folder: General Correspondence; Telegram May 1, 1918, Box 1, RG 18, Army Air Forces Field Installations Telegrams In, Barron Field, Everman, Texas, April, June 1918 Folder, National Archives SW; Telegram May 1, 1918, Box 24, RG 18; General Correspondence, Barron Field Flying Field Report, June, 1918; Letter Lt. Col. D. L. Roscoe, Signal Corps, to War Department Office of the Chief Signal Officer, Washington, D.C., Feb. 1, 1918, Box 29, RG 18, Barron Field Folder, General Correspondence, National Archives SW.

23. "Pronounce Field Name Correctly: Proper Way is 'Tolliver' Says Major Macaulay, Who Knew Officer for Whom Field Was Named—Public Hard to Educate on This Subject," *Taliaferro Target*, Sept. 20, 1918, 1; "Many Improvements Will Make Taliaferro Field Finest Gunnery School," *Taliaferro Target*, Aug. 1, 1918, 1; "Officers Report From Five Fields To Take Gunnery Course," *Taliaferro Target*, Oct. 4, 1918, 5; Memorandum, Aug. 8, 1918, Army Air Forces World War I Organization Records, Air Service Aviation Fields, Barron Field, Everman, Texas, Box 9, RG 18, Decimal File 210.8, National Archives SW.

24. Robert E. Hicks, "Big Marine Air Station at Quantico Is Named After Barron Field Head," *Fort Worth Star-Telegram*, Dec. 13, 1942, *Fort Worth Star-Telegram* Collection, Barron Field Folder, UTA; memo, Oct. 4, 1918, by order of Lt. Col. Turner, General Correspondence

Folder, Barron Field, Everman, Texas, Box 23, RG 18 National Archives SW; *Barron Field Review*, 9; untitled biography of Col. Thomas C. Turner (typescript), *Fort Worth Star-Telegram* Collection, Barron Field Folder, UTA.

25. "Barron Field Veterans Recall War at Picnic," *Fort Worth Star-Telegram*, Sept. 21, 1931, *Fort Worth Star-Telegram* Collection, Barron Field Folder, UTA.

26. Cecile Rider Craft (Mrs. John Craft), telephone interview with author, Feb. 27, 1997.

27. Mark Robertson, "Funny, but true stories" (one-page sheet in notebook about Benbrook history, Benbrook Public Library, Benbrook, Texas); War Department Memo from Division of Military Aeronautics to Commanding Officer, All Aviation Posts and Field, Dec. 31, 1918, Carruthers Field Shooting Birds Folder, Carruthers Field (formerly Taliaferro Field #3, Benbrook, Texas, General Correspondence, Box 1, RG 18, National Archives SW.

28. Robertson, "Funny, but true stories."

29. Ibid.

30. "Carruthers Field Special Orders Transfer RE: Jacob E. Fickel and Ervin Brockman," Army Air Forces Field Installations, Carruthers Field, General Correspondence of the Personnel Officer, 1918–1919. 201.3–220, HM 1999, Box 3, RG 18; Correspondence of the Flying School Detachment 1918–1919, AAF Field Installations, Carruthers Field, Officer Personnel Records, Flight Office. E368, RG 18, National Archives SW.

31. Leary, *Flyers of Barron Field*, 11–12, 98.

32. War Department Memo, Mar. 15, 1920, Barron Field Flying Teams Folder, Army Air Forces Barron Field, General Correspondence of the Office of the Aviation Supply Officer, 1919–1920, Box 3, RG 18, National Archives SW; "Cadet Note Book," 2, 5, in General Correspondence Folder, Proceedings of Board Court Martial Records, and Reports Relating to Personnel, Miscellaneous Correspondence, Army Air Forces Field Installations, Barron Field, Everman, Texas, Box 6, RG 18, National Archives SW.

33. Leary, *Flyers of Barron Field*, 83, 217–18.

34. [First name missing] Oglesby, untitled typescript in *Fort Worth Star-Telegram* Collection, Barron Field Folder, UTA; Morgan, "Royal Flying Corps in Texas," Part 2, 59; "Film Calendar for Week," *Fort Worth Star-Telegram*, Apr. 2, 1939, *Fort Worth Star-Telegram* Collection, Vernon Castle Folder, UTA

35. Morgan, "Royal Flying Corps in Texas," Part 2, 60; "Castle Funeral Cortege Leaving Undertaking Establishment," *Fort Worth Star-Telegram*, Feb. 17, 1918, 1; Jack Gordon, "Vernon Castle Gave Own Life To Save Cadet at Benbrook Airfield," in William E. Jary Jr., *Camp Bowie Fort Worth 1917–18: An Illustrated History of the 36th Division In The First World War* (Fort Worth: Thomason & Morrow, 1975), 51–52.

36. Oglesby, untitled typescript, 1; Carruthers logged 35,000 hours, Barron 26,608, and Taliaferro 32,488; Heinecke, "Fort Worth Aviation," 2; Morgan, "Royal Flying Corps in Texas," Part 2, 60; "Greenwood Cemetery," *Research Data* Vol. 52, 20774–20776; Chris Vaughn, "Saving History," *Fort Worth Star-Telegram*, May 29, 2005, 1, 8; Program, Veterans' Day, Nov. 11, 1966, Carswell Air Force Base (in possession of Gretchen Barrett); Program, Memorial Day, May 28, 2007 (in possession of author); 2009 Program; Ronnie, *Locklear*, 37; "Accident Reports," Barron Field Engineering Dept. Folder, Correspondence of the Office of the Engineer Officer, Box 2, RG 18, National Archives SW (quotations); telephone interview with Mary Mann Powell (Mrs. Gregory Powell), Gardendale, Texas, Aug. 15, 1997 (crashes quotation).

37. Memo to Commanding Officer, Barron Field, Subject Influenza, Sept. 29, 1918, Barron Field General Correspondence Folder, Office of Post Surgeon, Barron Field, Everman, Texas, Box 34, RG 18 (quotation); Telegram, Feb. 1, 1921, Army Air Forces Field Installations, Barron Field, Box 3, RG 18, National Archives SW; Leary, *Flyers of Barron Field*, 46–47; *Barron Field Review*, 48; "Quarantine Still Holds Taliaferro," *Taliaferro Target*, Oct. 4, 1918, 1; "Quarantine Lid to Lift in Morning," *Taliaferro Target*, Oct. 25, 1918, 1.

38. Alice C. Leary to Carol Hendrix, Oral Histories of Fort Worth, Inc. by the Junior League of Fort Worth, Inc. February 1978 (typed copy in Tarrant County Archives), 1–2, 5–10, 13 (quotation); Leary, *Flyers of Barron Field*, 10, 12. Alice later met a man named William Leary from Fort Worth whom she married. She returned to live the rest of her life in the city. She died in 1984.

39. Entertainment Folder, Barron Field, General Correspondence and Other Records of Training Squadron, RG 28, Box 2, National Archives SW; Hicks, "Big Marine Air Station at Quantico Is Named After Barron Field Head."

40. *The Strut* 1 (September 1918), Carruthers Field Magazines Folder, Carruthers Field, Benbrook, Texas, General Correspondence, Box 1, RG 18, National Archives SW; Public Entertainment Folder, Carruthers Field, General Correspondence, ibid.; Letter Air Service Flying School, Hicks, Texas Sept. 25, 1918, from Sgt. Ralph S. Granes, Chairman Entertainment Committee to CO Quartermaster Detachment Carruthers Field, Carruthers Field, General Correspondence, Box 22, RG 18, National Archives SW (first quotation); Entertainments Folder, Barron Field, General Correspondence and Other Records of Training Squadron, Box 2, RG 28, National Archives SW; Memo from Headquarters, Southern Department Fort Sam Houston, Texas, to Commanding Officer, Barron Field, Sept. 27, 1918, Barron Field, Box 22, RG 18, National Archives SW (second quotation).

41. Letter from Johnson County Fair to Barron Field, also Lt. Col. Turner's Reply, General Correspondence Folder, Barron Field, Box 24, RG 18, National Archives SW; Letter, Commanding Officer Rich Field, Waco to Carruthers Field, Carruthers Field Exhibitions Folder, Carruthers Field, General Correspondence, Box 1, ibid.

42. J'Nell L. Pate, "Ormer Leslie Locklear: The Epoch of Flying Has Arrived," in Ty Cashion and Jesús F. de la Teja (eds.) in *The Human Tradition in Texas* (Wilmington, Del: Scholarly Resources, Inc., 2001), 146–48.

43. Ibid.; Art Ronnie, *Locklear*, 17, 23–24, 33–35, 39.

44. Ronnie, *Locklear*, 44; Leary, *Flyers of Barron Field*, 124, 136–39.

45. *Fort Worth Star-Telegram*, untitled clipping, Locklear Collection, Pate Museum of Transportation, Cresson, Texas; Ronnie, *Locklear*, 52; Air Service Flying School Records, Barron Field, Special Orders, Box 7, RG 28, National Archives SW; *Fort Worth Record*, June 8, 1919; *Syracuse Journal*, Sept. 9, 1919; *San Francisco Examiner*, Sept. 12, 1919, Locklear Collection, Pate Museum of Transportation (quotation).

46. Ronnie, *Locklear*, 13, 273–74; *Dallas Times-Herald*, Oct. 17, 1919, Locklear Collection; Pate, "Ormer Leslie Locklear," 154–57.

47. "French Officers Leaving Taliaferro," *Taliaferro Target*, Sept. 27, 1918, 1; "Taliaferro Soon To Be Memory," *Taliaferro Target*, Jan. 10–17, 1919, 1.

48. Maurer Maurer, *Aviation in the U.S. Army, 1915–1939* (Washington, D.C.: Office of Air Force History, USAF, 1987), 24.

49. Ibid.; "Taliaferro Commander Successful Reaches the Pacific Coast in Pioneer Flight to Map Aerial Mail Route and Returns to Field After Many Thrilling Experiences," *Taliaferro Target*, Dec. 13, 1918, 1. The latter article was about an unsuccessful first attempt by Major Macaulay before his later successful one in early 1919. Fort Worth based pilots would complete the first non-stop around-the-world flight from Fort Worth's Carswell Air Force Base in 1949.

50. Maurer, *Aviation in the U.S. Army*, 24; Ronnie, *Locklear*, 54.

51. "Medical Department Memo Carruthers Field, May 3, 1919," Carruthers Field, Hospital 322.15 E365, General Correspondence of the Office of the Engineer Officer 1918–1919, AAF Field Installations, Carruthers Field, Benbrook, Texas. Box 12, RG 18; Letter, T. J. Hanley Jr., Commanding Officer, Carruthers Field, Nov. 1, 1919, to Department Air Service Officer, Fort Sam Houston, Texas, Carruthers Field Future of Field Folder, Box 26, RG 18, National Archives SW; Proceedings of Boards, Correspondence Relating to Deaths, Appli-

cations for Discharge, and Other Records of the Headquarters Cadet Detachment, Barron Field, Box 1, Folder A, RG 18, National Archives SW; "Headquarters Detachment Memo, Nov. 20, 1918 to Adjutant Barron Field, Box 23, RG 18, National Archives SW; Letter, Mrs. G. B. Bradley to Commanding Officer, Barron Field, with enclosed news article, "Soldier in Need At Home May Get Out," Barron Field General Correspondence, Box 48, RG 18, National Archives SW.

52. Memo Commanding Officer, Barron Field to Chief of Air Service, Washington, D.C. Oct. 2, 1920, General Correspondence Folder, Box 54, RG 18, National Archives SW (quotation); "Barron Field Prohibition Against Aerial Exhibitions," War Dept. Memo dated Mar. 24, 1920, General Correspondence of the Office of the Aviation Supply Officer, 1919–1920, Box 3, RG 18, National Archives SW; "National Airplane Co. Plans Purchase of Barron Field," *Fort Worth Record*, Aug. 29, 1919, clipping in General Correspondence Folder, Barron Field, Box 35, RG 18, National Archives SW; "Abandonment of Barron Field," General Correspondence of the Office of the Aviation Supply Officer, 1919–1920, Box 4, RG 18, National Archives SW; Memo Chief of Air Service to Commanding Officer Barron Field, Jan. 29, 1921, ibid.; "Telegrams," April–October 1920, Telegram Dec. 22, 1920, ibid.; Memo from C. W. Russell, Captain, Commanding Barron Field, Aug. 30, 1920 to Headquarters, Eighth Army Corps, Fort Sam Houston, General Correspondence, Box 37, RG 18, National Archives SW; "Barron Field 'Birds' To Meet."

53. *Selected Tarrant County Communities*, 188; Pat Castillon, "Club saves piece of history destined for wrecker's ball," *Fort Worth Star-Telegram*, Dec. 14, 1975, *Fort Worth Star-Telegram* Collection, Barron Field Folder, UTA.

54. Interview with Gretchen Brants Barrett, daughter of Harry Brants, May 11, 2006, Fort Worth; telephone interview with Gretchen Brants Barrett, Oct. 27, 2006; Scrapbook loaned to author by Mrs. Gretchen Barrett compiled in 1940 by Charles McClure, one of the flyers who remained in Fort Worth. He made the book for each of the men in his unit with whom he had kept in touch. Jack Moranz drawing, "Fort Worthers in Pen and Ink of Harry E. Brants in *Star-Telegram about 1940*," no page cited (in scrapbook obtained from Gretchen Barrett).

55. Interviews with Gretchen Barrett; "Scrapbook," compiled by McClure. Numerous pilots who served at the three airfields remained or returned to Fort Worth after the war. Some were Canadian, and others were American. Among these were Arno Behnke from Grand Rapids, Michigan; Tilford Warren Rhoads from Cowden, Illinois; Joseph Roman Pelich, born in Austria; and Charles F. A. McClure, Parkersburg, West Virginia.

56. "Haltom's" Advertisement in *Taliaferro Target*, Sept. 6, 1918, 5; telephone interview with Mrs. George L. (Irene) Grimes, 92 years old as of March 1, 1997, who was in the seventh and eighth grades when Taliaferro Field was located near where she lived.

57. Catherine Wakefield, "The Clell Wakefield Family," Special section of family histories accompanying *Saginaw Sentinel*, Sept. 2, 1982, 9; telephone interview with Catherine Wakefield, Saginaw Resident, Feb. 27, 1997.

58. Roger Bilstein and Jay Miller, *Aviation in Texas* (Austin: Texas Monthly Press, 1985), 52.

59. Morris and Smith, *Ceiling Unlimited*, 183.

CHAPTER THREE

1. Jary, *Camp Bowie Fort Worth*, 4.

2. Lonnie J. White, *Panthers to Arrowheads: The 36th Texas-Oklahoma Division in World War I* (Austin: Presidial Press, 1984), 16; "Camp Bowie Day, 9 Years Old. . . Holman Taylor Suggested Site. . . Army Plant Cost 2 Millions," *Fort Worth Star-Telegram*, Oct. 9, 1927, *Fort Worth Star-Telegram* Collection, Camp Bowie Folder, UTA (quotation); Jary, *Camp Bowie*, 4; Mack Williams, "In Old Fort Worth Growth of West Side Dates Back to WWI Camp Bowie," *Fort Worth News Tribune*, Sept. 19, 1986, 1C.

3. Chet Turnock, "Arlington Heights Story Brims With Color Action," in Jary, *Camp Bowie*, 8; "Over Here—Camp Bowie, Fort Worth, Texas, 1917–1919," Exhibit at Fort Worth Museum of Science and History, Feb. 9–Sept. 2, 1996; White, *Panthers to Arrowheads*, 16–17; Jary, *Camp Bowie*, 4; Williams, "In Old Fort Worth Growth of West Side Dates Back to WWI Camp Bowie"; "Camp Bowie Day 9 Years Old."

4. Bill Fairley, "Officers' club, bar a memorable home," *Fort Worth Star-Telegram*, Jan. 20, 1993, 3; "Camp Bowie Day, 9 Years Old. . ."; White, *Panthers to Arrowheads*, 18; W. B. Paddock to C. W. Hutchison, Aug. 6, 1917, in "Over Here—Camp Bowie" Exhibit at Fort Worth Museum of Science and History.

5. White, *Panthers to Arrowheads*, 20.

6. Ibid., 19–20; Jary, *Camp Bowie*, 9, 18; Talbert, *Cowtown-Metropolis*, 127.

7. White, *Panthers to Arrowheads*, 25–26; Jary, *Camp Bowie*, 5; "36th Division Record of Events," 9, typewritten in *Fort Worth Star-Telegram* Collection, Camp Bowie Folder, UTA.

8. "Over Here—Camp Bowie" Exhibit at Fort Worth Museum of Science and History; written interview, Hubert W. Hodges, obtained from Fort Worth Museum of Science and History, Fort Worth History Research Files, taped Dec. 1, 1994; Jary, *Camp Bowie*, 131, 5; Sharon Ware, "Like its brick streets, memories of war eras part of Camp Bowie heritage," *Fort Worth Star-Telegram*, Aug. 6, 1980 (quotation); Atkinson, *The Soldier's Chronology*, 298, 302.

9. "Recollections of Reed Craig Collier" (59 typewritten pages obtained from Charlotte Collier Grizzle, daughter of Collier).

10. "Over Here—Camp Bowie" Exhibit at Fort Worth Museum of Science and History; White, *Panthers to Arrowheads*, 26–27, 34; Jary, *Camp Bowie*, 4 (quotation).

11. White, *Panthers to Arrowheads*, 34.

12. Lelia McDugal, *Up Hill and Down: A History of the Texas National Guard* (Waco, Tex.: Texian Press, 1966), xi; White, *Panthers to Arrowheads*, 25, 28; "36th division record of Events," 9 (typewritten manuscript), "Camp Bowie" Folder, *Fort Worth Star-Telegram* Collection, UTA, cites July 18 as the date the War Department designated National Guard Troops of Texas and Oklahoma to form the 36th.

13. James Ward Lee, Carolyn N. Barnes, Kent A. Bowman, Laura Crow (eds.), *1941: Texas Goes to War* (Denton: University of North Texas Press, 1991), 63; "Over Here—Camp Bowie" Exhibit at Fort Worth Museum of Science and History.

14. White, *Panthers to Arrowheads*, 43, 45, 50. One soldier, Captain Augustine de Zavala, 143rd Infantry, a Spanish-American war veteran, was the grandson of Lorenzo de Zavala, Texas revolutionary war patriot and the first vice-president of the Republic of Texas. Atkinson, *The Soldier's Chronology*, 308.

15. White, *Panthers to Arrowheads*, 45.

16. Perry Stewart, "Over Here: Remembering when Camp Bowie meant a military base," *Fort Worth Star-Telegram*, Feb. 7, 1996, Sec. E, 2; Martin Blumenson, "The 36th Infantry Division in World War II," in Joseph G. Dawson III (ed.), *The Texas Military Experience: From the Texas Revolution through World War II* (College Station: Texas A&M University Press, 1995), 128.

17. Atkinson, *The Soldier's Chronology*, 30; *History of Texas World War Heroes* (Dallas: Army and Navy History Company, 1919), 45; White, *Panthers to Arrowheads*, 2, 27.

18. Stewart, "Over Here," 2; Jary, *Camp Bowie*, 99; interview with Jim Wright, Fritz Lanham Federal Building, Fort Worth, Feb. 11, 1997.

19. White, *Panthers to Arrowheads*, 49.

20. March, *The Nation at War*, 213–15 (quotation); Juliet George, *Images of America: Fort Worth's Arlington Heights* (Charleston, S.C.: Arcadia Publishing Co., 2010), 48.

21. Ware, "Like its brick streets, memories of war eras part of Camp Bowie heritage."

22. *History of Texas World War*, 38–41.

23. J'Nell L. Pate, "Boarding House Rosie: The Role of the Girls' Service League of Fort

Worth, Texas During World War II," (Paper delivered at the Texas State Historical Association Annual Meeting, March 1993, Houston, Texas), 4–5.

24. Lonnie J. White, "Texas Military Forces Museum 36th Division in World War I," Chapter 3 "Camp Bowie" <http://www.texasmilitaryforcesmuseum.org/36division/archives/wwi/white/Chap.3.htm> [Accessed April 5, 2007]

25. Atkinson, *The Soldier's Chronology*, 298; Ware, "Like its brick streets, memories of war eras part of Camp Bowie heritage"; Alfred F. Hurley, *Billy Mitchell: Crusader for Air Power* (New York: Franklin Watts, 1964), 181; "Over Here—Camp Bowie," Exhibit at Fort Worth Museum of Science and History.

26. Jary, *Camp Bowie*, 10, 17–18.

27. Ibid. 21, 36; written interview, Hubert W. Hodges.

28. Williams, "36th Division HQS Next Door To Country Club," in Jary, 10; Sanders and Tyler, *How Fort Worth Became the Texasmost City*, 191; "Over Here—Camp Bowie," Exhibit at Fort Worth Museum of Science and History; Atkinson, *The Soldier's Chronology*, 299.

29. Clay Reynolds with Marie-Madeleine Schein, *A Hundred Years of Heroes: A History of the Southwestern Exposition and Livestock Show* (Fort Worth: Texas Christian University Press, 1995), 119.

30. White, "Texas Military Forces Museum 36th Division in World War I," 4 of 7; David M. Kennedy, *Over Here The First World War and American Society* (New York: Oxford University Press, 1980), 185; Rupert N. Richardson, Adrian Anderson, and Ernest Wallace, *Texas The Lone Star State* (7th ed.; Upper Saddle River, N. J.: Prentice Hall, 1997), 332–33; "First Baptist Tabernacle Camp Bowie, J. Frank Norris Speaks Every Night," *Camp Bowie Texahoma Bugler*, Nov. 16, 1917, 1.

31. Telephone interview with Bill Crawford, May 2, 1998, Fort Worth.

32. Jary, *Camp Bowie*, 47; "Over Here—Camp Bowie" Exhibit at Fort Worth Museum of Science and History; Mae Biddison Benson, "Nursing Texans and Oklahomans Back to Health," *Fort Worth Star-Telegram*, Mar. 3, 1918, *Fort Worth Star-Telegram* Collection, Camp Bowie Folder, UTA.

33. James C. Miles, "Fort Worth and World War I," (M.A. thesis, Southern Methodist University, 1946), 24–25. See also *Fort Worth Star-Telegram*, Oct. 6, 1918, and Jim Atkinson and Judy Wood, *Fort Worth's Huge Deal: Unwinding Westside's Twisted Legend*, (privately published, 2010), PDF e-book, 161. Available at http://www.ruffbrickroad.com/HUGE%20DEAL%20AtkinsonWood.pdf [Accessed July 6, 2011].

34. Bill Fairley, "Nurse won long fight for justice," *Fort Worth Star-Telegram*, Dec. 13, 1995, Sect. A, 24.

35. Ibid.; Telephone conversation with Mary Virginia Simmons, May 28, 2007.

36. Kennedy, *Over Here*, 189; Atkinson, *The Soldier's Chronology*, 320 (latter source reveals that 4,526 troops were missing and 205,690 were wounded in World War I); William Berry, "Fort Worth as War Training Camp," 4, typewritten manuscript in "Camp Bowie" Folder, History Archives, Fort Worth Museum of Science and History; Sanders, *How Fort Worth Became the Texasmost City*, 169 (quotation); Benson, "Nursing Texans and Oklahomans Back to Health,"; Alvin A. Klein, "Alvin Klein Recalls Days With Division Quartermaster," in Jary, *Camp Bowie*, 116; L. H. Reeves, M.D., *The Medical History of Fort Worth and Tarrant County*, in Jary, *Camp Bowie*, 125; Ralph W. Lamb, "Trench Mortar Explosion Kills 15 Soldiers," in Jary, *Camp Bowie*, 15; Roy Harder, "Hominy Grits, McGee Was Overcome by Flagwaving," ibid., 90; Robert Campbell, "Fred Killough Armistice 1918; A Feeling of Pride," in Jary, *Camp Bowie*, 79.

37. Peyton C. March, *The Nation at War* (Westport, Conn.: Greenwood Press, Publishers, 1932), 1–2; Atkinson, *The Soldier's Chronology* , 296; Maurice Matloff (ed.), *American Military History* (Washington, D.C.: Office of the Chief of Military History, United States Army, 1969), 367; "Over Here—Camp Bowie, Fort Worth, Texas, 1917–1919," Exhibit at Fort Worth Museum of Science and History.

38. Jary, *Camp Bowie*, 41–42; Stewart, "Over Here: Remembering when Camp Bowie Meant a Military Base," p 2; "Over Here—Camp Bowie," Exhibit at Fort Worth Museum of Science and History; White, *Panthers to Arrowheads*, 89–90 (quotation).

39. Jary, *Camp Bowie*, 42, 82, 92; White, *Panthers to Arrowheads*, 93, 185; Blumenson, "The 36th Infantry Division in World War II," 128; "Officers Tell How 36th Division Fought," *Dallas Morning News*, Oct. 20, 1918, Section 1, 1 (first quotation); and "36th Division Made Record Near Rheims Work of Camp Bowie Boys Is Praised in Order Issued By Commander," *Dallas Morning News*, Nov. 27, 1918, 19 (second quotation).

40. White, *Panthers to Arrowheads*, 90; Skaggs, "Portrait of a Great Citizen-Soldier," in Jary, *Camp Bowie*, 93. The French government awarded General Hulen the Croix de Guerre twice, and the United States awarded him the Distinguished Service Medal. He served as head of the Texas National Guard after the war.

41. "Over Here: Camp Bowie," Exhibit at Fort Worth Museum of Science and History; Lelia McDugal, "The Texas National Guard Recap History of the 36th Division," as cited in Jary, *Camp Bowie*, 87; Sidney R. Weisiger, "Off to War With the 36th, *The Victoria Advocate*, Oct. 10, 1971, as cited in ibid., 89; Blumenson, "The 36th Infantry Division in World War II," in ibid., 129; "Camp Bowie Boulevard," Historical Marker at Veterans' Memorial Park, 4200 Camp Bowie Boulevard. Also Atkinson and Wood, *Fort Worth's Huge Deal*, 167.

42. Stewart, "Over Here," 1; "Major General W. R. Smith Addresses Farewell to Men of Thirty-Sixth Division Praises Courage of Texans and Oklahomans," *Fort Worth Star-Telegram*, June 22, 1919, 15 (quotation); Jary, *Camp Bowie*, 132–33; Williams, "36th Division HQS Next Door To Country Club," in ibid., 10 (the memorial was dedicated Oct. 29, 1950); Fund Raising Flyer on the wall at the Fort Worth Military Museum, 712 Dorothy Lane, Fort Worth, Texas.

43. "Camp Bowie Day, 9 Years Old. . . Holman Taylor Suggested Site . . . Army Plant Cost 2 Million"; Fairley, "Officers' Club, Bar a Memorable Home."; "Over Here—Camp Bowie," Exhibit at Fort Worth Museum of Science and History; Jean Wysatta, "Joe Driskill Returns to Develop His Old Stompin' Grounds," in Jary, *Camp Bowie*, 125.

44. Jary, *Camp Bowie*, 46; Atkinson, *The Soldier's Chronology*, 305.

45. J'Nell L. Pate, *Livestock Legacy The Fort Worth Stockyards 1887–1987* (College Station: Texas A&M University Press, 1988), 99–100; Sanders and Tyler, 69; White, *Panthers to Arrowheads*, 20.

CHAPTER FOUR

1. Fort Worth Chamber of Commerce, "Fort Worth—the New Metropolis of the Southwest" (June 1919), 23; Maurer, *Aviation in the U.S. Army*, 17; Jim Marrs, "GI Ordered to Close Air Field Talked Into Opening Meacham," *Fort Worth Star-Telegram*, Feb. 25, 1973; Air Center Gro (partial headline only)," *Fort Worth Star-Telegram*, Oct. 18, 1933, *Fort Worth Star-Telegram* Collection, Aviation History Folder, UTA.

2. Heinecke, "Fort Worth Aviation," 3–4.

3. Maurer, *Aviation in the U.S. Army*, 191; Atkinson, *The Soldier's Chronology*, 336.

4. Gurney, *A Chronology of World Aviation*, 40; Bilstein and Miller, *Aviation in Texas*, 45; G. R. Simonson (ed.), *The History of the American Aircraft Industry* (Cambridge, Mass.: The MIT Press, 1968), 23; "Air Center Gro"; George E. Haddaway, "Tribute to Our 'Airport Man'" *Fort Worth* (May 1961): 17; J'Nell Pate, *North of the River A Brief History of North Fort Worth* (Fort Worth: Texas Christian University Press, 1994), 120–21.

5. "Fort Worth—The New Metropolis of the Southwest," 28; "Industrial," *The Fort Worth Broadcaster* (October 1923): 5.

6. Pate, *North of the River*, 119–20; "Fourth Airways District," *Fort Worth Chamber of Commerce News* (August 1934): 5.

7. Bilstein and Miller, *Aviation in Texas*, 54; Gurney, *A Chronology of World Aviation*, 40;

"Ex-Navy Airman, Recalls Crashing in Shenandoah," *Convairiety*, Feb. 11, 1953, 8.

8. "A Cow Pasture Was First Air Port," *Fort Worth Star-Telegram*, Oct. 30, 1949, *Fort Worth Star-Telegram* Collection, Air Fields Folder, UTA.

9. Connelly, "The Silver Anniversary of Aviation," *Fort Worth Star-Telegram and Sunday Record Magazine* Section, Dec. 16, 1928, Aviation History Folder, ibid., 4–5.

10. D. W. Carlton, Manager, "Aviation," *Fort Worth Chamber of Commerce News* (January 1930): 18.

11. "American Airways Expands," *Fort Worth Chamber of Commerce News*, April 1930: 5 (quotation); John E. Wiltz, *From Isolation to War, 1931–1941* (New York: Thomas Y. Crowell Company, 1968), 16.

12. "Air Center Gro"; "United Air Line To Quit On 8th Anniversary," May 11, 1934, *Fort Worth Star-Telegram* Collection, Air Lines Folder, UTA; Bill Potts, "Three Lines Here Have Enviable Records," *Fort Worth Star-Telegram*, Jan. 13, 1939, *Fort Worth Star-Telegram* Collection, Aviation History Folder, ibid.; *Annual Report of the Manager of the Fort Worth Chamber of Commerce, 1935*, Aviation Department, *Fort Worth Chamber of Commerce News* (January 1936): 10; Sam Kinch, "Air Express Here Is Making Rapid Gain in Tonnage," *Fort Worth Star-Telegram*, Apr. 1, 1938, Aviation History Folder, *Fort Worth Star-Telegram* Collection, UTA.

13. Bilstein and Miller, *Aviation in Texas*, 43–44.

14. "Henry H. Arnold," The Associated Press Biographical Service, Sketch 3201, Issued Apr. 1, 1945, 2, in Arnold, H. H. Folder, *Fort Worth Star-Telegram* Collection, UTA; Morris and Smith, *Ceiling Unlimited*, 329; Wayne Biddle, *Barons of the Sky, From Early Flight to Strategic Warfare: The Story of the American Aerospace Industry* (New York: Simon and Schuster, 1991), 41; George Vecsey and George C. Dade, *Getting Off the Ground: The Pioneers of Aviation Speak for Themselves* (New York: E. Dutton, 1979), 176; Arnold, *Global Mission*, 169; William Wagner, *Reuben Fleet and the Story of Consolidated Aircraft* (Fallbrook, Calif.: Aero Publishers, 1976), 207; Niven, Canby, and Welsh (eds.), *Dynamic America: A History of General Dynamics Corporation and Its Predecessor Companies* (New York: General Dynamics Corporation and Doubleday & Company, Inc., 1958), 266; "Henry H. Arnold," The Associated Press Biographical Service, 2.

15. Morris and Smith, *Ceiling Unlimited*, 330; Copp, *A Few Great Captains*, 455–57 (quotation).

16. Copp, *A Few Great Captains*, 459, 461.

17. "XB-24 Designed, Built, Flown Within a Year," *Convairiety*, Mar. 30, 1960, 5; John Wegg, *General Dynamics Aircraft and Their Predecessors* (Annapolis, Md: Naval Institute Press, 1990), 46; "'Emergency' Cited By Air Corps Ahead," *Fort Worth Star-Telegram*, January 19, 1939, *Fort Worth Star-Telegram* Collection, Arnold, H. H. Folder, UTA; Niven, Canby, and Welsh, *Dynamic America*, 266.

18. "Air Training Plan Okayed By President," *Fort Worth Star-Telegram*, Dec. 28, 1938, *Fort Worth Star-Telegram* Collection, Aviation Defense Folder, UTA; "NTAC Chosen As Air School," ibid.

19. "Air Training Plan Okayed by President," (quotation); "XPB2Y Called Coronado, Result of Navy Contest," *Convairiety*, Mar. 16, 1960, 5; Gurney, *A Chronology of World Aviation*, 65.

20. "Aviation Department," *Annual Report of the Fort Worth Chamber of Commerce for 1939* in *This Month in Fort Worth* (January 1940): 9; Bilstein and Miller, *Aviation in Texas*, 91; *Annual Report of the Fort Worth Chamber of Commerce for 1940*, "Message From President B. B. Stone," *This Month in Fort Worth* (January 1941): 3.

21. "Aviation Department," *Annual Report of the Fort Worth Chamber of Commerce for 1939*, 9.

22. Jacqueline Cochran and Maryann Bucknum Brinley, *Jackie Cochran: An Autobiography* (New York: Bantam Books, 1987), 152; "Canada Plans Air School Here," *Fort Worth Star-Telegram*, June 28, 1940, *Fort Worth Star-Telegram* Collection, Air Fields Folder, UTA.

23. "Canada Plans Air School Here,"; "4 More Flying Fields Due Near Fort Worth," *Fort Worth Star-Telegram*, Sept. 27, 1940; McMullen, "Old World War Airfields in Fair Shape to Use Again"; Bill Potts, "U.S. May Re-establish Flying Fields Here, Rumors Assert," *Fort Worth Star-Telegram*, May 23, 1940, *Fort Worth Star-Telegram* Collection, Air Fields Folder, UTA.

24. William Holden, "Fort Worth Is Doing Its Part in National Defense Program," *This Month in Fort Worth* (June 1940): Inside Front Cover.

25. "Pilots Again May Train on World War Air Fields Here," *Fort Worth Star-Telegram*, May 24, 1940, *Fort Worth Star-Telegram* Collection, Air Fields Folder, UTA; McMullen, "Old World War Airfields in Fair Shape to Use Again."

26. *Selected Tarrant County Communities, Tarrant County Historic Resources Survey* (Fort Worth: Historic Preservation Council for Tarrant County, Texas, 1990), 167; "National Defense Activities Keep Chamber Staff Busy," *This Month in Fort Worth* (July 1940): Inside Front Cover; "Air Corps Training School Located at Hicks Field," ibid., 1; *Selected Tarrant County Communities*, 167; "Rapid Expansion at Hicks Field," *This Month in Fort Worth* (September 1940): 4; "Air Corps Training School Located at Hicks Field," 1; "Rapid Expansion at Hicks Field," 4. Colonel Daniel Edwin Hooks, a Fort Worthian, also commanded Hicks and later became commanding general of Andrews Air Force Base. One of the filers who gained his wings at Hicks prior to the war was George Gobel of later television and movie fame. *Oil Legends of Fort Worth*, 146.

27. "Chamber of Commerce Driving Hard on Prospective Plants Connected with National Defense Program," *This Month in Fort Worth* (August 1940): Inside Front Cover.

28. "Seaplane Base," *This Month in Fort Worth* (March 1940): 3; "Message From President B. B. Stone," *Annual Report of the Fort Worth Chamber of Commerce for 1940*, in *This Month in Fort Worth* (January 1941): 11; William Holden, "Our Chamber of Commerce In the War," *Annual Report of the Fort Worth Chamber of Commerce for 1944*, in *This Month in Fort Worth* (January 1945): 8; "1943 Finds Fort Worth Girding For War. . .In the Air. . . On Land and Over the Sea" *Annual Report of the Fort Worth Chamber of Commerce for 1942* in *This Month In Fort Worth* (January 1943): 4.

29. Simonson (ed.), *The History of the American Aircraft Industry*, 119 (quotation); *Of Men and Stars: Lockheed Aircraft Corporation* (Burbank, Calif.: 1958; reprint; New York: Arno Press, 1980), 15–16; Morris and Smith, *Ceiling Unlimited*, 377, 366; Arnold, *Global Mission*, 198, 203.

30. Arnold, *Global Mission*. 198, 203; Wagner, *Reuben Fleet and the Story of Consolidated Aircraft*, 221; Morris and Smith, *Ceiling Unlimited*, 336–37; *Of Men and Stars*, 15–16.

31. Arnold, *Global Mission*, 264–65.

32. Biddle, *Barons of the Sky*, 261.

33. "John Kennedy, Man of Many Careers Retains Interest in City of Saginaw," *Saginaw Sentinel*, July 8, 1971, 1: Bill Leader, "The First 11 Mayors Of Saginaw," *The Sentinel*, Sept. 2, 1982, 11; *Selected Tarrant County Communities*, 155; "Plywood Planes Soon Will Be in Production Here," *Fort Worth Star-Telegram*, Apr. 6, 1940, *Fort Worth Star-Telegram* Collection, Bennett Aircraft Folder, UTA.

34. "Plywood Planes Soon Will Be in Production Here"; "New Type Plane to Be Built Here," *This Month in Fort Worth* (November 1939): 10; "Plane Factory Here Expects British Order," *Fort Worth Star-Telegram*, Oct. 26, 1939, *Fort Worth Star-Telegram* Collection, Bennett Aircraft Folder, UTA; "Plane Factory Plans Will Be Revealed Here," *Fort Worth Star-Telegram*, Oct. 25, 1939, ibid.; "Globe. . . A Backward Glance and Forward Strides," *Bell Helicopter News*, July 10, 1959, 4; "This is Bell 1967 Globe: Busier than Ever," *Bell Helicopter News*, Mar. 10, 1967, 4; "Bennett Aircraft Plant Completed," *This Month in Fort Worth* (April 1940), 4.

35. "Plywood Planes Soon Will Be in Production Here"; "Globe . . . A Backward Glance And Forward Strides"; "Bennett Aircraft Organization Is Completed Here," *Fort Worth Star-Telegram*, Apr. 23, 1940, ibid.; "Bennett Aircraft Plant completed," 4.

36. "Globe. . .A Backward Glance And Forward Strides"; "First Plane Made Here Takes Off," *Fort Worth Star-Telegram*, Apr. 12, 1940, *Fort Worth Star-Telegram* Collection, Bennett Aircraft Folder, UTA; "Plane Factory Here Expects British Order"; "Industrial Department," *Annual Report of the Fort Worth Chamber of Commerce for 1939*, in *This Month in Fort Worth* (January 1940), 16; Bill Potts, "James Goodwin Hall Tells of Plan to Start Construction of Huge Cargo Planes at Bennett Aircraft Factory Here," *Fort Worth Star-Telegram*, June 9, 1940, *Fort Worth Star-Telegram* Collection, Bennett Aircraft Folder, UTA; "Bennett BTC-1 Will Make Bow," *Fort Worth Star-Telegram*, Apr. 11, 1940, ibid.

37. "Fort Worth Built Planes Considered," *Fort Worth Star-Telegram*, Aug. 2, 1940, ibid.

38. Leader, "The First 11 Mayors of Saginaw," 11; B. N. Timmons, "Globe Aircraft Awarded Army Plane Contract," *Fort Worth Star-Telegram*, Jan. 29, 1942, *Fort Worth Star-Telegram* Collection, Globe Aircraft Folder, UTA.

39. Bilstein and Miller, *Aviation in Texas*, 95; Morris and Smith, *Ceiling Unlimited*, 336–37.

CHAPTER 5

1. Wagner, *Reuben Fleet and The Story of Consolidated Aircraft*, ix.

2. Wegg, *General Dynamics Aircraft and Their Predecessors*, 42–43. For a time Fleet was a timber appraiser. Another young man who grew up in the lumbering business near Fleet in Washington State was William Boeing, who also later would become an aircraft manufacturer. Jacob Goodwin, *Brotherhood of Arms: General Dynamics and the Business of Defending America* (New York: Times Books, 1985), 50; Rae, *Climb to Greatness: The American Aircraft Industry, 1920–1960*, 11; and Niven, Canby, and Welsh (eds.), *Dynamic America*, 123. Gallaudet, who earned a Ph.D. from Johns Hopkins in electrical engineering, worked at Westinghouse Electric and later taught physics at Yale. Because he tinkered with "flying machines" on the side, the head of Yale's Physics Department told Gallaudet he had become a "laughingstock of the faculty" and must quit his experiments or resign.

3. Wegg, *General Dynamics Aircraft and Their Predecessors*, 43; Niven, Canby and Welsh (eds.), *Dynamic America* 201–202; Wagner, *Reuben Fleet and The Story of Consolidated Aircraft*, ix; Rae, *Climb To Greatness The American Aircraft Industry, 1920–1960*, 12–13; Gurney, *A Chronology of World Aviation*, 37.

4. Niven, Canby and Welsh (eds.), *Dynamic America*, 202; Rae, *Climb to Greatness*, 13; Wegg, *General Dynamics*, 45; Wagner, *Reuben Fleet and the Story of Consolidated Aircraft*, 180, 227.

5. Ethelbert C. Barksdale, *The Genesis of the Aviation Industry In North Texas* (Austin: Bureau of Business Research, University of Texas, 1958), 3.

6. Wagner, *Reuben Fleet and the Story of Consolidated Aircraft*, 221.

7. Barksdale, *The Genesis of the Aviation Industry in North Texas*, 2–3, 8; "Local History," 14, typewritten manuscript in loose-leaf scrapbook on History of Westworth Village, compiled in 1976 as a Sesquicentennial Project, City Secretary's Office, Westworth Village, Texas; Tolbert, *Cowtown-Metropolis*, 41; Bilstein and Miller, *Aviation in Texas*, 95; "White Settlement, Westworth Village, River Oaks," *Tarrant County Historic Resources Survey* (Fort Worth: Historic Preservation Council for Tarrant County, Texas, 1984), 7; "History of White Settlement" (75 page, mimeographed notebook prepared by Mrs. E. D. Head and students of Brewer High School history classes of 1952 and 1953); "Plant Produces Over 3,000 Libs and C-87s Plus 7,500,000 Spares," *The Eagle*, Dec. 15, 1944, 1; "Home of Colossal B-36s 10-Year-Old Air Industry Has $100,000,000 Output," *Fort Worth Star-Telegram*, Oct. 30, 1949, *Fort Worth Star-Telegram* Collection, Aviation Industry Folder, UTA; Wegg, *General Dynamics*, 47; "Fort Worth Plant Originally Built For Assembly of Wartime Bombers," *Convairiety*, Apr. 27, 1960, 5.

8. Holden, *Annual Report of the Fort Worth Chamber of Commerce for 1940*, 2 (quotation); Holden, "Membership and Budget Campaign," *This Month in Fort Worth* (March 1941): 1; "History of White Settlement," 33–34.

9. "City Gain Means New Services," *Fort Worth Star-Telegram*, Feb. 21, 1941, *Fort Worth Star-Telegram* Collection, Fort Worth Street Improvements Folder, UTA; Barksdale, *The Genesis of the Aviation Industry in North Texas*, 8–10; Holden, "Membership and Budget Campaign," 2.

10. Bilstein and Miller, *Aviation in Texas*, 95; Barksdale, *The Genesis of the Aviation Industry in North Texas*, 10; "Home of Colossal B-36s 10-Year-Old Air Industry Has $100,000,000 Output" (quotation); "City May Go Ahead With Airport Work," *Fort Worth Star-Telegram*, May 24, 1941, *Fort Worth Star-Telegram* Collection, Aviation History Folder, UTA.

11. Telephone Interview with Mrs. Edgar Deen Jr., Feb. 10, 1997, Fort Worth; Barksdale, *The Genesis of the Aviation Industry in North Texas*, 10; Bilstein and Miller, *Aviation in Texas*, 95; "Fort Worth 'Home' to B-32!" *The Eagle*, July 1945: 4; "No. 1 Citizen Picks Consair for Only Texas Plant Visit," *The Consolidated Eagle*, Oct. 8, 1942, 2; "Consolidated Vultee Provides Challenge to the Axis," *This Month in Fort Worth* (January 1944): 18; Wagner, *Reuben Fleet and the Story of Consolidated Aircraft*, 252.

12. "Three Million Spent on Roads," *The Consolidated Eagle*, Jan. 21, 1943, 1; Wagner, *Reuben Fleet and the Story of Consolidated Aircraft*, 241.

13. Wagner, *Reuben Fleet and the Story of Consolidated Aircraft*, 253; "Fort Worth Plant Originally Built For Assembly of Wartime Bombers," 5.

14. Wagner, *Reuben Fleet and the Story of Consolidated Aircraft*, 221, 297 (first quotation), 294 (third quotation); Goodwin, *Brotherhood of Arms*, 72 (second quotation); Wegg, *General Dynamics*, 48; "Control of Consolidated Aircraft Passes from Reuben Fleet to Avco," *Convairiety*, May 11, 1960, 5; Rae, *Climb to Greatness*, 128.

15. Rae, *Climb to Greatness*, 128; Wagner, *Reuben Fleet and the Story of Consolidated Aircraft*, ix, 242; Wegg, *General Dynamics*, 48–49.

16. Niven, Canby, and Welsh (eds.), *Dynamic America*, 273 (quotation); "First Powered Assembly Line Tried Out by Vultee at Downey," *Convairiety*, July 20, 1960, 5; Wegg, *General Dynamics*, 48–49; Wagner, *Reuben Fleet and the Story of Consolidated Aircraft*, 243.

17. "First Powered Assembly Line Tried Out by Vultee at Downey," 5; "Merger Creates One of World's Largest Aircraft Companies," *The Consolidated Eagle*, Mar. 18, 1943, 1; Niven, Canby, and Welsh (eds.), *Dynamic America*, 273; Wagner, *Reuben Fleet and the Story of Consolidated Aircraft*, 251; Wegg, *General Dynamics*, 49.

18. Wagner, *Reuben Fleet and the Story of Consolidated Aircraft*, 252; "More than 3,000 Multi-Engine Aircraft Produced by Fort Worth during War," *Convairiety*, Aug. 17, 1960, 5; "Plant Produced Over 3,000 Libs and C-87s Plus 7,500,000 Spares," 3.

19. Interview with J. D. McEachern, Mar. 4, 1997, Lockheed hangar where B-36 had been restored, Fort Worth; "No. 1 Off the Line," *This Month in Fort Worth* (May 1942): 5. Newman, an Englishman, came to America at age four when his father was hired to be factory manager for the Curtiss Company during World War I. Newman began work at Consolidated while it was still in the old Gallaudet factory on the East Coast. He transferred to Buffalo with Major Fleet and was assistant superintendent of Consolidated in San Francisco. On March 3, 1942, he became vice president in charge of operations for the Fort Worth plant. "No. 1 Off the Line," 5.

20. "No. 1 Off the Line," 5; interview with Enis M. Kerlee. Stockyards officials point out that Henry Ford did not invent the assembly line. Meatpacking plants conceived the idea in reverse by "disassembling" the animals from whole carcass to packaged meat by a slow moving line; interview with Harry Evans; "Work Around Clock Begun at Plant," *The Consolidated Eagle*, July 30, 1942, 1; "Plant Produces Over 3,000 Libs and C-87s Plus 7,500,000 Spares."

21. "Plant Produces Over 3,000 Libs and C-87s Plus 7,500,000 Spares," 3; Niven, Canby, and Welsh (eds.), *Dynamic America*, 275; Reginald M. Cleveland and Frank Graham, "Aviation Manufacturing Today in America," in *The History of the American Aircraft Industry: An Anthology*, 146.

22. Consolidated Vultee Aircraft Corporation Training Certificate in Foremanship and Job Instruction, issued to Vernon Rogers, June 19, 1943 (in possession of author); "Convair to Observe Lone 1943 Holiday," *The Eagle*, Dec. 16, 1943, 1; "Convair Leads In Production," *The Eagle*, Jan. 20, 1944, 1; The article did not cite the names of the companies that were second and third; Goodwin, *Brotherhood of Arms*, 72. See also Ann Markusen, Peter Hall, Scott Campbell, and Susan Deitrick, *The Rise of the Gunbelt* (New York: Oxford University Press, 1991), 93; "Plant Produces Over 3,000 Libs and C-87s Plus 7,500,000 Spares," 3; "Pacific War Demands to Bolster Plans Output Here," *Fort Worth Star-Telegram*, Apr. 20, 1945, *Fort Worth Star-Telegram* Collection, Aviation Industry Folder, UTA; "Progress Made on $3,000,000 Convair Construction Projects," *The Eagle*, Nov. 3, 1944, 1; "$2,000,000 Expansion Program Approved for Fort Worth Plant," *The Eagle*, May 11, 1944, 1.

23. "More Than 3,000 Multi-Engine Aircraft Produced by Fort Worth During War"; Conversation with Mr. Joe Wagner at Garden Club Open House, Botanic Gardens, Apr. 30, 1998; Maurice Lambert, *Memories of Liberator Village* (Fort Worth: Memorabiliacs Press, 2007), 81; "Moratorium Granted on Drafting Convair Employees Between 26–37," *The Eagle*, May 25, 1944, 1.

24. Alice Kessler-Harris, "Women, Work and War," in *The Private Side of American History*, ed. Thomas R. Frazier (4th ed.; New York: Harcourt Brace Jovanovich, Publisher, 1987), 283; Niven, Canby, and Welsh (eds.), *Dynamic America*, 277; interview with Gloria Doyle, Jan. 10, 1997, Haltom City; interview with Enis M. Kerlee, Dec. 3, 1996, Haltom City; Cynthia Guidici, "Women at War," in *1941: Texas Goes to War*, ed. James Ward Lee, Carolyn N. Barnes, Kent A. Bowman, and Laura Crow (Denton: University of North Texas Press, 1991), 149 (quotation).

25. Pate, "Boarding House Rosie: The Role of the Girls' Service League of Fort Worth, Texas during World War II,' 4, 6–7, 9–10, 12.

26. "Enough Said," *The Eagle*, May 20, 1943, 1.

27. "Open House Scheduled for Consair Employees," *The Eagle*, June 17, 1943, 1 (quotation); "250,000 in Bonds Subscribed Sunday, Final Figures Due," *The Eagle*, July 1, 1943, 1 (second quotation). The author's father, who was an assistant foreman at Consolidated Vultee, and her mother traveled to the plant that open-house Sunday afternoon after church. They left their two children, their son James, age thirteen, and the author, almost five, waiting in the family's 1939 Ford pickup in the parking lot. The tour took longer than expected, and the children sweltered in the cab of the pickup, even with the doors open. The author, who had brought a coloring book along to pass the time, was persuaded by her brother to put crayons on the metal dashboard of the vehicle and watch them melt! Neither remembers if they got into any trouble over the incident.

28. "No. 1 Citizen Picks Consair for Only Texas Plant Visit," 1–2.

29. Ibid.

30. "Gen. Arnold and Party End 5-State Inspection," *Fort Worth Star-Telegram*, July 11, 1942, *Fort Worth Star-Telegram* Collection, Arnold, H. H. Folder, UTA (first quotation); "Chief of AAF Praises Plant," *The Consolidated Eagle*, July 16, 1942, 1 (second quotation).

31. "Mayer Is Appointed Manager at Convair's Fort Worth Division," *The Eagle*, May 18, 1944, 1; "Girdler Resigns from Convair Board Post," *The Eagle*, Apr. 27, 1945, 1 (quotation).

32. "Arnold Thanks Convair Workers," *The Eagle*, Sept. 7, 1945, 4 (first quotation); "Mayer Says Convair In Top Shape for Postwar Production," *The Eagle*, Sept. 7, 1945, 1; "Convair Continues Three Projects; Work Week Cut to 40 Hours," *The Eagle*, Aug. 17, 1945, 1 (second quotation).

33. "Brief History of Fort Worth Operation of Convair Aerospace Division of General Dynamics," 6 in "History of White Settlement." 1; Wagner, *Reuben Fleet and the Story of Consolidated Aircraft*, 14; Barksdale, *The Genesis of the Aviation Industry in North Texas*, 11; "Convair Planes Since Pearl Harbor Total More Than 30,000," *The Eagle*, Jan. 5, 1945, 1; "History of

White Settlement," 41. Manufacturing plants were located at San Diego and Downey, California; Fort Worth, Texas; Nashville, Tennessee; Wayne, Michigan; Allentown, Pennsylvania; New Orleans, Louisiana; Miami, Florida; and modification plants at Tucson, Arizona; Louisville, Kentucky; Elizabeth City, North Carolina; and Dearborn, Michigan; and thirteenth, a trans-Pacific airline operated for the Air Transport Command. See also Markusen, Hall, Campbell, and Deitrick, *The Rise of the Gunbelt*, 93.

34. Talbert, *Cowtown-Metropolis*, 42; Barksdale, *The Genesis of the Aviation Industry in North Texas*, 10.

35. Niven, Candy, and Welsh (eds,), *Dynamic America*, 357; "Mr. Odlum Gets the Business," *Fortune* (September 1949): 92; Rae, *Climb To Greatness*, 181; Simonson (ed.), *The History of the American Aircraft Industry*, 181, 186; "Brief History of Fort Worth Operation of Convair Aerospace Division of General Dynamics," 1; "More than 3,000 Multi-Engine Aircraft Produced by Fort Worth During War," 5.

36. Richard C. Kirkland, *Tales of a War Pilot* (Washington, D.C.: Smithsonian Institution Press, 1999), 75; Jeffrey G. Barlow, *Revolt of the Admirals: The Fight for Naval Aviation 1945–1950* (Washington, D.C.: Brassey's, 1998), 145.

37. Charles D. Bright, *The Jet Makers: The Aerospace Industry from 1945 to 1972* (Lawrence: Regents Press of Kansas, 1978), 15; "Addition Will Make Concrete Runway 8,200 Feet Long," *The Eagle*, Aug. 20, 1945, 1; E. Hehs, "Beryl Arthur Erickson Test Pilot" *Code One* (October 1992), 19–20; Bill May, "Pilot Recalls Joy of Maiden Flight 37 Minutes Aloft Elates XB-36 Crew," *Fort Worth Star-Telegram*, Aug. 8, 1971, *Fort Worth Star-Telegram* Collection, B.A. Erickson Folder, UTA; "Story of B-36 Dates Back to Early in 1941," *Convairiety*, August 25, 1954, 8 (quotation).

38. Flyer of Aerodrome Press, The Aviation Art of Mike Machat, "Faster than a Speeding Bullet," (1996 Aerodrome Press information on Beryl A. Erickson; copy from B. A. Erickson); E. Hehs, "Beryl Arthur Erickson, Test Pilot," 18–19; telephone interview with Beryl Erickson, February 2, 1997.

39. "Memorable Day Recalled crew of XB-36 on Its Riskiest Flight Honored," *Fort Worth Star-Telegram*, May 26, 1947, *Fort Worth Star-Telegram* Collection, Fort Worth Army Air Field Folder, UTA (first quotation); Hehs, "Beryl Arthur Erickson Test Pilot" 20–21; interview, Loyd L. Turner, Sept. 6, 1996, Fort Worth, (second quotation).

40. McEachern interview.

41. Erickson interview (first quotation); telephone interview with Billye Erickson, Jan., 30, 1997 (second quotation); Hehs, "Beryl Arthur Erickson Test Pilot," 20–21; interview with Max Schelper, March 4, 1997, Fort Worth; McEachern interview.

42. "Boom and Bust: Aircraft Industry 'Collapse' Followed World War II's End," 5; "Mr. Odlum Gets the Business," 92.

43. Roger Franklin, *The Defender: The Story of General Dynamics* (New York: Harper and Row, 1986), 128–29; "Mr. Odlum Gets the Business": 90–92; Floyd Odlum was married to Jacqueline Cochran, a famous woman pilot who during World War II headed the Women's Airforce Service Pilots (WASPs). Some of the men who worked at Convair joked that they worked for a woman after they learned that the famous Cochran was married to the Convair owner. Interview with Harry Evans.

44. "Mr. Odlum Gets the Business," 93; "Troubled Times Mounting Convair-Liner Loss Created a 'Special Situation'," *Convairiety*, July 5, 1961, 5; "Convair Looks Back on 27 Years of Stirring History," *Convairiety*, May 24, 1950, 5; Niven, Canby, and Welsh (eds.), *Dynamic America*, 360; "Convair Shows Giant B-36 Close Up," *Fort Worth* (July 1947): 52.

45. "Mr. Odlum Gets the Business," 90 (quotations), 134, 138; "Here's Chance to Name B-36 Let's Start Thinking Now," *Convairiety*, Dec. 8, 1948, 1. *"Peacemaker": The History of the B-36 At Carswell Air Force Base Fort Worth, Texas 1948-1958*, 6.

46. "Troubled Times Mounting Convair-Liner Loss Created a 'Special Situation'," 5; "Ft.

Worth is Largest with 21 Blocks under Roof," *Convairiety*, Sept. 1, 1948, 4; "Profits Again AF, Navy and Airline Contracts Pulled Convair From Red in '49," *Convairiety*, July 19, 1961, 5.

47. "B-36 To Keep Convair Busy For Four Years," *Fort Worth Star-Telegram*, Apr. 27, 1950, *Fort Worth Star-Telegram* Collection, Aviation B-36 Folder, UTA.

48. "With 28,000 on Payroll, FW Now Biggest Air Plant," *Convairiety*, Apr. 11, 1951, 1 (quotation); "Brief History of Fort Worth Operation of Convair Aerospace Division of General Dynamics," 2. Also Don Pyeatt and Dennis R. Jenkins, *Cold War Peacemaker: The Story of Cowtown and the Convair B-36* (North Branch, Minn. Specialty Press, 2010), 51.

49. "History of White Settlement," 42; "Convair," *Fort Worth Annual Report Issue* (December 1952): 29; Bilstein and Miller, *Aviation in Texas*, 138.

50. "Brief History of Fort Worth Operation of Convair Aerospace Division of General Dynamics," 3; "Convair," *Fort Worth Annual Report Edition* (December 1955): 44; "Bomberettes Seek State Cage Title," *The Eagle*, March 16, 1945, 4.

51. "Convair," *Fort Worth Annual Report Edition* (December 1955): 44; "At Convair," *Fort Worth Annual Report Edition*, (December 1956): 34; "Good News : Convair's Payroll at All-Time High; Jobs Well Above 16-Year Average," *Fort Worth* (April 1958): 32.

CHAPTER SIX

1. W. E. Butterworth, *Flying Army The Modern Air Arm of the U.S. Army* (New York: Doubleday and Company, 1971), 32 (quotation); Alfred F. Hurley, *Billy Mitchell Crusader for Air Power* (New York: Franklin Watts, 1964), 11, 16–17, 107, 119, 135; John L. Frisbee (ed.), *Makers of the United States Air Force* (McLean, Va.: Pergamon-Brassey's International Defense Publishers, 1989) , 19; Arnold, *Global Mission*, 44; Arnold Brophy, *The Air Force: A Panorama of the Nation's Youngest Service* (New York: Gilbert Press, 1956), 52.

2. "History of Fort Worth Army Air Field," *The Lone Star Scanner*, Feb. 16, 1946, 4, Fort Worth Naval Air Station Joint Reserve Base Library, Fort Worth; "Consolidated Forced by Army To Build 50 PTs for $1 Apiece," *Convairiety*, June 24, 1959, 5; Gurney, *A Chronology of World Aviation*, 42.

3. Potts, "U.S. May Re-establish Flying Fields Here, Rumors Assert," *Fort Worth Star-Telegram*, May 23, 1940.

4. "Airport Sites Are Inspected," *Fort Worth Star-Telegram*, Sept. 4, 1941, *Fort Worth Star-Telegram* Collection, Airport Folder, UTA (quotation); "U.S. Bomber Unit May Be Placed Here," March 22, 1941, ibid.

5. "Airfield Work to Start Soon," June 12, 1941, Airport Folder, UTA (quotation); "City Freed of Airport Obligation."

6. "World Spotlight On City Aviation," *Fort Worth Star-Telegram*, Oct. 30, 1949, *Fort Worth Star-Telegram* Collection, Carswell Folder, UTA; "Army Ready to Speed Airfield," June 16, 1941, Airfield Folder, ibid; "Clearing Work Begins at Site of Airfield; Grading Bids to Be Asked Tuesday," June 23, 1941, Airport Folder, ibid.; "Base Has 7th Birthday Carswell, One of World's Major Airdromes, Marks Anniversary," *Fort Worth Star-Telegram*, Aug. 21, 1949, *Fort Worth Star-Telegram* Collection, Carswell Folder, UTA; "City Freed of Airport Obligation," Sept. 8, 1941, Aviation Folder, ibid.

7. Frisbee, Makers of the United States Air Force, 7; Maurer Maurer (ed.), *Air Force Combat Units of World War II* (1961; reprint, Washington, D.C.: U.S. Government Printing Office and Office of Air Force History, 1983) 8; Curtis E. Le May with MacKinlay Kantor, *Mission with Le May: My Story* (Garden City, N.Y.: Doubleday & Company, Inc., 1965), 197; Brophy, *The Air Force*, 55.

8. "Airport Sites Are Inspected" (quotation); "Bombardment Base 'Nearer'," *Fort Worth Star-Telegram*, Sept. 9, 1941, *Fort Worth Star-Telegram* Collection, Aviation Folder, UTA.

9. "Work Started on Runways," *Fort Worth Star-Telegram*, Dec. 1, 1941, ibid.; "World Spotlight on City Aviation."

10. John O. Lockwood, "Factual History of the Fort Worth Division Consolidated Vultee Aircraft Corporation," Nov. 22, 1945, mimeographed notebook, 1 (Lockheed Martin Corporation Library, Fort Worth, Texas); "Air Base Taken for Training," *Fort Worth Star-Telegram,* July 29, 1942, *Fort Worth Star-Telegram* Collection, U.S. Army Flying Training Command Folder, UTA; "Tarrant Field Combat Crew Classes Begin," *Fort Worth Star-Telegram,* Oct. 12, 1942, *Fort Worth Star-Telegram* Collection, Tarrant Field Folder, UTA; "Air Field Here Is Year Old," *Fort Worth Star-Telegram,* Aug. 7, 1943, Fort Worth Army Air Field Folder, ibid.; "History of White Settlement," 34; Ann Perliman, "Tarrant Field Hustling Community With 14 Busy on Ground to Keep One Flying," *Fort Worth Star-Telegram,* Dec. 10, 1942, Tarrant Field Folder, UTA.

11. "Tarrant Field Needs Recruits," *Fort Worth Star-Telegram,* Sept. 6, 1942, *Fort Worth Star-Telegram* Collection, Tarrant Field Folder, UTA (quotation); Perliman, "Tarrant Field Hustling Community With 14 Busy on Ground to Keep One Flying,"; Jack Douglas, "Old Soldiers Never Die; They Settle in Texas," *Fort Worth Star-Telegram,* Aug. 27, 1955, Carswell Folder, ibid.

12. "Tarrant Field Combat Crew Classes Begin"; "History of White Settlement," 34; Perliman, "Tarrant Field Hustling Community With 14 Busy on Ground to Keep One Flying," *Fort Worth Star-Telegram,* Dec. 10, 1942.

13. "Tarrant Field Combat Crew Classes Begin," *Fort Worth Star-Telegram,* Oct. 12, 1942; "Army Air Field Completes Its First Year of Training," *This Month in Fort Worth* (September 1943): 5; "Air Field Here Is Year Old," *Fort Worth Star-Telegram,* Aug. 7, 1943; "7th Bomb Wing commences with 40th anniversary celebration activities," *Carswell Sentinel,* Oct. 10, 1986, 1; "Tarrant Reveille Cannon Wakes Up Civilians Too," *Fort Worth Star-Telegram,* Jan. 6, 1943, *Fort Worth Star-Telegram* Collection, Tarrant Field, UTA.

14. "Army Air Field Completes Its First Year of Training."

15. "7th Bomb Wing commences with 40th anniversary celebration activities," *Carswell Sentinel,* Oct. 10, 1986; "World Spotlight on City Aviation"; "New Name for Tarrant Field," *This Month in Fort Worth* (May 1943): 23; "Army Air Field Completes Its First Year of Training," 5. Consistently throughout the country, airfields took the name of the city or town wherever located with the words "Army Air Field" following; "Air Field Here Is Year Old," *Fort Worth Star-Telegram,* Aug. 7, 1943; "Army Air Field Completes Its First Year of Training," 5.

16. "WACs Invade Key Jobs at Army Air Field Tower," *Fort Worth Star-Telegram,* Aug. 23, 1943, *Fort Worth Star-Telegram* Collection, Fort Worth Army Air Field Folder, UTA; "Canine Sentries Now on Post at Army Air Field," *Fort Worth Star-Telegram,* Aug. 15, 1943, ibid.

17. "Bomber School Adds Course in Target 'Run'" *Fort Worth Star-Telegram,* Sept. 27, 1943, *Fort Worth Star-Telegram* Collection, Tarrant Field Folder, UTA; "Fort Worth Army Air Field Has Impressive Safety Record," *Fort Worth Star-Telegram,* May 25, 1944, Fort Worth Army Air Field Folder, ibid.

18. Stanley Gunn, "Arnold Aim Is to Wipe Out Enemy, Go Fishing," *Fort Worth Star-Telegram,* Jan. 7, 1944, Arnold, H. H. Folder, ibid; Arnold, *Global Mission,* 608 (quotation); "'Must Grasp New Concept' General Arnold Here, Stresses Air Power," *Fort Worth Star-Telegram,* Dec. 12, 1946, *Fort Worth Star-Telegram* Collection, Arnold, H. H. Folder, UTA.

19. "FWAAF Holds Open House on Anniversary," *Fort Worth Star-Telegram,* August 2, 1944, Fort Worth Army Air Field Folder, UTA; "New Training Period for B-24 Pilots," *Fort Worth Star-Telegram,* Nov. 25, 1944, *Fort Worth Star-Telegram* Collection, FWAAF Folder, UTA; Harding and Long, *Dominator: The Story of the Consolidated B-32 Bomber,* 31.

20. Pat Nimmo Riddle, "Northeast People: Plane crash lasting vision for witnesses," *Fort Worth Star-Telegram,* Jan. 26, 1997, 1, 3, Northeast Metro Section B.

21. "Sororities Buy Amplifier for Combat Crew School," *Fort Worth Star-Telegram,* Oct. 15, 1942, *Fort Worth Star-Telegram* Collection, Tarrant Field Folder, UTA; "Tarrant Field Troops Get Recreation Breaks," Sept. 2, 1942, ibid.

22. "Tarrant Field Again Shares Spotlight on 'Army Hour,'" *Fort Worth Star-Telegram*, Sept. 14, 1943, *Fort Worth Star-Telegram* Collection, Tarrant Field Folder, UTA; "General Yount Speaks on Tarrant Field Broadcast," *Fort Worth Star-Telegram*, Apr. 5, 1943, ibid.

23 "New Airfield Newspaper will Appear on Saturday," *Fort Worth Star-Telegram*, Feb. 12, 1945, *Fort Worth Star-Telegram* Collection, FWAAF Folder, UTA.

24. Lucy Rountree Kuykendall, *P.S. to Pecos* (Houston: The Anson Jones Press, 1946), 94, 181 (quotation), 255.

25. Letter, Bill Carssow to J'Nell L. Pate, Apr. 18, 1997.

26. Kuykendall, *P.S. To Pecos*, 151.

27. Bill Carssow to J'Nell L. Pate.

28. Ibid.

29. "B-32 Crews Trained in Sight of Plant," *The Eagle* Special B-32 Dominator Edition, July 1945, 4; Stephen Harding and James Long, *Dominator: The Story of the Consolidated B-32 Bomber* (Missoula, Mont.: Pictorial Histories Publishing Company, 1983), 31; "World Spotlight on City Aviation"; "Conference Is Awaited To Arrange FWAAF Transfer," *Fort Worth Star-Telegram*, Oct. 23, 1945, *Fort Worth Star-Telegram* Collection, FWAAF Folder, UTA.

30. "FWAAF to Be Kept in Operation," *Fort Worth Star-Telegram*, Oct. 15, 1945, *Fort Worth Star-Telegram* Collection, Fort Worth Army Air Field Folder, UTA; "History of Fort Worth Army Air Field."

31. "FWAAF to Be Kept in Operation."

32. "Shooting Stars Live Up to Name as City Sees Air History in Making," *Fort Worth Star-Telegram*, May 16, 1946, *Fort Worth Star-Telegram* Collection, Fort Worth Army Air Field Folder, UTA; "World Spotlight on City Aviation"; Maurer (ed.), *Air Force Combat Units of World War II*, 464.

33. "FWAAF Population to Be Increased by About 700," *Fort Worth Star-Telegram*, Nov. 5, 1946, *Fort Worth Star-Telegram* Collection, Fort Worth Army Air Field Folder, UTA.

34. "City's Second Industry—Army Air Field Bids Being Let For 100 Quarters—Cost $750,000," *Fort Worth* (May 1947): 12, 48; "City's Second Biggest Industry: That's Fort Worth Army Air Field," *Fort Worth* (March 1947): 58; "Army Air Field," *Fort Worth*, April 1947: 7.

35. Robert Wear, "Flights From FWAAF Across the World Have Become Strictly Routine," *Fort Worth Star-Telegram*, Aug. 12, 1947, *Fort Worth Star-Telegram* Collection, Fort Worth Army Air Field Folder, UTA. Some additional publicity that General Ramey did not anticipate came from debris at a crash site near Roswell, New Mexico, that the government transferred to the FWAAF in June 1947. Residents of New Mexico had reported seeing an Unidentified Flying Object (UFO). A *Fort Worth Star-Telegram* reporter came to the airfield and took the only photograph of the remains as they lay on the carpet of General Ramey's office. They were described as looking like "beams of balsa wood and sheets of tinfoil." The Army reported that the remains were part of a downed weather balloon, but others believed the "flying saucer" story. Sixty years later, the photos of debris taken that day are the most requested photographs of any located at the University of Texas at Arlington's Special Collection Library. Matt Frazier, "Fame from outer space," *Fort Worth Star-Telegram*, July 15, 2007, 1B, 10B.

36. "50,000 Attend Open House At Air Field," *Fort Worth Star-Telegram*, Aug. 4, 1947, *Fort Worth Star-Telegram* Collection, Fort Worth Army Air Field Folder, UTA.

37. "Airfield Here 'Bars' Its Gates for Security Reasons," *Fort Worth Star-Telegram*, Oct. 23, 1947, ibid.

38. "City's Second Biggest Industry: That's Fort Worth Army Air Field," *Fort Worth*, March 1947: 19; "Army Air Field Will Spend $800,000 On Permanent Homes," *Fort Worth* (April 1947): 7; "Home of Colossal B-36s 10-Year-Old Air Industry Has $100,000,000 Output," *Fort Worth Star-Telegram*, Oct. 30, 1949, Aviation Industry Folder, UTA.

39. "F.W.A.F. Now: Word 'Army' Is Dropped By Air Force," *Fort Worth Star-Telegram*,

Dec. 4, 1947, *Fort Worth Star-Telegram* Collection, Aviation History Folder, UTA.

40. George Dolan, "Victory Spirit Spurred By Arnold in Ft. Worth," *Fort Worth Star-Telegram,* Jan. 16, 1950, *Fort Worth Star-Telegram* Collection, Arnold, H. H. Folder, UTA; Arnold, *Global Mission,* 608.

CHAPTER SEVEN

1. William Holden, "Our First Year in War," *Annual Report of the Fort Worth Chamber of Commerce for 1942* in *This Month in Fort Worth* (January 1943): 7.

2. Holden, "Our First Year in War," 7; "Fort Worth—Air Corps Capital," *This Month in Fort Worth* (May 1942): 3; "Army Engineers Guide $37,000,000 Building Projects," *Fort Worth* (August 1957): 18. Most of these offices were housed in the twelve-story Texas and Pacific building in downtown Fort Worth near the railroad network.

3. E. D. Rich, "Hub of Air Force Supplies," *This Month in Fort Worth,* July 1942: 4, 7; "In Fort Worth Air Force Office Watches Over Billion Dollars in Contracts," *Fort Worth,* (April 1951): 15. The twelve states were Colorado, New Mexico, Kansas, Oklahoma, Texas, Arkansas, Louisiana, Mississippi, Alabama, Georgia, South Carolina, and Florida. The Southern Air Procurement District had an office in what later became the Ridglea State Bank building in the west part of Fort Worth; Tom Williams, "Singleton Field, 1939–1945," Jack and Sue White, caption on photograph of Singleton/Russell Airfield South Freeway at Loop 820, 1935–1972 in "Fort Worth . . . the way we were," May 19, 2007 (e-mail to author). After the war Buck Russell acquired Singleton Field, renaming it Russell Field. Located at 6401 South Freeway, it lasted until 1972.

4. "Fort Worth—Air Corps Capital": 3; William Holden, "Our Chamber of Commerce In the War," *Annual Report of the Fort Worth Chamber of Commerce for 1944* in *This Month in Fort Worth* (January 1945): 8; Bilstein and Miller, *Aviation in Texas,* 92; Stanley Gunn, "AAF Training Command Controls Nationwide Flying Schools," *Fort Worth Star-Telegram,* Feb. 20, 1944, 5 (quotation); "Gen. Arnold and Party End 5-State Inspection," *Fort Worth Star-Telegram,* July 11, 1942, *Fort Worth Star-Telegram* Collection, Arnold, H. H. Folder, UTA.

5. "Fort Worth Selected As Headquarters For New Army Air Force Unit," *This Month In Fort Worth* (July 1943): 8; Atkinson, *The Soldier's Chronology,* 397; Gunn, "AAF Training Command Controls Nationwide Flying Schools," 5; "City Remains 'Home Office' for AAT Training," *Annual Report of the Fort Worth Chamber of Commerce for 1944* in *This Month In Fort Worth* (January 1945): 13. Also Thomas A. Manning, *A History of Military Aviation in San Antonio* (rev. ed. Washington, D.C.: USAF Air Education and Training Command, 2000), 89–90; "Fort Worth Selected As Headquarters For New Army Air Force Unit," 8; H. H. Arnold, Commanding General, Army Air Forces, *Second Report of the Commanding General of the Army Air Forces to the Secretary of War, February 27, 1945* (Washington, D.C.: U.S. Government Printing Office, 1945), 94 (quotation).

6. "They'll Earn Their Keep: War Prisoners to Be Assigned to Air Fields," *Fort Worth Star-Telegram,* Apr. 16, 1945, *Fort Worth Star-Telegram* Collection, Fort Worth Army Air Field Folder, UTA.

7. "Famous Aviatrix Stationed Here," *This Month In Fort Worth* (November 1942): 9; "WASPS . . . Women Airforce Service Pilots: Two Women Qualified to Pilot the B-29 during World War II," *The Sentinel,* July 8, 1994, 8; Marianne Verges, *On Silver Wings 1942–1944: The Women Airforce Service Pilots of World War II* (New York: Ballantine Books, 1991), 68–69. Ms. Cochran was named Outstanding Woman Flyer in the World in 1937. She was Outstanding Woman Pilot in America for four years straight, 1938–1941. Eventually she held more international speed, distance, and altitude records than any other pilot, man or woman. An orphan, she was on her own as a teenager and got a job at an exclusive beauty shop in New York. Through her clients she met Floyd Odlum, whom she married in 1936. He owned a majority share of Convair in 1947. Jacqueline Cochran and Maryann Bucknum Brinley, *Jackie*

Cochran: An Autobiography (New York: Bantam Books, 1987); and Jacqueline Cochran, *The Stars at Noon* (Boston: Little Brown and Company, 1954).

8. Verges, *On Silver Wings*, 65.

9. Sally Van Wagenen Keil, *These Wonderful Women in Their Flying Machines: The Unknown Heroines of World War II* (New York: Four Directions Press, 1979; reprint, 1990), 152; "Famous Aviatrix Stationed Here," 9.

10. Cochran, *The Stars at Noon*, 119, 122–23; Harry F. Snapp, "Pioneer Women in West Texas Skies: Women Airforce Service Pilots of World War II," *West Texas Historical Association Year Book*, Vol. 70 (1994): 19; Sarah Byrn Rickman, *Nancy Love and the WASP Ferry Pilots of World War II* (Denton: University of North Texas Press, 2008), 216.

11. Cochran, *The Stars at Noon*, 120–22; Keil, *These Wonderful Women in their Flying Machines*, 152, 170; "WASPS . . . Women Airforce Service Pilots: Two Women Qualified to Pilot the B-29 during World War II," 8 (quotation); Cochran, *The Stars at Noon*, 122; Marion Stegeman Hodgson, *Winning My Wings A Woman Airforce Service Pilot in World War II* (Albany, Tex.: Bright Sky Press, 1996), 106 (second quotation).

12. Keil, *These Wonderful Women in Their Flying Machines*, 171; Snapp, "Pioneer Women in West Texas Skies," 19–20, 23; Dora Strother, "Introduction," in Anne Noggle, *For God, Country, and the Thrill of It: Women Airforce Service Pilots of World War II* (College Station: Texas A&M University Press, 1990), 13.

13. "Women in the Military: a History of Service," *Carswell Sentinel*, Mar. 13, 1987, 17; Bilstein, *Flight in America*, 163; Strother, "Introduction," 13; Snapp, "Pioneer Women in West Texas Skies," 24–25.

14. Snapp, "Pioneer Women in West Texas Skies," 27–28.

15. Ibid., 28; Maria Recio, "The Long Flight to Glory," *The Fort Worth Star-Telegram*, Mar. 10, 2010, 1A; Gordon Lubold, "Decades Later, Women Pilots from World War II Get their Due," *Christian Science Monitor*, Mar. 10, 2010, <http://www.csmonitor.com/USA/2010/0310/Decades-later-women-pilots-from-World-War-II-get-their-due> [Accessed January 13, 2011].

16. *Fort Worth Quartermaster Depot Organization Manual, Organization Charts 1949–1950*, 1. Permanent Records, National Archives SW; David Larry Thomasson, "The Changing Economic Structure of the Fort Worth Metropolitan Area as Reflected by Changes in the Work Force" (M.A. thesis, Texas Christian University, 1964), 26.

17. Thomasson, "The Changing Economic Structure of the Fort Worth Metropolitan Area as Reflected by Changes in the Work Force," 26; *Fort Worth Quartermaster Depot Organization Manual, Organization Charts 1949–1950*, 1.

18. *Fort Worth Quartermaster Depot Organization Manual, Organization Charts 1949–1950*, 1–3; Holden, "Our Chamber of Commerce In the War," 33; Holden, "Our First Year in War," 15; Richard Walker, *Lone Star and the Swastika—Prisoners of War in Texas* (Austin: Eakin Press, 2001), xi, 47; telephone interview with Col. Willie H. Casper (Ret.) U.S. Army, July 27, 2007. He lives in Mineral Wells and wrote about POWs at Camp Wolters.

19. "Big Fort Worth Business Fort Worth General Depot," *Fort Worth* (May 1955): 17, 41.

20. *Report Concerning Possible Joint Utilization of Former U.S. Marine Corps Air Station Eagle Mountain Lake, Texas By Transportation Corps and Texas National Guard*, February 17, 1957, Department of the Army, Corps of Engineers, Fort Worth District, Fort Worth, Texas, 3, Eagle Mt. Marine Base Folder, Box 5 RG 77, EO5, National Archives SW; Holden, "Our First Year in War," 6.

21. Bill Fairley, "Early Unmanned Planes Tested at Eagle Mountain," *Fort Worth Star-Telegram*, Jan. 8, 2003, 1B, 6B.

22. Ibid., 6B. After the war the city leased the base to the Texas National Guard and to a company called Marine Aircraft Corporation. The latter built auxiliary fuel tanks for the Army and Navy before going bankrupt in 1954. *Report Concerning Possible Joint Utilization of*

Former U.S. Marine Corps Air Station Eagle Mountain Lake, Texas, Exhibit "A"; "Biggest Guard Center to Be At Fort Worth," *Fort Worth* (April 1947): 8; Reuben W. Strickland, "Marine Aircraft Plays Key Role In Fort Worth Aviation Picture," *Fort Worth* (October 1951): 12; "In Fort Worth Area Flying Machine Industry Provides Living for 65,000," *Fort Worth* (February 1952): 43–44. For a short time the facility became Eagle Mountain Air Force Base and as such received Bell's 3,000th helicopter. Letter, Carl E. Green, Colonel TC Commanding Eagle Mountain Base, to Adjutant General, Headquarters, Department of the Army, Washington, D.C., June 27, 1960, in Eagle Mountain AAF Folder, Box TX 177, RG 291, National Archives SW; Letter, W. H. Mathes, U.S. Army Corps of Engineers to Texas National Guard Armory Board, Feb. 24, 1960 in ibid.; "Military Affairs," *Annual Report of the Fort Worth Chamber of Commerce for 1960, Fort Worth* (November 1960): 21; Letter, O. W. Callis, Major, U.S. Army Corps Reserve, to Commanding General, Fourth U.S. Army, Fort Sam Houston, Texas, Dec. 16, 1958, in Eagle Mountain AAF Folder, Box TX 177 RG 291, National Archives SW, Fort Worth; "3,000th Texas Helicopter Delivered," *Bell Helicopter News*, Feb. 15, 1963, 2; The facility eventually closed and the Kenneth Copeland ministries purchased it in 1986. Telephone call to Kenneth Copeland Ministries, May 22, 2007, Newark, Texas.

23. "Selection of the Site for the Second United States Narcotic Farm," News Release by A. W. Melton, Secretary of the Treasury; Patrick J. Hurley Secretary of War; and William De Witt Mitchell, Attorney General of the U.S., June 1, 1931, Report on Selection of Sites Folder, United States Public Health Hospital Records, National Archives SW.

24. Letter, Jack H. Hott, Manager, Fort Worth Chamber of Commerce, to Dr. Walter L. Treadway, Assistant Surgeon General, United States Public Health Service and Chairman, Interdepartmental Sub-Committee, Treasury Department, Feb. 11, 1931, Original Proposal Folder, Narcotics Farm Records, National Archives SW (quotation); Letter, H. S. Cumming, Surgeon General, to Amon G. Carter, Sept. 30, 1930, in Original Proposals Folder, ibid.; Memo, H. S. Cumming, Surgeon General, to Dr. Treadway, Sept. 26, 1930, in ibid.; "Fort Worth Gets Narcotic Hospital," *Fort Worth Star-Telegram*, June 1, 1931, 1; "Report of Properties Inspected in the Vicinity of Fort Worth, Texas as Possible Location for the United States Narcotic Farm To Serve the Western Area of the United States," Sites Nos. 14 and 15, in Report on Selection of Sites Folder, Narcotics Farm Records, National Archives SW; "Narcotic Farm Will Provide Jobs for 500," *Fort Worth Star-Telegram*, June 23, 1934, 1; Info on back of Photo in NH Buildings Ground Breaking, Fort Worth, Folder in Narcotics Farm Records, National Archives SW; U.S. Narcotic Farm Stone Is Laid in Ceremony," *Fort Worth Star-Telegram*, Feb. 13, 1937, *Fort Worth Star-Telegram* Collection, Narcotic Farm Folder, UTA; Letter, Jack H. Hott, Manager, Fort Worth Chamber of Commerce, to Dr. Walter L. Treadway, Assistant Surgeon General, U.S. Public Health Service, Oct. 13, 1934, Narcotic Farm Records, National Archives SW; "Name Narcotic Farm Speakers," *Fort Worth Star-Telegram*, Jan. 30, 1937, *Fort Worth Star-Telegram* Collection, Narcotic Farm Folder, UTA; "Cornerstone Laying Today at U.S. Farm" *Fort Worth Star-Telegram*, Feb. 13, 1927, *Fort Worth Star-Telegram* Collection, Narcotics Farm Folder, UTA; Toni Heinzl, "Hospital at Prison to be Phased Out," *Fort Worth Star-Telegram*, July 8, 2004, 14A; "Air Raid Ward Outfitted Here," *Fort Worth Star-Telegram*, Apr. 18, 1942, ibid.; "Proposal For Expansion of Services of the United States Public Health Service Hospital at Fort Worth, Texas For Use as a Veterans Facility," Prepared by Fort Worth Chamber of Commerce, Harold S. Foster, Manager, Industrial Department, July 7, 1944, U.S. Public Health Hospital Records, National Archives SW.

25. "Dr. Kempf Will Head Hospital," *Fort Worth Star-Telegram*, Mar. 3, 1942, *Fort Worth Star-Telegram* Collection, Narcotic Farm Folder, UTA; Bess Stephenson, "Sheer Luck Makes U.S.P.H.S. Hospital Available for War's Mental Casualties," *Fort Worth Star-Telegram*, no date, ibid.

26. "Army Inspects U.S. Hospital," *Fort Worth Star-Telegram*, Nov. 6, 1941, *Fort Worth Star-Telegram* Collection, U.S. Public Health Hospital Folder, UTA; "Lunacy Court's Burden

Heavier," *Fort Worth Star-Telegram*, May 7, 1942, ibid.; Heinzl, "Hospital at Prison to be Phased Out," *Fort Worth Star-Telegram*, July 8, 2004, 14A; "Service Mental Cases Gaining," *Fort Worth Star-Telegram*, May 17, 1943, *Fort Worth Star-Telegram* Collection, U.S. Public Health Hospital Folder, UTA.; "U.S. Hospital Will Add 100 to Staff Here," *Fort Worth Star-Telegram*, Mar. 25, 1942, ibid.; Ruth Mahaffey, "War Neurosis Is Being Treated Near Fight Zones," *Fort Worth Star-Telegram*, Nov. 9, 1943, *Fort Worth Star-Telegram* Collection, U.S. Public Health Hospital Folder, UTA; "Plane Brings Navy Patients to Fort Worth," *Fort Worth Star-Telegram*, Feb. 3, 1944, *Fort Worth Star-Telegram* Collection, U.S. Public Health Hospital Folder, UTA.

27. "Hospital Patients Not Just 'Cases' to This Quintet," *Fort Worth Star-Telegram*, Dec. 3, 1942, *Fort Worth Star-Telegram* Collection, U.S. Public Service Hospital Folder, UTA.

28. "Mental Casualties of War Are Beating Path Back to Normal Life at Hospital Here," *Fort Worth Star-Telegram*, July 2, 1944, *Fort Worth Star-Telegram* Collection U.S. Public Service Hospital Folder, UTA; "U.S. Hospital Makes Money," *Fort Worth Star-Telegram*, Jan. 16, 1943, ibid.; "Proposal for Expansion of Facilities of the United States Public Health Service Hospital at Fort Worth, Texas," 2, Prepared by Fort Worth Chamber of Commerce, Harold S. Foster, Manager, Industrial Department, 1943, U.S. Public Health Hospital Records, National Archives SW.

29. Stephenson, "Sheer Luck Makes U.S.P.H.S. Hospital Available for War's Mental Casualties," *Fort Worth Star-Telegram*, no date.

30. Mahaffey, "War Neurosis Is Being Treated Near Fight Zones"; "Awards Made to Patients at Navy Unit," *Fort Worth Star-Telegram*, October 6, year not clear, *Fort Worth Star-Telegram* Collection, U.S. Public Health Hospital Folder, UTA.

31. Two telephone interviews with Clayborn Richard Harrison, June 16, 2005, and June 21, 2005, to Fort Smith, Arkansas.

32. Harrison interview.

33. Mahaffey, "War Neurosis Is Being Treated Near Fight Zones"; Stephenson, "Sheer Luck Makes U.S.P.H.S. Hospital Available for War's Mental Casualties."

34. "Police Catch Escaped Alien," *Fort Worth Star-Telegram*, Feb. 2, 1943, *Fort Worth Star-Telegram* Collection, U.S. Public Service Hospital Folder, UTA.

35. "Hospital Here Center for Navy Program," *Fort Worth Star-Telegram*, Jan. 15, 1944, ibid.

36. "Last of Red Cross Workers Have Gone From USPHSH," *Fort Worth Star-Telegram*, July 16, 1949, *Fort Worth Star-Telegram* Collection, U.S. Public Service Hospital Folder, UTA; Heinzl, "Hospital at Prison to be Phased Out," *Fort Worth Star-Telegram*, July 8, 2004, 14A. Letter, Robert H. Finch, Secretary, National Institutes of Mental Health's Fort Worth Clinical Research Center, to Honorable James C. Wright, House of Representatives, May 27, 1970, U.S. Public Health Hospital Records, National Archives SW; Letter, Elliot L. Richardson, Secretary, Department of Health, Education, and Welfare, to Honorable Lloyd Bentsen, U.S. Senator, May 11, 1971, ibid.; Letter, Bertram S. Brown, M.D., Director, Department Health, Education, and Welfare, to Mr. James W. Kerr, Jr., Assistant U. S. Attorney, U.S. Department of Justice, Western District of Texas, San Antonio, July 8, 1971, ibid.

37. Heinzl, "Hospital at Prison to be Phased Out," *Fort Worth Star-Telegram*, July 8, 2004; Letter, Brown to J. Kerr.

38. Holden, "Our Chamber of Commerce in the War," 11.

39. "Will Rogers Training Classrooms Expanded, Accommodate 5,000," *The Eagle*, May 11, 1944, 1.

40. Letters, Vernon Rogers to Berta Rogers, March 23, 1942, March 27, 1942, April 13, 1942 (in possession of author). Vernon Rogers, the author's father, took classes in the spring of 1942 at the downtown location. He left his Jack County farm and traveled to Fort Worth for six weeks of training. While cleaning out her parents' house after their deaths, the author

found letters her father had written home during that time. He told about the long hours of training.

41. Workers Trained in Skills . . . at Will Rogers School," *This Month in Fort Worth* (November 1943): 11.

42. Ibid.; "Government-Sponsored School To Occupy Horse Show Barns Near Coliseum, Train Skilled Workers for Defense Projects," *This Month in Fort Worth* (March 1942): 9.

43. "Housing Bids Are Due Soon," *The Consolidated Eagle*, June 18, 1942, 1.

44. "Bids Asked on Housing Units," *The Consolidated Eagle*, July 2, 1942, 2; "Housing Unit Contract Let," *The Consolidated Eagle*, Aug. 27, 1942, 1.; "Housing Units Named for B-24," *The Consolidated Eagle*, Nov. 19, 1942, 1 (quotation); "The Story of White Settlement A Pioneer Community at the Crossroads of Progress 1850–1992 (White Settlement Library, White Settlement, Texas), 3; Map, Department of the Army, Office of the District Engineer, Fort Worth, Texas, Aug. 12, 1952. "Fort Worth O.R.C. Site, Texas Military Reservation" in Victory Apartments Folder, Box TX 15, RG 269, National Archives SW.

45. "Village Units Ready Shortly," *The Consolidated Eagle*, Jan. 14, 1943, 1–2; "98 Mile Commuting Ends as Families Move Into Village," *The Consolidated Eagle*, Feb. 4, 1943, 1; "Half of First Village Units Are Occupied; Shop Center Planned," *The Consolidated Eagle*, Feb. 25, 1943, 1.

46. "10 Apply For Each of Village Units," *The Eagle*, Nov. 11, 1943, 1; "Apartments to Open Saturday," *The Eagle*, Apr. 29, 1943, 1; "Rental Application Office Opens Today For New Apartments," *The Eagle*, Apr. 15, 1943, 4; "Village Offers 3-Bedroom Units," *The Eagle*, Dec. 16, 1943, 1; Maurice G. Lambert, "Living in Liberator Village in the 1940s and '50s," manuscript (Tarrant County Archives, Fort Worth, Texas), 2.

47. Lambert, "Living in Liberator Village in the 1940s and '50s," 3-4; Weaver interview.

48. Weaver interview; Lambert, "Living in Liberator Village in the 1940s and '50s," 4; Lila Bunch Race, *Pioneer Fort Worth Texas: Life, Times and Families of South Tarrant County* (Dallas: Taylor Publishing Co., 1976), 262.

49. "Rental Application Office Opens Today For New Apartments," *The Eagle*, Apr. 15, 1943, 4; "Village Apartments Scheduled to Open; Third Contract Let," *The Consolidated Eagle*, Apr,, 1943, 1; "Village Units Ready Shortly," *The Consolidated Eagle*, Jan. 14, 1943, 1; Lambert, "Living in Liberator Village in the 1940s and '50s," 1-2, 9. The author's family moved to a tiny house on Camp Bowie Blvd. in June 1942 and were not able to get a telephone installed until after the war.

50. Lambert, 1–2, 9.

51. "New Housing Bill Passes," *The Consolidated Eagle*, Oct. 1, 1942, 1; "Village Shopping Center Contract Let for $90,850," *The Eagle*, Apr. 22, 1943, 1; Lambert, 1,7; Weaver interview.

52. "Village Recreation Program Planned," *The Eagle*, June 13, 1944, 1.

53. Interview, Norris Chambers, Apr. 17, 1997, White Settlement, Texas; Deed, State of Texas, U.S. General Services to Abe Meyer, City of Dallas, Aug. 8, 1956, Record Book 3021, 1, Deed Records of Tarrant County, Tarrant County Courthouse, Fort Worth, Texas.

54. "The Story of White Settlement: A Pioneer Community at the Crossroads of Progress 1850–1992," 3.

55. "Land History" 14, Westworth Village, 4; Shanan Johnson, "Town to Celebrate 50 Years Saturday," *Fort Worth Star Telegram*, June 8, 1991 (first quotation); Frank Blue (comp.), "History of River Oaks," 3, loose-leaf notebook (River Oaks Library), 1; Poll List in Loose-Leaf Scrapbook (City Secretary's Office Westworth Village City Hall, Westworth Village, Texas); Brooks Baker (civil engineer who surveyed Westworth Village), Field Notes, Mar. 15, 1941, Loose-Leaf Scrapbook (Westworth Village); Letter, Leo Brewster to Floyd Beard, Nov. 26, 1943, 2 in Loose-Leaf Scrapbook. (Westworth Village, second quotation).

56. George W. Hopkins, "From Naval Pauper to Naval Power: The Development of

Charleston's Metropolitan-Military Complex," in *The Martial Metropolis: U.S. Cities in War and Peace*, ed. Roger W. Lotchin (New York: Praeger Special Studies, 1984), 25; Roger W. Lotchin, "Conclusion: The Martial Metropolis," in *The Martial Metropolis*, 224, 229–30.

CHAPTER EIGHT

1. "Globe Plant Here to Make Army Planes," *Fort Worth Star-Telegram*, Jan. 29, 1942, *Fort Worth Star-Telegram* Collection, Globe Aircraft Folder, UTA; Bill Leader, "The First 11 Mayors of Saginaw," *The Sentinel*, Sept. 2, 1982: 11; "Hummingbird Plane—Fledgling of a New Industry," *This Month in Fort Worth* (July 1941): 4.

2. "Globe Aircraft Lands Contract for Army Planes," *This Month in Fort Worth* (February 1941): 9; "Globe Aircraft Tests Started," *Fort Worth Star-Telegram*, May 27, 1941, *Fort Worth Star-Telegram* Collection, Globe Aircraft Folder, UTA; Globe Aircraft Corporation Makers of Trainer Planes, Has Double Anniversary," *Fort Worth Star-Telegram*, Jan. 31, 1943, ibid.; "Hummingbird Plane—Fledgling of a New Industry," 4 (quotation); "Globe May Do Work for Army," *Fort Worth Star-Telegram*, June 7, 1941, *Fort Worth Star-Telegram* Collection, Globe Aircraft Corp Folder, UTA; "Home of Colossal B-36: 10-Year-Old Air Industry Has $100,000,000 Output"; "Globe Aircraft Gets Big Deal," *Fort Worth Star-Telegram*, June 6, 1941, *Fort Worth Star-Telegram* Collection, Globe Aircraft Folder, UTA.

3. "Those Who Can Not Speak or Hear Learn Air Crafts," *Fort Worth Star-Telegram*, Nov. 9, 1942, *Fort Worth Star-Telegram* Collection, Globe Aircraft Folder, UTA; "Globe Aircraft Trains Handicapped Workers," *This Month in Fort Worth* (November 1942): 5; "Women to Be Employed at Aircraft Plant," *Fort Worth Star-Telegram*, Feb. 11, 1942, *Fort Worth Star-Telegram* Collection, Globe Aircraft Folder, UTA; Jim Marrs, "GI Ordered to Close Air Field Talked Into Opening Meacham," *Fort Worth Star-Telegram*, Feb. 15, 1973, *Fort Worth Star-Telegram* Collection, Aviation History Folder, UTA; "Globe Aircraft Record Is Praised by Washington," *Fort Worth Star-Telegram*, Aug. 5, 1943, *Fort Worth Star-Telegram* Collection, Globe Aircraft Folder, UTA.

4. "Introduction," Globe Aircraft Corporation, Real Property Cases, Fort Worth, RG 121, Box TX 71A, Public Buildings Service (GSA), National Archives SW; "Globe Aircraft Emerges From 'Fledgling Stage,'" *Fort Worth Star-Telegram*, Apr. 17, 1942, *Fort Worth Star-Telegram* Collection, Globe Aircraft Folder, UTA.

5. "Globe Aircraft Firm Has U.S. Approval on Plane," *Fort Worth Star-Telegram*, Feb. 11, 1942, *Fort Worth Star-Telegram* Collection, Globe Aircraft Folder, UTA; "Kennedy Re-named Globe Aircraft Firm Head Here," *Fort Worth Star-Telegram*, Mar. 11, 1942, ibid.; Leader, "The First 11 Mayors Of Saginaw," 11; *Selected Tarrant County Communities*, 157; William Holden, *Fort Worth Chamber of Commerce Annual Report for 1942*, in *This Month in Fort Worth* (January 1943): 6; "Globe Aircraft Jobs Are Open," *Fort Worth Star-Telegram*, Sept. 23, 1942, *Fort Worth Star-Telegram* Collection, Globe Aircraft Folder UTA; "Globe Moves Job Office," *Fort Worth Star-Telegram*, Mar. 11, 1943, ibid.; "Globe Aircraft Plant Expands," *Fort Worth Star-Telegram*, Feb. 4, 1943, ibid.; "Globe Aircraft Expands Plants," *Fort Worth Star-Telegram*, Sept. 6, 1942, ibid.; Letter, Harry M. Katzen to W. G. Fuller, Globe Aircraft Corporation, Nov. 10, 1942. Fuller Collection, Box 51, Incoming Correspondence Folder, Special Collections (McDermott Library, University of Texas at Dallas, Richardson, Texas; quotation).

6. "Introduction," Globe Aircraft Corporation, Real Property Cases; "Globe Aircraft Is Commended," *Fort Worth Star-Telegram*, Dec. 5, 1943, "Globe Aircraft Receives Another Commendation," *Fort Worth Star-Telegram*, Nov. 7, 1943, *Fort Worth Star-Telegram* Collection, Globe Aircraft Folder, UTA; "Globe Aircraft Again Praised for Production," *Fort Worth Star-Telegram*, Apr. 7, 1944, ibid.; "Hundreds Go through Globe Plant as 'Family Day' Honors Record Producers," *Fort Worth Star-Telegram*, Apr. 17, 1944, ibid.

7. "Globe's Planes Go Directly to Training Centers," *Fort Worth Star-Telegram* [date too faint to read], Globe Aircraft Folder, UTA.; "New Contracts Announced For Globe," *This*

Month in Fort Worth (June 1944): 11; "Globe Delivers Army 600th Trainer, Fulfilling Contract," *Fort Worth Star-Telegram*, July 30, 1944, *Fort Worth Star-Telegram* Collection, Globe Aircraft Folder UTA; "Globe Aircraft Over Top on Quota by $11,332," *Fort Worth Star-Telegram*, July 11, 1944, ibid.; "Globe Plant Completes Its Last Trainer," *Fort Worth Star-Telegram*, [date not clear], ibid.

8. Charles Boatner, "Plans Announced for Feeder Airlines to Operate in Texas after the War," *Fort Worth Star-Telegram*, Dec. 1, 1944, *Fort Worth Star-Telegram* Collection, Globe Aircraft Folder, UTA; "Globe Is Tooling Up Plane Cutbacks Will Not Affect Convair," *Fort Worth Star-Telegram*, Apr. 20, 1945, ibid.; "Globe Is Converting Army Planes to Commercial Ships," *Fort Worth Star-Telegram*, May 4, 1945, ibid.; "Globe Aircraft Names Four New Officials," *Fort Worth Star-Telegram*, Mar. 14, 1945, ibid.; "Globe Builds First Postwar Plane," *This Month in Fort Worth* (November 1944): 8.

9. "Postwar Planning Underway At Globe Aircraft," *This Month in Fort Worth* (January 1945): 12 (quotation); Appraisal of Globe Aircraft Corporation Defense Plant Corporation, Plancor No. 898, Fort Worth, Texas, Appraisal Engineering Service Inc., Arthur E. Thomas, Architect, Appraisers, Dallas, Texas, Box 2, RG 270, War Assets Administration, Real Property Disposal Case Files, Globe Aircraft Corporation, National Archives SW.

10. "First Swift Plane Off Globe Assembly Line," *Fort Worth Star-Telegram*, Sept. 9, 1945, *Fort Worth Star-Telegram* Collection, Globe Aircraft Folder, UTA (quotation); "Globe Faces Production Task," *This Month in Fort Worth* (September 1945): 9; "Postwar Planning Underway At Globe Aircraft," 12.

11. "Globe Gives Sub-Contract," *Fort Worth Star-Telegram*, Dec. 28, 1945, *Fort Worth Star-Telegram* Collection, Globe Aircraft Folder, UTA; "Globe Faces Production Task," 9; "Globe Makes Public Plan for Financing," *Fort Worth Star-Telegram*, Feb. 24, 1946, *Fort Worth Star-Telegram* Collection, Globe Aircraft Folder, UTA; "Globe Aircraft Stock Issue Gets Approval," Mar. 20, 1946, ibid.

12. War Assets Corporation Press Release, Mar. 13, 1946, Box 1, RG 270, War Assets Administration Real Property Disposal, Case Files, "Globe Aircraft Corporation," National Archives SW; Lettergram, Powell D. Harris to Minot Mulligan, Treasurer, Reconstruction Finance Corporation, Washington, D.C., Apr. 5, 1946, in ibid.; Deed, Globe Plant, Aug.12, 1946, in Box TX71A, RG 121, Public Buildings Service (General Services Administration) Real Property Cases, Fort Worth, Globe Aircraft Corporation, ibid.; "Hummingbird Plane—Fledgling of a New Industry."

13. "Damage Suit Alleges Poisoning of Creek," *Fort Worth Star-Telegram*, Mar. 9, 1946, *Fort Worth Star-Telegram* Collection, Globe Aircraft Folder, UTA; *Globe Aircraft Corporation v. Thompson*, 203 S.W. 2d 865, No. 14836. Texas Civil Appeals, June 6, 1947; *B. G. Thompson v. Globe Aircraft Corporation*, No. 51065-A, District Court 67, Order for Dismissal, Dec. 12, 1947.

14. Robert Wear, "Globe's 'Swift' On View at NY Aviation Show," *Fort Worth Star-Telegram*, Apr. 5, 1946, *Fort Worth Star-Telegram* Collection, Globe Aircraft Folder, UTA; "Globe Aircraft Corp. Authorizes Dividend," *Fort Worth Star-Telegram*, May 27, 1946, Globe Aircraft Folder, UTA.; "CAA Certifies Third Globe Swift Plane," *Fort Worth Star-Telegram*, June 7, 1946, ibid.

15. "All Globe Swift Operations Here," *Fort Worth Star-Telegram*, Nov. 30, 1946, Globe Aircraft Folder, UTA; "Bankruptcy Is Asked for Globe Aircraft," *Fort Worth Star-Telegram*, Dec. 27, 1946, ibid.; "Globe Trustee Appointments Likely Today," *Fort Worth Star-Telegram*, Jan. 2, 1947, ibid. (quotation).

16. *Rosenberg v. Globe Aircraft Corporation*, 80 F, Su123 DC Pa 1938, June 18, 1948; "SEC Acted as Globe Aircraft Made Plans, Kennedy Says," *Fort Worth Star-Telegram*, Apr. 1, 1947, *Fort Worth Star-Telegram* Collection, Globe Aircraft Folder, UTA (first quotation); *U.S. v. Paddock*, 180F 2d 121, C.A.5 (Tex.) Feb. 18, 1950, No. 12738, U.S. Court of Appeals, Fifth Circuit, In re: Globe Aircraft Corporation; Waldemar A. Von Schoeler to Arthur H. May,

Director, Industrial Division, Office of Real Property Disposal, Sept. 30, 1947, Box 1, RG 270, War Assets Administration Real Property Disposal, Case Files, Globe Aircraft Corporation. National Archives SW (second quotation). Also, *B. G. Thompson v. Globe Aircraft Corporation*, No. 51065-A, District Court 67, Order for Dismissal, Dec. 12, 1947.

17. "Order to Liquidate Globe Aircraft Assets Issued," *Fort Worth Star-Telegram*, May 5, 1947, *Fort Worth Star-Telegram* Collection, Globe Aircraft Folder, UTA; "Bids Asked on Globe Assets," ibid., May 20, 1947, ibid.; "Globe Aircraft Denies Charges Made by SEC," *Fort Worth Star-Telegram*, June 13, 1947, ibid.; "U.S. May Get Globe funds," *Fort Worth Star-Telegram*, June 21, 1947, ibid.; "Globe Debts Are $5,366,131, Trustee Says," *Fort Worth Star-Telegram*, June 21, 1947, ibid.; "Financial Allowances Set in Globe Affairs," *Fort Worth Star-Telegram*, Dec. 11, 1947, ibid.; Waldemar A. Von Schoeler to Arthur H. May.

18. "Major Globe Assets Sold To Air Firm," *Fort Worth Star-Telegram*, June 20, 1947, *Fort Worth Star-Telegram* Collection, Globe Aircraft Folder, UTA; "Globe Aircraft Claim Hearing Set for Dec. 10," *Fort Worth Star-Telegram*, Nov. 16, 1947, ibid.; Letter, John Kennedy to L. B. Glidden, Manager, Reconstruction Finance Corporation, Dallas, Texas, Aug. 28, 1947, Box TX 71, RG 121, Public Buildings Service (GSA), Real Property Cases; Letter L. B. Glidden, to C. A. Saville, Office of Real Property Disposal, War Assets Administration, Feb. 10, 1948, ibid.; Letter, Waldemar A. Von Schoeler, Chief, Industrial Division, to L. B. Glidden, Manager Reconstruction Finance Corporation, Nov. 28, 1947, ibid. (quotation).

19. War Assets Administration, Zone V, Office of Real Property Disposal, Feb. 19, 1948, Box 1, RG 270, National Archives SW; Waldemar A. Von Schoeler to Arthur A. May, Mar. 26, 1948, Box TX71, RG 121; Memorandum to the Zone Administrator, Feb. 19, 1948, War Assets Administration, ibid.; Letter, L. B. Glidden, to Waldemar A. Von Schoeler, Jan. 28, 1948, Office of Real Property Disposal, Globe Aircraft Folder, Box TX71, RG 121; Letter, Pete Van Goethem, Mercer Lake Resort, Minocqua, Wisconsin, to Glidden, Jan. 1, 1948, ibid.

20. Letter, Harley Hise, Chairman, Reconstruction Finance Corp, Washington, D.C. to Mr. Jess Larson, Administrator, Federal Works Agency, Washington, D.C., July 1, 1949, Box 2, RG 270, War Assets Administration, Real Property Disposal Case Files, Globe Aircraft Corporation, National Archives SW; M. H. Elliott General Counsel, Jan. 26, 1951, "Plancor 898" Folder, ibid. Box 1; Deed, State of Texas, County of Tarrant whereby Reconstruction Finance Corp acquired the 149.762 acres of land, June 30, 1949, ibid., Box 2; Letter, Paul McDonald, Director of Administrative Services to Jess Larson, Administrator, War Assets Administration, Washington, DC May 6, 1948, Box TX71A, RG 121, Real Property Cases, Globe Aircraft Corporation, National Archives SW; "Globe . . . A Backward Glance: And Forward Strides," *Bell Helicopter News*, July 10, 1959, 6; "Bell's Globe Plant Scheduled for $377,000 Rehabilitation Program," *Bell Aircraft News*, Mar. 13, 1953, 2; Telephone Interview with Yvonne Flippo, Librarian, Saginaw Public Library, Saginaw, Texas, May 26, 2006; Bilstein and Miller, *Aviation in Texas*, 132.

21. Leader, "The First 11 Mayors Of Saginaw," 14; An organization called the National Swift Association composed of Globe/TEMCO Swift airplane owners and an International Swift Association both still existed in the first decade of the twenty-first century.

CHAPTER NINE

1. Dick Tipton, "Larry Bell—Aviation Trailblazer (Part 6)," *Bell Helicopter News*, (October 1982): 4; Simonson (ed.), *The History of the American Aircraft Industry*, 206.

2. Carroll V. Glines Jr., *The Compact History of the United States Air Force* (New York: Hawthorn Books, Inc., 1963), 14 (quotation); Atkinson, *The Soldier's Chronology*, 332, 439; Gurney, *A Chronology of World Aviation*, 36–37, 45, 60; Rae, *Climb to Greatness*, 162; Butterworth, *Flying Army*, 56–58.

3. Butterworth, *Flying Army*, 29; Rae, *Climb to Greatness*, 16, 163; Bilstein, *Flight in America*, 117.

4. Rae, *Climb to Greatness*, 203; Robert J. Serling, *Legend and Legacy: The Story of Boeing and Its People* (New York: St. Martin's Press, 1992), 203–204.

5. Dick Tipton, "Larry Bell—Aviation Trailblazer (Part 1)," *Bell Helicopter News* (October 1981): 4–5; Donald J. Norton, *Larry: A Biography of Lawrence D. Bell* (Chicago: Nelson-Hall, 1981), 2–3.

6. David A. Brown, *The Bell Helicopter Textron Story: Changing the Way the World Flies* (Arlington, Tex.: Aerofax, Inc., 1995), 14; Tipton, "Larry Bell—Aviation Trailblazer (Part 1)", 5; Norton, *Larry: A Biography of Lawrence D. Bell*, 3, 7, 15–16.

7. Dick Tipton, "Larry Bell—Aviation Trailblazer (Part 2)," *Bell Helicopter News* (January 1982): 5; Norton, *Larry: A Biography of Lawrence D. Bell*, 18, 30, 34, 40-41; Brown, *The Bell Helicopter Textron Story*, 15; 13. Dick Tipton, "Larry Bell—Aviation Trailblazer (Part 3)," *Bell Helicopter News* (March 1982): 4; Wagner, *Reuben Fleet and the Story of Consolidated Aircraft*, 140; Wegg, *General Dynamics Aircraft and Their Predecessors*, 45.

8. Wagner, *Reuben Fleet and the Story of Consolidated Aircraft*, 181.

9. Ibid., 182.

10. Tipton, "Larry Bell—Aviation Trailblazer (Part 3)," 4.

11. Norton, *Larry: A Biography of Lawrence D. Bell*, 69–70, 72, 82, 103, 106, 133; Brophy, *The Air Force*, 329–30; Tipton, "Larry Bell—Aviation Trailblazer (Part 3)," 5; "Aircraft Manufacturing in the United States," The Aircraft Industries Association of America, 167, in *Aviation Annual of 1946* as cited in Simonson (ed.), *The History of the American Aircraft Industry*, 167; Rae, *Climb to Greatness*, 143; "In Fort Worth Area Flying Machine Industry Provides Living for 65,000," *Fort Worth* (February 1952): 42.

12. Norton, *Larry: A Biography of Lawrence D. Bell*, 123; Tipton, "Larry Bell—Aviation Trailblazer (Part 1)," 4; Brophy, *The Air Force*, 330; Jim Winchester, *X-Planes and Prototypes: From Nazi Secret Weapons to the Warplanes of the Future* (New York: Barnes and Noble Books, 2005), 16.

13. "Arthur Young . . . The Maker of the Bell (Part 1)," *Bell Helicopter News*, April 4, 1980, 4; "40 years of making history," *Bell Helicopter News* (March 1986): 4; "History of How Bell Aircraft Pioneered Rotary-Wing Flight," *Bell Aircraft News*, Apr. 10, 1953, 3.

14. "History of How Bell Aircraft Pioneered Rotary-Wing Flight," 4 (first quotation); Dick Tipton, "Arthur Young—The Maker of the Bell," (Part 2), *Bell Helicopter News*, May 16, 1980, 5; "From Research to Rotary Wings, the Bell Helicopter Story," *Bell Helicopter News*, Aug. 3, 1962, 7; Dick Tipton, "Arthur Young—The Maker of the Bell (Part 3)," *Bell Helicopter News*, July 18, 1980, 4–5 (second quotation).

15. "From Research to Rotary Wings," 7; "History of How Bell Aircraft Pioneered Rotary-Wing Flight," 4; Tipton, "Arthur Young—The Maker of the Bell (Part 3)," 4–5.

16. Dick Tipton, "Arthur Young—The Maker of the Bell (Part 4)," *Bell Helicopter News*, Sept. 26, 1980, 4–5 (first quotation); Norton, *Larry: A Biography of Lawrence D. Bell*, 159; Brown, *The Bell Helicopter Textron Story*, 122 (second quotation).

17. Dick Tipton, "Larry Bell—Aviation Trailblazer (Part 4)," *Bell Helicopter News* (May 1982): 4; Dick Tipton, "Arthur Young—The Maker of the Bell (Part 5)," *Bell Helicopter News*, Nov. 21, 1980, 4–5; "First Commercial License Issued March 8: Rotary Wing Milestone," *Bell Helicopter News*, Feb. 25, 1966, 2; Dick Tipton, "Larry Bell—Aviation Trailblazer (Part 5)," *Bell Helicopter News* (July 1982)," 2; Tipton, "Larry Bell—Aviation Trailblazer (Part 1)," 1, 4; Brown, *The Bell Helicopter Textron Story*, 40.

18. Butterworth, *Flying Army*, 61; "From Research to Rotary Wings," 7; "History of How Bell Aircraft Pioneered Rotary-Wing Flight," 4; Norton, *Larry: A Biography of Lawrence D. Bell*, 165 (quotation); "Texas Ranch First to Use Copter To Beat Mesquite In Cattle Drive,"

Bell Aircraft News, Sept. 26, 1952, 2; "Bell," *Fort Worth Chamber of Commerce Annual Report for 1952, Fort Worth* (December 1952): 21, 62.

19. Norton, *Larry: A Biography of Lawrence D. Bell*, 161, 164; Brown, *The Bell Helicopter Textron Story*, 13 (quotation).

20. Tipton, "Larry Bell—Aviation Trailblazer (Part 6)," 4; Brophy, *The Air Force*, 331; Atkinson, *The Soldier's Chronology*, 425, 419; Brown, *The Bell Helicopter Textron Story*, 60.

21. Tipton, "Larry Bell—Aviation Trailblazer (Part 6)," 4; "From Research to Rotary Wings The Bell Helicopter Story," 7; "President Bell Welcomes Division's Inspection Guests," *Bell Aircraft News*, June 6–8, 1952, 1; Brown, *The Bell Helicopter Textron Story*, 83.

22. Norton, *Larry: A Biography of Lawrence D. Bell*, 165 (quotation); Brown, *The Bell Helicopter Textron Story*, 80–82.

23. "Bell Sets Copter Production Record," *Bell Aircraft News*, Jan. 30, 1953, 1; Brown, *The Bell Helicopter Textron Story*, 83, 85, 91, 93; "Bell Helicopter Highlights," *Bell Aircraft News*, June 6–8, 1952, 4; Tipton, "Larry Bell—Aviation Trailblazer (Part 6)," 4; "10 Big Years in Texas," *Bell Helicopter News*, May 12, 1961, 3; "*Wall Street Journal* Says Texas May Take Laurels in Aircraft Production," *Fort Worth Star-Telegram*, Nov. 9, 1951, *Fort Worth Star-Telegram* Collection, Aviation History Folder, UTA; "They've Seen Hurst Grow. . ." *Bell Helicopter News*, Jan. 8, 1960, 6; "Teamed for Success—Bell and Hurst," *Bell Helicopter News*, Jan. 8, 1960, 5.

24. "They've Seen Hurst Grow. . ." *Bell Helicopter News*, Jan. 8, 1960, 6; "Teamed for Success—Bell and Hurst," *Bell Helicopter News*, Jan. 8, 1960, 5.

25. Barksdale, *The Genesis of the Aviation Industry in North Texas*, 22; "Bell," *Fort Worth Chamber of Commerce Annual Report for 1952, Fort Worth* (December 1952): 21; "Growth and Achievements: That's the story of Bell Texas," *Bell Helicopter News*, Aug. 17, 1962, 5; "This Is Bell, 1967: The Changing Face of Hurst," *Bell Helicopter News*, Mar. 24, 1967, 5; Brown, *The Bell Helicopter Textron Story*, 84; "Bell's First Assembly Facility is Vacated after 38 Years of Service," *Bell Helicopter News* (February 1989): 4; "Globe Delivers Last B-36 Jet Pod to Convair," *Bell Aircraft News*, Apr. 9, 1954, 2; "XHSF-1 Flight Highlights 1953," *Bell Aircraft News*, Jan. 1, 1954, 5.

26. Dick Tipton, "Larry Bell—Aviation Trailblazer (Part 7)," *Bell Helicopter News*, (January 1983): 4; "Bell Copter Sets World Distance Mark," *Bell Aircraft News*, Sept. 26, 1952, 1; "First Jet Flight in U.S. Made by Bell '59' in '42," *Bell Aircraft News*, Oct. 10, 1952, 2; "Bell to Address First Texas Division Dinner," *Bell Aircraft News*, Oct. 24, 1952, 1.

27. Interview, Joe Fuchs Jr. Dec. 5, 1996, Hurst, Texas. His father worked at Bell from 1935 to 1968, both in Buffalo and Hurst; "Joe Fuchs: Hopeful Immigrant to Supervisor," *Bell Aircraft News*, Apr. 6, 1956, 3. Joe Fuchs died in 1985. His son remained in the business in Hurst that his father began. He said that his father traveled to Germany right before he retired with a group of Bell people who were setting up helicopter assembly there. Fuchs helped translate for them.

28. "Bell Resigns as General Manager, Faneuf Elected," *Bell Aircraft News*, Oct. 8, 1954, 2 (quotation); "Bell Aircraft," *Fort Worth Chamber of Commerce Annual Report for 1955, Fort Worth* (December 1955): 21 (quotation).

29. "Stockholders Approve Autonomy for Division," *Bell Aircraft News*, Aug. 10, 1956, 2; "Texas Division Assumes Status As Bell Helicopter Corporation," *Bell Helicopter News*, Jan. 4, 1957, 2; "Hurst Facility: 10 Years Old This Week," *Bell Helicopter News*, Dec. 8, 1961, 5; Tipton, "Larry Bell —Aviation Trailblazer (Part 7)," *Bell Helicopter News*, Dec. 8, 1961, 5; "Lawrence Dale Bell: His Life: Search for Tomorrow," *Bell Aircraft News*, Oct. 26, 1956, 3; "Larry Bell, The Man," *Bell Aircraft News*, Oct. 26, 1956, 7.

30. "Board Names School After President Bell," *Bell Aircraft News*, Jan. 13, 1956, 3; "Bell Foundation, Inc. Grants $1,000 to Larry Bell School," *Bell Helicopter News*, Nov. 22, 1957, 7; "Will Be Ready Sept. 7: New Bell High School Nears Completion," *Bell Helicopter News*, Aug. 27, 1965, 8; "Bell in Aviation Hall of Fame," *Bell Helicopter News*, June 17, 1977, 4; "Larry

Bell inducted into Army Aviation Hall of Fame," *Bell Helicopter News* (February 1987): 1.

31. "Senator Johnson Clips Ribbon as Bell Rolls Out 2000 R [headline not clear] '47," *Bell Helicopter News*, Jan. 10, 1958, 2; "By Appointment of the President Bell: Helicopter Delivers Two Trim Craft to Fly Eisenhower," *Fort Worth* (June 1957): 19; "Model of Presidential Helicopter Presented to Eisenhower Library," *Bell Helicopter News*, Aug. 7, 1970, 2.

32. "Woman Scientist Flying High in Helicopter and Laboratory," 15, 41–42 (quotation); "President Reagan's Letter Takes Strother by Surprise," *Bell Helicopter News* (February 1987): 2; "WASPS—Women Airforce Service Pilots: After the War, For Some, the Air Adventure Continued," *The Sentinel*, July 22, 1994, 6. Strother was Dora Dougherty's married name.

33. "WASPS—Women Airforce Service Pilots: After the War, For Some, the Air Adventure Continued," 6; "Woman Scientist Flying High In Helicopter and Laboratory," 42; "WASPS . . . Women Airforce Service Pilots: Two Women Qualified to Pilot the B-29 during World War II," 11; "Ronald Reagan to Dr. Dora Dougherty Strother," as cited in *Bell Helicopter News* (February 1987): 2 (quotation). After being widowed, Strother married Colonel Harry McKeown, a fellow pilot and veteran.

34. "Bell Helicopter Joins Textron: A Family of 22 Divisions, 90 Plants," *Bell Helicopter News*, July 8, 1960, 5; "Parent Gives Bell New Name! It's Now Bell Helicopter Textron," *Bell Helicopter News*, Jan. 16, 1976, 3; "A Brief History of Textron," *Bell Helicopter News*, June 17, 1977, 5; Rae, *Climb to Greatness*, 213; "Bell is up for SALE," *Bell Helicopter News* (March 1985): 1.

35. "Humphrey Praises Company, Products," *Bell Helicopter News*, July 29, 1966, 3; "10 Years on Schedule!" *Bell Helicopter News*, Oct. 21, 1966, 4; "Presentation of 5,000th Huey, Marks Production Milestone," *Bell Helicopter News*, Nov. 17, 1967, 3; Wayne Mutza, *Helicopter Gunships Deadly Combat Weapon Systems* (North Branch, Minn.: Specialty Press, 2010), 64.

36. "Plant 5 Delivers First Part," *Bell Helicopter News*, Nov. 19, 1965, 3; Press Conference of Bell President Jim Atkins at Helicopter Association of America's Annual Meeting in Las Vegas, 1979 as cited in "Atkins Sees $20 Billion Helicopter Industry by Year 2000," *Bell Helicopter News*, Feb. 9, 1979, 4.

37. Brown, *The Bell Helicopter Textron Story*, 181; Robert R. Williams, "BHI [Bell Helicopter International] celebrates third anniversary," *BHI News* (April 1976): 1 (motto); Press Briefing by Jim Atkins at annual conference of Helicopter Association of America as cited in "Our 10,000 People Keep Us on Top—Atkins," *Bell Helicopter News*, Feb. 13, 1981, 5; "Bell is up for SALE," *Bell Helicopter News* (March 1985): 1; "25,000th Bell Helicopter Delivered at HAA," *Bell Helicopter News*, Jan. 30, 1981, 2; "Company is Created to Serve Southeast Asia," *Bell Helicopter News*, November 1983, 1; "Plans to Co-produce Helicopter in South Korea Are Announced," *Bell Helicopter News* (August 1986): 1; "New agreement established with Canadian government," ibid.

38. "Bell's First Assembly Facility is Vacated after 38 Years of Service," *Bell Helicopter News* (February 1989): 4.

39. *Of Men and Stars*, Chapter 9, 5; "Bell Aircraft," *Fort Worth Chamber of Commerce Annual Report for 1953*, Fort Worth (December 1953): 36; Gurney, *A Chronology of World Aviation*, 178; "Convertiplane Flies," *Bell Aircraft News*, Aug. 26, 1955, 4–5; "Bell Aircraft," *Fort Worth Chamber of Commerce Annual Report for 1955*, Fort Worth (December 1955): 21; "Bell Unveils New 'Copter Airplane," *Fort Worth* (February 1955): 17.

40. Gurney, *A Chronology of World Aviation*, 230, 237, 242; Brown, *The Bell Helicopter Textron Story*, 139; Paul Hussey, "The First VTOL Harrier Jump Jet—A British Icon," Posted July 20, 2010 <www.articlesbase.com/culture-articles/the-first-vtol-harrier-jump-jet-a-british-icon-2> [Accessed May 27, 2011]; "Navy Says Go on V-22 Full Scale Development," *Bell Helicopter News* (May 1986): 1 (quotation).

41. "Navy Says Go on V-22 Full Scale Development," 1; Serling, *Legend and Legacy*, 217.

42. Terry Arnold, "Horner Calls Flight One of the Greatest Aeronautical Accomplish-

ments," *Bell Helicopter News* (April 1989): 2 (quotation); Terry Arnold, "V-22 Osprey Flies in Airplane Mode," *Bell Helicopter News* (October 1989): 1; "Bell Helicopter Highlights for 1989," *Bell Helicopter News* (February 1990): 3; "XV-15 Goes to Washington for Civil Tilt Rotor Hearings," *Bell Helicopter News* (June 1990): 1; Jim Wright interview (quotation).

43. Interview, Webb Joiner, President and CEO, Bell Helicopter Textron, Feb. 4, 1998, Hurst, Texas.

44. Dave Montgomery, "With Little Fanfare, Squadron of V-22s is Heading for Iraq," *Fort Worth Star-Telegram*, Sept. 20, 2007, 1C, 6C; Bob Cox, "Pentagon to Buy 167 Tilt-Rotor Ospreys," *Fort Worth Star-Telegram*, Mar. 29, 2008, 1C; Bob Cox, "V-22 Contract Means Production till 2012," *Fort Worth Star-Telegram*, Feb. 23, 2008, 1C; Jay Price, "Afghanistan Battle Marks V-22's Debut in Combat," *Fort Worth Star-Telegram*, Dec. 6, 2009, 1A.

45. Serling, *Legend and Legacy*, 219; Joiner interview.

46. "The Town That Bell Built," *Bell Aircraft News*, Sept. 10, 1954, 8; "'Town' That Bell Aircraft People Built," *Fort Worth* (March 1955): 15.

47. "Texas Division Assumes Status as Bell Helicopter Corporation," *Bell Aircraft News*, Jan. 4, 1957, 2; "23 Million Copter Order Bell Gets Big Army Contract," *Fort Worth* (March 1959): 9.

48. "Teamed for Success—Bell and Hurst," *Bell Helicopter News*, Jan. 8, 1960, 6; "10 Big Years in Texas," 3; "This Is Bell, 1967," *Bell Helicopter News*, Jan. 13, 1967, 4; "City longtime leader in aviation field," *Fort Worth Star-Telegram*, Jan. 19, 1975, *Fort Worth Star-Telegram* Collection, Aviation History Folder, UTA.

49. Bob Cox, "Bell Keeping Faith in Its Civil Copter," *Fort Worth Star-Telegram*, July 22, 2010, 3C (quotation); Bob Cox, "Bell Says New Copter to be Ready in a Year," *Fort Worth Star-Telegram*, Oct. 12, 2007, 1C, 3C; Bob Cox, "Bell to Cut Mid-Level Management and Non-Factory Jobs," *Fort Worth Star-Telegram*, Jan. 26, 2008, 1C; Greg Hubbard, "The Bell 429 Makes Successful Flying Debut at Recent Heli-Expo," Press Release, Bell Helicopter/ Textron, Inc., Feb. 26, 2009, 1 (copy in author's possession; second quotation).

50. *Congressional Record*, Nov. 19, 1971 as cited in *Bell Helicopter News*, Dec. 10, 1971, 5 (quotation); "World's First! Dick Smith Returns to Bell to End Around-World Flight," *Bell Helicopter News* (August 1983): 4; Joiner interview.

CHAPTER TEN

1. Atkinson, *The Soldier's Chronology*, 412.

2. Brophy, 31–32; Strategic Air Command," in *Historical Dictionary of the U.S. Air Force*, ed. Charles D. Bright (New York: Greenwood Press, 1992), 540; Le May, the oldest of six children of a migrant iron worker from the Midwest, wanted to be appointed to West Point, but his local Congressman ignored him. He worked his way through Ohio State University and applied for Army Air Cadet training through the ROTC and was accepted in 1928. Richard G. Hubler, *SAC :The Strategic Air Command* (New York: Duell, Sloan and Pearce, 1958), 156–57; Le May, *Mission With Le May*, 6 (quotation); "Movie Makers Arrive For 'Location' Scenes," *Fort Worth Star-Telegram*, Apr. 1, 1954, *Fort Worth Star-Telegram* Collection, Carswell Folder, UTA; "June Allyson Will Arrive Ahead of Paramount Crew," ibid.; "Jimmy Stewart Pays Convair Visit While Acting in Movie About B-36," *Convairiety*, Apr. 21, 1954, 1; Eleanor Wilson, "Carswell to Resemble Hollywood Sound Stage," *Fort Worth Star-Telegram*, Apr. 4, 1954, *Fort Worth Star-Telegram* Collection, Carswell Folder, UTA; Ann Jones, "For Moviemaking Purposes Film Actor James Stewart Puts In Bid for Sunshine, Fleecy Clouds," *Fort Worth Star-Telegram*, Apr. 5, 1954, ibid. George Peyton Cole, son of the commander of Carswell at the time, took a bit part in the movie. Years later, he came back to be stationed at Carswell and completed his career as a two-star general. The film's southwestern premier took place in Fort Worth in May 1955. Interview, Stanley Cole, Mar. 13, 1997, Fort Worth, Texas. See also "Carswell Air Base," *Annual Report of the Fort Worth Chamber of Commerce*, Fort Worth (December

1955): 19. The author, who saw the film in 1955 as a teenager, viewed it again in July 2007 on television. After years of military research, even climbing into a restored B-36 at Lockheed, she was enthralled at the movie scenes of the big Peacemaker in flight.

3. Glines, *The Compact History of the United States Air Force*, 289; Harry Truman, "Special Message to the Congress Recommending the Establishment of a Department of National Defense, Dec. 19, 1945," Public Papers of the Presidents of the United States, Harry S. Truman, 1945, 551 as cited in Charles J. Hitch, *Decision-Making for Defense* (Berkeley and Los Angeles: University of California Press, 1965), 71 (quotation); Gurney, *A Chronology of World Aviation*, 129.

4. "Separate Air Force, Union Of Services Elate Eaker," *Fort Worth Star-Telegram*, July 27, 1947, *Fort Worth Star Telegram* Collection, Eaker, Ira C. Folder, UTA (quotation); Brophy, *The Air Force*, 70; Glines, *The Compact History of the United States Air Force*, 290.

5. Atkinson, *The Soldier's Chronology*, 415; Gurney, *A Chronology of World Aviation*, 17, 138; Butterworth, *Flying Army*, 66; "Fact Sheet," Naval Air Station Joint Reserve Base, Fort Worth, Texas, 1; *A Defense Reorganization Act of 1986 Attempted to Improve Inter-Operability among the Military Services* (copy in author's possession); Bilstein, *Flight in America*, 179; Brophy, *The Air Force*, 75.

6. "FWAF Is Griffiss Air Force Base," *Fort Worth Star-Telegram*, Jan. 19, 1948, *Fort Worth Star-Telegram* Collection, Fort Worth Air Base Folder, UTA; Leslie Carpenter, "Townshend Griffiss Was Due A Star Hero for Whom Air Field Here Is Named Called 'One of Finest Men,'" *Fort Worth Star-Telegram*, Jan. 21, 1948, ibid.; "Name Change Due to Union of Services," *Fort Worth Star-Telegram*, Jan. 30, 1948, "Carswell" Folder, ibid.

7. Horace Seaver Carswell Jr., Official Birth Certificate, Copy in Military Personnel Records (in author's possession); interview with Bobby Capps, Oct. 26, 2001, Fort Worth; interview with Bobby Capps, Mar. 19, 1997, Fort Worth; "Major Horace Seaver Carswell Jr." in Barrett Tillman, *Above and Beyond: The Aviation Medals of Honor* (Washington, D.C.: Smithsonian Institution Press, 2002), 117; "FWAF's New Name Honors Ft. Worth Man," *Fort Worth Star-Telegram*, Jan. 30, 1948, *Fort Worth Star-Telegram* Collection, Carswell Folder, UTA; "Horace Seaver Carswell, Jr.," Department of the Air Force, Statement of Military Service, Military Personnel Records (in author's possession).

8. "Horace Seaver Carswell, Jr." Department of the Air Force, Statement of Military Service, Military Personnel Records.

9. Ibid.; "Fort Worth B-24 Pilot Gives His Life To Save Crew," *The Eagle*, Dec. 1, 1944, 3; "Major Horace Seaver Carswell, Jr." in Barrett, *Above and Beyond*, 118; "Base named after local native Medal of Honor recipient," *Carswell Sentinel*, Oct. 30, 1987, 6; "Horace Seaver Carswell, Jr." Department of the Air Force, Statement of Military Service, Military Personnel Records; Sgt. John Van Winkle, "History: Pilot Dies Trying to Save His Crew," *Carswell Sentinel*, Oct. 23, 1992, 13 (quotation).

10. Citation, Medal of Honor, Military Personnel Records (in author's possession; quotation); "Medal of Honor Given Posthumously to Flier," *Fort Worth Star-Telegram*, Jan. 8, 1946, *Fort Worth Star-Telegram* Collection, Carswell Folder, UTA; "Major Horace Seaver Carswell, Jr." in Barrett, *Above and Beyond*, 119. Major Carswell's body was buried five times: in China by missionaries, in Hawaii by the Air Corps, at Rose Hill Cemetery in Fort Worth, at Carswell Air Force Base, and at Oakwood Cemetery in Fort Worth after Carswell closed.

11. Tribune Paid To Namesake Of Carswell," *Fort Worth Star-Telegram*, May 30, 1951, *Fort Worth Star-Telegram* Collection, Carswell, Horace Folder, UTA (quotation); "Carswell Base Dedicated In Army Aviator's Honor," *Fort Worth Star-Telegram*, Feb. 28, 1948, ibid. (quotation).

12. "Carswell's Widow to Unveil Memorial at Ceremonies," *Fort Worth Star-Telegram*, Feb. 26, 1948, *Fort Worth Star-Telegram* Collection, Carswell Folder, UTA; "Carswell Air Base Naming This Afternoon," *Fort Worth Star-Telegram*, Feb. 27, 1948, ibid.; "Redesignation

FWAF's New Name Honors Ft. Worth Man," *Fort Worth Star-Telegram*, Jan. 30, 1948, *Fort Worth Star-Telegram* Collection, FWAF Folder, UTA; "Air Field Renamed for Only Native Honor Medal Winner," *Fort Worth Star-Telegram*, Jan. 30, 1948, ibid. In 1983 Griffiss AFB covered 4,000 acres in northeast Rome, New York, and had 7,000 military and civilian personnel. As a result of the Base Realignment and Closure (BRAC) military cutbacks, Griffiss AFB closed September 30, 1995. A Business and Technology Park now covers the former Air Force base grounds.

13. *"Peacemaker": The History of the B-36 at Carswell Air Force Base Fort Worth, Texas 1948–1958* (Fort Worth: 7th Bomb Wing Association, 1995), 2, 9, 25. See also "World Spotlight on City Aviation," *Fort Worth Star-Telegram*, Oct. 30, 1949, *Fort Worth Star-Telegram* Collection, Carswell Folder, UTA. The last B-36 to roll off the flight line also was named "The City of Fort Worth," creating some confusion in later years; "Base Has 7th Birthday Carswell, One of World's Major Airdromes, Marks Anniversary" (quotation). General Ramey also directed bomber bases at Tucson, Roswell, El Paso, and Savannah, plus a fighter wing at Austin. Ibid.; "Aircraft Industry Is Recent Boom," in *Fort Worth 1849–1949: 100 Years of Progress*, Reprinted from *Fort Worth Chamber of Commerce Magazine* (1949), 23.

14. Robert F. Dorr, *7th Bombardment Group/Wing 1918–1995* (Paducah, Ky: Turner Publishing Co., 1996), 7; "Carswell recalls vast history during park dedication," *Carswell Sentinel*, Oct. 17, 1986, 9; *"Peacemaker,"* 66.

15. Interview, Colonel Frank Kleinwechter, Apr. 14, 1997, Benbrook, Texas. While Kleinwechter still served as a bombardier, entertainer Arthur Godfrey once visited Carswell. Kleinwechter's crew was preparing to go on a six- to eight-hour flight mission to Midland to drop a practice bomb. Somehow Godfrey obtained permission to ride along. General Hoyt Vandenburg came on the radio, and the two men talked, although Vandenburg did not know in advance that Godfrey would be on the airplane. The men let Godfey drop a bomb, and he did pretty well; *"Peacemaker,"* 27; Retirees like Kleinwechter, who either flew B-36s, maintained them, or built them at Convair, began a B-36 Association in 1982 with reunions organized semi-annually. Ibid. Eventually the retirees conceived the idea to restore a B-36 that sat out in the weather for many years at Amon Carter Field between Dallas and Fort Worth. Over several years the volunteers donated a total of 43,000 hours restoring the B-36, named "City of Fort Worth." The retirees in their B-36 Association tried to raise enough money for a museum for the large B-36, but did not meet a deadline set by the Air Force. Even though the city of Fort Worth had acquired the big bomber on loan from the Air Force in 1959 when it ceased flying, through failure to allocate funds for an inside location for the big B-36, they lost it when the Air Force transferred it in 2005 to Davis-Monthan AFB at Tucson, Arizona. The author took part in the attempt to "save" the B-36 for Fort Worth; *"Peacemaker,"* 30, 39. "7 BMW B-36 Chronology," 19. See slso *Real Estate Planning Report Acquisition of Land By Lease in Crockett and Val Verde Counties, Texas for a Proposed Bombing Range Said Land to be Used by Carswell Air Force Base, Texas, for the Department of the United States Army Air Force Headquarters*, Washington, D.C., U.S. Army Corps of Engineers, Fort Worth District, Fort Worth, Texas 16 February 1954, Prepared by C. K. Wildermuth, Appraiser, RG 341, Box 23, National Archives SW.

16. *"Peacemaker,"* 17 (quotation); Pete Trent, "Second 'Sneak Attack' Proves Point," *The Sentinel*, Jan. 17, 1993, 1, 14 (second quotation).

17. *"Peacemaker,"* 52 (quotation); Kleinwechter interview.

18. Trent, "Second 'Sneak Attack' Proves Point," 14; Michael J. Ramsey Sr. "Second 'Sneak Attack' Proves Point," *Carswell Sentinel*, Dec. 6, 1985, 6. Two articles about the same attack appeared in the *Carswell Sentinel* eight years apart. Information also came from Kleinwechter interview, and *"Peacemaker,"* 22, 52. See also "7BMW B-36 Chronology," TSgt Gregory S. Byard, Historian, U.S.A.F. Office of Base Historian, Dyess AFB, Abilene, Texas, 9. (7th Bomb Wing Records were moved from Carswell after it closed in 1993.)

19. Kleinwechter interview; Trent, "Second 'Sneak Attack' Proves Point," 14 (quotation); Frisbee, *Makers of the United States Air Force*, 215 (second quotation); Barlow, 268.

20. Department of Defense, *Second Report of the Secretary of Defense 1949. Annual Report of the Secretary of the Air Force for the Fiscal Year 1949* (Washington, D.C.: Government Printing Office, 1950), 106; Frisbee, *Makers of the United States Air Force*, 229.

21. Le May, *Mission with Le May*, 439.

22. Ibid., 499 (first quotation); Bilstein, *Flight in America*, 329 (second quotation); Hubler, *SAC*, 211; Jack Anderson and Fred Blumenthal, "Target Moscow: Our Global Bombing Crews Get Ready," *Parade Magazine*, Aug. 15, 1954, 6–7 (final quotation).

23. Chris Vaughn, "Life after Carswell: West Fort Worth Comes Back since 1991 Base Closing," *Fort Worth Star-Telegram*, Apr. 11, 2001, 1A; Report of Ammunition Storage Site Location for Carswell Air Force Base Tarrant County, Texas, Department of the Army Corps of Engineers Fort Worth District, Fort Worth, Texas, Carswell Ordnance Storage Area Folder, Box 24, RG 341, National Archives SW; Real Estate Report Ammunition Storage Area Carswell Air Force Base Fort Worth, Tarrant County, Texas, Date of Original Report, September, 1951, Department of the Army, Corps of Engineers Fort Worth District, Carswell AFB Ammo Folder, Box 5, RG 341. Prior to the government's dismantling the concrete bunkers and selling the land to developers early in the twenty-first century, this author met with local media and environmental scientists at the site, and even took a peek inside the large, empty bunkers. The environmental specialists that the Air Force hired ran special equipment all over the bunkers and the surrounding grounds to test for radioactive substances.

24. "Current Issues and the Asian Challenge," in Williamson Murray and Allan R. Millett, *Brassey's Mershon American Defense Annual* (Washington, D.C.: Brassey's, 1996), 31.

25. Mark O. Webb, "'*Lucky Lady*' Soared to Lucky Day," *Carswell Sentinel*, Mar. 3, 1989, 4; Heinecke, "Fort Worth Aviation," copy of 5 typed notes dated October 1950 in "Aviation" Folder, *Fort Worth Star-Telegram* Collection, UTA, 5; Norman Polmar (ed.) *Strategic Air Command: People, Aircraft, and Missiles* (Annapolis, Md.: Nautical and Aviation Publishing Company of America, 1979), 18; "History of the 7th Bomb Wing and Carswell AFB," Office of History, 7th Bomb Wing, Carswell AFB, Tex. Obtained from Office of History, Dyess, AFB, Abilene, Tex., 28; *Department of Defense Second Report of the Secretary of Defense 1949, Annual Report of the Secretary of the Air Force for the Fiscal Year 1949*, 243 (second quotation), 268 (first quotation); "Aviation Makes History at Carswell," *Carswell Sentinel*, Sept. 22, 1978, 14A; James N. Eastman Jr., "*Lucky Lady II* Takes off into History," *Carswell Sentinel*, Mar. 2, 1979, 13; Crew members of the *Lucky Lady II* may not have known that a couple of pioneering aerial refuelings took place nearly three decades earlier. The very first air-to-air event occurred on November 12, 1921, when Wesley May, with a five-gallon can of gasoline strapped to his back, jumped from the wing of a Lincoln Standard, flown by Frank Hawks, to the wing skid of a JN-4 flown by Earl S. Daugherty. May climbed to the engine, opened the gas cap, and poured fuel into the tank. The second refueling occurred April 20, 1923, at Rockwell Field, San Diego, between two DH-4B aircraft under the direction of Henry H. Arnold, at that time in the U.S. Air Service. The 1949 Carswell crew, even had they known, would not have taken the two early attempts too seriously. Gurney, *A Chronology of World Aviation*, 34, 37.

26. Hubler, *SAC*, 97; "*Peacemaker*," 23; Polmar (ed.), *Strategic Air Command*, 18; "Carswell AF Base," *Fort Worth* (December 1951): 56.

27. "5,000 Placed On Alert Duty at Carswell," *Fort Worth Star-Telegram*, May 17, 1949, *Fort Worth Star-Telegram* Collection, Carswell Folder, UTA.

28. Dick Gorton, "Fisherman Sees Plane Plunge 'Looked Like Huge Fish Slithering in Water' Crash Eye-Witness Says," *Fort Worth Star-Telegram*, Sept. 16, 1949, *Fort Worth Star Telegram* Collection, Aviation B-36 Folder, UTA (first quotation); Irvin Farman, "Like A Dying Whale Gnarled Monster Lies Deep in Oily Lake Mud," *Fort Worth Star-Telegram*, Sept. 16, 1949, ibid. (second quotation); Ira Cain, "Only One Question Brings Smiles to Grim Faces

of B-36 Crash Survivors," ibid.; Robert Wear, "Power Failure Balks Takeoff at Carswell," *Fort Worth Star-Telegram*, Sept. 16, 1949, *Fort Worth Star-Telegram* Collection, Carswell Folder, UTA.

29. Bob Considine, "On the Line," Column in *Fort Worth Star-Telegram*, Sept. 16, 1952, *Fort Worth Star-Telegram* Collection, Carswell Folder, UTA (first quotation); *"Peacemaker,"* 63 (second quotation); "Preliminary Report of Damage Caused by Wind Storm, Carswell AFB, 4 September 1952, To Director of Installations, Headquarters USAF Washington, DC from Robert R. Conner, Colonel USAF, Representative Office Southwestern Division, Dallas, Texas, Carswell Collection, Box 24, RG 341, National Archives SW; "C.A.F.B. Storm Loss Estimate Cut in Half By Finletter," *Fort Worth Star-Telegram*, Jan. 15, 1953, *Fort Worth Star-Telegram* Collection, Carswell Folder, UTA (third quotation); "History of the 7th Bomb Wing and Carswell AFB, 8; Also "7 BMW B-36 Chronology," 29, 32; "Monthly Progress Analysis of Activities and Achievements, September, 1952," History of the 7th Bombardment Wing Heavy, 19th Air Division, Carswell Air Force Base, Fort Worth, Texas, September, 1952, Office of Base Historian, MSgt Robert Romanelli, Dyess Air Force Base, Abilene, Tex; "Carswell Air Base Open to Traffic, After Million-Dollar Storm Damage," *Fort Worth Star-Telegram*, Sept. 2, 1952, *Fort Worth Star-Telegram* Collection, Carswell Folder, UTA.

30. "5 States Alerted For Man Who Took Carswell Photos," *Fort Worth Star-Telegram*, Aug. 9, 1952, *Fort Worth Star-Telegram* Collection, Carswell Folder, UTA; "Focuses on Lake, Not B-36s Unregistered Camera Trips Carswell Alarm," ibid.; Jack Anderson and Fred Blumenthal, "Target Moscow: Our Global Bombing Crews Get Ready," *Parade Magazine*, Aug. 15, 1954, 6–7 (quotation).

31. Ira Cain, "Carswell Plane Dropped South Pacific H-Bomb," *Fort Worth Star-Telegram*, Jan. 27, 1953, *Fort Worth Star-Telegram* Collection, Carswell Folder, UTA (first three quotations); "B-36 Back, Blackened By H-Bomb," *Fort Worth Star-Telegram*, Jan. 28, 1953, ibid. (last quotation).

32. "Bent on B-36 'Sabotage' Five 'Agents' Fail to Gain Entry to Carswell AFB in Security Exercise," *Fort Worth Star-Telegram*, Nov. 4, 1953, *Fort Worth Star-Telegram* Collection, Carswell Folder, UTA.

33. Pete Bowles, "No Intruder Can Pass: Watchdog Patrol Is Guarantee of Security," *Fort Worth Star-Telegram*, June 29, 1960, *Fort Worth Star-Telegram* Collection, Carswell Folder, UTA (quotation).

34. "Antiaircraft Guns Manned 24 Hours Daily to Protect Convair FW, Carswell," *Convairiety*, Nov. 3, 1954, 5; "Antiaircraft Will Protect Fort Worth," *Fort Worth Star-Telegram*, Dec. 18, 1953, *Fort Worth-Star Telegram* Collection, Carswell Folder, UTA; Real Estate Planning Report Acquisition of Leasehold Interest and Easements for Access Roads and Utility Lines, Carswell Air Force Base, Texas, May 10, 1954, Department of the Army, Corps of Engineers, Fort Worth District, Fort Worth, Texas, Andrew J. Landry, Appraiser. Carswell Records, Box 5, RG 77, National Archives SW; "Antiaircraft Unit, Personal Guardian Of City Since 1954, Leaving June 15," *Fort Worth Star-Telegram*, May 26, 1957, *Fort Worth Star-Telegram* Collection, Carswell Folder, UTA.

35. Alfred Goldberg (ed.), *A History of the United States Air Force 1907–1957* (New York: Arno Press, 1957; Reprint, 1972), 123; Ira Cain, "8th AF Headquarters at Carswell to be Moved to Massachusetts February 1," *Fort Worth Star-Telegram*, Oct. 6, 1954, *Fort Worth Star-Telegram* Collection, Carswell Folder, UTA; "Carswell Air Base," *Fort Worth Chamber of Commerce Annual Report*, Fort Worth (December 1955): 19; Mark O. Webb, "Carswell's B-52s plan for role in 21st century," *Carswell Sentinel*, Apr. 28, 1989, 10; "Profits Again AF, Navy and Airline Contracts Pulled Convair From Red in '49," *Convairiety*, July 19, 1961, 5; Mark O. Webb, "Carswell tankers support global mission," *Carswell Sentinel*, Oct. 30, 1987, 23 (quotation).

36. "Carswell to Bid 'Farewell to B-36' On Memorial Day," *Convairiety*, Sept. 3, 1958, 1; *"Peacemaker,"* 49; "Last B-36 To Leave Carswell" *Fort Worth Star-Telegram*, Apr. 20, 1958, *Fort*

Worth Star-Telegram Collection, Carswell Folder, UTA. Also "7 BMW B-36 Chronology," 47; "Last B-36 Comes to Rest at Air Terminal Shrine," *Convairiety*, Feb. 18, 1959, 1 (quotation); Herbert Molloy Mason Jr., *The United States Air Force: A Turbulent History* (New York: Mason/Charter, 1976), 228.

37. Dave Brown, "'Routine Flight' Becomes Nightmare B-52 Survives Battering Hailstorm," *Fort Worth Star-Telegram*, Nov. 2, 1958, *Fort Worth Star-Telegram* Collection, Carswell Folder, UTA.

38. "Facts About the Fort Worth Operation of Convair Aerospace Division of General Dynamics," in "History of White Settlement," 2; Niven, Canby, and Welsh (eds.), *Dynamic America*, 360; "AF Asks $29,000,000 for B-58s at Carswell," *Fort Worth Star-Telegram*, May 9, 1959, *Fort Worth Star-Telegram* Collection, Carswell Folder, UTA.

39. "New York to Paris Flight Gives B-58 Another Record," *Convairiety*, June 7, 1961, 2 (quotation); "Facts About the Fort Worth Operation of Convair Aerospace Division of General Dynamics," 2.

40. Evans interview (quotation); Ford Dixon, "McNamara, General Dynamics and the F-111: A Business and Political History" (Ph.D. diss., Texas Christian University, 1972), 34–35 (second quotation); B. A. Erickson, B-58 Development Chief Test Pilot, "Flight Characteristics of the B-58 Mach 2 Bomber," Research Paper Presented to the Royal Aeronautical Society, London, England, November 23, 1961, 4, 10 (Erickson's quotation); Hehs, "Beryl Arthur Erickson Test Pilot," 25; Wright interview; Jim Wright, *Balance of Power Presidents and Congress from the Era of McCarthy to the Age of Gingrich* (Atlanta: Turner Publishing, Inc., 1996), 81.

41. Wright, *Balance of Power*, 78; Wright interview.

42. "Retirement of Hustlers Effective Next Year," *General Dynamics News*, Dec. 3, 1969, 6; "Problems Shared: Teamwork of Convair And Carswell Effective," ibid.; "Fort Worth's Growth Linked to Carswell," *Carswell Sentinel Introspect* (Spring 1979): 15A. The F-111 will be discussed more thoroughly in Chapter 11.

43. Roger C. Groce, "As Fort Worth Slept—Carswell Bombers Flew Off To War the Other Night," *Fort Worth* (March 1964): 17, 41–42; Cashion, *The New Frontier*, 127–28.

44. "Fort Worth's growth linked to Carswell," 15A.

45. *"Peacemaker,"* 28; Also Jim Wright interview.

46. Ira Cain, "Carswell Expansion Details Announced," *Fort Worth Star-Telegram*, Oct. 25, 1951, 1; "Carswell Funds For Expansion Cut by Congress," *Fort Worth Star-Telegram*, Aug. 27, 1952; Marshall Lynam, "Carswell's Growth to Gulp Homes," *Fort Worth Press*, Oct. 25, 1951, 1; *Supplement No. 2 To Real Estate Report Carswell Air Force Base Proposed North-South Runway and Taxiway Extensions and Warm-Up Pad Site, 17 January 1952*, Department of the Army, Corps of Engineers, Fort Worth District, Fort Worth, Texas, 14 April 1952, Box 24, RG 341, National Archives SW.

47. Letter, C. Carlisle, Fort Worth, Texas, to President [Dwight] Eisenhower, U.S.A., Apr. 29, 1954, Carswell Records, RG 341, Box 23, Carswell AFB Folder, National Archives SW (quotation).

48. "Many Achievements 1954 Outstanding Year for Carswell Progress," *Fort Worth Star-Telegram*, Jan. 9, 1955, *Fort Worth Star-Telegram* Collection, Carswell Folder, UTA. A total of $5 million spent in 1957 resulted in a 250-bed base hospital. "Army Engineers Guide $37,000,000 Building Projects," *Fort Worth* (August 1957): 18.

49. "Groundbreaking ceremony starts new commissary," *Carswell Sentinel*, May 27, 1983, 1; Wright interview.

50. *"Peacemaker,"* 67; Dan Cragg, *Guide to Military Installation.* (2nd ed.; Harrisburg, Pa.: Stackpole Books, 1988), 245–46.

51. Nancy Shea, *The Air Force Wife* (New York: Harper & Row, 1951), 2 (first quotation); telephone interview, Elaina Pyle, Apr. 17, 2011, N. Charleston, S.C.

52. Cragg, *Guide to Military Installations,* 245; Andrew G. B. Vallance, *The Air Weapon: Doctrines of Air Power Strategy and Operational Art* (London: Macmillan Press, 1996), 20; "B-52 Remains Primary Bomber," *Carswell Sentinel,* June 21, 1991, 19; "History of the 7th Bomb Wing and Carswell AFB," 6.

53. Chris Vaughn and Maria Recio, "Closing of Bases Possible in Texas," *Fort Worth Star-Telegram,* Mar. 25, 2001, 1A, 23A (quotation); Sgt. Mark Kinkade, "Base Closure List Shakes up SAC," *Carswell Sentinel,* Apr. 19, 1991, 2.

54. *Socioeconomic Impact Analysis Study: March 1993 Disposal and Reuse of Carswell Air Force Base, Texas* (Washington, D.C.: Department of the Air Force, 1993), S-1; Ethan B. Kapstein (ed.), *Downsizing Defense* (Washington, D.C.: Congressional Quarterly, Inc., 1993), 90; "Aircraft Industry Is Recent Boom," 23.

55. Kleinwechter interview; Bobby N. Petty, "Oldest Bomb Squadron Celebrates 75 Years," *Carswell Sentinel,* June 5, 1992, 8; Mark Kinkade, "Standing down," *Carswell Sentinel,* Oct. 4, 1991, 1 (quotation). Obviously, the world did not remain a safer place. Within less than a decade, a new enemy and a new war erupted in the Middle East, particularly after the destruction of the World Trade Center on September 11, 2001.

56. "Moves to Dyess: Carswell's 7th Bomb Wing Lowers Colors for the Last Time," *The Sentinel,* Oct. 14, 1993, 1; Lance A. Jay, "7th Wing Leaves in '93," *Carswell Sentinel,* Oct. 4, 1991, 1; Author's Personal Tour of Carswell, November 6, 1996, as a member of the Carswell Restoration Advisory Board; "William J. Allen, History of the 7th Wing," July 1, 1995 (7th Wing Office of History 7th Wing Dyess Air Force Base, Texas), 4; Interview with Bobby Skipper, former Carswell Librarian and later Naval Air Station Fort Worth Librarian, Nov. 7, 1996; Kapstein (ed.), *Downsizing Defense,* 107; "Federal Medical Center Carswell Prison program starts this month at Carswell," *The Sentinel,* July 22, 1994, 1.

57. *Socioeconomic Impact Analysis Study March 1993, Disposal and Reuse of Carswell Air Force Base, Texas,* S-1, S-2; Chris Vaughn, "Life after Carswell: West Fort Worth Comes Back since 1991 Base Closing," *Fort Worth Star-Telegram,* Apr. 11, 2001, 17A.

58. One Air Force brat who later became quite well known as a folk singer, John Denver, attended and graduated from Arlington Heights High School in 1961 as John Deutschendorf Jr. His father was an Air Force flight instructor stationed at Carswell. The author J'Nell Pate is a graduate of the same high school and is aware of its famous or infamous graduates. Gregory Fontenot, "Junction City-Fort Riley: A Case of Symbiosis," in *The Martial Metropolis,* 37.

59. Cole interview. Also Ann Markusen, Peter Hall, Scott Campbell, and Sabina Deitrick, *The Rise of the Gunbelt,* 39; Jackson Bechetta, "Western Suburbs Home to Fewer Kids as Residents Age," *Fort Worth Star-Telegram,* May 23, 2001, 20A.

60. Vaughn, "Life after Carswell," 17A; "BRAC Sides with Fort Worth: 301st Air Wing to stay at NAS Fort Worth Joint Reserve Base," *The Sentinel,* June 30, 1995, 1; Michael B. Wood, "Carswell's Air Force Reserve 301st Fighter Wing is Now Flying 'Operation Deny Flight' in Europe," *The Sentinel,* Dec. 1993, 11; Program, Change of Command Ceremony, Naval Air Station Joint Reserve Base (copy in possession of author).

61. Vaughn, "Life after Carswell," 1A, 17A; Program, Change of Command Ceremony, 10; Jo Ann Dennis, "Around the Town Joint Base Has Assured Future," *River Oaks News,* June 29, 1995, 1.

62. "Monument Inscription," *The Sentinel,* Dec. 23, 1994, 7; "It's All In the Way You Say It: NAS Fort Worth, Joint Reserve Base, Carswell Field," *The Sentinel,* Sept. 30, 1993, 16; "Carswell Field Dedication All Services—A Joint Reserve Base," *The Sentinel,* Feb. 10, 1995, 1; "Carswell Field Memorial Dedicated," *The Sentinel,* Feb. 24, 1995, 1, 19.

63. Remarks, Commander John Werner, executive officer, Naval Air Station Fort Worth Joint Reserve Base to luncheon of Carswell Officers Wives Club, Los Vaqueros Restaurant, Fort Worth, Texas, Feb. 11, 1997 (author's notes); "Current and Past Aircraft on Display: NAS Fort Worth Gets New Street Names," *The Sentinel,* Oct. 28, 1994, 1; Vaughn, "Life after

Carswell," 17A; Fort Worth Chamber of Commerce Offices and Public Affairs Office, Fort Worth JRB, May 29, 2007.

64. Letter, Col. H. R. Hallock to Division Engineer Southwestern Division, Corps of Engineers, Dallas, Texas, June 12, 1954, in Carswell AFB Operational FACs Folder, Box 61, RG 341, National Archives SW (quotation).

65. The author is a member of the RAB and learned this information at meetings and tours of the cleanup sites, including the former nuclear bunkers.

66. Chris Vaughn, "Security at Base Affects Retirees," *Fort Worth Star-Telegram*, Sept. 20, 2001, 1B (quotation).

67. News Announcement, WFAA, Channel 8 Television, Fort Worth, Nov. 16, 1998.

68. Thomasson, "The Changing Economic Structure of the Fort Worth Metropolitan Area as Reflected by Changes in the Work Force," 25.

69. "Carswell Pay Means $1,500,000 Each Month," *Fort Worth Star-Telegram*, Oct. 1, 1950, *Fort Worth Star-Telegram* Collection, Carswell Folder, UTA; "Aspirin Tablets, Autos and Paper Clips $3 Million Spent by Carswell Buyers On Purchases From Fort Worth Firms," *Fort Worth Star-Telegram*, Aug. 26, 1951, Carswell Folder, UTA; "Carswell," *Fort Worth Chamber of Commerce Annual Report for 1953, Fort Worth* (December 1953): 51 (quotation); "Carswell Grows With Fort Worth," *Fort Worth* (March 1956): 25, 46; "Base Boost Economy Benefits by Location," *Fort Worth Star-Telegram*, June 29, 1960, *Fort Worth Star-Telegram* Collection, Carswell Folder, UTA; Dave Brown, "Military Payrolls Hit $50 Millions," *Fort Worth Star-Telegram*, Jan. 10, 1960, ibid.; "Carswell begins briefing leaders on major report," *Fort Worth Star-Telegram*, Feb. 3, 1978, clipping, Tarrant County Archives.

70. Cragg, *The Guide to Military Installations*, vii–xxiii. California had 37 military bases, Texas, 17; Florida, 13; and Virginia, 12. Advertisement in *Carswell Sentinel*, Mar. 23, 1984, 13; Floyd Durham, "Military Retirement, Golf, and the Size of the Fort Worth Market," 2 (economic report in possession of author). See also Chris Vaughn, "Military Commissary Makes a Comeback," *Fort Worth Star-Telegram*, Mar. 24, 2008, 14B; "NCTCOG North Central Texas Council of Governments, Major Employers, Top Ten Employers," <http://www.nctcog.org/print.asp.> [Accessed May 2, 2011].

71. Chris Vaughn, "N. Texas Native Takes the Reins at Naval Air Station," *Fort Worth Star-Telegram*, Apr. 12, 2008, 7B; interview with Captain T. D. Smyers, Commanding Officer, Naval Air Station Fort Worth Joint Reserve Base, Carswell Field, Dec. 22, 2009; Chris Vaughn, "Meet the Highflying Stars of the Naval Air Station's Biggest Show Yet," *Fort Worth Star-Telegram*, Apr. 15, 2011: 1A, 11B; Kathleen Bynum, "Air Power Expo Draws Record Crowds," *Sky Ranger* (May 2011): 1 (quotation).

CHAPTER ELEVEN

1. Bright, *The Jet Makers*, 182.

2. Goodwin, *Brotherhood of Arms*, 4–6, 21. Holland, an Irish immigrant, came to the U.S. in 1873, taught school, and tinkered on the side with his submarine, at first called an underwater ship. He spent decades trying to interest the Navy in his invention, but the admirals called it comic and awkward. Fortunately, he interested President Theodore Roosevelt, who helped influence the Navy to purchase it. Niven, Canby, and Welsh (eds.), *Dynamic America*, 337; Franklin, *The Defender*, 127. Hopkins, after several years in private law practice, became a director of Electric Boat in 1937. He moved up to vice president, then president. He developed a philosophy of expansion for Electric Boat/General Dynamics from the first. His motto became "Grow or die." "Hopkins Guiding Force behind Great Growth of General Dynamics," *Convairiety*, May 15, 1957, 1; "Directors Approve Merger of General Dynamics and Convair," *Convairiety*, Mar. 3, 1954, 1.

3. "Directors Approve Merger of General Dynamics and Convair."; Franklin, *The Defender*, 146; John Mort, "Atomic Reactor Being Flown Over Fort Worth Area in B-36," *Fort*

Worth Star-Telegram, Jan. 8, 1956, *Fort Worth Star-Telegram* Collection, Carswell Folder, UTA; "1700 Mainly Engineers Will Occupy New Building on Montgomery Street," *Convairiety*, Feb. 20, 1957, 1, 8.

4. Niven, Canby, and Welsh (eds.), *Dynamic America*, 337–38; Franklin, 160; "Former Army, Secy. Elected To Presidency," *Convairiety*, May 15, 1957, 1.

5. "New 2½ Million Nuclear Airplane Contract Signed," *Convairiety*, Nov. 12, 1958, 1; "Nuclear Research Important Part of GD/Fort Worth Task," *General Dynamics News*, Nov. 27, 1963, 2; "Versatile Fort Worth Division Makes Transition to Aerospace," ibid. (quotation); Don Pyeatt, "Efforts to Produce a Nuclear-powered Aircraft at Air Force Plant 4 in Fort Worth," presentation, B-36 Peacemaker Museum, Inc. meeting, Sept. 15, 2009, University of North Texas Health Science Center, Fort Worth, Texas (author notes).

6. "Brief History of Fort Worth Operation of Convair Aerospace Division of General Dynamics," 3; Franklin, *The Defender*, 126; "Atlas 109–D Puts Astronaut Glenn In Earth Orbit," *General Dynamics News*, Feb. 28, 1962, 1; Dixon, "McNamara, General Dynamics and the F-111: A Business and Political History," 26.

7. Henry L. Trewhitt, *McNamara* (New York: Harper & Row Publishers, 1971), 137; Robert J. Art, *The TFX Decision McNamara and the Military* (Boston: Little, Brown & Co., 1968), 29, 39–40; Goodwin, *Brotherhood of Arms General Dynamics and the Business of Defending America*, 13.

8. Dixon, "McNamara, General Dynamics and the F-111," 28.

9. "Brief History of Fort Worth Operation of Convair Aerospace Division of General Dynamics," 3.

10. Trewhitt, *McNamara*, 138–39; Dixon, "McNamara, General Dynamics and the F-111: A Business and Political History," 81–82, 122–23, 93–94.

11. Dixon, 98–99, 103, 105–06; Markusen, Hall, Campbell, Deitrick, *The Rise of the Gunbelt*, 163; TFX Hearings (1963) Vol. 2, 375, as cited in Dixon, 114 (quotation).

12. Wegg, *General Dynamics Aircraft and Their Predecessors*, 228; Trewhitt, *McNamara*, 151; Dixon, "McNamara, General Dynamics and the F-111," 179, 152; William T. Allen, "Speech to B-36 Peacemaker Inc. Group, Aug. 21, 2006, Meacham Field Terminal, Saginaw (author's notes); "Named, Retired . . .F-111 Leaves Air Force Service," *The Sentinel*, Aug. 16, 1996, 1. Other countries purchased the F-111. Australia was still using it in the first decade of the twenty-first century.

13. Franklin, *The Defender*, 224–25, 233; Dorfer, *Arms Deal*, 77; Goodwin, *Brotherhood of Arms*, 86, 89-90, 93. After acquiring a degree in aeronautical engineering in 1939, Lewis began working for Glenn L. Martin's aircraft plant in Baltimore. After seven years with Martin, Lewis joined McDonnell Aircraft in St. Louis in 1946, rising to president by 1962. In 1967 he engineered the merger of McDonnell with Douglas Aircraft and turned the DC-10 commercial project into profitability; "Directors Elect David S. Lewis as Board Chairman," *General Dynamics News*, Oct. 28, 1970, 1.

14. Wegg, *General Dynamics Aircraft and Their Predecessors*, 229; Bob Cox, "He Was the 'Father of the F-16': General Dynamics Engineer Helped Design the Legendary fighter Jet," *Fort Worth Star-Telegram*, Feb. 10, 2009, 1, 3C (first, third quotations); Goodwin, *Brotherhood of Arms*, 325 ("Deal of Century" quotation).

15. Dixon, "McNamara, General Dynamics and the F-111: A Business and Political History," 171 (The *Chicago Sun-Times* article was dated Feb. 19, 1982 (quotation); Goodwin, *Brotherhood of Arms*, 87, 204, 238; Franklin, *The Defender*, 309.

16. Markusen, Hall, Campbell, Deitrick, *The Rise of the Gunbelt*, 25 (quotation).

17. Franklin, *The Defender*, 12, 237, 283, 285--86, 317, 339; Goodwin, *Brotherhood of Arms*, 9–10, 310; Wegg, *General Dynamics Aircraft and Their Predecessors*, 229.

18. Wegg, 229-30. The ten divisions were: Convair, Electronic, Space Systems, all in San

Diego; Pomona, and Valley Systems Divisions, east of Los Angeles; Electric Boat at Groton, Conn.; Data Systems at St. Louis Mo.; Land Systems at Troy, Mich.; Flight Training Systems at Wichita, Kans.; and the Fort Worth Division. In addition, GD also owned six subsidiaries; Franklin, *The Defender*, ix; Cox, "He Was the 'Father of the F-16,'" 1C. Hillaker, a senior engineer at GD, retired in 1985 after forty-four years with the company. He died in Fort Worth on February 8, 2009, at the age of eighty-nine, ibid. See also Bob Cox, "F-16 Jets Are Still Drawing Interest," *Fort Worth Star-Telegram*, Aug. 5, 2010, 1C.

19. Wegg, *General Dynamics Aircraft and Their Predecessors*, 229; Walter J. Boyne, *Beyond the Horizons: The Lockheed Story* (New York: St. Martin's Press, 1998), 49.

20. Kapstein (ed.), *Downsizing Defense*, xiv, 2.

21. Boyne, *Beyond the Horizons*, 459–461. The Scot-Irish brothers with exhibition flights at county fairs earned money to be able to build airplanes. They also worked as auto mechanics. Their first attempt was a wood and fabric hydroplane that flew for twenty minutes over San Francisco Bay on June 15, 1913. *Of Men and Stars* Chapter 2, 2, 6–9; Kapstein (ed.), *Downsizing Defense*, 135.

22. Boyne, *Beyond the Horizons*, 2, 6, 11; *Of Men and Stars*, Chapter 2, 11–12; Harris, *The First To Fly*, 214; Anthony Sampson, *The Arms Bazaar: From Lebanon to Lockheed* (New York: The Viking Press, 1977), 90–91. The company's early success was a monoplane called a Vega that Northrop designed. Amelia Earhart made headlines when she flew a Vega solo over the Atlantic. Wiley Post and Harold Gatty flew a single-engine Lockheed Vega monoplane named the *Winnie Mae* in the first around-the-world flight from July 15 to July 22, 1933. James F. Sunderman (ed.) *Early Air Pioneers, 1862–1935* (New York: Franklin Watts, 1961), 253.

23. Sampson, *The Arms Bazaar*, 90–91; *Of Men and Stars*, 2–3; Rae, *Climb to Greatness*, 66.

24. Sampson, *The Arms Bazaar*, 98, 211, 275, 287; Robert T. Minnich, "Defense Downsizing and Economic Conversion: An Industry Perspective," in *Downsizing Defense*, 121.

25. Boyne, *Beyond the Horizons*, 462 (quotation).

26. Wayne Biddle, *Barons of the Sky: From Early Flight to Strategic Warfare, The Story of the American Aerospace Industry* (New York: Simon and Schuster, 1991), 44–47, 59–60; 64–65, 88, 322; *Los Angeles Express*, Dec. 5, 1912, as cited in Biddle, *Barons of the Sky*, 61 (quotation); Bright, *The Jet Makers*, 176; Rae, *Climb to Greatness*, 213; Boyne, *Beyond the Horizons*, 468–69. A list of the honorary pallbearers at Martin's funeral read like an honor roll of aircraft giants: Donald Douglas, Lawrence Bell, William Boeing, and Robert Gross (of Lockheed). Many of them had worked for Martin.

27. Boyne, *Beyond the Horizons*, 470–71, 476–77.

28. Ibid., 422–23 (quotation).

29. Ibid., 478, 482; Jim Wilson, "'Flexible Flier' The Joint Strike Fighter Puts the Best of Every 20th Century Warplane into One Nimble and Stealthy Package," *Popular Mechanics* (May 2002): 3–4,

30. "It's Lockheed!" [Huge headline], Maria Recio and Dan Piller, "Decision to Secure Thousands of Jobs," *Fort Worth Star-Telegram*, Oct. 27, 2001, 1A, 18A (Hutchison quotation); Wilson, "'Flexible Flier' The Joint Strike Fighter puts the best of every 20th century warplane into one nimble and stealthy package," 4 (Roche quotation).

31. Wilson, "Flexible Flier," 2–3, 5; Bob Cox, "New 2011 Budget Would Cut 10 F-35 Purchases," *Fort Worth Star-Telegram*, Sept. 15, 2010, 1C; Bob Cox, "Lockheed: Goal is $20 Billion Annual Revenue within 5 Years," *Fort Worth Star-Telegram*, May 4, 2010, 3C; David A. Dietsch, "The Pentagon and Americans Should Keep Faith with the F-35," *Fort Worth Star-Telegram*, Apr. 13, 2010, 5A (quotation).

32. Tony Capaccio, "F-35 Cuts Are on Table as Pentagon Eyes Budget," *Fort Worth Star-Telegram*, Feb. 7, 2009, 1, 3C; "Gates Would End 2 Lockheed Programs, Expand Another,"

Fort Worth Star-Telegram, Apr. 7, 2009, 1, 4C (Gates quotation); Bob Cox, "It's a Critical Year for the Joint Strike Fighter," *Fort Worth Star-Telegram,* Mar. 9, 2009, 1C; "Pentagon Chief Strongly Endorses Fighter Program on Fort Worth Visit," *Fort Worth Star-Telegram,* Sept. 1, 2009, 1A.; Bob Cox, "Norway Chooses Joint Strike Fighter for Frontline Combat," *Fort Worth Star-Telegram,* Nov. 21, 2008, 1C.

33. The speaker asked to remain anonymous.

34. Barksdale, *The Genesis of the Aviation Industry in North Texas,* 12; Talbert, *Cowtown-Metropolis,* 133. The county population grew from 225,521 to 361,253 in the decade from 1940 to 1950, a growth of over 50 percent. *Texas Almanac and State Industrial Guide, 1941–42* (Dallas: A. H. Belo and Company, 1941, 106; *Texas Almanac 1954–1955* (Dallas: A.H. Belo and Company, 1953), 609; "Turner Files for School Board," *Convairiety,* Feb. 11, 1953, 1, 3(Turner quote); Thomasson, "The Changing Economic Structure of the Fort Worth Metropolitan Area as Reflected by Changes in the Work Force," 84; "$12 Million A Month Pours into Payrolls at Convair Plant," *Fort Worth* (October 1951): 24; "In Fort Worth Area, Flying Machine Industry Provides Living for 65,000," *Fort Worth* (February 1952): 40 (quotation); Barksdale, *The Genesis of the Aviation Industry in North Texas,* 12; "Convair Has Produced 3,000 Planes During Decade at Fort Worth," *Convairiety,* Apr. 11, 1951, 1 (paychecks quotation); "Aircraft Built in Fort Worth Fill The Skies Of The World," *Fort Worth* (March 1959): 12; Kapstein (ed.), *Downsizing Defense,* 129 (final quotation); "Fort Worth Division Looks Back On Crowded 28 Years of Aircraft Mfg." *General Dynamics News,* June 11, 1969, 2.

35. Jacques S. Gansler, *The Defense Industry* (Cambridge, Mass.: The MIT Press, 1980), 1, 7, 11, 83, 89.

36. Ibid., 171; Kapstein (ed.), *Downsizing Defense,* 123–24.

37. Interview with B. J. Clark, Azle, Texas, June 6, 2007; Conversation with Betty Clark, Oct. 24, 1996.

38. "Rockets and Atoms at General Dynamics," *Fort Worth* (March 1964): 18–19 (nuclear quotation); Gopal Ratnam and Juliann Neher, "Lockheed Says 25% of Execs Took Buyouts," *Fort Worth Star-Telegram,* Sept. 9, 2010, 1C.

39. "Lockheed, Air Force Come to F-35's Defense," *Fort Worth Star-Telegram,* Sept. 20, 2008, 3C.

CHAPTER TWELVE

1. Ralph Heath, "Pioneers, Promoters of Flight Have Roots Deep in Texas," *Fort Worth Star-Telegram,* Sept. 13, 2010, 7A (quotation); Ralph J. Schmidt and Clare D. Wright (comps.), *The Menasco Story 1926 through 1991* (Charlotte, N.C.: Coltec Industries, 1994), 24, 35. Coltec Industries bought Menasco, and in 1999 Goodrich Aerospace acquired both. interview, J. W. Greenwood, Haltom City, Texas, Oct. 30, 2005. Albert Menasco was a classmate at Manual Arts High School in Los Angeles with World War II hero Jimmie Doolittle. Menasco quit school in 1912 to work for a friend who had an airplane. William Boeing once lent Menasco money to start his own company, and later his next-door neighbor Clark Gable became an investor. Menasco resigned and severed all ties with the company before a division of it moved to Fort Worth. He died in 1988 at age ninety-one. *The Menasco Story,* 10.

2. Thomasson, "The Changing Economic Structure of the Fort Worth Metropolitan Area as Reflected by Changes in the Work Force," 87; "This Area Is 2nd Largest In Aircraft Manufacturing," *Fort Worth Star-Telegram,* May 31, 1953, *Fort Worth Star-Telegram* Collection, Aviation History Folder, UTA; "In Fort Worth Area Flying Machine Industry Provides Living for 65,000," 7; Loyd L. Turner, "Aircraft Construction The South's Biggest 'War Baby,'" *Editor and Publisher,* Oct. 31, 1953: 170; "Aviation—a Blue Ribbon Industry," *Fort Worth* (February 1954): 7.

3. "Teamed for Success—Bell and Hurst," 5.

4. "State Plane Work One of Big Three," *Fort Worth Star-Telegram,* Jan. 25, 1959, *Fort Worth*

Star-Telegram Collection, Aviation Industry Folder, UTA.

5. Roger W. Lotchin, "Introduction," in *The Martial Metropolis*, xii (quotations).

6. Johnson, "A Study of the Effect of Convair Employment Fluctuations on Fort Worth Business Activity," 19; *U.S. Census of Population 1960*, Vol. I, Part 38, U.S. Department of Commerce, Bureau of the Census (Washington, D.C:. Government Printing Office, 1961), 59–76. *Texas Almanac and State Industrial Guide, 1941–1942*, 106; *Texas Almanac and State Industrial Guide, 1954–1955*, 609; "Census Extremely Gratifying—Thornton," *Fort Worth* (June 1960): 21, 42: George Green, *Hurst, Euless, Bedford Heart of the Metroplex* (Austin: Eakin Press, 1995), 65, 68–69; telephone calls to the City Hall of each of the three major mid-cities, Hurst, Euless, and Bedford, Sept. 24, 2009.

7. "Aircraft Built in Fort Worth Fill The Skies Of The World," 12; Thomasson, "The Changing Economic Structure of the Fort Worth Metropolitan Area as Reflected by Changes in the Work Force," 84 (quotation); 1980 U.S. Census data in *Texas Almanac and State Industrial Guide, 1982–1983* (Dallas: *Dallas Morning News*, 1981), 336; Gordon Dickson, "We're No. 4! We're No. 4!" *Fort Worth Star-Telegram*, Jan. 7, 2008, 2B; "North Texas Population Boom," *Fort Worth Star-Telegram*, Jan. 27, 2008, 1A.

8. *Texas Almanac, 1941–1942*, 508; *Texas Almanac, 1949–1950*, 591; "Aircraft Built in Fort Worth Fill the Skies of the World," *Fort Worth* (March 1959): 12 (quotation); "Aviation Europe Discovers F-111 and Iroquois," *Fort Worth* (May 1965): 47.

9. *Socioeconomic Impact Analysis Study March 1993 Disposal and Reuse of Carswell Air Force Base, Texas*, 2–7; Simonson, *The History of the American Aircraft Industry*, 227; *Texas Almanac and State Industrial Guide, 1982–1983*, 336; *Texas Almanac, 2002–2003*, 265; Bob Cox, "Army Cites Runaway Costs in Bell Copter Cancellation," *Fort Worth Star-Telegram*, Oct. 18, 2008, 1C; "Gates Would End 2 Lockheed Programs, Expand Another," *Fort Worth Star-Telegram*, Apr. 7, 2009, 1.

10. "Texas 2nd in Plane Industry," *Fort Worth Star-Telegram*, Aug.13, 1952, *Fort Worth Star-Telegram* Collection, Aviation Industry Folder, UTA.

11. The author heard this comment numerous times and even thought it as well.

12. Carter, the publisher of the *Fort Worth Star-Telegram*, began the motto "the city where the West begins" and placed it on the front page of his daily newspaper early in the twentieth century. In the first decade of the twenty-first century, it still is there.

13. Gerald D. Nash, *The American West Transformed: The Impact of the Second World War.* (Lincoln: University of Nebraska Press, 1985), 19.

14. Ibid., vii, 17–18; Roger W. Lotchin, *Fortress California, 1910–1961: From Warfare to Welfare* (New York: Oxford University Press, 1992), 19.

15. Nash, *The American West Transformed*, 39 (first quotation), 14 (second quotation); Kevin J. Fernlund, (ed.) *The Cold War American West 1945–1989* (Albuquerque: University of New Mexico Press, 1998), 2–3, 102.

16. Markusen, Hall, Campbell, Deitrick, *The Rise of the Gunbelt*, 9, 13, 25.

17. Ibid., 25, 82, 234 (quotations).

18. Ibid., 88–89.

19. Ibid., 148 (quotation), 161, 168.

20. Ibid., 176–77.

21. Ibid., 233, 236 (quotation).

22. Ibid., 230, 6.

23. Lotchin, *Fortress California, 1910–1961*, 329 (second quotation), 352–53 (first quotation); Kenneth T. Jackson, "The City Loses the Sword: The Decline of Major Military Activity in the New York Metropolitan Region," in *The Martial Metropolis*, 160; William Holden, "Our Year In Defense—and War," *Fort Worth Chamber of Commerce Annual Report for 1941*, *Fort Worth* (January 1942): 4.

24. "Important Fort Worth Industry: American Manufacturing Products Are Sought by Many Industries," *Fort Worth* (October 1951): 18; Holden, "Our Chamber of Commerce In the War," 7.

25. Lotchin, *Fortress California, 1910–1961*, xviii.

26. Thomas A. Manning, Command Historian, *A History of Military Aviation in San Antonio* (rev. ed.; Washington, D.C.: USAF Air Education and Training Command, 2000), 83, 105, 111–112.

Bibliography

ARCHIVAL MATERIALS

Manuscripts and Collections

Angelo State University. San Angelo, Texas. West Texas Collection. "Major Horace S. Carswell Jr." Colonel Alan Clark, "Welcome to Carswell Air Force Base."

Bandy, Charles C. Personal Files. "Camp Bowie: Shaper of Destiny," Research Paper prepared for Retrofest Competition, Tarrant County Junior College, Northeast Campus, March 15, 1996.

Barker, Dee. Personal Collection. "Bird's Fort as Recorded in Official Documents and Letters from Jonathan Bird."

Bell Helicopter. Library. Bound Volumes of Company Newspapers.

Benbrook Public Library. Benbrook, Texas. Scrapbook on Benbrook History. "Carruthers Field." "Benbrook's Name: What's in a Name!" "Brief History of Benbrook, Texas." Excerpts from the Benbrook Comprehensive Plan, June 2, 1994.

Brunk, Arthur E. "A Memory Voyage." 1996.

Collier, Reed Craig. "Recollections of Reed Craig Collier." Typewritten manuscript. Obtained from Charlotte Grizzle, daughter.

Consolidated Vultee Aircraft Corporation. Training Certificate in Foremanship and Job Instruction Issued to Vernon Rogers. June 19, 1943.

Durham, Floyd. "Military Retirement, Golf and the Size of the Fort Worth Market." Typewritten manuscript. In possession of author.

Erickson, Beryl A., Personal Collection. Articles shared with author: "Convair Chief Test Pilot Revisits Two 'Old Friends.'" "History of the B-58." Also, "Flight Characteristics of the B-58 Mach 2 Bomber," Research Paper by Erickson Presented to the Royal Aeronautical Society, London, England, November 23, 1961.

Fort Worth Chamber of Commerce. Bound copies of monthly newsletter.

———. "Lease Contract and Option to Purchase Land Owned by Mary E. Gantt to the Chamber of Commerce on August 7, 1917, for use by the U.S. Government.

———. "Proposal For Expansion of Services of the United States Public Health Service Hospital at Fort Worth, Texas For Use as a Veterans' Facility." Prepared by Harold S. Foster, Manager, Industrial Department. July 7, 1944.

Fort Worth Museum of Science and History. History Archives. Camp Bowie Folder. William Berry, "Fort Worth as War Training Camp."

Fuchs, Joe, Jr. Collection, Hurst, Texas. Letter, information about his father.

Lockheed Martin Corporation. Fort Worth, Texas. Library. Bound Copies of Company Newspapers. Also, John O. Lockwood, "Factual History of the Fort Worth Division Consolidated Vultee Aircraft Corporation," November 22, 1945. Mimeographed notebook.

McClure, Charles. Scrapbook Compiled in 1940 of McClure's fellow fliers who were in his same unit in Fort Worth in World War I. Information on Harry Brants and Jack Moranz drawing of him.

Murphey, Dr. Griffin. Personal Collection. Manuscript on Dermott Allen and other articles on Canadian Fliers in Fort Worth in World War I.

Neubroch, Hans. Personal Manuscript. "The Extraordinary Life of Wing Commander Dermott Allen, Late Royal Irish Fuseliers."

Pate, J'Nell L. Personal Manuscript. "Boarding House Rosie: The Role of the Girls' Service League of Fort Worth, Texas During World War II."

Pate Museum of Transportation. Cresson, Texas. Locklear Collection. Newspaper Clippings about Ormer Leslie Locklear.

River Oaks Library. River Oaks, Texas. Loose-Leaf Notebook: "History of River Oaks." Compiled by Frank Blue.

Saginaw Public Library. Saginaw, Texas. "Saginaw History" Folder. Handwritten account of a history of Saginaw written by Mary Yarbrough, November 1985.

Skinner, Alan. "Concrete Fokker in Tarrant County." Paper delivered at Texas State Historical Association Annual Meeting. March 3, 2005. Radisson Plaza Hotel. Fort Worth.

Tarrant County Archives. Fort Worth. "Barron Field Review," 1919. Also Maurice G. Lambert, "Living in Liberator Village in the 1940's and 50's." Updated February 26, 2001.

Texas. Bureau of Economic Geology and Technology. Bulletin No. 1750. September 5, 1917. "The Geology of Camp Bowie and Vicinity."

Texas Tech University. Southwest Collection. Khleber Van Zandt Papers. "History of the Seventh Texas Regiment, Infantry, C.S.A."

University of Texas at Arlington. Arlington, Texas. Special Collections Library. *Fort Worth Star-Telegram* Collection. Numerous Clippings Folders: Amon Carter, Aviation History, B-36, Barron Field, Bell Helicopter, Camp Bowie, Carswell, Consolidated, Fort Worth Army Air Field, General Dynamics, Globe Aircraft, Marine Glider Base, Narcotics Farm, U.S. Public Health Service Hospital.

University of Texas at Dallas. Richardson, Texas. McDermott Library. Special Collections. Globe Aircraft Collection.

Veterans' Memorial Park, 4100 Camp Bowie Boulevard, Fort Worth, Texas. Historical Markers: "Camp Bowie Boulevard," "Camp Bowie in World War I."

Westworth Village Town Hall. City Secretary's Office. Local History Collection. Scrapbook: "History of Westworth Village," compiled 1976. Clipping: "Town to Celebrate 50 Years Saturday." By Shanan Johnson, June 8, 1991.

White Settlement Historical Museum. White Settlement, Texas. Scrapbook: "Liberator Village."

White Settlement Library, White Settlement, Texas. "History of White Settlement." Mimeographed notebook prepared by Mrs. E. D. Head and students of Brewer High School history classes of 1952 and 1953, included with the notebook "Brief History of Fort Worth Operation of Convair Aerospace Division of General Dynamics." "The Story of White Settlement A Pioneer Community at the Crossroads of Progress 1850–1992." Booklet by Norris Chambers. "The Story of White Settlement." 1978.

GOVERNMENT DOCUMENTS AND PUBLICATIONS

Texas

Texas. "No. 203 Proclamation by Sam Houston Bird's Fort Treaty [September 29, 1843]," in *The Indian Papers of Texas and the Southwest, 1825–1916*, Edited by Dorman H. Winfrey and James M. Day, with a new Introduction by Michael L. Tate. Austin: Texas State Historical Association, 1995.

United States

National Archives and Records Administration, Southwest Region. Fort Worth Quartermaster Depot Organization Manual. Organization Charts. 1949–1950. Permanent Records.

———. Barron Field Records.

———. Carruthers Field Records.

———. Carswell Air Force Base Land Acquisition Records.

———. Eagle Mountain Army Air Field Records.

———. Globe Aircraft Acquisition Records.

———. Narcotics' Farm and United States Public Health Service Hospital Records.

———. Taliaferro Field Records.

National Park Service, Washington, D.C. "San Diego: Three Centuries of Defense, 1769–1988." By Erwin N. Thompson. Historic Resources Study. Cabrillo National Monument, California, 1988.

Tarrant County, Texas. Deed. U.S. General Services Administration to Abe Meyer, City of Dallas. August 8, 1956. Record Book 3021, p. 1.

———. Deed whereby Reconstruction Finance Corporation acquired the 149.762 Acres of land belonging to Globe Aircraft Corporation.

———. 67th District Court. *Rosenberg v. Globe Aircraft Corporation*. 80F Supp. 123. June 18, 1948.

———. 67th District Court. *B. G. Thompson v. Globe Aircraft Corporation*. NO. 51065-A. December 12, 1947.

Texas. Court of Civil Appeals. Fort Worth. *Globe Aircraft Corporation v. Thompson* 203 S.W. 2d 865. June 6, 1947. (No. 14836).

United States Air Force. *Annual Report of the Secretary of the Air Force for the Fiscal Year 1949.*

———. Carswell Air Force Base. Program. Veteran's Day, November 11, 1966.

———. Historical Report. Prepared by Historical Division, 7th Bombardment Wing, Heavy, Headquarters 19th Air Division, Carswell Air Force Base, Fort Worth, Texas. May 1951. Obtained from Office of Base Historian. Dyess Air Force Base, Abilene, Texas.

———. "A History of Military Aviation in San Antonio," by Thomas A. Manning, Command Historian. USAF Air Education and Training Command. Government Publication 01061. Revised 2000.

———. "History of the 7th Wing." July 1, 1955. MSgt. William J. Allen. Obtained from Dyess Air Force Base, Abilene, Texas.

———. "History of the 7th Bomb Wing and Carswell AFB." Office of History. 7th Bomb Wing Carswell AFB, Texas. Obtained from Office of History, Dyess Air Force Base, Abilene, Texas.

———. "Monthly Progress Analysis of Activities and Achievements. September 1952." History of the 7th Bombardment Wing, Heavy, 19th Air Division, Carswell Air Force Base, Fort Worth, Texas. Office of Base Historian, MSgt. Robert Romanelli, Dyess Air Force Base, Abilene, Texas.

———. "Monthly Progress Analysis of Activity and Achievement. August 1952." Ibid.

———. Office of Air Force History. *The United States Air Force Basic Documents on Roles and Missions*. Richard I. Wolf, ed. 1987.

———. "Organization." History of the 7th Bombardment Wing, Heavy, 19th Air Division. Carswell Air Force Base, Fort Worth, Texas. December 1955. Office of Base Historian. MSgt. Robert Romanelli, Dyess Air Force Base, Abilene, Texas.

———. "Preliminary Report of Damage caused by Wind Storm, Carswell AFB, 4 Sept. 1952 To Director of Installations." Robert R. Conner, Colonel, U.S.A.F., Southwestern Division, Dallas, Texas.

———. Seventh Bombardment Wing. Office of Public Affairs, Carswell, Air Force Base, Texas. "Fact Sheet."

———. "7 BMW B-36 Chronology." TSgt. Gregory S. Byard, Historian, U.S.A.F. Office of Base Historian, Dyess Air Force Base, Abilene, Texas.

———. *Socioeconomic Impact Analysis Study Disposal and Reuse of Carswell Air Force Base, Texas*. March 1993.

United States Army Air Forces. "Agreements as to the Initial Implementation of the National Security Act of 1947." September 15, 1947. "Separation of the Air Force from the U.S. Army." Kenneth C. Royall, Secretary of War.

———. Barron Field. Everman, Texas. Field Installations. Telegrams In. April-June 1918.

———. Barron Field, Everman, Texas. Field Installations. Proceedings of Board, Court Martial Records, and Reports Relating to Personnel Miscellaneous Correspondence. Incoming Office Reports.

———. Barron Field, Everman, Texas. General Correspondence of the Office of the Aviation Supply Officer, 1919–1920.

———. Second Report of the Commanding General of the Army Air Forces to the Secretary of War. February 27, 1945. H. H. Arnold, Commanding General.

———. Third Report of the Commanding General of the Army Air Forces to the Secretary of War. November 12, 1945. H. H. Arnold, Commanding General.

United States Congress. *Congressional Record.* November 19, 1971.

———. *Congressional Record.* "Comments on F-111 Program During House Debate of Fiscal Year 1971 Defense Appropriations Bill. October 8, 1970.

United States Congress. Senate Permanent Subcommittee on Government Operations. "Statement of Frank W. Davis, president of GD/Fort Worth." May 1963.

———. Senate Permanent Subcommittee on Government Operations. "Statement of Roger Lewis, President of General Dynamics Corp."

United States Department of the Army. Corps of Engineers, Southern Department 1918–1919. "Map." Prepared under the direction of Col. W. P. Stokey, Department Engineer. Note: Camp Bowie, Carruthers Field, Barron Field, Taliaferro Field and Aerial Gunnery Range Abandoned.

———. Corps of Engineers, Fort Worth District. Fort Worth, Texas. "Map." Fort Worth O.R.C. Site Texas Military Reservation." August 12, 1952.

———. Corps of Engineers, Fort Worth District. Fort Worth, Texas. Real Estate Planning Report. "Acquisition of Leasehold Interest and Easements for Access Roads and Utility Lines." Carswell Air Force Base, Texas. May 10, 1954. Prepared by Andrew J. Landry, Appraiser.

———. Corps of Engineers, Fort Worth District. Fort Worth, Texas. Real Estate Planning Report. *Acquisition of Land By Lease in Crockett and Val Verde Counties, Texas For A Proposed Bombing Range, Said Land To Be Used for Carswell Air Force Base Texas.* February 16, 1954. Prepared by C. K. Wildermuth, Appraiser.

———. Corps of Engineers, Fort Worth District. Fort Worth, Texas. Real Estate Report, Ammunition Storage Area. Carswell Air Force Base Fort Worth, Tarrant County, Texas. September 1951.

———. Corps of Engineers. Fort Worth District. Fort Worth, Texas. *Supplement No. 2 to Real Estate Report: Carswell Air Force Base Proposed North-South Runway and Taxiway Extensions and Warm-up Pad Site.* January 17, 1952.

———. Corps of Engineers. Fort Worth District. Fort Worth, Texas. *Report of Ammunitions Storage Site Location for Carswell Air Force Base Tarrant County, Texas.*

———. Corps of Engineers. Fort Worth District. Fort Worth, Texas. *Report Concerning Possible Joint Utilization of Former U.S. Marine Corps Air Station Eagle Mountain Lake, Texas.* Transportation Corps and Texas National Guard. February 27, 1957.

United States Court of Appeals. *U.S. v. Paddock.* 180 F 2d 121, C.A. 5 (Tex.) February 18, 1950. (No. 12738).

United States Department of Defense. Second Primary Report of the Secretary of Defense, 1949.

United States Department of Labor. Women's Bureau. "The Woman Worker, 1942."

United States Military. National Personnel Records Center. St. Louis, Missouri. Military Records of Major Horace Seaver Carswell Jr.

United States Navy. Naval Air Station Joint Reserve Base Fort Worth, Texas. "Fact Sheet."

———. Naval Air Station Joint Reserve Base Fort Worth, Texas. "Supplementary Fact Sheet."

———. Program, Change of Command Ceremony. Naval Air Station Joint Reserve Base Fort Worth/Naval Air Station Dallas. August 22, 1998.

United States Secretary of the Treasury. "Selection of the Site for the Second United States Narcotic Farm." News Release by A. W. Melton, Secretary of the Treasury; Patrick J. Hurley, Secretary of War; and William DeWitt Mitchell, Attorney General of the United States. June 1, 1931.

United States Supreme Court. *Paddock v. U. S.* 340 U.S. 813. October 9, 1950. (No. 79).

Unpublished Sources

Theses and Dissertations

Brown, Jerold Edward. "Where Eagles Roost: A History of Army Airfields Before World War II." Ph.D. dissertation, Duke University, 1977.

Dixon, Ford. "McNamara, General Dynamics, and the F-111: A Business and Political History." Ph.D. dissertation, Texas Christian University, 1972.

Farrington, Michael Walter. "Middleton Tate Johnson: Texas' Would-Be Governor, General and Railroad Entrepreneur." Master's thesis, University of Texas at Arlington, 1980.

Ferguson, John Craig. "A History of Goodfellow Air Force Base, San Angelo, Texas 1940–1958." Master's thesis, Angelo State University, 1996.

Johnson, Warren Eugene. "A Study of the Effect of Convair Employment Fluctuations on Fort Worth Business Activity." Master's thesis, Texas Christian University, 1960.

Miles, James C. "Fort Worth and World War I." Master's thesis, Southern Methodist University, 1946.

Thomasson, David Larry. "The Changing Economic Structure of the Fort Worth Metropolitan Area As Reflected By Changes in the Work Force." Master's thesis, Texas Christian University, 1964.

Interviews

Arnold, Terry. Bell Helicopter Employee. Hurst, Texas. October 18, 1996.

Barrett, Gretchen. Daughter of Harry Brants. Fort Worth, Texas. May 11, 2006; October 27, 2006.

Capps, Bobby. Childhood friend of Horace Carswell Jr. Fort Worth, Texas. March 19, 1997; October 26, 2001.

Carswell, Robert E. Son of Major Horace Carswell Jr. Telephone Interviews. April 7, 2002; February 20, 2003.

Casper, Col. Willie H. (Ret.) Telephone Interview. July 27, 2007.

Chambers, Norris. White Settlement, Texas. April 17, 1997.

Clark, B. J. Owner, Clark's Precision Machine and Tool. Azle, Texas. May 24, 2007.

Clark, Betty. Wife of owner of Clark's Precision Machine and Tool. Azle, Texas. October 24, 1996.

Cole, Stanley, Publisher, *Carswell Sentinel*. Fort Worth, Texas. March 13, 1997.

Craft, Cecile. (Mrs. John Craft). Telephone interview. February 27, 1997.

Crawford, Bill. Telephone interview. May 2, 1998.

Deen, Mrs. Edgar "Eddie" Deen Jr. Telephone interview. February 10, 1997.

Douglas, Walt. On B-36 Restoration Team. Fort Worth, Texas. March 4, 1997.

Doyle, Gloria. Former Consolidated worker. Haltom City, Texas. January 10, 1997.

Erickson, Beryl A. Consolidated/Convair Test Pilot. Telephone Interview. February 2, 1997.

Erickson, Billie. Wife of Convair Test Pilot Beryl A. Erickson. Telephone interview. January 30, 1997; February 19, 1997.

Evans, Harry. Worked at General Dynamics. Azle, Texas. December 30, 1996.

Faulks, Earl. Worked at General Dynamics on B-36. Fort Worth, Texas. Telephone Interview. October 4, 2006.

Feeley, Mike. City of Fort Worth Aviation Department. Telephone Interview. July 29, 2005.

Fisher, Ray. Telephone interview. February 19, 1997.

Flippo, Yvonne, Librarian, Saginaw Public Library, Saginaw, Texas. Telephone Interview. May 26, 2006.

Fox, Sue. Texas Star Books. Fort Worth, Texas. March 5, 2005.

Fuchs, Joe, Jr. His father worked at Bell in Buffalo, New York, and then came to Texas after the company moved. Hurst, Texas. December 5, 1996.

Gill, Jimmie. Haltom City, Texas. January 15, 2007.

Glover, Billy. Azle, Texas. January 19, 2007.

Greenwood, J. W. Worked at Menasco. Haltom City, Texas. October 30, 2005.

Grimes, Irene. Was in seventh or eighth grade when Taliaferro Field was operated in World War I. Telephone interview. March 1, 1997.

Harrison, C. Richard. Fort Smith, Arkansas. Telephone Interviews. June 16, 2005; June 21, 2005.

Hodges, Hubert W. Written Interview. Fort Worth Museum of Science and History, Fort Worth History Research Files. Taped December 1, 1994. Subject: "Camp Bowie."

Host, Patricia. City Secretary, Westworth Village. Westworth Village, Texas. April 8, 1997.

Howard, Charles. School Friend of Horace Carswell Jr. River Oaks, Texas. July 8, 2005.

Hunter, Grace Imogene "Johnnie" Johnston. Worked at Eagle Mountain Marine Base. Telephone Interviews. February 7, 1997; February 8, 1997; January 17, 2007.

Joiner, Webb. President and CEO, Bell Helicopter/Textron. Hurst, Texas. February 4, 1998.

Kerlee, Enis M. Worked at Consolidated. Fort Worth, Texas. December 30, 1996.

Kibbe, Tech. Sergeant Craig. Offutt AFB, Nebraska. Telephone interview. November 20, 1996.

Kleinwechter, Colonel Frank. Stationed at Carswell, Navigator on B-36. Benbrook, Texas. April 14, 1997.

Korth, Fred. Secretary of the Navy in John F. Kennedy Administration. Telephone Interview. February 23, 1998.

Krause, Paul. Fort Worth, Texas. February 11, 1997.

Leavy, Alice C. Oral Histories of Fort Worth, Inc. by the Junior League of Fort Worth, Inc. Typed Copy in Tarrant County Archives, Carol Hendrix, Interviewer. February 1978.

Long, Olen. Took Restoration Advisory Board Members on Tour of Carswell to Show Environmental Cleanup. Carswell AFB. November 6, 1996.

McDaniel, Jack. Worked at Hicks Field. Telephone interview. February 27, 1997.

McKeown, Colonel Harry. Fort Worth, Texas. May 28, 2007.

McKeown, Dora Dougherty Strother. Fort Worth, Texas. May 28, 2007.

McEachern, J. D. On B-36 Restoration Team. Fort Worth, Texas. March 4, 1997.

McGovern, George. Former U.S. Senator from South Dakota. Lincoln, Nebraska. October 4, 1996.

Mahon, George. U.S. Congressman. Written Oral Interview. George Mahon Papers. Southwest Collection, Texas Tech University.

Plumlee, Bill. Fort Worth Aviation Heritage Association. Fort Worth, Texas. March 4, 1997.

Powell, Mary Mann. Telephone interview. August 15, 1997.

Pritchett, Captain R. N. Westover Hills Police Officer. Westover Hills, Texas. April 8, 1997.

Pyle, Elaina. Telephone interview. April 17, 2011.

Schelper, Max. On B-36 Restoration Team. Fort Worth, Texas. March 4, 1997.

Schulte, Gene. Bridgeport, Texas. March 12, 1997.

Simmons, Mary Virginia. Telephone interview. May 28, 2007.

Skipper, Bobbie. Former Carswell Librarian; NAS Fort Worth JRB Librarian. November 7, 1996.

Smyers, Captain T. D., Commanding Officer, Naval Air Station Fort Worth Joint Reserve Base, Carswell Field, December 22, 2009.

Turner, Loyd L. Public Relations Director at Convair/General Dynamics, 1948–1971. Fort Worth, Texas. September 6, 1996.

Wagner, Joe. Fort Worth, Texas. April 30, 1998.

Wakefield, Catherine. Saginaw. Telephone interview. February 27, 1997.

Weaver, Jimmie. Former resident of Liberator Village. White Settlement, Texas. April 20, 1997.

Werner, Commander John. Executive Officer Naval Air Station Fort Worth, JRB. Fort Worth, Texas. February 11, 1997.

Wright, Jim. U.S. Congressman, Twelfth Congressional District, 1955–1989. Fort Worth, Texas. February 11, 1997.

PUBLISHED SOURCES

Newspapers and Periodicals

Bell Aircraft News. 1950s.

Bell Helicopter News. 1960s–1990s (weekly publication that went monthly in the early 1980s)

Bell Helicopter International News

Bellringer, The. Bell Aircraft Newspaper. Mid-1940s.

Camp Bowie Texahoma Bugler.

Carswell Sentinel. 1970s–1980s.

Consolidated Eagle, The. Early 1940s.

Convairiety. Convair newspaper. Late 1940s–1950s.

Eagle, The. Consolidated newspaper. 1940s.

Fort Worth. Fort Worth Chamber of Commerce Magazine. Mid-1940s.

Fort Worth Association of Commerce News Bulletin. 1925.

Fort Worth Broadcaster. Fort Worth Chamber of Commerce Magazine. 1920s.

Fort Worth Magazine. Fort Worth Chamber of Commerce Magazine. Late-1940s.

Fort Worth News-Tribune.

Fort Worth Press.

Fort Worth Record. 1919.

Fort Worth Star-Telegram.

Fort Worth Today. Fort Worth Chamber of Commerce Magazine. 1980s.

General Dynamics News. 1960s–1980s.

Horned Frog. Yearbook. Texas Christian University. 1936–1940.

Lone Star Scanner, The. 1940s.

Northwest Sentinel. Saginaw newspaper. Late 1980s.

Pass in Review. Magazine for Camp Bowie.

River Oaks News.

Saginaw Sentinel. Saginaw newspaper. 1970s.

Sentinel, The. Saginaw newspaper. Early 1980s.

Sentinel, The. Serving Texas's military retirees after Carswell closed. 1990s.

San Angelo Standard-Times.

Strut, The. Magazine at Carruthers Field. 1918.

Taliaferro Target. Newspaper at Taliaferro Field. 1918.

Texas Almanac.

Texas Monthly.

This Month in Fort Worth. Fort Worth Chamber of Commerce Magazine. 1930s, early 1940s.

Books and Articles

Air Force Bases: A Directory of U.S. Air Force Installations, Both in the Continental U.S. and Overseas with Useful Information on Each Base and its Nearby Community. Harrisburg, Pa.: The Stackpole Company, 1965.

Alexander, Thomas E. *The Stars Were Big and Bright: The United States Army Air*

Forces and Texas During World War II. Vol. 2. Austin: Eakin Press, 2001.

Allen, Richard Sanders. *Revolution in the Sky: The Lockheeds of Aviation's Golden Age.* 1964. Revised ed. New York: Orion Books, 1988.

Anderson, Jack, and Fred Blumenthal. "Target Moscow: Our Global Bombing Crews Get Ready." *Parade*, August 15, 1954: 6–7.

Arbingast, Stanley A., and Robert H. Ryan. "Texas: Diversified Resources Spark Economy." *Editor and Publisher*, October 31, 1953: 157–164.

Arnold, Henry H. *Airmen and Aircraft: An Introduction to Aeronautics.* New York: The Ronald Press Company, 1926.

———. *Global Mission.* New York: Harper and Brothers, Publishers, 1949.

Art, Robert J. *The TFX Decision: McNamara and the Military.* Boston: Little, Brown & Co., 1968.

Atkinson, James W. *The Soldier's Chronology.* New York: Garland Publishing, 1993.

Atkinson, James W., and Judy Wood. *Fort Worth's Huge Deal Unwinding Westside's Twisted Legend,* 2010. PDF e-book.

"B-36's 50th anniversary to be celebrated." *The Azle News,* July 25, 1996, p. 7a.

Barksdale, Ethelbert C. *The Genesis of the Aviation Industry in North Texas.* Austin: Bureau of Business Research, University of Texas, 1958.

Barlow, Jeffrey G. *Revolt of the Admirals: The Fight for Naval Aviation, 1945–1950.* Washington, D.C.: Brassey's, 1998.

Biddle, Wayne. *Barons of the Sky: From Early Flight to Strategic Warfare, The Story of the American Aerospace Industry.* New York: Simon and Schuster, 1991.

Bilstein, Roger E. *Flight in America, 1900–1983: From the Wrights to the Astronauts.* Baltimore: The Johns Hopkins University Press, 1984.

Bilstein, Roger E., and Jay Miller. *Aviation in Texas.* Austin: Texas Monthly Press, 1985.

Birdsall, Steve. *Log of the Liberators: An Illustrated History of the B-24.* Garden City, N.Y.: Doubleday & Co., 1973.

Boyne, Walter J. *Beyond the Horizons: The Lockheed Story.* New York: St. Martin's Press, Thomas Dunne Books, 1998.

A Brief History of Goodfellow AFB and the 17th Training Wing. San Angelo, Tex.: Office of History HQ 17th Training Wing Goodfellow Air Force Base, Texas, 1995.

Bright, Charles D. *The Jet Makers: The Aerospace Industry from 1945 to 1972.* Lawrence: The Regents Press of Kansas, 1978.

Bright, Charles D., ed. *Historical Dictionary of the U.S. Air Force.* New York: Greenwood Press, 1992.

Brokaw, Tom. *The Greatest Generation.* New York: Random House, 1998.

Brown, Carol, ed. *America through the Eyes of Its People: A Collection of Primary Sources.* New York: Harper Collins College Publishers, 1993.

Brown, David A. *The Bell Helicopter Textron Story: Changing the Way the World Flies.* Arlington, Tex.: Aerofax, 1995.

Brown, Stanley H. *Ling: The Rise, Fall, and Return of a Texas Titan.* New York: Athenaeum, 1972.

Brown, Stuart F., and Steve Douglass. "Swing Wing Stealth Attack Plane." *Popular Science,* January 1995: 54–56, 86.

Brophy, Arnold. *The Air Force: A Panorama of the Nation's Youngest Service.* New York: Gilbert Press, 1956.

Butterworth, W. E. *Flying Army: The Modern Air Arm of the U.S. Army.* New York: Doubleday & Company, Inc., 1971.

Cadogan, Mary. *Women with Wings.* Chicago: Academy Chicago Publishers, 1993.

Cagle, Eldon, Jr. *Fort Sam: The Story of Fort Sam Houston, Texas.* San Antonio: Maverick Publishing Company, 2003.

Califano, Joseph A., Jr. *The Triumph and Tragedy of Lyndon Johnson: The White House Years.* New York: Simon & Schuster, 1991.

Calvert, Robert A., and Arnoldo DeLeón. *The History of Texas.* 2nd ed. Wheeling, Ill.: Harlan Davidson, 1996.

Campbell, Randolph C. *Gone To Texas: A History of the Lone Star State.* New York: Oxford University Press, 2003.

Capp, De Witt S. *A Few Great Captains: The Men and Events That Shaped the Development of U.S. Air Power.* Garden City, N.Y.: Doubleday & Company., 1980.

Cashion, Ty, and Jesús F. de la Teja, eds. *The Human Tradition in Texas.* Wilmington, Del.: Scholarly Resources, 2001.

Cashion, Ty. *The New Frontier: A Contemporary History of Fort Worth and Tarrant County.* San Antonio: Historical Publishing Network, 2006.

Chamberlin, Clarence D. *Record Flights.* Philadelphia: Dorrance and Company Publishers, 1928.

Chandler, Charles De Forest and Frank P. Lahm. *How Our Army Grew Wings: Airmen and Aircraft Before 1914.* New York: The Ronald Press Company, 1943.

Chastaine, Ben H. *Story of the 36th: The Experiences of the 36th Division in the World War.* Oklahoma City: Harlow Publishing Company, 1920.

Clark, Don. *Wild Blue Yonder An Air Epic.* Seattle: Superior Publishing Company, 1972.

Coffman, Edward M. *The War to End All Wars: The American Military Experience in World War I.* New York: Oxford University Press, 1968.

Cochran, Jacqueline, and Maryann Bucknum Brinley *Jackie Cochran: An Autobiography.* New York: Bantam Books, 1987.

———. *The Stars at Noon.* Boston: Little, Brown and Company, 1954.

Coleman, Ted, with Robert Wenkam. *Jack Northrop and the Flying Wing The Story Behind the Stealth Bomber.* New York: Paragon House, 1988.

Colwell, Frances, comp. *White Settlement.* White Settlement, Tex.: White Settlement Sesquicentennial Committee, 1986.

Conlin, J. R., and C. H. Peterson, eds. *An American Harvest: Readings in American History.* Vol. 2. San Diego: Harcourt Brace Jovanovich, Publishers, 1986.

Cook, David C. *Sky Battle, 1914–1918: The Story of Aviation in World War I.* New York: W.W. Norton & Company, Inc., 1970.

Corn, Joseph J. *The Winged Gospel: America's Romance with Aviation, 1900–1950.* New York: Oxford University Press, 1983.

Coulam, Robert F. *Illusions of Choice: The F-111 and the Problem of Weapons Acquisition Reform.* Princeton, N.J.: Princeton University Press, 1977.

Cragg, Dan. *Guide to Military Installations.* Harrisburg, Pa.: Stackpole Books, 1983.

Cunningham, Robert E. *Aces High.* St. Louis: General Dynamics Corporation, 1977.

Dawson, Joseph G. III, ed. *The Texas Military Experience from the Texas Revolution through World War II.* College Station: Texas A&M University Press, 1995.

DeSeversky, Alexander P. *Victory through Air Power.* New York: Simon and Schuster, 1942.

Dickey, Betty. *Echoes of Yesterday: A History of White Settlement Schools.* White Settlement, Tex.: Betty McCrary Dickey, 1990.

Dorfer, Ingemar. *Arms Deal: The Selling of the F-16.* Westport, Conn.: Praeger Publishers, 1983.

Dorr, Robert F. *7th Bombardment Group/Wing 1918–1995.* Paducah, Ky.: Turner Publishing Co., 1996.

Elliott, Charles Winslow. *Winfield Scott: The Soldier and the Man.* New York: The Macmillan Company, 1937.

Farber, James. *Fort Worth in the Civil War.* Belton, Tex.: Peter Hansbrough Bell Press, 1960.

Fernlund, Kevin J., ed. *The Cold War American West 1945–1989.* Albuquerque: University of New Mexico Press, 1998.

Flemmons, Jerry. *Amon: The Life of Amon Carter, Sr. of Texas.* Austin: Jenkins Publishing Company, 1978.

Flynn, John T. *The Roosevelt Myth.* Garden City, N.Y.: Garden City Publishing Co., 1948.

Fort Worth, 1849–1949: 100 Years of Progress. Reprinted from Fort Worth Chamber of Commerce Magazine, *Fort Worth,* 1949.

Fort Worth Official Pocket Guide. Fort Worth: C. S. Rogers, 1920.

Fox, J. Ronald. *Arming America: How the U.S. Buys Weapons.* Boston: Harvard University, 1974.

Francillon, Rene J. *Lockheed Aircraft since 1913.* Annapolis, Md.: Naval Institute Press, 1987.

Franklin, Roger. *The Defender: The Story of General Dynamics.* New York: Harper and Row, Publishers, 1986.

Frazer, Robert W., ed. *Mansfield on the Condition of the Western Forts 1853–54.* Norman: University of Oklahoma Press, 1963.

Frazier, Thomas R., ed. *The Private Side of American History.* 4th ed. New York: Harcourt Brace Jovanovich, Publisher, 1987.

Frisbee, John L. ed. *Makers of the United States Air Force.* McLean, Va.: Pergamon-Brassey's International Defense Publishers, 1989.

Gansler, Jacques S. *The Defense Industry.* Cambridge, Mass.: The MIT Press, 1980.

George, Juliet. *Images of America: Fort Worth's Arlington Heights.* Charleston, S.C.: Arcadia Publishing, 2010.

Glines, Carroll V., Jr. *The Compact Military History of the United States Air Force.* New York: Hawthorn Books, 1963.

———. *Jimmy Doolittle: Master of the Calculated Risk.* New York: Van Nostrand Reinhold Company, 1972.

Goldberg, Alfred., ed. *A History of the United States Air Force 1907–1957.* New York: Arno Press, 1957. Reprinted, 1972.

Goodwin, Jacob. *Brotherhood of Arms General Dynamics and the Business of Defending America.* New York: Times Books, 1985.

Grant, Ulysses S. *Personal Memoirs of U .S. Grant.* Vols. 1 and 2. 1885. Reprint New York: Konecky & Konecky, 1992.

Green, George. *Hurst, Euless, Bedford: Heart of the Metroplex.* Austin: Eakin Press, 1995.

Gurney, Gene. *A Chronology of World Aviation.* New York: Franklin Watts, Inc., 1965.

Haley, J. Evetts. *A Texan Looks At Lyndon.* Canyon, Tex.: Palo Duro Press, 1964.

Harding, Stephen, and James Long. *Dominator: The Story of the Consolidated B-32 Bomber.* Missoula, Mont.: Pictorial Histories Publishing Company, 1983.

Harris, Sherwood. "Coast to Coast in 12 Crashes." *American Heritage,* October 1964: 46–49; 76–81.

Harris, Sherwood. *The First to Fly: Aviation's Pioneer Days.* New York: Simon & Schuster, 1970.

Hart, Archibald. *Company K of Yesterday.* New York: Vantage Press, 1969.

Hehs, E. "Beryl Arthur Erickson, Test Pilot." *Code One.* October 1992: 17–25.

History of Texas: World War Heroes. Dallas: Army and Navy History Company, 1919.

Hitch, Charles J. *Decision-Making for Defense.* Berkeley & Los Angeles: University of California Press, 1965.

Hobbs, James. *Wild Life in the Far West: Personal Adventures of a Border Mountain Man.* 1872, Reprint. Glorieta, N. Mex.: The Rio Grande Press, Inc., 1969.

Hodgson, Marion Stegeman. *Winning My Wings: A Woman Airforce Service Pilot in World War II.* Albany, Tex.: Bright Sky Press, 1996.

Holms, Cecil J. "Tale of an Early Bird." *Airforce: The Magazine of Canada's Air Force Heritage* 26. Fall 2002: 36–40.

Hubler, Richard G. *SAC: The Strategic Air Command.* New York: Duell, Sloan and Pearce, 1958.

Hunt, C. W. *Dancing in the Sky: The Royal Flying Corps in Canada.* Toronto: Dundurn Press, 2009.

Hurley, Alfred F. *Billy Mitchell: Crusader for Air Power.* New York: Franklin Watts, 1964.

James, Peter N. *The Air Force Mafia.* New Rochelle, N.Y.: Arlington House Publishers, 1975.

Jary, William E., Jr. *Camp Bowie Fort Worth, 1917–1919: An Illustrated History of the 36th Division in The First World War.* Fort Worth: Thomason & Morrow, 1975.

Jaynes, Jack B. *Eagles Must Fly.* Edited by Charles H. Young. Dallas: Taylor Publishing Company, 1982.

Johnson, Clarence L. "Kelly." *Kelly: More than My Share of It All.* Washington, D.C. Smithsonian Institution Press, 1985.

Johnston, Alva. "Colonel Carter of Cartersville." *The Saturday Evening Post,* November 26, 1938, pp. 8-9, 31–32, 34.

Kapstein, Ethan B., ed. *Downsizing Defense.* Washington, D.C.: Congressional Quarterly, Inc., 1993.

Keil, Sally Van Wagenen. *These Wonderful Women in Their Flying Machines: The*

Unknown Heroines of World War II. New York: Four Directions Press, 1979. Reprint, 1990.

Kennedy, David M. *Over Here: The First World War and American Society*. New York: Oxford University Press, 1980.

Kirkland, Richard C. *Tales of a War Pilot*. Washington, D.C.: Smithsonian Institution Press, 1999.

Knightley, Phillip. *The First Casualty from the Crimean to Vietnam: The War Correspondent as Hero, Propagandist, and Myth Maker*. New York: Harcourt Brace Jovanovich, 1975.

Kuykendall, Lucy Rountree. *P.S. to Pecos*. Houston: The Anson Jones Press, 1946.

Lambert, Maurice. *Memories of Liberator Village*. Fort Worth: Memorabiliacs Press, 2007.

Leary, Bill. *Flyers of Barron Field: A Chronicle of the Wild Antics of Flyers Stationed Around Fort Worth in World War I*. Fort Worth: The Yrael Publishing Co., 2003.

Lebow, Eileen F. *Cal Rodgers and the Vin Fiz: The First Transcontinental Flight*. Washington: Smithsonian Institution Press, 1989.

Lee, James Ward, Carolyn N. Barnes, Kent A. Bowman, and Laura Crow. *1941: Texas Goes To War*. Denton.: University of North Texas Press, 1991.

Le May, Curtis E., with MacKinlay Kantor. *Mission with Le May: My Story*. Garden City, N.Y.: Doubleday & Company, Inc., 1965.

Lindbergh, Charles A. *The Wartime Journals of Charles A. Lindbergh*. New York: Harcourt Brace Jovanovich, Inc., 1970.

Livingston-Little, D. E., ed. *The Mexican War Diary of Thomas D. Tennery*. Norman: University of Oklahoma Press, 1970.

Lomax, Judy. *Women of the Air*. New York: Dodd, Mead & Company, 1986.

Lotchin, Roger W. *Fortress California, 1910–1961: From Warfare to Welfare*. New York: Oxford University Press, 1992.

Lotchin, Roger W., ed. *The Martial Metropolis: U.S. Cities in War and Peace*. New York: Praeger Special Studies, 1984.

Loughead, Victor. *Vehicles of the Air A Popular Exposition of Modern Aeronautics with Working Drawings*. Chicago: The Reilly and Britton Co., 1909. Reprint, New York: Arno Press, Inc., 1972.

Luttwak, Edward N. *The Pentagon and the Art of War: The Question of Military Reform*. New York: Simon and Schuster Publishers, 1985.

"Major General William J. Worth." *U.S. Veterans Memorial Institute News* 9 (1985).

March, Peyton C. *The Nation at War*. Westport, Conn.: Greenwood Press, Publishers, 1932.

Marcus, Robert D., and David Burner, eds. *America Firsthand*. Vol. 2. New York: St. Martin's Press, 1992.

Markusen, Ann, Peter Hall, Scott Campbell, and Sabina Deitrick. *The Rise of the Gunbelt: The Military Remapping of Industrial America*. New York: Oxford University Press, 1991.

Mason, Herbert Molloy, Jr. *The United States Air Force: A Turbulent History*. New York: Mason/Charter, 1976.

Matloff, Maurice, ed. *American Military History*. Washington, D.C.: Office of the Chief of Military History, United States Army, 1969.

Maurer, Maurer. *Air Force Combat Units of World War II*. 1961. Reprint: Washington, D.C.: Office of Air Force History, 1983.

_____. *Aviation in the U.S. Army, 1919–1939*. Washington, D.C:. Office of Air Force History, 1987.

McDugal, Lelia. *Up Hill and Down: A History of the Texas National Guard*. Waco, Tex.: Texian Press, 1966.

Mitchell, William. *Winged Defense: The Development and Possibilities of Modern Air Power—Economic and Military*. New York: G. P. Putnam's Sons, 1925.

Moolman, Valerie. *Women Aloft*. Alexandria, Va.: Time-Life Books, 1981.

Morgan, Hugh. "Royal Flying Corps in Texas." Part I. *Aeroplane Monthly*, November 1992: 48–51.

_____. Royal Flying Corps in Texas." Part II *Aeroplane Monthly*, December 1992: 58–60.

Morris, Lloyd, and Kendall Smith. *Ceiling Unlimited: The Story of Aviation From Kitty Hawk to Supersonics*. New York: The Macmillan Company, 1953.

"Mr. Odlum Gets the Business." *Fortune*, September 1949: 90–94, 134–45.

Mueller, Robert. *Air Force Bases*. Vol. I.: Active Air Force Bases within the United States of America on 17 September 1982. Washington, D.C.: Office of Air Force History, United States Air Force, 1989.

Murray, Williamson, and Allan R. Millett. *Brassey's Mershon American Defense Annual*. Washington, D.C. Brassey's, 1996.

Mutza, Wayne. *Helicopter Gunships: Deadly Combat Weapon Systems*. North Branch, Minn.: Specialty Press, 2010.

Nash, Gerald D. *The American West Transformed: The Impact of the Second World War*. Lincoln: University of Nebraska Press, 1985.

Nemir, Marina. "WASP (Women Air Force Service Pilots) and the Avenger Field in Sweetwater." Paper presented at West Texas A&M, Canyon, Texas, at the West Texas Historical Association Convention, April 5, 2008.

Niven, John, Courtlandt Canby, and Vernon Welsh, eds. *Dynamic America: A History of General Dynamics Corporation and Its Predecessor Companies*. New York: General Dynamics Corporation and Doubleday & Company, Inc., 1958.

Noggle, Anne. *For God, Country, and the Thrill of It: Women Airforce Service Pilots of World War II*. College Station: Texas A&M University Press, 1990.

Norton, Donald J. *Larry: A Biography of Lawrence D. Bell*. Chicago: Nelson-Hall, 1981.

Of Men and Stars. Burbank, Calif.: Lockheed Aircraft Corporation, 1958; Reprint, New York: Arno Press, 1980.

Oil Legends of Fort Worth. Dallas: Taylor Publishing Company, 1993.

Paddock, B. B., ed. *History of Fort Worth and the Texas Northwest*. 4 Vols. Chicago: The Lewis Publishing Co., 1922.

Palmer, Gregory. *The McNamara Strategy and the Vietnam War*. Westport, Conn.: Greenwood Press, 1978.

Parton, James. *"Air Force Spoken Here": General Ira Eaker and the Command of the Air.* Bethesda, Md.: Adler & Adler, 1986.

Pate, J'Nell L. *Livestock Legacy: The Fort Worth Stockyards, 1887–1987.* College Station: Texas A&M University Press, 1988.

_____. *North of the River: A Brief History of North Fort Worth.* Fort Worth: Texas Christian University Press, 1994.

Patterson, Mike. *Fort Worth: New Frontiers in Excellence.* Chatsworth, Calif.: Windsor Publications., 1990.

"Peacemaker": The History of the B-36 at Carswell Air Force Base Fort Worth, Texas, 1948–1958. Fort Worth: 7th Bomb Wing Association, 1995.

Polmar, Norman, ed. *Strategic Air Command People, Aircraft, and Missiles.* Annapolis, Md.: The Nautical and Aviation Publishing Company of America, 1979.

Proxmire, William. *Report from Wasteland: America's Military-Industrial Complex.* New York: Praeger Publishers, 1970.

Prucha, Francis Paul. *The Sword of the Republic: The United States Army on the Frontier 1783–1846.* New York: The Macmillan Company, 1969.

Pyeatt, Don, and Dennis R. Jenkins. *Cold War Peacemaker: The Story of Cowtown and the B-36.* North Branch, Minn.: Specialty Press, 2010.

Race, Lila Bunch. *Pioneer Fort Worth, Texas: Life, Times and Families of South Tarrant County.* Dallas: Taylor Publishing Co., 1976.

Rae, John B. *Climb to Greatness: The American Aircraft Industry, 1920–1960.* Cambridge, Mass.: The MIT Press, 1968.

Reynolds, Clay, with Marie-Madeleine Schein. *A Hundred Years of Heroes: A History of the Southwestern Exposition and Livestock Show.* Fort Worth: Texas Christian University Press, 1995.

Rich, Ben R., and Leo Janos. *Skunk Works : A Personal Memoir of My Years at Lockheed.* Boston: Little, Brown and Company, 1994.

Richardson, Doug. *Classic Warplanes: General Dynamics F-16 Fighting Falcon.* New York: Gallery Books, 1990.

Richardson, Rupert N., Adrian Anderson, and Ernest Wallace. *Texas: The Lone Star State.* 7th ed. Upper Saddle River, N.J.: Prentice Hall, 1997.

Rickenbacker, Edward V. *Rickenbacker.* Englewood Cliffs, N. J.: Prentice-Hall, Inc., 1967.

Rickman, Sarah Byrn. *Nancy Love and the WASP Ferry Pilots of World War II.* Denton: University of North Texas Press, 2008.

Roherty, James M. *Decisions of Robert S. McNamara A Study of the Role of the Secretary of Defense.* Coral Gables, Fla.: University of Miami Press, 1970.

Ronnie, Art. *Locklear: The Man Who Walked on Wings.* New York: A. S. Barnes and Company, 1973.

"The Round-Up." *National Institute of Mental Health Clinical Research Center Newsletter.* II (December 1970).

Rundquist, Barry S., and Thomas M. Carsey. *Congress and Defense Spending: The Distributive Politics of Military Procurement.* Norman: University of Oklahoma Press, 2002.

Russell, Ronald D. "Canada's Airmen and Airwomen in the First World War." *Airforce: The Magazine of Canada's Air Force Heritage* 28 (Summer 2004): 30–37.

Sampson, Anthony. *The Arms Bazaar: From Lebanon to Lockheed.* New York: The Viking Press, 1977.

Sanders, Leonard, and Ronnie C. Tyler. *How Fort Worth Became the Texasmost City.* Fort Worth: Amon Carter Museum of Western Art, 1973.

Sarkesian, Sam C., ed. *The Military-Industrial Complex: A Reassessment.* Beverly Hills, Cal.: Sage Publications, 1972.

Schlafly, Phyllis, and Chester Ward. *Kissinger on the Couch.* New Rochelle, N.Y.: Arlington House Publishers, 1975.

Schmidt, Ralph J., and Clare D. Wright, comps. *The Menasco Story: 1926 through 1991.* Charlotte, N.C.: Coltec Industries, 1994.

Scott, Florence Johnson. *"Old Rough and Ready" on the Rio Grande.* 1935; Revised ed. Waco, Tex.: Texian Press, 1969.

Scott, Winfield. *Memoirs.* Vol. 2. 1864. Reprint. Freeport, N.Y.: Books for Libraries Press, 1970.

Selcer, Richard F., and William B. Potter. *The Fort That Became A City: An Illustrated Reconstruction of Fort Worth, Texas, 1849–1953.* Fort Worth: Texas Christian University Press, 1995.

Selected Tarrant County Communities. Fort Worth: Historic Preservation Council for Tarrant County, Texas, 1990.

Serling, Robert J. *Legend and Legacy: The Story of Boeing and Its People.* New York: St. Martin's Press, 1992.

Shea, Nancy. *The Air Force Wife.* New York: Harper & Row, Publishers, 1951.

Sherry, Michael S. *The Rise of American Air Power.* New Haven: Yale University Press, 1987.

Sherwood, Robert E. *Roosevelt and Hopkins: An Intimate History.* New York: Harper & Brothers, 1948.

Shiner, John F. *Foulois and the U.S. Army Air Corps 1931–1935.* Washington, D.C.: Office of Air Force History, 1983.

Shirley, Noel. "An Interview with Ralph A. O'Neill." *Over the Front,* Summer 1987: 116–121.

Simonson, G. R., ed. *The History of the American Aircraft Industry: An Anthology.* Cambridge, Mass.: The Massachusetts Institute of Technology Press, 1968.

Simpson, Harold B., ed. *Texas in the War 1861–1865.* Hillsboro, Tex.: The Hill Junior College Press, 1965.

Skaggs, Jimmy M. "Portrait of a Great Citizen-Soldier: John A. Hulen." *Texas Military History* 8 (1970): 135–143.

Smith, George Winston, and Charles Judah, eds. *Chronicles of the Gringos: The U.S. Army in the Mexican War, 1846–1848, Accounts of Eyewitnesses & Combatants.* Albuquerque: University of New Mexico Press, 1968.

Smith, Thomas T. *The U.S. Army and the Texas Frontier Economy, 1845–1900.* College Station: Texas A&M University Press, 1999.

Snapp, Harry F. "Pioneer Women in West Texas Skies: Women Airforce Service

Pilots of World War II." *West Texas Historical Association Year Book* 70 (1994): 19–39.

Sontag, Raymond J. *A Broken World, 1919–1939.* New York: Harper and Row, Publishers, 1971.

Sorensen, Theodore C. *Kennedy.* New York: Harper & Row Publishers, 1965.

Stein, E. P. *Flight of the Vin Fiz.* New York: Arbor House, 1985.

Sullivan, Alan. *Aviation in Canada, 1917–1918.* Toronto: Rous & Mann Limited, 1919.

Sunderman, James F., ed. *Early Air Pioneers 1862–1935.* New York: Franklin Watts, 1961.

Sweetman, Bill. "Venture Star: 21st Century Space Shuttle." *Popular Science,* October 1996: 43-47.

Talbert, Robert H. *Cowtown-Metropolis: Case Study of a City's Growth and Structure.* Fort Worth: Texas Christian University, 1956.

Thayer, George. *The War Business: The International Trade in Armaments.* New York: Simon and Schuster, 1969.

Thompson, Robert D. *We'll Find the Way: The History of Hondo Army Air Field During World War II.* Austin: Eakin Press, 1992.

Tillman, Barrett. *Above and Beyond: The Aviation Medals of Honor.* Washington, D.C. Smithsonian Institution Press, 2002.

Tillman, Stephen F. *Man Unafraid.* Washington, D.C. Army Times Publishing Company, 1958.

Tipps, Don. *The Story of Bird's Fort: Birthplace of the Metroplex.* Haltom City, Tex.: Privately Printed, 2003.

Tompkins, Walker A. *Santa Barbara History Makers.* Santa Barbara, Calif.: McNally & Loftin Publishers, 1983.

Toulmin, Harry A., Jr. *Air Service: American Expeditionary Force 1918.* New York: D. Van Nostrand Company, 1927.

Turner, Loyd L. "Aircraft Construction: The South's Biggest 'War Baby.'" *Editor and Publisher,* October 31, 1953: 166–172.

Trewhitt, Henry L. *McNamara.* New York: Harper & Row, 1971.

Underwood, Jeffery S. *The Wings of Democracy: The Influence of Air Power on the Roosevelt Administration, 1933–1941.* College Station: Texas A&M University Press, 1991.

Vallance, Andrew G. B. *The Air Weapon Doctrines of Air Power Strategy and Operational Art.* London: Macmillan Press, Ltd., 1996.

Vandiver, Frank E. *Black Jack: The Life and Times of John J. Pershing.* College Station: Texas A&M University Press, 1977.

Van Zandt, K. M. *Force without Fanfare: The Autobiography of K. M. Van Zandt.* Edited and with an Introduction by Sandra L. Myres. Fort Worth: Texas Christian University Press, 1968.

Vecsey, George, and George C. Dade. *Getting off the Ground: The Pioneers of Aviation Speak for Themselves.* New York: E. P. Dutton, 1979.

Verges, Marianne. *On Silver Wings 1942–1944: The Women Airforce Service Pilots of World War II.* New York: Ballantine Books, 1991.

Villard, Henry Serrano. *Contact! The Story of the Early Birds.* New York: Thomas Y. Crowell Company, 1968.

Vosburgh, Frederick G. "Flying in the 'Blowtorch' Era," *The National Geographic Magazine* 98, September 1950: 281–322.

Wagner, William. *Reuben Fleet and the Story of Consolidated Aircraft.* Fallbrook, Calif.: Aero Publishers, Inc. 1976.

Walker, Richard P. *The Lone Star and the Swastika: Prisoners of War in Texas.* Austin: Eakin Press, 2001.

Wallace, Edward S. *General William Jenkins Worth: Monterey's Forgotten Hero.* Dallas: Southern Methodist University Press, 1953.

Wallace, Lane E. "The Wing Will Fly," *Aopa Pilot,* October 1996: 48–4.

Wegg, John. *General Dynamics Aircraft and Their Predecessors.* Annapolis, Md.: Naval Institute Press, 1990.

Weigley, Russell F. *History of the United States Army.* New York: The Macmillan Company, 1967.

Weisier, Sidney R. "Off to War With the 36th," *The Victoria Advocate,* October 10, 1971: 4.

White, Lonnie J. *Panthers to Arrowheads: The 36th Division in World War I.* Austin: Presidial Press, 1984.

Whiteley, John F. *Early Army Aviation: The Emerging Air Force.* Manhattan, Kans.: Aerospace Historian for the Air Force Historical Foundation, 1974.

Williams, Mack. *In Old Fort Worth.* Fort Worth: *The News-Tribune,* 1977.

Wiltz, John E. *From Isolation to War, 1931–1941.* New York: Thomas Y. Crowell Company, 1968.

Winchester, Jim. *X-Planes and Prototypes: From Nazi Secret Weapons to the Warplanes of the Future.* New York: Barnes and Noble Books, 2005.

Wise, S. F. *Canadian Airmen and the First World War.* Toronto: The University of Toronto Press, 1980.

Wolk, Herman S. *Planning and Organizing the Postwar Air Force, 1943–1947.* Washington, D. C.: United States Air Force, 1982.

Wright, Jim. *Balance of Power: Presidents and Congress from the Era of McCarthy to the Age of Gingrich.* Atlanta: Turner Publishing, 1996.

Yarmolinsky, Adam. *The Military Establishment: Its Impact on American Society.* New York: Harper & Row, 1971.

Index